OPERATION
HOMECOMING

NATIONAL ENDOWMENT FOR THE ARTS

OPERATION
HOMECOMING

IRAQ, AFGHANISTAN, AND THE HOME FRONT,
IN THE WORDS OF U.S. TROOPS
AND THEIR FAMILIES

PREFACE BY
Dana Gioia

EDITED BY
Andrew Carroll

RANDOM HOUSE / NEW YORK

Published in the United States by Random House, an imprint
of The Random House Publishing Group, a division of Random House, Inc., New York.

RANDOM HOUSE and colophon are registered trademarks of Random House, Inc.

The Operation Homecoming: Writing the Wartime Experience program
was created by the National Endowment for the Arts and is presented
in partnership with the Southern Arts Federation.

The Operation Homecoming program is funded by The Boeing Company.

The contents of Operation Homecoming do not reflect the opinions of the National Endowment
for the Arts, the Department of Defense, or The Boeing Company.

Proceeds from this book will be used to provide arts and cultural programming to U.S. military
communities. For more information, please go to www.OperationHomecoming.gov.

LIBRARY OF CONGRESS CATALOGING-IN-PUBLICATION DATA
Operation homecoming : Iraq, Afghanistan, and the Home Front, in the words of
U.S. troops and their families / edited by Andrew Carroll.
p. cm.
ISBN-10: 1-4000-6562-3
1. Iraq War, 2003– Personal narratives, American. 2. Afghan War, 2001– Personal narratives,
American. 3. Families of military personnel—United States. I. Carroll, Andrew.
DS79.76.O634 2006
956.7044092'273—dc22   2006045838

Printed in the United States of America on acid-free paper

www.atrandom.com

2 4 6 8 9 7 5 3

Book design by Casey Hampton

To our nation's troops and their families—
and to all who went before them

OPERATION HOMECOMING
PARTICIPATING WRITERS

Operation Homecoming Director

Jon Parrish Peede

Editorial Panel

Donald Anderson	McKay Jenkins	Dan Rifenburgh
John Barr	Stephen Lang	Jeff Shaara
Andrew Carroll	Erin McGraw	Cindy Simmons
Richard Currey	E. Ethelbert Miller	Larry Smith
Joe Haldeman	Marilyn Nelson	Karen Spears Zacharias
Barry Hannah	Kathleen Norris	
Andrew Hudgins	Quang Pham	

Workshop Teachers

Richard Bausch	Barry Hannah	Marilyn Nelson
Mark Bowden	Victor Davis Hanson	Wyatt Prunty
Andrew Carroll	Andrew Hudgins	Dan Rifenburgh
Lawrence Christon	McKay Jenkins	Jeff Shaara
Tom Clancy	Stephen Lang	Larry Smith
Judith Ortiz Cofer	Bobbie Ann Mason	Evan J. Wallach
Richard Currey	Erin McGraw	Tobias Wolff
Joe Haldeman	E. Ethelbert Miller	

Audio CD Participants

Will D. Campbell	Bobbie Ann Mason	Richard Wilbur
Shelby Foote	Marilyn Nelson	Tobias Wolff
Barry Hannah	James Salter	
Victor Davis Hanson	Louis Simpson	

PREFACE

Dana Gioia

Chairman, National Endowment for the Arts

There are countless books of military history and wartime reminiscence, but I don't believe that there ever has been a collection quite like *Operation Homecoming*. This volume contains writing by members of the U.S. military who have been involved in the war in Afghanistan and Iraq. It is not an official publication. The writing did not emerge from an armed forces or congressional history project but grew out of a series of workshops sponsored by the National Endowment for the Arts and conducted by a group of distinguished American writers. The volume was edited by a civilian panel of writers, editors, and historians. Most important, the writing was not composed after the conflicts it describes had concluded. It was created in the midst of the war, sometimes even on the front lines. Finally, as *Operation Homecoming* is published, the war it discusses is still under way.

The idea for *Operation Homecoming* emerged—oddly enough—in a tavern full of poets. In April 2003, at the first gathering of the nation's state poet laureates, the conversation turned to the war in Iraq and Afghanistan. Marilyn Nelson, poet laureate of Connecticut, talked about the stress and uncertainty faced by the troops being mobilized for combat. The daughter of a Tuskegee Airman, Nelson knew the pressures on military families. Having re-

cently taught as a visiting writer at the United States Military Academy at
West Point, she suggested that the enlisted men and women might benefit
from the opportunity to write about their experiences. We spoke about how
separate the worlds of literature and the military are in our society, and how
crucially important the art of literature might be to military personnel under-
going huge changes in their lives. What would happen if the nation fostered
a conversation between its writers and its troops?

The National Endowment for the Arts exists to bring the best of the arts to
all Americans, but up to this point, the agency had never done anything to
serve the more than three million Americans in the military or military families. Perhaps this omission reflected a sort of unexamined cultural snobbism.
At the very least, it reflected a failure of imagination on the agency's part. The
new project, which was soon named Operation Homecoming, allowed us to
both democratize and extend the reach of the agency's programs.

Operation Homecoming is a unique program in American literary history. It invited troops and their families to discuss and write about their
wartime experiences while the events were still happening, rather than years
later. Participants were encouraged to write in any form—fiction, poetry,
drama, memoir, journal, or letters. Most of the workshops were conducted
among troops who had just been rotated out of frontline combat. These sessions were also open to spouses, to discuss their experience on the home
front. (This may be the first American war in which many of those spouses
are male.) In some cases, workshops were held with military personnel still
serving in combat zones, such as the sessions on the aircraft carrier USS *Carl
Vinson* in the Persian Gulf. The writings contained in this book are not ret-
rospective accounts of a completed conflict, but rather episodes from a war
still unfolding and unfinished. Furthermore, these accounts did not emerge
from a traditional military history program but grew out of a unique series of
lectures, seminars, and workshops conducted by a distinguished group of
American writers—nearly three dozen novelists, historians, poets, dramatists,
and journalists—who operated free from any official constraints other than
basic security guidelines.

There seemed many good reasons to create Operation Homecoming.
First, the program met genuine human needs by providing people facing
enormous challenges with the opportunity for reflection and clarity that the
reading and writing of literature afford. Second, the program had historic importance, creating personal accounts of the war—from the combat zone to

the home front—by individuals who would not normally be heard. The reports on the war from politicians and journalists were printed and broadcast daily. Now there would be an opportunity to give voice to the troops themselves. Third, the project had literary potential: Some new literary talent would almost certainly emerge from the hundreds of novice writers engaged in the NEA workshops. Finally, the workshops themselves had a social and cultural importance by bringing together writers and military personnel—two groups who do not customarily mix in contemporary America.

The original plan for Operation Homecoming was to offer ten workshops on five bases. Each base would host two visiting writers, who would teach and lecture. To prepare for the workshops, each base would receive copies of books by visiting writers and a CD audiobook featuring selections of American war literature from the Civil War through the Vietnam era. So that this new program would not divert funds from other Arts Endowment grants, we secured private support from The Boeing Company. We then chose one of the agency's regional partners, the Southern Arts Federation, to help administer the program.

Assembling the writers to conduct the workshops, the Arts Endowment consciously sought a faculty of distinction and diversity. We wanted writers who represented a variety of literary genres and who spanned the political spectrum. Virtually everyone we invited agreed to participate. Our initial faculty represented an impressive sampling of America's finest writers, including Richard Bausch, Mark Bowden, Tom Clancy, Judith Ortiz Cofer, Barry Hannah, Victor Davis Hanson, Bobbie Ann Mason, Marilyn Nelson, Jeff Shaara, and Tobias Wolff. Meanwhile, a number of other writers were interviewed and recorded for the audiobook, including Shelby Foote, James Salter, Louis Simpson, and Richard Wilbur. Since we planned to publish the best of the writing in an anthology, the project also needed an editor. Once again we were fortunate to secure our first choice—Andrew Carroll, editor of *War Letters* and *Letters of a Nation*. Neither we nor Carroll, however, yet realized the ultimate scope of the burgeoning project we had initiated.

As it turned out, our original plan proved utterly inadequate. We announced the program to the public on April 20, 2004. When news of Operation Homecoming appeared in the media the next day, NEA phones began ringing, fax machines whirred, and e-mails poured into our headquarters at the Old Post Office in Washington, D.C., as military personnel and their families asked to participate. Some soldiers even called from Baghdad and

Kabul on their satellite phones, eager to sign up for workshops. For weeks, letters and manuscripts continued to arrive, including several powerful testimonies by Vietnam War veterans who wished they had been offered a similar chance to come to terms with their difficult wartime experiences. All of this happened before the program had even begun. We realized that our initial plan would need to be expanded. The Boeing Company graciously agreed to increase its support, and several new faculty were recruited, including actor-playwright Stephen Lang, who agreed to visit bases abroad.

The Arts Endowment gave the visiting writers total freedom in conducting their workshops. They were not told what to teach, and they in turn gave their participants complete freedom on how and what to write. The objective of the program was to give voice to the American troops and their families. There was no way to accomplish this mission except by allowing them complete liberty.

Eventually, the Arts Endowment conducted not ten but fifty writing workshops, which reached twenty-five bases in five countries, as well as an aircraft carrier and fleet ship in the Persian Gulf. More than 6,000 troops and spouses attended small-group writing workshops. Another 25,000 troops received our audiobooks. Nearly 2,000 manuscripts were submitted for the anthology, totaling well over 10,000 pages. (The staff eventually stopped counting.) Two independent editorial panels of writers, historians, journalists, and editors sifted through the copious material to make the final selection—ultimately only 5 percent of the total submissions. Once again, the editorial panel had no mandate except to find the best writing possible, without reference to point of view or political content. The Department of Defense played no role in selecting the contents of the book.

There is something in *Operation Homecoming* to support every viewpoint on the war—whatever the political stance. There is also something to contradict every viewpoint on the war. I have no doubt that certain readers (or reviewers) will quote some individual passage to prove or disprove some political theory. But such selective reading misses the true character of this volume. *Operation Homecoming* has no single author or common point of view. The volume comprises a chorus of one hundred voices heard as much in counterpoint as in harmony. These independent-minded people have earned their right to speak, and they do so candidly.

No one who reads the entire book will emerge with his or her views on the war unchanged—no matter what those initial views may be. *Operation*

Homecoming is a book about a war, America's current war in Iraq and Afghanistan. The book presents a stark and powerful composite, full of passionate, diverging individual accounts. It's a book not about politics but about particulars. Someone suggested the book be marketed as the first "official" account of the war, but "official" is exactly what *Operation Homecoming* is not. The book presents some one hundred unofficial accounts of the war—from the battleground to the home base. Official language strives for objectivity, scope, and balance. These stories are personal, emotional, and focused. These testimonies seem precise because they are individual and authentic.

One cannot tell the story of a nation without telling the story of its wars, and these often harrowing tales are most vividly told by the men and women who lived them. Today's American military is the best trained and best educated in our nation's history. They have witnessed events that are changing both our nation and the world. Their perspectives enlarge and refine our sense of current history. It is time to let them speak.

CONTENTS

INTRODUCTION

Andrew Carroll

"Emotionally," U.S. Navy Captain William J. Toti writes of those who serve in the American armed forces, "we pretend we're bulletproof."

Toti was at the Pentagon on the morning of September 11 when a commercial airliner carrying fifty-nine innocent civilians slammed into the building at more than five hundred miles an hour. It would be months before he could speak about the carnage he had seen, and he did not express how fully traumatized he was by the terrorist attack until he began putting his feelings down on paper. Some veterans, particularly those who have witnessed firsthand the horrors of war, go their entire lives without ever discussing their experiences.

Their reluctance is understandable. Many do not want to burden friends or relatives with their memories, and others question whether their loved ones would even be able to comprehend the harsh realities of life on the front lines. Some are also unwilling to confide in their fellow troops for fear of appearing weak or unstable. Despite increased efforts by the government to promote counseling for servicemen and women, military traditions and training have fostered a culture that ultimately values silent forbearance—not individual self-expression—in the face of adversity.

Which is why, when the National Endowment for the Arts first ap-

proached me about editing an anthology based on their Operation Homecoming initiative, my immediate reaction was to say no. Sending prominent
novelists, poets, and historians to lead workshops on military bases was, I
thought, an inspired and truly commendable idea. But I doubted much would
come of it. Expecting active-duty personnel and their families to divulge their
most private thoughts in stories, poems, memoirs, and other writings and then
forward these submissions to an agency within the executive branch of the U.S.
government seemed unrealistic, to say the least.

Though past generations of troops have produced their share of authors,
the percentage is minuscule compared to the number who served. And most
of the veterans who became literary giants—Ambrose Bierce, E. E. Cummings,
Kurt Vonnegut, Joseph Heller, Norman Mailer, Tim O'Brien, Tobias Wolff—
were published years, if not decades, after they returned home. This distance
not only gave them the opportunity to process their thoughts, it enabled them
to write freely, unconstrained by military censorship or oversight. The official
language of war tends to downplay and sanitize combat through euphemisms
and slang, covering it with layers of verbal camouflage; dead civilians are "col-
lateral damage," the accidental killing of a comrade is "friendly fire," the *in-
tentional* killing of one is "fragging," and a GI who steps on a land mine and
explodes in a shower of flesh and blood is "pink mist." Would men and women
in uniform today reveal the true brutality of warfare in any of their writings?
And if so, would the NEA allow them to be published?

Less than twenty-four hours after the launch of Operation Homecoming,
service members and their families began inundating the agency with diaries,
essays, song lyrics, haikus, eulogies, sketches, self-published newsletters,
e-mails, letters, short fiction, and full-length novels and autobiographies. Although the submissions centered primarily on life in the military, the contributors displayed a knowledge of and passion for literature, religion,
geography, and culture. One soldier paid homage to Thornton Wilder by
composing a humorous, sharply written play titled "Our Post." Kathy Roth-
Douquet, the wife of a Marine Corps officer commanding a helicopter
squadron in Iraq, alluded to Emily Dickinson's "Hope Is the Thing with
Feathers" in her more contemporary version, "Emily, Updated":

> *Helicopters*
> *fly without*
> *feathers*

Hope
is the thing
with armor.

In an e-mail to his two young boys, Cavan and Crew, an Air Force lieutenant colonel named Chris Cohoes marveled at the ancient history of the land that passed below him as he flew across Iraq. "Have you ever heard of Mesopotamia?" he asked his sons. "This is where civilization began on earth (the Sumarians)!" "Heard of Babylon?" Cohoes continued:

> The city was built about 3,800 years ago by King Hammurabi. King Nebuchadnezzar (I can't say it either) built the Hanging Gardens of Babylon about 2,600 years ago. It is one of the Seven Ancient Wonders of the World. This is where many great battles took place. The Romans fought here. One of the Egyptian Pharaohs fought here. Now I'm fighting here.

Contributors also related stories about the wars in Iraq and Afghanistan that had yet to be told. Army Sergeant Clint Douglas recounted the surreal experience of dining with an Afghan warlord and his band of thugs in a dilapidated castle. Dr. Edward Jewell, a commander in the Navy Reserve, chronicled life aboard the hospital ship USNS *Comfort* in the early weeks of Operation Iraqi Freedom (OIF) and the medical team's exhausting efforts to treat the wounded—even though their patients were not the people they were expecting. Several U.S. soldiers, including a twenty-four-year-old first lieutenant named Sangjoon Han, portrayed the fighting in Iraq through the eyes of innocent civilians caught in the crossfire. And Marine Corps Lieutenant Colonel John Berens reflected on a mission he was assigned to carry out in Al Kut, Iraq, involving British troops who had marched through and died in the same region. During World War I.

On the home front, a helicopter pilot named Peter Madsen, who had trained as both a soldier and a Marine, admitted how difficult it was to say goodbye to his wife—as *she* headed off to Iraq. Another Army spouse, Billie Hill-Hunt, wrote in verse about her rather ingenious solution to dealing with the emptiness of a lonely bedroom while her husband was deployed. In a poignant letter to her soon-to-be-born baby, Staff Sergeant Sharon McBride explained the challenges that awaited them because of her decision to stay in the military. "I can see why some single mommies choose to get out of the Army," McBride acknowledged, "but my resolve is true."

Not all of the submissions were somber or full of anguish. There is levity even in wartime, and servicemen and women used humor to help break the monotony of daily routines and, most important, cope with unrelenting stress and anxiety. They readily poked fun at their superiors, recalled with satisfaction the practical jokes they played on one another, and laced their journals with sarcastic commentary about their love of everything from port-o-johns and MREs (prepackaged "meals, ready to eat") to the scorpions and hand-sized camel spiders that frequently crept into their tents and gear.

Troops wrote as well about the thrill of combat. "There is nothing so exhilarating as being shot at and missed," Winston Churchill famously remarked, and generations of warriors have described the electric surge of adrenaline that rushes through the veins when bombs and bullets start to fly. The men and women in today's armed forces are no different. "As long as I can remember, I've wanted to fight in a war," the main character in Paul Stieglitz's story "Get Some" states unabashedly. Based on Lieutenant Stieglitz's own thoughts in the first days of OIF, the semifictional account underscored how eager he and his fellow Marines were to see action and, they hoped, to kill. What made the narrative especially compelling, however, was the revelation that their bravado was not impenetrable. After confronting a sight he literally found sickening, the protagonist could barely keep himself together. This was the first combat-related story I read, and I was stunned by its emotional intensity. There were many more like it to come.

One after another, the submissions depicted the barbarity of combat in explicit and unflinching detail. "The ambulance in the middle of my six-vehicle column pulls forward, and I get out to find where the casualties are," Captain Brian Humphreys recorded in his journal about the aftermath of an insurgent attack.

"What the hell is that?" I ask a Marine. Perhaps the explosion had somehow killed a farm animal of some sort who wandered out on the road. A sheep maybe? Or a cow. No, not big enough. Well, what is that and how did it happen? The Marine gives his buddy's name and asks me to help find his head.

The troops were also open about the degree to which the incessant blood-shed was affecting them psychologically. "We are dying," Sergeant John McCary wrote bluntly at the beginning of an e-mail to his family after his unit lost several soldiers. "Not in some philosophical, chronological, 'the end comes for all of us sooner or later' sense. Just dying." McCary knew how worried his mother was about his well-being, and he assured her that he was physically un-harmed. Emotionally, however, he was not unscathed.

> I'm ok, Mom. I'm just a little . . . shaken, a little sad. I know this isn't any Divine mission. No God, Allah, Jesus, Buddha or other divinity ever de-creed "Go get your body ripped to shreds, it's for the better." This is Man's doing. This is Man's War. And War it is.

Whether they were Air Force nurses describing wave after wave of critically wounded young troops being loaded onto medevac flights or frontline military psychiatrists observing the toughest, most battle-hardened grunts suddenly break down sobbing after a firefight, contributors did not hold back in reporting the full damage of combat to body and soul. And in doing so they were not looking for pity or a pat on the back, and they certainly did not mean to frighten their loved ones on the home front. They only wished to ensure that the sacri-fices made by their brothers and sisters in arms are never forgotten, and they know that words like *courage* and *honor* are hollow without an understanding of the horrific conditions in which they are forged.

Within a year of announcing Operation Homecoming, the NEA had ac-cumulated a towering, ten-thousand-page stack of submissions, and by this time I had enthusiastically signed on to help edit the book. (In retrospect, I could not have been more wrong about the influence of the project or the re-action it would trigger.) The question was no longer whether there would be enough material to produce an anthology, but how to distill into a single col-lection the richness and scope of these writings, which ranged from long, riv-eting accounts of massive ground assaults and air rescue missions to short, contemplative poems about Afghan poppies and the beauty of a nighttime Iraqi desert illuminated by lightning.

Novels and other literary works rarely begin with an introduction ex-plaining how the book was created, but anthologies are different; they—or, at least, their editors—are obliged to elaborate on how the volume is structured and why certain pieces were chosen over others. A collection such as this one, which is the result of a government effort, requires perhaps even greater transparency.

Before immersing myself in the editing process, I served on a panel of professional writers (selected by the NEA), several of whom are veterans themselves. For three months we carefully read every submission, and then, after scoring each piece, we convened for two intense days to discuss and debate how we envisioned the book and which submissions merited inclusion.

Our first challenge concerned the architecture of the anthology and whether it should be constructed by war, genre, military branch, or some other criterion. We decided that organizing by literary type or military branch might result in a lopsided book that lacked cohesiveness, as there are significantly more submissions by soldiers, airmen, and Marines than by sailors. We were tempted to arrange the writings sequentially by date, but, with the wars still unfolding, the book would abruptly conclude with whatever the last Operation Homecoming submission happened to be.

There was strong consensus in the end that the anthology was not intended to be a chronology of the fighting in Afghanistan and Iraq or an analysis of why or how these campaigns were being waged. Like the project that inspired it, the book was about the troops and their loved ones, and it should convey the personal perspective of going to war—packing up and heading into a combat zone, interacting with local civilians, enduring the daily grind of life "in the sandbox," longing for family and friends back home, facing the very real possibility of being killed, and, finally, returning to the States—alive, wounded, or dead. Within this narrative arc, the chapters and submissions would emphasize the individual human experience, as opposed to the sweeping history, of the wars in Afghanistan and Iraq.

To maximize the number of writers featured in the book, we also agreed that certain submissions—with the permission of their authors—should be edited for length and clarity. Most contributors wanted to hone and polish their works, and we encouraged this in all cases except one: correspondence. There is a raw immediacy to letters and e-mails sent from the front lines, and they lose their potency, I think, if the words are tidied up later. (We did cut some down for space reasons, adding an ellipsis with four periods to indicate where deletions were made. Any other ellipses were in the original.) I knew the contributors would not be thrilled that their typos and misspellings would remain uncorrected, but I believe that their letters and e-mails, because of the rough spontaneity of the prose, are among the most powerful writings in the entire Operation Homecoming collection.

As the panel reviewed the specific pieces to be considered for publication, the NEA offered four criteria to guide us in our deliberations: the work's artistic quality, its historical significance, and its contribution to the book's overall diversity in terms of genre—for instance, poetry, fiction, personal narrative—and life experience. By the end of our two-day meeting, we had whittled the initially overwhelming pile of submissions down to a manageable but still formidable one thousand pages. I had asked the other panel members to leave me with an abundance of material so that I would have some flexibility in crafting the manuscript, and they kindly obliged.

Over the next eight months I collaborated with Nancy Miller at Random House and Jon Peede at the NEA to shape the chapters and edit the final submissions line by line. (After the poet Marilyn Nelson and NEA Chairman Dana Gioia proposed the idea for Operation Homecoming, Jon spearheaded the project as a whole and worked tirelessly—including weekends, evenings, and vacations—to oversee its success.) Whatever concerns I had that the NEA might try to exert control over the manuscript, censor any of the material, or advance a political cause proved completely unfounded. At no time did I feel even a hint of pressure.

The only "agenda" I could detect, and I supported it wholeheartedly, was for the book to be as faithful as possible to the heart and soul of the writings themselves, regardless of how jarring or potentially upsetting they might be. There are contributors who voice staunchly antiwar opinions and accentuate in their writings the pain and destruction the hostilities in Iraq and Afghanistan have inflicted, while others express a strong sense of pride about going off to serve and focus on the positive achievements made in both countries over the past few years. Many contributors lash out at the media for only reporting when a bomb is detonated and not when a school or water treatment plant has been rebuilt, while others blame politicians in the United States for not calling on the nation to sacrifice more, as government leaders have done in past conflicts. And some, in words that are more pained than angry, cannot believe that as two major wars rage overseas, claiming the lives of American men and women on an almost daily basis, the conflicts are often overshadowed by the latest movie-star gossip, celebrity wedding, or reality-show winner. Instead of diluting these impassioned and disparate sentiments, I felt the anthology would have more integrity and authenticity if it featured a full spectrum of viewpoints and experiences.

Most of all, the book had to make the conflicts—and the people fighting them—real. Even in an age of twenty-four-hour cable news, Internet blogs, and live webcasts, war can seem abstract and remote. Its true impact cannot be communicated through third-person reports or the latest casualty statistics, no matter how staggering in size. It is best captured viscerally in the first-person words of those who have lived it. For Captain Robert W. Schaefer, the reality of war is watching helplessly from afar as two soldiers find themselves in a minefield and, after a split-second mistake, essentially vanish into thin air. For Myrna Bein, the mother of a soldier who lost part of his leg in Iraq, it's walking the halls of Walter Reed Army Medical Center as her son recuperates and catching glimpses of teenage troops maimed and disfigured for life. For Major Theodore Granger, it's the fear of coming home after a six-month deployment and finding that his infant son has no memory of his father. For Captain William J. Toti, it's observing a chaplain rush from one burn victim to the next outside the Pentagon and administer last rites over their bodies.

As I worked with the contributors on the final edits of their submissions and wrote the short biographical introductions to each piece, one question kept coming to mind: What compelled these men and women to share their writings? This could be asked of any author, I suppose, but the response to this project has been so enormous that it has clearly touched a nerve within the military. What was prompting veterans and troops to let their guard down and be so forthcoming? Not everything that they sent in, of course, was provocative or outspoken, and some potentially incendiary issues like desertion, infidelity, suicide, and substance abuse were addressed only peripherally. (Ideally, as the Operation Homecoming archive continues to grow, these and other relevant topics will be represented.) But the vast majority of the material submitted to date is remarkably intimate and candid, especially for members of a community renowned for its reticence and stoicism.

When I asked the troops about their motives for writing, the responses were as diverse as the individuals themselves. Some explained that they do so purely for enjoyment: It's a hobby, a way to pass the time. Others consider it a necessity. They find the act of writing to be cathartic, enabling them to gain a measure of control over their feelings as they unravel tangled knots of emotions, one thread after another.

Time and time again, I also heard contributors lament how little civilians know about the armed forces, and they hoped that these writings would foster a greater understanding of the military. "Until I married my husband," the wife of a National Guardsman said to me, "I had no idea how demanding the life of a soldier is. He almost never talks about it, but it's harder than anyone can imagine."

Many veterans told me as well that they decided to share their words so that troops overcome with grief, anger, or depression after being deployed would realize that they weren't alone. For a young combatant suffering from post-traumatic stress disorder, alcoholism, or persistent nightmares, there can be solace in knowing that others have struggled with these problems, too—and gotten through them.

The answer that proved to be the most memorable, however, was actually the first I was given. It came from a noncommissioned officer in the Army's Special Forces during an Operation Homecoming workshop at Fort Bragg, North Carolina. After I posed the question about what inspired him to participate, he said quietly: "This is the first time anyone's asked us to write about what we think of all that's going on." The small semicircle of soldiers around him nodded in agreement.

This anthology marks not the completion of the Operation Homecoming mission, but its expansion. And there is, on a personal level, a kind of heartbreak and joy to working on a project like this. Not all of the writings forwarded to the NEA are literary masterpieces, and many—especially the private e-mails, letters, and journals—were not, it seems evident, originally produced with any intention of later being published. But in even the most hastily dashed-off messages, there are flashes of poetry and wisdom. These authors demonstrate in submission after submission that they are more than just stenographers mechanically recording history. They are true artists crafting works of profound beauty, depth, and imagination. They have exceptional eyes for detail, for the small, searing images that infuse characters and moments with drama and vitality. And although composed in the context of war, their pieces transcend the subject. They are about resilience, faith, loss, terror, heroism, despair, hope, camaraderie, and the extremes of human nature, from its astonishing capacity for destruction to its limitless potential for compassion and mercy. The value of these insights lies in what they reveal to us not only about warfare, but about ourselves.

The excitement of seeing a new generation of extraordinary writers receive the attention they deserve is tempered only by the realization that so many others, before this effort was launched, were never encouraged to put their wartime experiences down on paper or preserve their correspondences and journals. But as discouraging as it is to consider what has been lost or gone unrecognized before this initiative began, now that the idea of seeking out the undiscovered literature of our nation's troops and their loved ones has taken hold, it is exhilarating to think of all that is yet to be found and of every-thing, ultimately, that is still to be written.

—*Andrew Carroll*
Washington, D.C.

OPERATION
HOMECOMING

CHAPTER ONE

AND NOW IT BEGINS

HEADING INTO COMBAT

The World Trade Center's North Tower and the Empire State Building, as seen from the South Tower, c. 1987. *Photo by Gregory S. Cleghorne; used by permission.*

I remember the golden globe in the vast courtyard between the two buildings and a spattering fountain next to cold stone benches. Inside, I would look up in awe at the cathedral-like glass, the suspended walkways, and the grand, vaulted ceilings rising ten stories, crowned with a diadem of crystal chandeliers. I remember the large fabric hanging artwork. I can still smell the concourse level's red carpets when they were new. I was eleven. I remember sitting on those red carpets with my schoolbooks, imagining I was in the city's most elegant reading room.

Now, up there on floors so high no hook and ladder could ever reach, a man in a tattered and burned white business shirt stands in a broken window with flames licking at him and smoke billowing around him. I see someone let go, briefly flying. I read later hundreds did the same. Hundreds.

I remember spending many summer afternoons and twilights as a teenager sitting on top of the South Tower, sometimes reading poetry or a book, the raucous sound of the city muted and far below. I was listening only to the air passing by me, my mind wandering.

A second plane slams into the South Tower. The explosion sounds like thunder.

I remember closing my eyes outside in the open air up there and feeling the sun's warmth on my face. No matter how hot it was on those city streets below, there were always cool breezes at more than a thousand feet up. The Tower would gently sway from the wind. It was unnerving at first, but after a while, I remember feeling comforted like a child being rocked back and forth. I wasn't worried she'd tip over. Ever.

The president addresses the nation and the world. He says to us, the armed forces, "Be ready."

I am.

— Forty-four-year-old Petty Officer First Class Gregory S. Cleghorne, born and raised in Brooklyn, New York.

ANTOINETTE
Personal Narrative
Captain William J. Toti

Just before 9:00 a.m., as word spread rapidly throughout the Pentagon, military and civilian personnel alike began huddling around television sets to watch breaking news about a plane crashing into one of the World Trade Center towers in New York City. "I am sitting at my desk when I hear someone yell, 'Oh my God!'" forty-four-year-old Captain William J. Toti wrote in a detailed, present-tense account of what he was doing on September 11, 2001. Toti had enlisted in the U.S. Navy at age seventeen, while he was still in high school, and eventually became a career submariner. In 1997, he was given command of the nuclear fast-attack submarine USS Indianapolis, which was based in Pearl Harbor, Hawaii, and named after the legendary World War II cruiser. On the morning of September 11, Toti was in the Pentagon, serving as the special assistant to the vice chief of naval operations. "I glance up at the television to see the World Trade Center on fire," he continued in his narrative.

I walk into my outer office, turn up the volume, and hear the anchor theorize that the cause of impact is some sort of technological malfunction. We know immediately that there is no way navigational failure could cause an airliner to fly accidentally into a building on a bright clear day. By the time the second plane hits the Trade Center's South Tower, we all realize this is a major terrorist attack.

What Toti and his colleagues did not know was that a third plane, American Airlines flight 77, was heading straight for them.

I quickly go back to my desk to call my wife, but nobody is there. I leave a voice message, telling her to take the kids out of school, stay home, and keep the telephone lines open.

As I hang up the phone and walk back to the outer office, I hear the sound of an approaching airplane, the whine of the engines growing louder and louder. And then impact—a massive earthquake-like jolt. There is screaming everywhere, and the halls immediately fill with dust and smoke. There is no time to think. I sprint down the hall behind two other Navy officers toward the point of impact.

My office is on the fourth floor of the E-ring, which is between the fifth and sixth corridors of the Pentagon. The plane has hit between the third and fourth corridors. We run through a brown haze that I learn weeks later was a combination of vaporized aviation fuel and particle asbestos that had been shaken loose from the ceiling. We pass through an area that recently had been abandoned for renovation and into a newly renovated, fully occupied area containing our operations center.

I finally reach the fissure—a gaping hole of sunlight where there should be building. The floor simply has dropped out, and parts of the airplane are visible, burning not fifty feet below us. It does not take us long to figure out that everybody on our floor who is still alive has evacuated, and that there is nothing we can do for anybody in the pit.

I run outside to the point of impact, and I encounter total devastation. Aircraft parts, most no larger than a sheet of paper, litter the field. I can make out, on one of the larger pieces of aluminum, a red A from AMERICAN AIRLINES. A column of black smoke rises into the air, bending toward the Potomac over the top of the building.

I start to wonder, *Where is everybody? Thousands of people work in that building, there should be hundreds streaming out of the emergency exits right now.* But at first I see no evacuees. Then as I round the corner of the heliport utility building, I notice a very small number of walking wounded, and then, on the ground before me, one gravely injured man. He is a Pentagon maintenance worker who is burned so badly that I can't tell whether he is white or black. Amazingly, he is still conscious. An Army officer is kneeling beside him, and since we are just a few feet from the still-burning building, the soldier says, "Let's get him out of here." A few more military men gather, and we carry him away from the building to the edge of Route 27, where the first ambulance has just pulled up.

As the EMTs tend to him, I look back down toward the building and see an open emergency exit, thick black smoke billowing out. There's some sort of movement inside the doorway, and it appears as if someone has fallen, so I run back down the hill and into the building.

Just a few feet inside I almost stumble over a lady crawling toward the door. She can't stand up, and I try to lift her, but I'm having trouble because sheets of her skin are coming off in my hands. I call for help, and two Army officers respond immediately. Then, as we hear—and feel—a series of secondary explosions just a few yards away, the three of us half-carry, half-drag the woman to the top of the hill, where we place her by the maintenance worker as a second ambulance arrives.

Third-degree burns cover her. But she is conscious and lucid, and a man with a blue traffic vest proclaiming PENTAGON PHYSICIAN stops to examine her. So I leave, confident that she is in good hands, and run back down the hill to help evacuate another of the wounded.

When we attempt to lift a badly burned man, he screams out, "Let go! Don't touch me!" Just then we hear more explosions coming from the fissure which we fear are bombs (but later learn are the airliner's oxygen tanks cooking off), so we carry this man out of there with him screaming the whole way.

When we arrive at the top of the hill with the second man, I notice that the woman we had just carried up the hill is becoming agitated, saying, "I can't breathe." I call over to an EMT, "Do you have any oxygen?" He runs to the back of his rig, pulls out a bottle, and puts it on her. As the flow begins and she starts to calm down, she looks at me like she wants to say something. I kneel down beside her and ask, "Is that better, are you all right?"

And then comes the moment I'll never forget. She blinks and asks, "Doctor, am I going to die?" Wham. Just like that. That is a question that I never imagined myself having to answer. I look around our little triage area on the side of the road—

The first injured man I had come across is no longer conscious and is doing poorly.

Another young lady is standing nearby with severely burned hands, screaming hysterically.

A soldier is trying to chase down a fire truck that has become lost in the maze of roads surrounding the Pentagon.

Other officers are attending to the walking wounded, and someone is pouring water from a five-gallon cooler bottle onto people as they exit the building to extinguish the small fires on their clothing.

—And here lies this woman, with no one to attend to her but me. What should I say? Should I tell her I am not a doctor? But there are no answers to be found, so I lean over the lady and ask, "What's your name?"

"Antoinette," she says.

"No, Antoinette, you're not going to die. We have a helicopter coming for you. I'm going to stay with you until you're on it."

She nods, and I feel relieved for having said this.

The medevac helicopter arrives a few minutes later. Since the Pentagon's heliport is in the middle of the attack area, the helo has to land up the hill toward the Navy Annex, on the other side of Route 27. The trek up the hill is surprisingly long and difficult. When we finally get her to the helicopter I yell out over the noise, "I'll visit you in the hospital!" Then I turn and run down the hill without looking back.

When I arrive, the "Pentagon Physician" (who, it turns out, is actually a dentist) asks me to take charge of establishing a station to receive the "expectants," which means I am in charge of caring for those who are not expected to live. Just then one of the Defense Protective Service police shouts, "Clear the area! Another plane is coming in!" So we cram the rest of the wounded into the few ambulances present and they drive away. We move farther from the building to wait for a second attack, which never happens. This is the first of many false alarms that day.

I try several times during the morning to call my wife, but the cell phone circuits are jammed, and eventually I kill my battery trying to get through. Hence, it is several hours before she knows I am still alive.

The day is full of vivid images. At one point, a group of firefighters is inside the building, knocking out windows to vent the heat, when they come across a Marine Corps flag. They extend the bright red flag out the window to a wave of cheers.

Another time, I am going to the fissure to help an FBI agent plan his evidence walk-down. As I approach the burning core, I see a single yellow flower in a clay pot, miraculously sitting untouched amid smoldering embers and soot.

I also watch as a Catholic priest, who I later find out had walked three miles to the Pentagon from his parish in Arlington, stands over a dying man to give him his last rites. The priest then moves to another man, who is severely burned but still lucid enough to be screaming, and he repeats the sacrament. Overwhelmed by the enormity of the event, the priest walks up to the gaping hole in the building and gives absolution to all of the dead at once.

One of the great ironies of the day is that earlier, when we were saturated by wounded, there was almost no medical help available. Then later, when we had hundreds of doctors, nurses, and paramedics on the scene, we had a profound shortage of injuries that needed treatment. Those who were rescued were saved not by trained first responders, but by people who were on the scene at the moment of impact.

At about 2100, almost eleven hours after the Pentagon attack, a wave of exhaustion hits me, and I decide there is nothing more I can do. I need my wife to come for me, but I realize she will be unable to get anywhere near us. So I borrow a cell phone and tell her to start driving north on Interstate 395. I start walking south, and after about fifteen minutes a state trooper pulls over beside me and asks me if I want a ride. I tell him that if I get into his car I am afraid that my wife will never find me, so I continue walking for almost a mile, with him creeping along behind me in his patrol car, both of us traveling south in the northbound lane, until I arrive at the barricade and see my wife.

Not surprisingly, I have trouble sleeping that night. I receive calls from some friends who, during World War II, survived the sinking of the cruiser USS *Indianapolis*. One says, "You got hit by a kamikaze just like us." Another remarks, "You got too close to us, now you have to share our fate." And through it all, I keep thinking about things we might have done better, the possibility that we might have been able to save more people. I am comforted, however, by the thought that at least we saved one individual: Antoinette.

The days immediately after the attack are a continuous stream of fifteen-hour workdays. I never find the time to make good on my promise to visit Antoinette. I know that she is in the Washington Hospital Center, and I call to check up on her, but then move on to what seem like more pressing matters. The urgent eclipses the important.

On September 19, I open *The Washington Post* and find a story about Antoinette. Thirty-five years old, budget analyst, raising a teenage foster child by herself. Two dogs, Oreo and Rex. Had been on the phone with a friend before the plane hit the Pentagon, planning a cruise together, just a month later. She was wheeled into the emergency room fully conscious. But despite hours of surgery, she never opened her eyes again. She had been burned over 70 percent of her body. She died on September 18.

I had only known Antoinette for a few moments, but I am shocked by the news and feel as if I have lost someone very close to me. I will never forget her.

During a memorial service near Ground Zero in New York, Rabbi Marc Gellman said that it is improper to think that on September 11 approximately three thousand people died. To understand the enormity of the loss, we have to recognize that what really happened was that a single individual died three thousand times.

There were three thousand Antoinettes that day, every one of them searching for a human savior who never arrived.

Toti was awarded the Legion of Merit for his actions on September 11 by Chief of Naval Operations Admiral Vern Clark. In 2003, he was promoted to serve as commodore of a squadron of nuclear-powered fast-attack submarines, and in 2006, he retired from the Navy after twenty-six years of service.

IN-COUNTRY
Personal Narrative
Lieutenant Colonel Brian D. Perry, Sr.

In a favorite café on the outskirts of New Orleans, Karla Perry and her children were enjoying breakfast on September 11, 2001, when the waitress came over and asked, "Your husband is on military duty, isn't he?" Mrs. Perry answered that he was. The waitress said, "You need to come look at the television right now." After seeing the images on the screen, Mrs. Perry turned to her children and remarked, "Our whole life has just changed." Within weeks, in fact, her husband, Brian, would be on a plane heading overseas to hunt down the terrorists responsible for masterminding the attacks on the United States. Lieutenant Colonel Brian Perry was, coincidentally, visiting CENTCOM (Central Command, which has been responsible for U.S. military operations in most of the Middle East for more than two decades) in Tampa, Florida, on the morning of September 11. He had just come out of one briefing and was about to step into another when he heard the news. A full-time attorney in New Orleans, Perry was one of 815,000 Americans serving in the reserve or Guard (another 1.4 million are on active duty), and he would have to temporarily shut down his law practice and help his family prepare for his abrupt departure. And because the mission was classified, he could not tell them exactly what he was doing or where he was going. Perry would later write about certain aspects of his deployment, and in the following narrative he describes his first impressions of the base where he would be stationed and what was going through his mind during the seventy-two hours it took him to get there.

From the time I departed New Orleans to the moment we landed in-country, I had been traveling almost nonstop for three days. There were only two passengers on the MC-130 taking us to our final destination: me and a Marine who had recently retired but was called back to active duty.

On the last leg of the journey, fatigue was getting the best of me. I would doze off and on, but the web seats were uncomfortable and made sleeping a challenge. Time became difficult to track.

My mind drifted back to New Orleans. It was just a few days ago that I had served my last trial as a judge ad hoc. It was a coveted position, but, unfortunately, the appointment came just a week before September 11, 2001. My lovely wife, Karla, and our six children spent part of the day in the courtroom with me, and it was an emotional moment for all of us. The youngest, our seven-year-old son, had hidden behind the massive bench and secretly handed me small notes telling me how proud they all were of me.

The stench of diesel fuel brought me back to the present. I set my watch to Zulu (Greenwich Mean) time, which would be my way of keeping track of operations no matter where we were. The place we were going was one of the few countries in the world to have its time thirty minutes different from others in the same longitude.

The sluggish sway of the plane began to lull me to sleep again. Not the deep sleep my body desired, but the type where your mind is moving too rapidly to unwind.

I thought back on my decision to stay in Tampa in the days immediately after 9/11. I did not want to leave headquarters, as there was so much to do to get ready for war, and I remained on duty until my wife received my mobilization orders. One week was all the time I had to close down my law office and return to CENTCOM.

A sudden movement in front of me brought me back to the plane, to the mission. The loadmaster was no longer asleep. He was aggressively searching through one of the military duffel bags, from which he pulled out a helmet, flak vest, and what in the darkness appeared to be a pistol. He opened his hand and dropped the weapon onto the pallet beside him. The Marine and I watched the crew member retrieve and strap on the pistol, which we could now see was a military-issue 9mm. He had already worked his way into the flak jacket.

"We are going in hot," he shouted over the pulsating engine noise. He started making movements with his hands indicating that, to avoid surface-to-air missile attack, we were going to zigzag in.

The plane shifted and swayed in the air, jerking us back and forth and pressing us hard into the unforgiving seats. This was part of the "corkscrew" landing procedure to evade surface-to-air fire against the unarmed plane.

The plane then rose in altitude. We watched the crew members, now in full battle gear, pull their seat belts tighter. We did the same. I heard the familiar rumbling of the plane's flaps extending, followed by the clamor of the wheels extending beneath us. The engines were slowing and then increasing in no discernible pattern, as if the plane were faltering. Losing, then gaining altitude. Suddenly I felt the jolt of the wheels contacting the pavement.

The loadmaster was out of his chair in a flash. After struggling with the side door, he was finally able to force it open, and the noise and rush of air startled me. The prop wash blew into the plane with a deafening roar. I expected the propellers to be slowing to a stop, but we still seemed to be at full power. The Marine bolted out of his seat while I fumbled for a second with the double latch of the seat belt. The crew was throwing our gear out of the door, and another crew member made frantic hand signals for us to exit.

The Marine made it to the door first but stopped abruptly before descending the ladder. I felt a hand on my shoulder pushing me out of the plane, but the Marine hadn't started moving yet.

"Go!" the crew member yelled at us as he prodded the Marine forward with his hand. The Marine glared back at the crew member, but finally he was down the stepladder into the darkness, and I was right behind him.

Mines, I thought, *beware of the mines*. This was why the Marine had hesitated. We had been forewarned that the place was full of them. Stay on the hardstand. The airplane took up most of the width of the runway and there was no place for us to go. Darkness surrounded us. I pulled a small flashlight from my pocket and, aware of the need for light discipline, lit the area around us for only a split second. We were right on the edge of the cement. The minefield lay just beyond where we stood, out there in the darkness. The Marine was standing next to me but I could barely see him.

Above, a million stars shone. The sight was overwhelming. In that moment I felt totally alone but surprisingly at peace. I knew I was where I was supposed to be. I thought of my wife and family, left behind with my closed law practice. I was comforted knowing that they, too, believed I was where I needed to be. Here in the fight.

A chill wind blew down on us from the snowcapped mountains. I searched in vain for some way to get off the runway before the MC-130 went to full power for takeoff. But it was not to be. I heard the four heavy propellers grab more air as the plane inched forward. There was no place for us to go.

We huddled deeper into our field jackets. The windblast forced our hands over our ears and we tightly closed our eyes. Dirt and small rocks peppered us. In a few minutes the wind abruptly and unexpectedly subsided. No lights were visible on the plane. I could just see its outline turning sharply into the night.

We waited, not moving until the MC-130 was out of earshot. The plane and its crew were safe. But were we? We looked around, squinting into the pitch black nothingness. There was no one there to meet us. We had no radios on us, no way to communicate with anyone. We had rushed to get on that plane back in Uzbekistan, and even though we weren't on the manifest, they had agreed to drop us off in-country. We knew that our final destination, the Task Force Headquarters building, was near the runway, but it was about 0130 (one-thirty in the morning), and we didn't dare walk blindly off into the darkness.

After about fifteen minutes of standing in the cold night, we heard a slight rumbling in the distance. The silhouette of a truck started to grow larger and larger as it approached. Unarmed and exhausted, we hoped it was friendly. The headlights were mostly blacked out but still projected a faint glow, and we walked quickly over to where the truck seemed to be heading. It stopped. A young airman looked out and, by the expression on his face, appeared more surprised to see us than we were to see him. To our relief, he gave us a ride.

It was two o'clock in the morning by the time we made our way to the support base, which was not really a base at all but just an old bullet-riddled roofless building. A makeshift entranceway was added to keep light from seeping out of the cracks of the front doorway. A sliding hatch opened into a vestibule of hefty tarps. No security guards were posted, no barbed wire protected the perimeter. The American troops we met inside all had beards and wore civilian clothes. Their defense was being low key, and they relied on the Northern Alliance and their own intelligence to notify them of an attack. Any Taliban in the area would be dealt with quickly, long before they could get close to the special operations forces.

The light was dim inside the building. Special Forces teams slept in two large rooms off the main hall. Camouflaged poncho liners acted as interior doorways. Plywood and two-by-fours were used to fashion a separate operations area at one end of the main room. Maps with overlays hung professionally on the bare wood walls. Radios and field telephones of different types were silent. The light was brighter here.

"I'll take you to the general," a bearded man who identified himself as the unit's sergeant major said, obviously not happy that he was awakened to greet the two lieutenant colonels unexpectedly dropping in.

"You were brought to the wrong place. Follow me." We grabbed our heavy bags and dragged them along the dirt road to our headquarters. Our task force was separate from the war fighters here. We had a special mission. The sergeant major carried two of our bags and used a small flashlight strapped onto a headband to find his way as we moved clumsily through the darkness.

Out of breath and disoriented in the blackness, we made it to our destination and into a dusty old building. The lights here were dim. There was a hole in the door where the handle was supposed to be. A water bottle filled with sand as ballast was used instead of a spring to keep the door closed. A lanyard tied to the upper corner of the wooden door fit through a small hole in the doorjamb. The sand weight pulled the door tightly closed.

A lone figure sat in a chair guarding a plywood door. He was a bearded, tired-looking young man, in jeans and a heavy sweater. Even with his longish hair and coarse wool hat I could tell he was an American soldier. He stood slowly as we entered, adjusting his M-16.

"These officers belong here," the sergeant major said while he moved quickly back to the door. The young man just nodded.

As we made our way through the darkness to our sleeping quarters, I was struck by the contrast between the building's decrepit condition and the twenty-first-century technology I knew was in these rooms, installed by the first troops who had arrived at this desolate base. There would be STU-III secure telephones, state-of-the-art computers monitored continually by signals technicians and information analysts, and a video-teleconferencing uplink system that enabled the general and his staff to communicate with fellow commanders back in the States. This was the "the cell," the nerve center for the task force in the region.

We were led into a small, cramped room with no heat. It was cold enough that I could see my own breath. Military equipment and weapons were suspended haphazardly from nails in the wall. A bare lightbulb seemed to be hanging precariously from frayed wires in the center of the ceiling, and I could make out the dark outline of men sleeping in cots. For the next five months, this was home. The Marine and I looked at each other. We had finally made it. I could tell by the half smile on his face that he, too, knew that this whole experience was history in the making and we were now a part of it.

Before leaving, the sergeant major turned toward us and said respectfully but matter-of-factly, "Gentlemen, welcome to Afghanistan."

TIC

Journal
Lieutenant Colonel Stephen McAllister

A philosophy major who joined the U.S. Air Force not long after he graduated from college, Stephen McAllister would go on to serve in Operation Desert Storm in 1991 and Operation Enduring Freedom more than ten years later. McAllister's deployment to Afghanistan was originally scheduled to last for three months. It was extended to eight. McAllister worked at Bagram Air Base for the Air Component Coordination Element (ACCE) in the headquarters of the Combined Joint Task Force (CJTF-180), and during his time there he began writing a journal. McAllister mused on both the serious and the relatively insignificant, from the plight of the Afghan people and mortar attacks on Bagram to poisonous snakes and port-o-johns that were almost as terrifying in their own way. (McAllister's observations about the bathroom facilities on base are featured on p. 143.) In one of his entries, which is intentionally vague in parts for reasons of operational security, he wrote about the military euphemisms and terminology used to describe the harsh, real-life brutality of combat.

E arly in the afternoon, another map is projected on the screen at the front of the headquarters, prompting everyone to stop and take notice. Along with its graphic terrain depiction, contour lines, and named geographic features, there are bright yellow crosshairs in a circle. And above it are the words—Troops-In-Contact. The acronym is TIC, and it is shorthand for U.S. soldiers either engaging hostile forces or receiving fire from the enemy. It is a polite and dispassionate way of saying that someone is trying to kill an American's son or daughter, husband or wife, boyfriend or girlfriend.

At the beginning of this mission, a convoy of vehicles, mostly Humvees, is traveling down a gully between steeply rising hills. A single, two-lane dirt road winds next to a dried streambed. It serves as the sole link between two relatively large villages. Inside the lead and rear Humvees, soldiers sit in the driver and passenger seats, and a soldier stands in the turret manning the M240D machine gun. The other vehicles contain two soldiers each. All have their flak vests and helmets donned. The driver and passenger have their M-16s "locked and loaded," on safe with a round in the chamber. The muzzles rest on the floorboard. The more senior soldier is in the passenger seat, though all three of the troops are under twenty-five years old. I can imagine the driver and passenger joking about getting home to toilets that actually flush as they are constantly scanning the terrain for something out of the ordinary. The soldier in the turret can't hear the joking below and shifts his focus in segments to look for the "bad guys."

And now it begins. The lead vehicle jumps violently and dirt flies. A deafening explosion echoes through the valley like a thunderclap. The driver and passenger are numb from the shock. Shards of metal and glass rip through the air. The turret gunner, knocked off balance, is on his knees holding on to whatever feels solid. Pain like they have never known before surges through the driver and passenger like an electric current. The convoy behind them lurches to a stop. I can almost hear the soldiers in the number-two vehicle say "Jesus Christ" in unison and instinctively pick up their M-16s. The ranking soldier yells into a microphone slung over his shoulder and clipped to the front of his flak vest: "Dragon Base, Dragon Base! This is Convoy Alpha. We are under fire! We are under fire! Coordinates 42S WD 964 629. Vehicle number one disabled. Crew status unknown. Direction of attack unknown. Request immediate assistance." The microphone transmits every word and breath. "Stay in the vehicle! Everybody stay in the vehicle! No one move!"

Two soldiers cautiously approach the lead Humvee. One door is missing, the rest intact. The turret gunner opens a back door and slides onto the ground, trying to keep a low profile.

"Jesus, what was that?"

"Stay here."

The driver and passenger are both conscious but obviously in shock. Blood covers the right side of the driver's face. The passenger's mouth is also bleeding profusely and he's wincing in agony. They're taken from the vehicle and laid on the ground. "Dragon Base, Dragon Base, Convoy Alpha requesting immediate medevac. Two injuries—both stable."

The headquarters is all business. Is there close air support available? What caused the explosion? What time did the explosion happen? Where's the nearest medevac? Launch the HH-60 and support it with an AH-64. Take the patients to the nearest airfield where we can stabilize them and put them on a bird to Bagram. We've heard reports that it was an RPG (rocket-propelled grenade). Can we get confirmation? We need to launch a Chinook to sling-load the damaged Humvee and bring it to Bagram for analysis. The HH-60 is en route, expect arrival in fifteen minutes. Hold the C-130. We'll put the patients on it. Remainder of the convoy reports negative contact. Close air support reports negative contact. Chinook estimating arrival in twenty minutes. HH-60 arrived. Patients stable. Transload to C-130. Expect departure in twenty-five minutes; arrival at Bagram in one hour and twenty-five minutes. We now believe they struck a mine. Chinook sling-loading Humvee now. Second explosion. RPG? No injuries, no damage. Convoy reports mines. Professional and dispassionate.

The moon is out now, casting shadows everywhere. A patrol is investigating reports of suspicious activity within a kilometer of base camp. Twelve soldiers struggle with the moon's brightness, which washes out the NVGs (night vision goggles). They stumble on rocks, cursing. Approaching the reported coordinates they find twenty individuals fully armed with AK-47s and RPGs. Suddenly, the armed men turn and run. The patrol begins pursuit. The armed men stop and turn, shooting into the darkness. The patrol returns fire. One soldier abruptly stops shooting and doesn't respond. Another is cursing and swearing. The assailants get away. The first soldier has been shot in the head and is covered in blood. The second soldier is lucky. The bullet grazed his cheek and exited the back of his helmet. The squad leader radios for medevac and again the HH-60s and AH-64s scramble. The soldier with the head wound dies before getting to a hospital.

I stand at the gate to the flight line for the arrival of a C-130, which is carrying the remains of the soldier. The moon's gone and the clouds are thickening. The only stars visible are running from the advancing storm front and the blackness is penetrating. A crowd of troops gathers, though it's difficult to tell how many have come. Uniforms stand next to sweat clothes, young next to old, men next to women. Some strain to see as the aft ramp lowers, others look blankly at their feet. We watch intently as the body, entirely covered, is removed on a stretcher and put in the waiting ambulance. The general salutes as the ambulance passes. Some follow suit. Others, lost in prayer, deep thoughts, tears, salute in their own private way. Once the ambulance disappears into the darkness, some of the gathered start to walk back to their tents. It takes a little longer for others to start moving. No one says a word.

As I walk slowly to work, I wonder if the young dead soldier has a wife and children. Would his son or daughter be allowed to see him? Would they recognize him when he comes home? Would they remember him as they walked across their high school commencement stage or at their wedding? Would his grandchildren ever know how their grandfather died? How long before his memory would disappear? Fifteen seconds on CNN.

It's still dark when I start the daily reports. There isn't an airlift mission of special note today. Airpower didn't dispense any flares, drop any bombs, fire any guns. Combat air support covers the next twenty-four hours.

The bottom line on the report—NSTR. Nothing Significant to Report.

FRIENDLY FIRE

Personal Narrative

Captain Michael S. Daftarian

As American and Coalition infantry units poured into Southwest Asia to serve in Operation Enduring Freedom, thousands of airmen flew over the region to bomb Al Qaeda and Taliban targets and provide close air support for the troops on the ground. Thirty-two-year-old U.S. Air Force Reserve captain Michael S. Daftarian, a civilian pilot and firefighter prior

to his active-duty service, was deployed to Bagram, Afghanistan, in Au-
gust 2002 for six months with the 354th Fighter Squadron of the 355th
Fighter Wing from Arizona. In the following account, Daftarian describes
not only the technical and logistical challenges of flying an A-10 Warthog in
the chaos of combat, but the split-second decisions that have to be made
while traveling at more than four hundred miles an hour—in the dark.

The particular area we're headed to contains a small U.S. outpost located on the Pakistan border surrounded by hilly and moderately mountainous terrain. I've provided support to the ground forward air controllers, or GFACs, there before, but never on a dark night like this one. Conversely, my lead pilot is on his second flight in-country and his first night flight here, having only arrived three days prior.

As we continue south, passing off my four o'clock are the lights of Kabul, the last, and really only, major city or town of any kind in this vast region. Off to the distant east is the well-lit Pakistani city of Peshawar. To the south is nothingness, and that's where we are directly headed. A faint something begins to appear. It almost looks like Saint Elmo's fire dancing around. My lead and I are coordinating on our interflight radio, cross-checking the map location, and quickly reviewing available tactics to use. As we get closer, it becomes clear that what I'm seeing are tracers from automatic weapons fire.

Lead gives a call on the designated UHF freq and uses the ground unit's call sign: "Playmate, this is Misty One-One."

No answer; we're still too far out. Approaching twenty miles from the area, it's now apparent that there's a serious battle going on down there. The tracers are heavy coming from the northeast, while the return fire from what must be our guys is not as intense. I also see what looks like strobe-light flashes appear on the southwest side of the fighting. The scene is difficult to describe, but it's akin to a fireworks show gone insane, with Roman candles shooting in every direction on the ground.

Lead tries the call again, "Playmate, Misty One-One."

Immediately we get a response. "Misty One-One, Playmate, we got a situation here," the guy on the radio is yelling. "We're under automatic weapons fire at this time from our north. What's your location and what you got?"

Normally, in close air support, there's a standard litany of information that's passed back and forth when checking in with a ground unit, and prior to expending munitions. Called the "9-line," it's nine essential elements of coordination information passed from the ground unit to the supporting aircraft. It contains such items as target coordinates, target elevation, target type, friendly location, any restrictions, any marking devices to be used, heading and distance to the target if running in from an initial point, etc. Right now, there is no time to go through a standard coordination drill, and most of the information we need is readily apparent just by what we are looking at on the ground.

"Misty, Playmate, we're taking a beating from the hills to our north, heavy fire. We need that suppressed. You got that area in sight?" the GFAC asks.

"Affirmative," lead answers. "I'm contact that, we can be there in one mike with strafe. What restrictions you got for us?" The GFAC reads us the restrictions of northwest to southeast or vice versa, in order to keep stray rounds from hitting friendlies. What is so surreal about this situation is that from my jet, I can see what can only be described as a beautiful light show. The significance of the destruction being sent back and forth down there is apparent only each time the GFAC keys his mike. Each time he transmits, I can hear automatic weapons, rifle fire, and men shouting in the background.

The GFAC keys up, yelling into the mike (probably due to being nearly deaf from all the close gunfire), "Misty, Playmate, you got your restrictions, you're cleared hot, call in with direction and target in sight, you've— INCOMING!"

At that exact moment Playmate's radio cuts off, and I see what appears from my vantage point to be two bottle rockets zing across the ground from the hillside and impact the camp with two bright, instantaneous glows.

Playmate had been talking into his handset with us, and had seen the RPG-7 rocket-propelled grenades coming his way. I could hear the *whoosh-bang* of the explosion as Playmate yelled the "INCOMING" warning to his comrades, while at the same time watching it happen from the air.

Lead calls, "Misty, Playmate, you up? You all right?"

No answer.

In a few seconds, Playmate comes back up, yelling into the handset, somewhat incoherent and breathing heavily, as if he'd just been punched in the gut: "You . . . Copy? . . . you're cleared . . . hot . . . need the munitions now . . . Juliet Papa."

Juliet Papa is the confirmation code. In close air support ops, if you're dropping bombs in support of troops-in-contact, they must verify that they know, approve, and accept the risk of your dropping munitions close to their position, mindful of the fact that they could potentially get hit. This was not only troops-in-contact, this was danger-close. The enemy is located only about seven hundred to eight hundred meters from the friendly position. Considering that a 500-pound bomb has a minimum safe distance of 425 meters, there is no room for error here. As I set up my switches for my first pass, I mentally rehearse the pilot prayer: "Please God, don't let me fuck up."

Lead and I quickly confirm our game plan: we will start our first pass with strafe from the 30 mm cannon and work from there. Tonight, my weapons loadout is 1,170 rounds of 30 mm gun, two Mk-82 500-pound bombs, one seven-shot pod of rockets, and one Maverick air-ground missile. I quickly double-check my switches: Heads Up Display (HUD) on top of the dash panel is set to guns, gunsight cross visible, backup gunsight mil-setting dialed in, 30 mm cannon selected to ON/HIGH, master arm selected to ARM, green "gun ready" light visible on the top center of the instrument panel. Lead calls, "Misty One's in from the southeast hot, target in sight."

"Cleared . . . hot," comes the exhausted response from Playmate amid the ever-present staccato of gunfire.

Lead calls, "Off target, west," just as Playmate, watching our strike, comes up with "Two, work further north from there along the hill. . . ." I acknowledge Playmate's correction.

Shortly thereafter, I call, "Two's in from the southeast, target in sight."

"You're cleared hot, Two," comes the reply.

The target is just to my left. I roll into a 140-degree bank, simultaneously cracking the throttles back to half and letting the nose fall through the horizon. I then pull it up in a slicing maneuver through seventy degrees nose low towards the target as I roll wings-level, stabilizing in a level, fifty-degree dive.

The altimeter is rapidly unwinding, going full-circle counterclockwise about once a second. I roll in at 17,000, and am now passing 14,000 in a fifty-degree dive. I fan out the speed brakes as the airspeed begins passing 370 knots, while simultaneously centering up the target in the gun sight.

BRRRRRRRRRRRRIPPPPPPP goes the cannon as I squeeze the trigger, sending seventy rounds per second down into the hillside below.

I see the enemy tracer fire still going as my rounds impact like so many sparklers, reminding me of a dark concert hall with tons of camera flashbulbs going off. I keep the trigger squeezed and move the stick forward and aft about one inch, spreading out the death and destruction on the hillside instead of just keeping it focused on one area. When shooting tanks you want to concentrate your gunfire, a method commonly known as track-shoot-track. Here, I want to spread the bullets—share the love, if you will—with as many of the enemy as I can. I hold the trigger for what seems like an eternity, getting blinded by the flame now coming from the front of the jet.

Mindful that I am screaming towards mountainous terrain in a fifty-degree dive with an airspeed of 440 knots and the altimeter wildly spinning through 8,000 feet, I come off the gun trigger and haul the stick into my lap and shove the throttles forward. I pull up into a forty-degree climb and roll into a ninety-degree left bank, letting the nose fall to the horizon as I reenter my left-hand orbit of the target.

I can see that there's still enemy fire coming from the northern side of the hill, though the overall volume is less than it was before. Lead gets to his roll-in point and calls in from the southeast again. He receives a "cleared hot" from Playmate.

He calls off target to the west again, and Playmate comes on freq with a request: "Two, can you give me those bombs on this next pass? I wanna waste the hillside. We still got movers up there firing . . . and we're heading towards that location."

I respond with affirmative and ask if I can be in from the south this next pass to give me a varied run-in heading (don't want to use the same tactics too many times), and to buy me a little more breathing room from the friendlies, who are now starting to fan out from the camp perimeter. I reset my switches for bombs now: 30 mm cannon still set to ON as backup, weapons stations four and eight selected, fuzing sequence set to RIPPLE-SINGLE, two bombs selected with thirty-one-millisecond interval, master arm checked in ARM, green RR ready lights on the bomb panel. Passing on the south side of the target, I call, "Two's in from the south, target in sight."

Playmate passes the "cleared hot" and I roll in.

I stabilize in a fifty-degree dive again. The altimeter madly unwinds and the airspeed increases as I watch the bombsight, or "pipper," slowly track up the HUD to the area of enemy fire on the center of the hillside. As the pipper tracks over that point, I press the "pickle" button, and feel a slight jolt as the jet rids itself of two 500-pound bombs from its underside. Pulling off target into a thirty-degree climb and rolling back down to the horizon, I see my two bombs detonate: one on the center of the hill, and one on the northwest side, both creating a large "photoflash" effect as they explode. Both land slightly left of where I've aimed them, closer to the friendlies. Instantly, I get on the radio. "Playmate, Misty Two, how were those bombs?"

Static.

No response from Playmate. A huge lump forms in my throat. I come back with "Playmate, Misty Two, how'd those bombs look?"

Nothing.

"Playmate, Misty Two, acknowledge!" Still nothing but broken static.

Looking down at the hillside, there are no more tracers. None from anywhere. A few fires burning here and there, but no signs of any weapon fire, either from the enemy in the hills or from the friendlies near the outpost.

Goddammit! Dammit to hell. Nothing can compare to the feeling that you've just bombed your own troops, the very guys you came to support. "Playmate, Misty Two, what's your SITREP?" (situation report). Nothing.

Then there's the sound of a mike keying. Once, twice. Playmate comes up: "Two . . . good hits, we're still hunkering down. . . . We still got shrapnel raining down here, but the hillside is gone! Break, break . . . One, put your bombs on the far-north side of the hill."

Damn that was close, too close for comfort. But an indescribable relief. Lead drops his bombs on the north side of the hill. We each make two more passes, expending our rockets and some more gunfire on the eastern side of the hill near the border, in order to try to get anyone attempting to escape back across to Pakistan.

Playmate reports all clear, thanks us, and promises to forward the BDA (bomb damage assessment) come daylight. Then he clears us off-target.

"Copy that, Playmate. We can be back in a hurry if you need us," I say, and then turn the plane around to begin the forty-minute flight to Bagram. Less than two and a half hours later, after returning to base, debriefing the intelligence officers, and reviewing the videotapes of the mission, I'm back in my bunk.

Seven months after returning to Arizona from Afghanistan, Daftarian was called up to serve again—this time to provide close air support to U.S. ground troops fighting in the early stages of Operation Iraqi Freedom.

A QUICK LOOK AT WHO IS FIGHTING THIS WAR
Letter
Captain Ryan Kelly

As a blinding sandstorm whipped through Camp Buehring in Udairi, Kuwait, thirty-five-year-old U.S. Army Captain Ryan Kelly sat in a tent typing out a letter to his mother back in Colorado. "The worst thing here is not the searing heat or the cold nights," Kelly wrote. "It's the waiting."

> *Waiting for the wind to quit blowing and the sand to quit grinding against your skin. Waiting for a moment of privacy in a tent packed with 70 other men, in a camp packed with 700 other tents, in a base packed with 15,000 soldiers, all looking for a clean place to go to the bathroom. . . . Waiting for the bone-rattling coughs from dust finer than powdered sugar to stop attacking the lungs. Waiting for the generals to order the battalion to move north, toward Tikrit, where others—Iraqis—are also waiting: waiting for us. . . .*

While stuck at Camp Buehring preparing himself for battle, Kelly had the opportunity to reflect not only on the imminent charge into Iraq, but on the men and women who would be going with him. His letter to his mother continued:

A quick look around my tent will show you who is fighting this war. There's Ed, a 58-year-old grandfather from Delaware. He never complains about his age, but his body does, in aches and creaks and in the slowness of his movements on late nights and cold mornings. . . .

There's Lindon, a 31-year-old black-as-coal ex-Navy man from Trinidad who speaks every word with a smile. His grandfather owned an animal farm and lived next to his grandmother, who owned an adjacent cocoa field. They met as children.

There's SGT Lilian, a single mother who left her five-year-old daughter at home with a frail and aging mother because nobody else was there to help.

There's Melissa and Mike, two sergeants who got married inside the Ft. Dix chapel a month before we deployed—so in love, yet forbidden, because of fraternization policies, even to hold hands in front of other soldiers. But if you watch them closely, you can catch them stealing secret glances at each other. Sometimes I'll see them sitting together on a box of bottled water tenderly sharing a lunch. They are so focused on each other, that the world seems to dissolve around them. If they were on a picnic in Sheep's Meadow in Central Park, instead of here, surrounded by sand and war machines, it would be the same. War's a hell of a way to spend your honeymoon.

There's SFC Ernesto, 38, a professional soldier whose father owns a coffee plantation in Puerto Rico and whose four-year-old daughter cries when he calls.

There's Noah, a 23-year-old motor cross stuntman, who wears his hair on the ragged edge of army regulations. He's been asking me for months to let him ship his motorcycle to the desert. I keep telling him no.

There's CW4 Jerry, the "Linedog" of aviation maintenance, whose father was wounded in WWII a month after he arrived in combat. On D-Day, a bouncing betty popped up from behind a hedge grove near Normandy Beach and spewed burning white phosphorus all over his body, consigning the man to a cane and a stutter for the rest of his life. CW4 Jerry lives out on the flight line, going from aircraft to aircraft with his odd bag of tools, like a doctor making house calls. He works so hard I often have to order him to take a day off.

There's Martina, 22, a jet-black-haired girl, who fled Macedonia with her family to escape the genocide of the Bosnia-Croatian civil war. Her family ran away to prevent the draft from snatching up her older brother and consuming him in a war they considered absurd and illegal. A few years later, the family, with no place else to run, watched helplessly as the US flew their daughter into Iraq. She's not even a US citizen, just a foreigner fighting for a foreign country on foreign soil for a foreign cause. She has become one of my best soldiers.

There is William "Wild Bill," a 23-year-old kid from Jersey with a strong chin and a James Dean–like grin. The day before we went on leave, he roared up in front of the barracks and beamed at me from behind the wheel of a gleaming-white monster truck that he bought for $1500. Three days later, he drove it into the heart of Amish country where the transmission clanked and clattered it to a stop. He drank beer all night at some stranger's house, and in the morning, sold them the truck. Kicker is, he made it back to post in time for my formation.

There's my 1SG, my no-nonsense right-hand man. He's my counsel, my confidant, my friend. He's the top enlisted man in the company with 28 years in the army, and would snap his back, and anybody else's for that matter, for any one of our men. Last year, his pit bull attacked his wife's smaller dog—a terrier of some sort, I think. As she tried to pry them apart, the pit bit off the tip of her ring finger. Top punched the pit bull in the skull and eventually separated the two. A hospital visit and a half a pack of cigarettes later, he learned the blow broke his hand. He bought her a new wedding ring in Kuwait.

And on, and on and on. . . .

I hope you are doing well, mom. I'm doing my best. For them. For me. For you. I hope it's good enough.

Tell everyone I said hello and that I love and miss them. Talk to you soon.

Love,
Ryan

Captain Kelly was responsible for every one of these individuals, as well as more than seventy other soldiers. He—and all of them—would come home alive after almost a year of combat in Iraq.

DISTANT THUNDER
Personal Narrative
Sergeant Denis Prior

"I hate the idea of war and I can't wait for it to begin," Denis Prior writes at the beginning of a moment-by-moment account of the days just before and after the launch of the March 2003 invasion into Iraq. A thirty-year-old U.S. Army sergeant originally from Mobile, Alabama, Prior was attached to the 3/7 Cavalry Squadron, 3rd Infantry Division. After being trained in Arabic, he was designated as a HUMINT (human intelligence) collector—or, as it is more commonly known, an interrogator. Prior was deployed to Kuwait in October 2002, and after six months in the desert, he was anxious for the war to start. "Every soldier in Kuwait feels the same way," Prior goes on to explain in his narrative,

even though we never say so, never in fact talk about it. Every day as
we inch closer to the inevitable but still unknown date when we will
charge across the berm we grow more certain it is a terrible idea and
grow more apprehensive partly because we want to begin before the
horrifying heat of summer starts to simmer, partly because we just
want to get it over with, but mostly, deep down, we are afraid it may
not happen, and even though we don't want it to happen we have
grown to count on it. We are, however reluctant, soldiers, and we have
trained and trained, lived eaten and slept a hundred pretend wars,
and we are desperately ready to commence with a real one, however
much we dread it.

And then, almost before Prior himself realizes it, the war has begun.

We haven't even crossed the border yet when an explosion rocks our left side. Later we will find out that it is an errant Iraqi missile aimed at Kuwait City, but we all assume now a battle is starting, except that nothing else follows and we proceed uneasily to the border. Just as planned, the berms and fences are breached, the line through marked, the other side secure. We hear sporadic small-arms fire in the distance, but it dies down quickly, and nothing about it comes over the net, so we don't figure it to be real resistance. Still, everyone is tense, and within an hour the lead hunter-killer team spots an enemy tank to his two o'clock and asks Apache Six for permission to fire.

"Are you sure it's an enemy tank?" Six asks.

"Roger, Six, it's a T-54."

"Kill it."

We hear the boom of the Abrams's big gun, and the team leader reports a direct hit.

"Six, we have some movement on our left, can't make it out yet, but it could be a group of tanks."

Meanwhile nothing stirs from the burning tank to our right. The CO has the first team keep moving while a trail team sweeps out for a better look at the tank.

"Six, I think it's at least three T-62s, eleven o'clock. Permission to engage."

"You're sure they're not our tracks?"

No response.

"Why don't you wait till you see what you're shooting, Blue."

"Roger."

"Six, this is White Four. Coming around the tank on the right."

"Send it, Four."

"The good news is, it's an enemy tank, and it's destroyed. The bad news is, it looks like it was destroyed in Desert Storm."

We all chuckle.

"Apache Six, this is Blue One. Negative enemy contact on the left here."

"Well, what was it, Blue?"

"It looks like it's, uh . . . a herd of camels."

We could hear a collective groan from the entire troop.

"All right, Apache, everybody settle down," Six said. "Every blip on the radar's not gonna be Godzilla. Scan your lane, and wait till you can identify something. Six out."

A sandstorm hits just after dark, and it gets harder and harder to follow the order of march. We are traveling with no lights except our blackouts, the dim bulbs that are only visible by NVGs. The air is full of sand, and there is only a bare sliver of a waning moon. Chief Wilder raises Chaos on the radio and asks who they are following. "Nobody," they yell, "we can't see anything!"

Chief tells them to follow us and, cursing, Gene veers off in the direction he thinks he saw the convoy, and the rest of the train falls in behind us. Mike and I, in the back and without NVGs, can see nothing except dim swirls of sand and the occasional faint bouncing set of lights from roving parts of the convoy. The terrain gets rockier and hillier, and our gear, so carefully placed, is bouncing up and down and around. By the time we catch up with the vehicles ahead of us, the convoy is in shambles. There are vehicles all over the rocky desert. Captain Lyle is anxious to get to Samawah because Crazy Horse is taking the canal bridge and we are supposed to immediately take the river bridges. He is shouting on the radio, back and forth with the first sergeant, trying to locate the sprawling pieces of his unit.

"Band-Aid, where are you?" he yells into the radio.

"We're just right of Apache Seven," they answer.

"That's a negative," the first sergeant cuts in. "I don't see anybody on my right."

"Don't give me this right-left shit," the captain counters, "give me a goddamn grid!"

Band-Aid reads off a grid, and the captain is silent, plotting it, while the first sergeant stays on the radio trying to consolidate the trains.

"Where the fuck are we?" Chief Wilder asks, his eyes jumping from the plugger to the map.

"We're right behind the 113s. That's either Rock or Thunder up there."

"Is Apache Seven behind us?"

"Must be."

"Band-Aid, you are nowhere near Apache Seven," says the commander. "Who is the last in the convoy?" There is silence on the radio. "Goddammit," Seven yells, "Apache Eight, you're supposed to be the trail vehicle! Is there anyone behind you?"

"This is Apache Eight. I can't see anybody anywhere."

In the truck, we groan.

"All right, listen up, trains," Apache Six says. "We are going to take those damn bridges, whether you come along or not. Unless you want to stay here in the middle of fucking nowhere by yourselves, you better keep up." A moment later he gets back on the radio. "Guide ons, guide ons, guide ons: I want everyone to stop in place. I say again, the convoy is halting now. Drivers, take off your NODs and switch to white light. I say again, everyone in the convoy, switch to white light." Slowly the desert lights up, and through the haze of sand lights pop up in every direction, amid the humming of idling engines.

"Good God," someone in our truck mutters. There is no semblance of order at all.

We start sprinting north, rolling over absurdly rough terrain, jagged rocky hills and ravines with no trail. I expect to flip the trailer or puncture a tire at any moment. There is less talk over the radio, but we hear several M-113 armored personnel carriers lose their tracks, and one of the trucks snaps its steering column. We hit the road just before dawn and come upon the combat tracks waiting for us. Remarkably, the whole convoy, minus the downed vehicles, quickly regroups in the gray light, and as the sun rises we roll into the muddy fields below Samawah. There are groves of palm trees along the road, the first green things we have seen in months, and some simple block houses. We veer off the road in front of the canal, where Crazy has set checkpoints, and drive along to a muddy bank just south of the city. We park next to a CNN truck and eavesdrop on the correspondent's broadcast. He seems to be practicing his lead-in.

"Thirty-six hours after the war officially started, I stand here with members of the Seventh Cavalry Regiment—"

"It's been thirty-six hours since the war started, and the Seventh Cavalry Regiment is poised in front of the first engagement—"

"After thirty-six hours of driving through the desert, the Seventh Cavalry Regiment is—"

We quickly lose interest. It has begun to rain lightly, and we get in the truck and close our eyes, too tired to sleep.

Shots ring out just ahead of us.

"Contact on left side," the lead platoon leader calls out on the radio. Apache Six orders the convoy to speed up and fire on any confirmed targets.

"Three dismounts, ten o'clock!" a squad leader calls out.

"Watch out on the left side," I yell, inanely, since our truck has no gunner, and all we can do is shoot out of whatever window we are sitting by. The only other person on the left side besides myself is Gene, who is driving and can't very well scan and shoot at the same time.

Tracers flash up at the head of the convoy, and the 25 mm guns start booming. I hear a bullet hit my side of the truck, and instinctively I fire a couple of rounds into the darkness.

"What are you shooting at?" Chief yells, and I scream back, "They hit our truck," not answering his question, so he yells again, "*But what are you shooting at?*"

I don't answer, and tell myself to settle down. Members of the lead element start identifying the attackers better: they are wearing black, they are driving white trucks, they are firing rifles and RPGs.

"White truck, eleven o'clock," Gene calls out.

I lean out the window and fire at the truck until it disappears behind us. In front of me, Gene is yelling. "Are you all right?" I call out, thinking he's been hit. "It's your goddamn brass!" he yells back. With every shot my rifle was flinging hot empty casings onto Gene's head, neck, and lap.

"Was there anybody in it?" Chief asks, meaning the truck. I replay the truck flashing by in my head. Not only was there no one in it, it was riddled with bullet holes from every rifle in every previous vehicle in the convoy. Afterwards, the Chief, Mike, and Gene will often bring up the deadly white Toyota. "You sure took out that empty truck," Chief will cackle. "You whipped the shit out of that thing."

Apache Six gets us back into a more orderly formation, and we continue down the road. Soon there is more shooting, and we race through it without stopping, then drive on, and then more shooting. Finally we stop and our team jumps out onto the ground and begins scanning for targets. Scanning is hopeless without night vision goggles; there is no moon and we can't see where the earth stops and the sky begins. It is just an endless expanse of black, with only the tracers from the .50-cal guns blazing into the darkness.

Then we hear the hum from the sky, the sweet sound of close air support. An A-10 screams down with its cannon blazing, and then it, or another plane, drops its payload, the last bomb so powerful it almost makes my insides collapse. Throughout the firefight I hear a clicking from the other side of the truck, and after the last bomb, when there is nothing but dead silence, I ask Chief Wilder what it was.

"Were you taking pictures?" Gene asks from the truck.

Chief grins. "I got some good ones."

"Just don't leave the flash on," I say.

Apache Six calls on the radio to move on. As we roll out he gives the troop some words of encouragement, and then the XO, who is apparently at the point tracking the route, says he wants to change it to avoid some built-up areas ahead. The commander assents, and after driving through a silent town and over a small bridge and along a canal, we turn right off the main road and stop for a moment.

I take Chief Wilder's NVGs and pull guard while he monitors the radio. There is a road far out to the left, and occasionally a car drives by with headlights. I can hear voices on the radio, but I'm not close enough to understand what they are saying. Gradually the gunfire subsides.

Daniel, the interpreter working for Civil Affairs, comes up to me with a roll of toilet paper. It seems that all the excitement has loosened his bowels, and he absolutely has to relieve himself.

"Can you cover me?" he asks, looking sheepish.

"You're serious?"

"Yes, I *have* to," he insists.

I nod, and he runs over and squats in the culvert across the road. Beyond the culvert is a flat dusty field with patches of palms. Off in the distance there is more gunfire, then shouting on the radio.

"Apache Six, Apache Seven. We are taking direct fire! Direct fire from the north side of the road!"

"Apache Seven, Apache Six. Set up a tight perimeter and return fire. Do you have eyes on the enemy?"

"Negative, no eyes on."

"Lay down suppressive fire, but watch those houses! Do not fire on the houses unless you have positively identified a target."

I am looking in the direction of the gunfire, and when I turn back toward Daniel I freeze. In the green haze of the NVGs there are five green figures creeping stealthily through the palms just behind Daniel.

"Mike!" I hiss, "five people, nine o'clock, can't see who." We both drop to a knee and aim our rifles. Mike doesn't have NVGs so he is blind, just waiting to do what I do. The figures are dead silent and still moving cautiously. Slowly I rotate the selector from SAFE to SEMI, and hear a faint click as Mike does the same. Two of the figures are cradling what look like weapons in their arms.

I should shoot them now. I should not give them a chance to shoot first. The trigger is cold against my finger. I struggle to keep Daniel and the five figures in the screen at the same time. I should shoot.

"*Qif!*" I yell as loud as I can. "*Irmee salahik!*" [Stop! Throw down your weapon!]

They freeze. A quivering voice calls out, "*Ma termee. Medeniyoun.*" [Don't shoot. We're civilians.]

I walk up a few steps. It is a family of five shivering next to the road, actually a family of seven. What I had seen as the two weapons in their arms are babies wrapped up in blankets. "Ease up, Mike, they're civilians." Daniel, crouching behind a bush practically underneath them, tells them to go to a safe place. They quickly cross the road between our trucks and disappear into the trees, silent as ghosts.

When we approach the Euphrates again, we jump from Apache to Bone Crusher, another troop in the cavalry squadron. We stop just outside the town and hear gunfire ahead. Soon we start moving again as the Iraqi fighters up front are killed or driven off, and a light sandstorm kicks up. We quickly lose sight of the horizon as it disappears into the orange-gray haze. When we reach the river, the convoy stops and the tanks move up and take the first bridge. They receive fire immediately, and we listen to the battle as they fight their way across the bridge. They advance through the town, getting fire from all over.

As we pull up to the bridge, we see an old man carrying a paper bag and wearing a ratty blue blazer over the light robe called a *dishdasha*. He is patiently standing in front of a scout who is holding him in place with his rifle.

There is some sporadic small-arms fire in the distance, but it is quiet here by the bridge. I approach the old man and ask him what he was doing.

"I am trying to cross the bridge. My house is over there."

"What is in your bag?"

"Just ordinary items from the *dukhan* [small convenience store]."

"Show me."

I make sure the scout is covering me as I peer over the old man's shoulder while he sifts through the eggs and milk and sugar in the bag.

"Listen," I say, "it is not safe here. It is not safe to cross the bridge, and it is not safe to go to your house. Find some place safe here—maybe the *dukhan*—where you can wait until we are gone."

"How long will that take?"

"I don't know how long, it could be a few hours, it could be all day."

"I will sit here and wait."

"Listen, it is not safe to be near our forces or the *muselaheen* [armed fighters]. There is fighting all around here."

"I can't sit here?" he asks, pointing at the railing that lines the road approaching the bridge.

"You can sit anywhere you want, as long as you stay out of the way, but I would prefer you stay away until the fighting is over."

He looks at me wearily and shuffles back up the road away from the bridge. I turn to the scout, who asks what the old man wanted. When I tell him, he says, "What the hell? Doesn't he know we're trying to fight a war here?"

I shrug and head back to the truck. The old man has not, as I had hoped, gone back to the *dukhan.* He has stopped farther up the road and sat on the railing. After a while a younger man walks by. The old man shouts something at him, and the younger man smiles and keeps walking until the scout stops him. Gene and I get out, and Gene searches him while I ask him what he wants. His cousins live across the river and he wants to see if they are safe. I tell him he has to wait and then ask him several questions about the *muselaheen,* and he pleads ignorance, and I tell him he should find a safe place to wait until we are gone. He nods again, and walks back up the road and sits next to the old man. Soon another man comes and then another. We search and question them, and they sit down on the railing. By the time we get the call that the convoy is being relieved, there is a line of ten men sitting, talking, and smoking, waiting for our battle for their town to end. One is a doctor who speaks a little English, and I give him some general instructions for the crowd: raise their hands if they approach American troops, keep out in the open if they insist on going outside, avoid the *muselaheen*. Then I go back to the truck and listen to the radio, and we wait anxiously for orders to get the hell out of town, which finally come. Just before we drive off to find our place in the convoy I jump out and run back to them.

"Listen, there are more American soldiers coming. Do not cross any of the bridges until all the Americans are gone, or they will stop you, and maybe shoot you. Stay out of their way. Do you understand me?"

They all nod, and I jump back in the truck. As we pull out I look back and they are all waving.

We continue driving, and, as the sandstorm gets worse, the dim light from the sky begins to fail altogether. No one knows where we are going, and the radio is mostly silent. I nod off for a moment, and when my head clears I think about relieving Gene with the driving so he can get some sleep. Then the shooting starts again.

This time they are smart: instead of hitting us up front, they have waited until the front of the convoy has passed and strike us in the middle. Bone Six yells at everyone to hit the gas and punch through. With all of us cursing the vehicle in front of us, which is not moving fast enough for our liking, Gene stomps on the gas. The Iraqis have set the ambush on a sharp turn, and we can hear the bullets zipping across our hood and tail end as we hit the turn and haul ass. I see muzzle flashes off the road on our left and shoot at them, and Gene yelps in surprise as my hot brass lands in his lap.

A rocket whooshes by, then another. Tracers are flying all over, from every direction.

There is havoc on the radio, all the leaders screaming at once. Some kind of a rocket screams over our left flank and lands up ahead somewhere in the convoy.

"CEASE FIRE! CEASE FIRE!" someone yells on the radio, not identifying himself. "You're shooting friendlies!"

No one ceases fire.

"Who's shooting?" Bone Six asks someone, everyone. "Who said that?"

We fly by an Abrams on fire and watch as the crew scrambles out of the tank and into another track that's pulled up alongside it.

"Holy shit," Chief says. "Did you see that?"

"There's dismounts up front!" one of the platoon leaders yells in the radio. "I see ten, maybe twenty, small arms, RPGs."

"BRAD DOWN! BRAD DOWN!" someone starts screaming, then, "They're swarming all over here! There's a hundred, maybe two hundred! Abandoning Brad!"

We listen in horror, bullets still flying around us, at the nightmare up front, in the very direction we are racing.

"This is Bone Six. Turn around, Bone Crusher! Every vehicle turn around and drive!"

"What the fuck?" Gene yells as he brakes. "We're going back through the kill zone?"

"Just turn around," Chief says.

The road is still on top of a narrow berm, so there is precious little room to turn around, but Gene executes a lightning-fast three-point turn, yelling at the vehicle behind us to get the fuck out of our way. When the other truck takes too long he veers around it. There are some M-113 assault vehicles interspersed among the train, and we swerve around the slower trucks to get in the shade of their firepower. We pass the burning Abrams again, lifeless now, and the shooting increases as we whip around the turn. We don't stop until we reach squadron's rally point.

Before sunrise the next morning we are already moving out. We are back in open desert, and we cut off the road through the sand. We quickly sink into soft beds of dust, and churn through it to the next road, and stick to improved surfaces for the most part after that. It is hot and the convoy throws up clouds of dust into the air, but the sandstorms seem to have left us, and for the first time since we reached Samawah, no one is shooting at us. It is a comforting feeling, but as we get closer to Baghdad we are getting closer and closer to Iraq's proper armies, and I dread the thought, after weathering Kalashnikov and RPG and mortar fire, of getting shot at by tanks and heavy artillery. Occasionally we hear snatches of reports of Iraqi heavy units, but we never seem to get a sense of where or how large they are.

In the late afternoon there is a skirmish with an Iraqi checkpoint on a road parallel to the one we are traveling on. Apache is dispatched, and soon after they call for Bull, so we ride out with a Bradley to our east, following the Brad as it crosses right through a farm field with a small house. There are several figures standing in front of the doorway, staring toward us blankly.

When we get to the checkpoint, there are three zip-tied Iraqis surrounded by some Apache soldiers. We hop out and separate the prisoners, talking to each in quick succession. Two of them are willing to talk, though they don't know much. They were put in place by their unit as a routine checkpoint. The poor bastards were ordered to resist any force and then left to wait for American tanks. To add insult to injury, their lieutenant fled the post a few hours before we found them.

The third prisoner, a sergeant, is as defiant as I've ever seen any EPW. "I still resist the Americans," he tells me. "I would still be fighting if it wasn't for your superior technology." I try not to laugh; I admire his gumption. It turns out that, in what may be a first in war, the three surrendered themselves to an American helicopter hovering over them. It was a couple of Kiowas that found the checkpoint and rained down 25 mm fire on them until they raised the white flag, and then the helos hovered in place until some ground troops could reach them and take them into custody.

The prisoner is uncooperative, but he is also furious with his unit and particularly his lieutenant. I ask him why he is protecting the officers who betrayed him, while his silence means more of his fellow enlisted troops will die, and soon I have him talking. Unfortunately, he knows almost nothing. The Iraqi command's reputation for keeping their soldiers, even their NCOs, in the dark is proving true. It may not be an effective way to run an army, but it is an effective way to stymie an interrogation.

We drive back to Apache's train where they have set up camp and spend the night on an open plain. I've lost track of exactly where we are, but we seem to be surrounded by friendlies, since our security posture is low. I expect there to be an argument about who will guard the prisoners, but Civil Affairs all of a sudden seems happy to hang out with them. They camp next to us and are up half the night talking with their prisoners, about Iraqi culture, Islam, war, peace, and so on. By the time I drop off, nestled in my spot on the hood of the Humvee, they are all great friends, even the defiant Iraqi sergeant, laughing and cutting up while the rest of the troops slumber.

CENTCOM has ordered a pause for the entire Operation Iraqi Freedom. We are all to stay put indefinitely to refit, which everyone desperately needs. Some of the troops' vehicles are on their last legs, and Apache Eight starts making the rounds as everyone else breaks open their vehicles for some serious maintenance. While Mike and Gene tend to our equipment, Chief and I walk to our squadron headquarters, and I stop by a familiar-looking cargo truck. Inside, with their hands tied behind their backs, are all of the prisoners we have collected so far. Their eyes light up when they recognize me. They assault me with questions. It takes me a minute to realize they are all saying the same desperate thing: "Please give us cigarettes."

I tell the guard standing at the foot of the truck that they are asking for cigarettes. "Is it OK?" he asks.

"It's not good for them," I tell him. "It causes cancer."

"But, I mean," he says, not smiling, "is it . . . ?" I know what he means. He wants to know if it is all right to be nice to the enemy.

"Sure, if you want," I say. "They're your cigarettes."

He pulls out his pack, spurring the prisoners to rush to the door, and we stick the cigarettes in their mouths and light them, and they ask me more questions: Where are they going? How long will they be in custody? When will the handcuffs come off? Will the food get any better? Will they get cigarettes? Will they go to America? I tell them the truth, that they are going to a detention facility, they will stay there until the war is over, the food will not get any better, they will rarely if ever get cigarettes, and they will not get sent to America. They seem pleased that they are being fed and not being beaten, but disappointed that they are not going to America, and crushed by the news about the cigarettes.

That night the sky lights up with artillery. We are shelling Hillah, we are shelling Karbala, we are shelling Baghdad. Since we paused the artillery has caught up with us, so after dark we watch the streaks of fire thrusting up into the sky, and listen for the cool free fall back down to earth, and then see the flash, then the boom, as it pummels the cities, like the lightning, then the thunder, of a rainstorm. The shelling cleaves me in two, one side shaken, knowing each flash and boom means more innocent Iraqis dying in their homes; the other side stilled, knowing it also means less of the enemy likely to shoot at me. I sit and watch, picturing the Fedayeen and Republican Guard getting annihilated. Die, motherfuckers, die, I say to them all. You, not me. Not me.

We drive toward Baghdad, past Karbala, through the Karbala Gap. We are finally confronting Saddam's conventional army and the tank battles are commencing. We come upon the carnage as the burnt-out enemy vehicles are cooling, as the dead bodies are stiffening. This is when the tourism begins;

the soldiers start taking pictures of the corpses, stripping them of mementos—weapons, web gear, belt buckles, anything shiny that you can carry easily and wipe the blood off quickly. Our team is scouring through the wreckage looking for survivors to interrogate. The stench leaves us reeling.

We bypass the twisted smoking metal of the vehicles hit by rockets and bombs, where the corpses are simply blackened effigies of former human beings, and concentrate on the fighting positions riddled with bullets, where the bodies are untouched by fire, harmed only by bullets and the loss of blood. But still they are all dead. By the time we pass Yusifiyah and swing west to Abu Ghraib, there is grass on the ground and we can see palm trees. Apache Six sends us to scout out a car that has attacked them. A Bradley shot it up, but there may be a survivor. We slowly approach the car on foot, weapons pointed ahead. I call out, but there is no reply, and we quickly determine the three men inside are dead. Gene pulls something out of the clutches of the corpse in the driver's seat.

"What are you doing?" I ask him.

"It's a Dragunov," he says, brandishing the long sniper's rifle. "Fifty cal."

I start to tell him to put it down, then change my mind. What do I care? Gene grabs a corner of the dead man's shirt and wipes the blood off the barrel. When we get back to Apache he scrubs the weapon down, then until sunset he scans the horizon with the sights, the muzzle fanning right, then left. The dead man didn't have any ammo left, so there are no rounds for Gene to shoot.

"I'll find some," he says. "We got time."

Second Brigade is approaching Baghdad, just east of us, and we follow their progress over the radio in between talking to Iraqis. The Iraqis can't stand the idea of unburied bodies, and the civilians quickly organize themselves into burial teams; we supervise them as they cross our line of control, dragging corpses out of tanks and foxholes, digging shallow graves on the side of the road and quickly filling them. They wrap their headdresses around their faces to protect themselves from the stench, but it does little good. The smell of death can't be avoided. It drowns out the smell of smoke from the fires that have broken out in Abu Ghraib, western Baghdad, and out towards Fallujah.

"I'll find some," Gene repeats to himself. "We got time." He squints into the sun. A sandstorm is kicking up, tilting the pillars of smoke on the horizon to the east, and the sun brightens, even though it is setting.

GET SOME

Fiction

First Lieutenant Paul A. Stieglitz

At the same time that soldiers with the U.S. Army's 3rd Infantry Division were pushing northward through the desert toward Baghdad, U.S. Marines with the 1st Marine Division were also converging on the Iraqi capital by way of An Nasiriyah. The Marines were—to the disappointment of many of them—encountering minimal resistance as they charged through one town after another. Twenty-eight-year-old First Lieutenant Paul A. Stieglitz was a ground intelligence officer in the 1st Battalion, 4th Marines, and served as the commander of the battalion's Scout Sniper Platoon. The following story, although a work of fiction, is based substantially on what Stieglitz saw as he and his platoon, every one of them eager to experience actual combat, rushed almost nonstop through Iraq.

I stand up and look at the horizon through my binos. Big surprise. Not a goddamn thing. Doc Q has the other side of the road. I bring up my M-40 sniper rifle and place it in the 550-cord sling we made on the Humvee's frame. I'm stiff from the cold and from sitting in the back for too long. The drivers are pushing on nothing but coffee grounds. The forward-thinking ones brought some Ripped Fuel or some other over-the-counter stimulant, and now they pass it around like candy.

"Keene, go see what's going on up with the lieutenant's vehicle," I say. Azuela comes back to the vehicle from his two minutes of fun.

"How you doing, Azuela?" I say as we glance at each other.

"Where's the fight?" he replies.

Good question. We started with such high hopes and an adrenaline rush. Intel passed that we would not have any resistance for a while, until we got further north, but still. It was hard to not get pumped up when we were finally moving into Iraq. We sat in Kuwait for one long-ass month, and before that, we were on the ship for forty-five days. I had said goodbye to my wife, Karen, almost three months earlier. Before that, we trained with the expectation of going to Iraq, based on what the president was saying in the news for around five or six months. Talk about a buildup. And now those goddamn Iraqis don't even have the class to meet us at the border. After two days of driving, the excitement has eased into bitterness. Most of the guys here just want a chance to kill someone, and now it looks like we came all this way and aren't even going to get a Combat Action Ribbon.

Sergeant Azuela rummages through his gear until he finds his cigarettes. He pulls two out and gives me one. I take it without a word and he lights us. I never smoked but started to in Kuwait. Just something to do. Most of the guys in the infantry are just ordinary men doing an extraordinarily painful job. It makes working with a true psychopath like Azuela all the more refreshing.

He's a real American hero. His parents are Puerto Rican immigrants who came to America when he was five or so and settled in Brooklyn. Never call him Puerto Rican or Mexican or Hispanic. All he is, he says, is American. I've never heard him speak Spanish. He came into the Marines as a cook and quickly worked his way to sergeant. And then after 9/11, he wanted to get back at those motherfuckers and went about it the only way he knew how, by transferring to the infantry. All he ever talks about is killing and fighting. He really lives the Marine Corps. He has a wife, but I don't know anybody who ever met her. He took a few different types of martial arts in his free time and is missing a front tooth that he lost in a fight. He just never bothered to get it replaced. He is always demonstrating his tricks on the guys, "teaching" them. Things like how to kill a man silently by disemboweling him with one of the small samurai swords he keeps in his boots.

"Two minutes!" yells Lance Corporal Levick. Finally, we're getting ready to roll.

Lance Corporal Keene runs back and hands his M-16 rifle to Doc as he climbs in.

"What's up? The lieutenant got any good intel?" I ask.

"Fifth Marines has been fighting in that oil field, I guess they have had some casualties."

"Any dead?" asks Doc.

"Yeah. I don't know how many."

"Cool. Maybe we'll get some," says Azuela with a smile.

We settle in on our piled-up gear as the convoy starts up again.

I wake up and it's dark. The convoy has stopped and we have been sitting in the same spot for around five hours. Earlier today, our biggest excitement was when a single car drove up onto the embankment around 1,800 meters to the east. As soon as it was visible, every gun in the battalion was on it. The radio traffic was hilarious. You would have thought we were being flanked by the Red Guard. It turned out to be just some guy in his car. This country does have like forty million people in it, right? People do sometimes drive around, right? Everyone needs to chill the fuck out.

It's my turn on watch, so I take the NVGs from Doc and start my surveillance of the horizon. The companies have pushed out Marines on security, and they are in groups around five hundred meters out. I am looking out past them, sitting on the hood of our vehicle. After about an hour and a half, Captain Madrigal makes his way back to our vehicle. He's the commanding officer of the Headquarters and Service Company, which in an infantry battalion is pretty much everyone but those actually doing the fighting. He slaps the hood and yells, "All right, gents, we're moving out real soon. We're going right through the city and they've got heavy fighting up there! I need you to stay alert and stay alive!" and he's off to the next vehicle with the same speech. What a crazy, spastic bastard.

Over the radio, they call for all of the drivers for a route brief and Sergeant Azuela and PFC Claybuck go. I have my guys clean their weapons and do a function check and go over all their gear. We all have M-16s and pistols. I also have my M-40 sniper rifle complete with night-vision scope, and one of only two monstrous M-82 Barrett .50-cal sniper rifles. Plus extra rounds, radios (both handheld and back mounted), grenades, claymore antipersonnel mines, antitank rockets, food, and other miscellaneous crap.

"How's it going?" asks our lieutenant, who sauntered up quietly in the dark.

"Good, sir," says Levick.

"Cleaning your weapons? Good. I guess I don't have to micromanage you all, right?" He looks at me with a smile and I just stare back. He is an all-right guy, but he has a knack of saying the wrong things that just get under my skin. I thought that the biggest part of officer training was to make them feel like invincible leading machines, so they can pass off their crap to the troops. But I guess it didn't work on this guy.

"Look, you all know the plan, right?" asks the lieutenant. "Stay flexible, we need to be able to adapt to any situation."

"Aye, sir," I answer with an inward roll of the eyes. Despite my frustration, one of the good things about our lieutenant is that he knows the value of the sniper team leader, and even though he sounds like a Marine Corps leadership pamphlet, he always stresses initiative and judgment. He's not the kind of guy to micromanage me. Hell, let's see him try it. I am almost nine years older than him and have a few tricks in my bag.

And no, I'm not some screwed-up sergeant who can't get promoted. I got out of the Corps after my first enlistment. Nothing really seemed to be going on back in 1997. So I went to college to be a paramedic and worked that job until 2001.

Two days after 9/11 I went to the recruiter and asked about coming back in with broken time. Like everyone else I was pissed off beyond belief about the attack. I didn't even tell Karen about it until after. They let me back in with a reduction in rank to corporal and I joined again on November 12.

People always ask why I came back in. As long as I can remember, I've wanted to fight in a war. I figured if I could put my desires to good use, it would be okay, so I joined up with the Marines. When I got to my first battalion it felt like home. After 9/11, I returned because I knew there was going to be some major shit going down and the Marines were going to be doing most of the hard-core fighting, as always. Fuck if I was going to miss it.

The lieutenant returns to his vehicle, and I go through some possible scenarios with my team. We practice actions on ambush and talk through room clearing and entering buildings again, just to make sure everyone has their heads in the game. I talk a little about sniper/observer dialogue with my observer and radio operator, Lance Corporal Keene. My four-man team is made up of me, Keene, Levick, and Doc. As the team leader and only school-trained sniper, I would be the one shooting the M-40. Lance Corporal Levick is my assistant team leader and carries our new M-16 A-4, which has a heavier barrel and is supposed to be accurate to eight hundred meters. It also comes with a good magnified sight and night vision, so Levick is able to split from me and act as a de facto sniper. Doc is our team's medic. He also carries a radio. A real good group of guys. They are all experienced, relatively, and they were chosen for the platoon for their maturity and intelligence. In a sniper team, each one needs to be able to do it all. I can't babysit them like I would if I were in the rifle companies. They need to be able to act without instructions, which is a rare thing in the companies for lance corporals.

Sergeant Azuela says, "They just gave the five-minute warning," and we all get in the back. Me and Keene on the right, Levick and Doc on the left facing outboard. Up and down the convoy, Marines are running back to their vehicles. Claybuck is in the passenger seat up front and is monitoring the battalion TACNET. If anything goes down, Azuela and Claybuck stay in the vehicle. Unless of course it's an ambush, in which case we either drive through it or everyone gets out and fights.

The vehicles all start at the same time so that our numbers can't be detected by sound. We start moving. We can see and hear artillery firing in the direction of the city. They fire constantly, like popping popcorn. After a half hour of moving at a snail's pace, we pass the artillery, probably a full battalion firing, spread out in a line perpendicular to our route on both sides of us. The noise punches you in the gut every time they fire.

"Whoa, check it out," Azuela calls over his shoulder. "Up ahead."

We look and can see the Euphrates River that marks the southern boundary of Nasiriyah. We will be crossing a bridge and on the right side of it we notice a burning tank, glowing in the night sky.

"Sweet!"

"I guess this is the real thing, huh?"

"Get some!"

The convoy comes to a stop for a minute with the burning tank in our view, with us on the south side of the bridge.

"Hey Azuela, where's the convoy?" I ask after a few minutes. I look ahead and see nothing; only the bridge and blackness beyond. Azuela had whited out his NVGs by looking at the fire and didn't see when the convoy took off. Azuela punches it, going maybe forty miles an hour, which seems like a hundred after driving fifteen for all this time. Levick's M-16 is pointed over the side, and he goes back to watching the darkness. I know that my guys are all just praying to see action.

Low buildings line the street, two or three stories max. Third-world-type buildings. Tropical plants contrast with the desert environment we've driven through up to this point. Palm trees and thick, unkempt vegetation grow between the buildings.

We come to another bridge and Azuela slows down a little. There is a burned-out shell of an amtrac, one of ours, on the bridge. Up ahead we can see tracers flashing across the road from both sides. An artillery illumination round goes off and lights up the sky. We are driving full into a fight.

Levick says that the convoy is up ahead waiting until the fighting dies down.

"Who's getting some?" I ask. Charlie Company is first in the procession, but they aren't necessarily the ones fighting.

"Bravo," answers Levick. Right. They are second in line followed by Alpha, so I assume that Bravo had been ambushed or hit after Charlie passed. I hear the popping sound of small arms punctuated by the boom of AT-4s or SMAWs, probably used to punch a hole in a wall while breeching.

I look at my team. They are patiently watching over the side of the Humvee, scanning with NVGs. "Give me the headset," I say to Levick, "and switch it over to regimental intel net."

"Desperado Six, this is Desperado One," I call, trying to get our platoon commander.

"Desperado One, this is Desperado Six," he answers.

"Disco," using the code to switch to our own battalion intel net.

"Roger."

Levick switches freqs and I wait for my platoon commander.

"Desperado One, go ahead."

"Roger, we should be up in the fight, I can see a good building from back here that we can get up on and provide covering fire. Requesting permission."

"Roger, get a grid ready and I'll get permission from Palehorse Three."

I lied about the building. I couldn't see shit, we were too far away, but I was counting on the lieutenant being so into his radio that he wasn't looking at the fight up ahead. I know we can find something, though. So, we wait for permission from Palehorse Three, the operations officer who controls, or at least keeps track of, all of the moving pieces of the battalion. Each of my guys turns and gives me either a big smile, or with Doc, a little lower-lip biting complete with flared nostrils.

The lieutenant calls back and gives us our permission. "Just make sure you stay on the west side of the road when you move into position. There is a big concentration of bad guys up there, east of the road. Their ambush was pretty well coordinated."

"Roger, Desperado One out."

I have Sergeant Azuela drive up to the beginning of the convoy and then we get out to walk up to the fight, maybe five hundred meters ahead. Levick radios in as we leave convoy security and we spread out in patrol formation on the west of the road.

There are a few one-story buildings, and we go behind those to move up and stay back from the road. Keene is point, then me, and then Levick, with Doc bringing up the rear. We aren't doing the typical sniper stalking-type movement, trying to stay hidden from all observation; the situation doesn't call for it. We need to get up there as quickly as possible, and I don't want these eighteen-year-old kids on Bravo's security thinking we are trying to sneak into their lines.

We move almost at a run, staying behind buildings and in vegetation as much as possible. This is easy because the whole area is overgrown. The chemical protective suits are really difficult to move in. It's like wearing an extra-large set of pajamas over a three-piece suit and then trying to look smooth as you dance a tango.

We come around the corner of a building. "Halt!" a bush yells at us. "I have a book on my desk," he challenges us, using the challenge word "desk." The password is "waiter."

"Your mother fucked a waiter," answers Keene.

We continue moving parallel to the road, keeping back about a hundred meters until we come to the biggest building we can see. Three stories. Close to the road, on our right, we can see the amtracs of Bravo Company and a lot of Marines lying prostrate on the ground. Some seem to be in decent cover, but most are just lined up near the road. Looks a little too close together, but who am I to second-guess?

I get on Bravo's TACNET and ask if anyone is in the building that we want to go into. The company XO tells us no and I ask permission to go in and occupy the roof. "Be my guest," he says like the jackass he is.

I'd like to have some suppressive fire on the building, just in case there is someone in there, but it would take too long to coordinate, plus stealth would be out the window with a squad of machine guns shooting the place to hell. We are going to go in all at once, in a stack, just like we practiced before coming over here.

This part gets me nervous and I decide to move up to the building and look in the windows to check it out. It's all dark, just like all the buildings in the city, because the power is out. We peer in one window and it looks like an ordinary office building, with desks and office furniture inside. We move to the back and more of the same. Fuck it, I think as I get impatient, we need to get in there.

I signal to my team that we're going through the window. Doc gets on his hands and knees and Keene stands on his back and looks into the window for a few seconds. Levick and I are keeping security and watching to the left and right. I motion for him to go in, and Keene breaks the window with the butt of his rifle. He clears the glass from the pane and heaves himself in. Next I go through and then Landers. Keene is on one knee pointing his rifle at the door leading out of the office. Levick and I reach out the window and pull in Doc.

Once in, we listen for a minute. All quiet. The air smells like dust and mold. We get back in order and proceed out of the room. I can tell that we are all nervous; a little sharpness in movements, quickness maybe that isn't always there in training. We stack up by the door, and I give Keene a knee in his leg, which is his signal to open the door. We explode into the other room, each of us covering his corners like we practiced time and time again. I feel warm feelings of pride for a second, before I make myself concentrate on what we're doing. There'll be time for pride if we all make it back.

We move through two more rooms this way before we find the hallway and the stairwell. We move up the stairs to the second and then third floors. Now to find a way to the roof. We move through each room, looking for a hatch, or better yet, a stairway up, but there isn't one. There might be a ladder on the outside of the building, going up from a window, but I decide not to waste time looking for it. I motion to go to the forward window, the one that looks out over the street and at our potential targets.

We set up. Keene and I drag a desk to make a good, stable shooting position as Doc opens all the windows. Not just the one I will be shooting out of, because that would alert the not-so-casual observer of our location. I arrange my shooting position on the desk, Keene sets up his observation position next to me, and Levick and Doc move to the rear of the building to cover security.

I set my pack on the desk in order to provide a platform to place the barrel of my M-40 on. The desk is in the middle of the room so that we aren't too close to the window, silhouetting ourselves in the frame. I grab a bunch of binders from a bookshelf in the office and stack them on the desk to rest my shooting elbow on, setting up a makeshift platform that is angled down at the street and buildings ahead of us. When Keene is ready, sitting Indian style on another desk with his elbows on his knees and his binos on his tripod in front of him, I tell him to call to Bravo and give them our position and say that we're ready to shoot.

We begin. We're in a good position, a little to the north of all of Bravo's amtracs. I can see the furthest northern amtrac about a hundred meters to our south. Charlie is to the north, but they aren't visible from here. I start looking for guys with guns that I can shoot.

I see two buildings on the other side of the street, one of which is two stories tall and the other, one story. In between the two buildings is a nice field with plenty of concealment from bushes and trees. Lots of shadows and good places to hide. Were I an Iraqi, I would definitely use it to move through, and that's what I'm counting on. We hear over Keene's radio that Bravo is preparing to clear a building they think has the most enemy in it, to our south. We hear the explosions of two rockets and several machine guns providing suppressive fire. A textbook attack. Keene and I keep looking at our field, hoping that we can get some of the Iraqis running away to the north.

"I think I got one," says Keene. "Two to the left of the center palm tree. I saw movement."

"Got it." I move my gaze to that area, and with my night vision scope, I can see a suspicious dark spot. My rifle's scope is set at 300 yards, and this spot is roughly 350 yards away. No wind. Just aim a little high, I tell myself. I wait until we can get a definite target; no sense in possibly giving our position away. And then the dumb fucker stands up, just like that, in the open. Maybe he thinks he's hidden behind that tree because of the angles. Even better, he has an AK.

I'm about to get my first kill. There's no way I can miss at this range, the guy fills my whole scope, but I take my time anyway, just like I've done thousands of times in training. On my exhale I slowly and gently squeeze the trigger, pulling straight back. The slow controlled motion feels like it takes an eternity, and the guy is raising his rifle up to his shoulder to fire a shot. My crosshairs rest directly on the line that connects his shoulders—he is at about a forty-five degree angle. . . .

BANG!!!

My rifle jumps and I lose sight of anything as it recoils. I quickly bring it back down and look for my target, but I see nothing.

I work the bolt to rack another round. Like butter.

"Center mass, you got him," reports Keene. My heart is racing and I feel a light-headed euphoria. Giddy. I did it. Fucking sweet. Felt just like I always imagined it would.

Some might think that is a little extreme, to imagine shooting someone during training. Maybe it is, but then again, shooting a man is a little extreme as well, and this is what we were sent here to do. I knew if I ever had to use this weapon for real, it would end someone's life. No doubt about it. And if I weren't mentally prepared for that, right now I would probably be a little more worried about what I had just done and not have my head in the game.

Maybe I'd be shaking and trembling, unable to focus. But that guy is a memory to me now. Only the present matters, and I've got more people to shoot.

"Good job, Sergeant," Keene says. I can feel him looking at me.

"Shut the fuck up and keep looking. There should be some more fuckers back there . . . or some running through soon," I say as I slow my breathing to a nice calm, even pace. More shooting by Bravo a few hundred yards away. We listen to the radio chatter on their net.

"I got one . . . four hundred out . . . he's running away from the building," says Keene. I move my rifle to the left and see the guy instantly. He's running, but having a hard time of it with the tall grass and uneven ground. Aim high. I relax my left hand, which my rifle butt rests on, lowering the butt and elevating the crosshairs until they are at his head level. I trail him for a second or two. This one is harder because he's moving, but luckily, or unluckily for him, he's moving perpendicularly to me. Easier to lead. He's not moving quickly, so I keep my crosshairs a fraction of a mil ahead of him and start to squeeze. Lightly, steady . . .

BANG!

The rifle always startles me; just like it should. I bring the scope back down and work the bolt.

"You got him. . . . He went down."

"Impact?"

"I couldn't tell. He just went down."

"Call this in to Bravo. Both kills. Tell them we've got this area covered."

I get two more kills in the same way, bringing my total to four for the night. After about an hour and a half, we move out again. There has not been any shooting for about twenty minutes and Bravo has cleared the three buildings that had been giving trouble. I guess our mission was not to clear the town or route, but merely to go through it and this was a sidetrack, self-defense. When I look at my watch, we've only been in the building for about two hours.

The sun is coming up again as we roll out.

"How was the shooting, Sergeant?" Claybuck asks with his usual wide-eyed enthusiasm.

"Four," I answer. I reach into my pack and take out an MRE. I eat some pound cake as I heat beef ravioli. Doc is already asleep, lying on our gear, and Levick and Keene are talking while they eat. The city looks different in the light. Looks much more like a small town than a city with a million people in it. The air's cool and fresh and there's dew on the plants. Before I know it, we're out of the city and into the suburbs. The city was even smaller than it looked on the map.

We pass a burning little car in the median. I can see the driver's door open and an Iraqi is lying out of the driver's seat with his head on the ground. Dead as a . . . whatever. Just dead.

"Holy shit, look at that." Doc is awake now, watching the view. Then I see what they're talking about. There's a bus ahead completely shot to fuck, still burning a little. Then I catch a whiff of the indescribably revolting smell of burning flesh. Driving past at five miles an hour we get a slo-mo show of the gore inside. Bodies. Maybe fifteen or twenty. All dead. Some charred, black and crisp, windows shot out and a few dead fuckers half in, half out, trying to escape. A few had made it out of the bus and were lying in the road, their bodies contorted in every position imaginable. We drive over the smear of a body already driven over countless times by tracks and tires. There's a pair of boots in the road, sitting in the normal position, as if someone was still wearing them, attached to them, with feet and a few inches of calf inside.

We continue to see the aftermath of last night. Another bus. Same condition. A torn leg in the road. Severed at the hip.

"Holy shit!" says Sergeant Azuela.

I look to see what he's looking at. "Stop the vehicle," I tell him. "Come on, Doc."

We jump over the side of the vehicle and walk over to a body in the road. A small body. A small moving body. A boy about seven or eight years old, lying on his back and raising one of his hands to the sky.

As we walk over to him, I think, *How many vehicles have passed and not stopped for this boy?* I stand over him, looking with a paramedic's critical eye, and gasp a little inside. He is fucked, there is no other way to say it. His eyes move to me and we meet. His big, black, Arab eyes. He moves his arms as if he wants me to pick him up and he lets out a labored, wheezing whine. His eyes are huge with pleading, huge and beautiful and black. His head is split open and there's a large spot of dark sticky blood pooled in a heart shape above his head. He's bleeding from his chest. Old blood, dark blood, is dried on his tank-top T-shirt and pooled at his left. He has crusted, dried blood tracing down both cheeks from his mouth. I can't believe he's still alive. Barefoot with torn shorts.

I take in all of this in an instant. Doc looks through his bag for something and pulls out a stethoscope and listens to his chest as those eyes tear me to pieces. I want to reach down and pick him up and hug him and make everything better. I kneel down beside him and put my hand on his head and hold his forehead. Dried tears have left tracks in the dirt on his face; his eyes stay on me and he tries to say something but just opens his mouth as he looks at me, pleads with me to take care of him, but I can't, we can't. This boy is dead. *Fuck!!!!!* I scream inside.

"Come on, Doc, we gotta go. They're waiting." I pull Doc up and we run back to the Humvee and continue on. Back in the vehicle no one talks. I feel a powerful wave of rage flowing inside and try to let it flow out of me, not resist it, just let it disperse without showing it. Thinking about that boy, scared, all alone, pain, just wanting his mother, confused, not knowing what he did to deserve this or why it happened, just scared and wanting his mother to make it better, but no one comes, cold, night, noise, pain.

Nausea hits. Oh God, please don't let me throw up in front of my guys. I need to keep it together, stay cool, be cool, man. I try to concentrate on my breathing, but my mouth is watering, watering with that bitter alkaline taste. Too late, fuck, here it comes. I'm not going to let it. My back is turned to my guys, I'm looking out the side and I brace myself.

Fuck it, I'm keeping it down, I'm not puking in front of my guys. Not after that. Every muscle in my body tenses and I feel the spasm of my guts. My throat tightens and I will myself to keep it down. My mind and guts are duking it out, and it comes up but I keep my mouth clamped shut. I am not going to let this happen, I squeeze and squeeze and finally it stops and I swallow the majority. I spit a little out and cough. Some went down my windpipe and I cough and cough like I'm dying. But I pull through it. My eyes are watering and I wipe 'em and my mouth and look back at my guys, but no one noticed, thank God. I'm sweating as I take a drink of stale, dirty-tasting water.

I sit back and think about why that affected me so much. I've seen children die before when I was a paramedic and it always bothered me. I once worked on a pretty little eight-year-old girl who was hit by a car crossing the road. Her head had smashed the windshield and she was lying maybe twenty feet from the car when we got there. We did everything we could, which was basically nothing, but she stopped breathing on the way to the hospital. We breathed for her, but they pronounced her dead at the hospital during surgery. I thought that after I quit, I would never need to see anything like that again.

We drive on. The sun is high in the sky now and we're the lead battalion for the division, pushing our way to Baghdad. I settle in for more of the same.

LIFE ON THE USNS *COMFORT*
Journal
Commander Edward W. Jewell, M.D.

After weighing anchor in January 2003, the hospital ship USNS Comfort left Baltimore, Maryland, and slowly chugged across thousands of miles of ocean to its final destination in the Persian Gulf. What the Comfort lacks in speed (and firepower), it makes up for in size and advanced medical technology: the bright white hospital ship, the length of almost three football fields, has one thousand patient beds, twelve fully equipped operating rooms, full state-of-the-art radiological capabilities, several labs, CAT-scan machines, and two oxygen-producing plant systems. In early March, just weeks before the launch of Operation Iraqi Freedom, forty-eight-year-old Commander Edward W. Jewell said goodbye to his wife, Clara, and left their home in Washington, D.C., to fly out to the Middle East. Jewell specializes in diagnostic radiology and was sent to the Comfort for a two-month deployment to evaluate X-rays and determine the severity of internal wounds sustained by American forces. The following excerpts are taken from the journal entries that Jewell wrote aboard ship and then edited later.

March 27
Q: The *Comfort* is a large noncombat hospital ship protected by the most powerful Navy, Army, and Air Force in history. What is there to be afraid of?
A: Everything. Danger is all around us. We are really very close to the action. At times we see oil fires near the shore. However, we cannot really see the combat. We are not afraid of the Iraqi military. If they try to fire a rocket at us it would be easily shot down by artillery on the ground, aircraft, or naval gunnery/rockets. However, we believe there are mines in the Gulf. Purportedly, small boats have approached the *Comfort* several times. When this happens we call in a helo and launch our small boat to run them off. How can we possibly see one of these things in the dark? I think it would be very easy for a ter-

rorist to attack this ship with an explosive-laden small boat. Very easy. The *Comfort* is the slowest ship in the water. We couldn't outrun a rowboat. Huge red crosses on our sides and decks mark the optimum spots to aim a torpedo or rocket to sink us. As a noncombatant ship, *Comfort* is, of course, unarmed. Would the Iraqis attack a hospital ship if they could? Why not? In their view, they were invaded by mercenary infidels who deserve no better. A surgeon buddy of mine Mike from Massachusetts thinks an attack on our ship is a near given, with a 50 percent chance of success. However, he is a proctologist and Red Sox fan and naturally pessimistic.

March 28
Sickening sight: a helicopter's downwash blows a stack of letters overboard. Who knows what was lost? Last letter to save a troubled relationship? A fat check? Notice of tax audit? We'll never know. That's war.

The doctors are all bored from underutilization, but the surgeons seem particularly restless. There are so many of them and not enough cases to fill the time.

The Army helos cannot fly patients out to us in bad weather. The visibility has been poor the last three days, with choppy seas. We were to have received twenty or thirty new patients but they never made it because of the weather. This will all change markedly very soon. A new scheme for casualty movement has *Comfort* playing a more pivotal role. Two all-weather CH-46 Marine helos will be permanently assigned to us. They will be bringing patients to us who have had only basic stabilizing medical care or none at all, coming directly from the battlefield. We hear they will be mostly Americans.

Rumor is an Iraqi speedboat loaded with explosives was intercepted today. It is believed it was headed towards one of our ships, maybe us. I notice today there are more gray-hulled (regular Navy) ships protecting *Comfort*. I hope it stays that way.

March 29
Old Navy jargon "belay my last," meaning disregard my last statement, applies to my commentary from yesterday. We got creamed with fresh casualties last night, thirty new patients, both sides, all needing immediate and significant intervention. The injuries are horrifying. Ruptured eyeballs. Children missing limbs. Large burns. Genitals and buttocks blown off. Grotesque frac-

tures. Gunshot wounds to the head. Faces blown apart. Paraplegics from spine injuries. The number of X-ray studies performed last night in a short period of time is so great it causes the entire system to crash under the burden of the electronic data it is being fed. Miraculously, Cathy and John are able to reboot it.

Our patients are mostly Iraqis. Along with their combat wounds, they are dirty, undernourished, and dehydrated. One rumor says we will treat all the wounded Iraqi EPWs (enemy prisoners of war) for the duration of the war and these are the only patients we will see. If true, this would, in effect, make the *Comfort* a prison hospital ship. The corpsmen on the wards have to guard the prisoners and keep them from communicating with one another to prevent rebellion. As medical people we are trained to care for the sick; it is difficult to stay mindful that these patients are the enemy and could fight back against us.

April 4

A.m.: We will be taking on fuel, food, supplies, mail(?), and off-loading garbage most of the day. This will limit opportunities to bring on new patients and pave the way for an easy day. We hope.

P.m.: Well, no mail but they did bring in eight more Iraqis, so I had a busy afternoon and evening. Worst case was a middle-aged civilian female shot in the head. Her CAT scan showed major brain damage and her prognosis is very dim. Nonetheless, they chose to operate on her. She will not do well.

So far, sixty coalition fatalities, twelve of which were due to friendly fire.

April 5

The Saturday entertainment is karaoke. I usually like it, but tonight it's not for me. The room is hot and crowded, and the whole event is just too loud for me. I step out for air. On deck is a different world. For safety we are on "darken ship" status now. This means no external lights and all windows are covered to block light transmission. The night is moonless, skies only a slight haze. It is very dark outside. So dark my eyes need ten minutes to fully accommodate. There is a magnificent display of stars, and the night has a misty, impressionist feel. People moving about in the night are just vague dark shapes. Voices are low. Boys and girls being what they are, couples are forming on *Comfort*. They drift into obscure corners. Ghostlike green blobs of fluorescence rise and fall in the water. Jellyfish. Thousands of jellyfish, they drift and bob around the ship. I watch the stars until my neck hurts. Someone is singing in the dark in a beautiful, strange language. He tells me it is Hindi, and he is actually practicing for karaoke. I hope he wins.

April 7

Unusual experience today. I visited the inpatient ward holding the Iraqi EPWs. I accompany one of the internists on his rounds. This doctor created a niche for himself by volunteering to serve as the attending physician on the prisoner ward. The experience will be unforgettable for him—and be a unique item on his curriculum vitae.

The prisoners are kept on a separate ward, deep in the bowels of the ship, for security reasons, and the location is kept obscure. There is concern for the security of the prisoners. Lawyers run everything now, and we actually have a lawyer on board whose primary job is to ensure we comply with all tenets of the Geneva Convention. There are press on board all the time.

The ward is real creepy. Burly armed guards keep a watchful eye on the prisoners. There is an interpreter on board most of the time. The prisoners are not allowed to talk to one another. Some are strapped down to the bed. There is an isolation room for the unruly. Medical attendants have to remove their belts before entering the ward and empty their pockets of pens and other sharp objects (remember Hannibal Lecter).

Most of the Iraqis show real appreciation for the care rendered them. I would love to talk to them about family, etc., but we have been firmly warned not to do this. It is contrary to our training in medicine not to show at least some warmth towards the patient, but these are our marching orders. The prisoners are a sad lot. I feel for them. Most were not real soldiers, just conscripts forced to fight for the Big Lie, Saddam Hussein. Some of these guys, however, were Republican Guards, some of them the feared Fedayeen suicide commandos. In general, the prisoners are badly wounded. They look defeated and glad to be out of combat.

April 11

The number of patients coming aboard *Comfort* is simply out of control. Like the characters on *M*A*S*H*, we have grown to hate the rumble of helos on the flight deck, since it usually means another load of Iraqi patients. Today we received at least thirty-five more. New in the last twenty-four hours is a big influx of sick and injured children. We have only one doctor with residency training in pediatrics. Some of the kids are very ill. One was DOA from drinking kerosene. "They" are sending everyone here. We don't know who "they" are, and no one seems to have a handle on where these patients come from, when they are arriving, or who is sending them. We take them all and do our best. Patients are beginning to die because their injuries are so severe and they are getting to us too late.

There is no long-term care plan for all these patients, and the ones who survive will need long-term care. Where will they go? Who will care for them after we leave? We have become deeply involved in a humanitarian crisis we will not be able to extricate ourselves from.

April 12
It had to happen. Boys and girls together. Sex. People are having sex on board, and rumor has it that finally somebody(s) got caught. It may have been more than just a couple. A ménage à trois had been the subject of rumors for some time and they were finally caught in flagrante. They were sent to captain's mast, a form of internal Navy investigation and trial where the accused Stand Tall in front of The Captain to answer allegations. Mast is swift and final. They get to the point quickly and mete out punishment on the spot. Whatever punishment was assigned here is unknown to the crew. Most of the men just want to know who the girl(s?) were!

April 15
Tim and John were up all night helping with a Marine who was run over by an eighteen-wheel truck in an accident. Amazingly he lived despite a crushed pelvis and massive blood loss.

Civilian Iraqi patients are being allowed to move around the ship more (with escort, of course) as their conditions improve. I saw a teenager today smiling and shaking hands with everyone. As he bent to tie his shoe, his sleeve slid up. I saw he had a tattoo on his upper arm. A fresh Marine Corps "Globe and Anchor." Wow! Hearts and minds, indeed.

April 17
We began in earnest to discharge stable EPW patients from the *Comfort*. Close to thirty sent back today. Sent somewhere. Sadly, these guys don't realize they are not being repatriated. For security reasons they cannot be told where they are really going. Looking at these pathetic-looking fellows, it is easy to forget they were the enemy, and many probably still wish us harm. Ac-

cording to an ICU doctor, one of the most timid-looking teenage patients is actually an identified terrorist. Another patient awoke from surgery disoriented as to place; he asked if he had been sent home to Syria! Apparently many anti-American Syrians had joined Saddam's army to fight us.

In a Pavlovian way, the patients now associate the presence of the Big Nurse Administrator with the Clipboard with imminent departure of fellow Iraqis. As soon as she sets foot on the wards they circle their arms overhead like helo blades in motion and make woop-woop sounds. They know helos are in-bound for evacuation.

April 21

Comfort receives a visit from CENTCOM, the name for the headquarters group for the entire war. A group of their medical admin bureaucrats, primarily Army, are on board to give us an overview of the medical situation in Iraq and Kuwait. We hope to hear something concrete about our own status—what is planned for us, how can we off-load our patients, and mostly, when can we go home? Instead of insight and clarity, we got more obscuring mud in the eye. The formal presentation is tiresome, trite, and uninformative. It takes fifteen minutes to get the PowerPoint working. The speaker uses too much Army-specific jargon. He admits the *Comfort* is the most stable, established, and productive medical unit in theater. The hospitals in Iraq have been looted and are barely functioning.

A Q&A session follows. The discussion is as overheated as the room. Several doctors are really pissed about how hard we worked and how we got stuck taking all the EPWs. Pointed questions regarding why we got so stuck with so many patients go ignored or glossed over. It is explained that the Iraqi casualties were put on helicopters by well-meaning, altruistic U.S. troops, even though they were told not to do this. They offer no explanation for why all the Iraqis ended up in our hospital. They thank us for all our hard work, tell us they "feel our pain," and say war is hell. It is not convincing or reassuring to us. These guys all look rested, tanned, and pain-free.

The meeting ended inconclusively. We are no clearer on finding out when this will be over for us. If anything, the Army brief made it appear we may be here for a long time to come.

The USNS Comfort *returned to Baltimore in June 2003, having treated almost seven hundred patients (nearly two hundred of whom were Iraqi civil-*

ians and prisoners of war). Dr. Jewell remained on active duty until the end of September 2004, when he officially retired from the Navy. But he continues to work for the military as a civilian doctor.

HERE AMONG THESE RUINS

E-mail

Specialist Helen Gerhardt

Of the estimated 2.2 million troops serving in the United States military, approximately one out of every six is a woman. Officially, women are not allowed to fight in frontline infantry combat units. But, just as in wars past, they are frequently placed—or put themselves—in harm's way. At the age of thirty-three, Helen Gerhardt enlisted in the U.S. Army in May 2000. Three years later, having just completed a double undergraduate major in fine arts and English literature, she found herself in the Middle East with the Missouri Army National Guard, 1221st Transportation Company. The job entailed driving 915 A1s (eighteen-wheeler tractor-trailers) throughout Iraq to move everything from large cases of food and water to charred Humvees incapacitated by roadside bombs. The work was demanding and often extremely dangerous. (Soon after the invasion commenced, eleven U.S. soldiers with the 507th Maintenance Company were killed when their convoy was hit by rocket-propelled grenades and small-arms fire.) In the following e-mail to loved ones back in Missouri, Specialist Gerhardt shared her first impressions of the Iraqi people and their country, which seemed to be a curious mix of the ancient and the modern.

Dear friends and family,

A few days ago I sat in the passenger seat of a truck with my M16 pointing out the window as I crossed the border into Iraq for the first time. All of us methodically scanned the landscape for the flesh and blood snipers or grenade launchers we had envisioned during training and constantly glanced in the rear view mirror to make sure the truck behind us was at a safe distance. I felt greedy for every concrete detail to dispel the figments of the Iraq I had constructed in my own imagination over the months of waiting.

Our convoy of nine trucks and a humvee felt very small to all of us. Our

request for an MP escort had been denied without the required 48 hours notice, never mind that we'd been ordered onto the road with only about 36
hours warning. The MPs are stretched very thin, and although officially all
convoys are supposed to be escorted, in reality most small groups go without.
We'd been advised to make our own firepower very apparent as the next best
deterrent to an attack. The convoy commanders traveled in the Humvee with
a machine gun mounted on top and the other saw gunners in the 915s were
placed at front, middle, and end of the convoy. Combat Lifesaver drivers and
their first aid bags were also spaced evenly throughout the line. We'd been in-
structed to look as wide-awake as we could. I didn't find this difficult.

The border is a real border. In Kuwait, high status sports cars, Islamic sky-
scrapers, gleaming ranks of enormous oil drums, and slickly designed bill-
boards all shouted the thriving economy of our hosts. Light poles, power
lines, and little green trees marched beside the near-flawless highway, unre-
markable until they abruptly halted where the demilitarized zone was
marked by bulldozed ridges topped with concertina wire. On the other side
of the DMZ null and void, the village of Safwan straggled loosely north and
south along the road. Rusted, carefully stripped car frames rested on both
shoulders of the road, uncomfortably reminding me of the props at our live-
fire training range. Small windowless houses shed grey bricks like worn-out
lizard scales on patches of thick, fine dust and rocky sand. . . .

The first face I saw closely was a girl maybe ten-years-old, thin, but beating time on a half-full water bottle as she danced up and down on the shoulder of the road with confident grace. She looked straight into my eyes with no
trace of humility, her brilliant smile seemed to command acknowledgement
of a beauty impossible to deny anything to, her cinnamon and curry-colored
gown waved like a flag of bold pleasure in her past triumphs. I wished I could
throw roses and roast beef, confetti and corndogs, wanted to celebrate her
gutsy contrast to my worst fears and to get a good square meal into her belly.
Behind her an older woman stood still and straight, wrapped in black, staring
through her daughter and me to the desert beyond.

As we passed the last house, beyond the line of other children, two young
boys squatted with hands on knees, one in shorts and a Western-style oxford
shirt, the other in a white knee-length Islamic gown. They ignored our obe-
diently tight-fisted caravan as they examined and seriously discussed some
mechanical contraption between them.

Everywhere as we progressed north, the middle ages met the modern; a satellite dish protruded from a mud hut, a donkey hauled a cart with two women sharing a cell phone back and forth, a large black and white cow tried to keep its feet in the bed of a small Toyota pick up truck. Roadside stands sold Snapple and long blocks of ice. Men dressed in shiny green U.S. football jerseys waved to us with one hand as they scooped salt from cracked-ivory flats into glinting white pyramids. Lines of camels were urged onward by little boys with big sticks and bigger walkmans. . . .

We stayed overnight in a little dustbowl of a new Army camp, Cedar II, setting up our cots on the empty trailer beds out of reach of scorpions and snakes. The next day we were scheduled to pass through the outskirts of Baghdad, near where the members of another mission had seen the smoking remains of a 915 truck after it had been rocket grenaded. We took a wrong turn off the highway and, unable to read the Arabic street signs, wandered into the slums of Sadr City where children pointed and laughed as our long convoy of illiterates passed back and forth through the narrow streets looking for a way out. The adults barely glanced at us, faces surely schooled into stone by years of threats by those who held rifles and the keys to prisons that swallowed many sons, fathers, and husbands whole without a word. We finally found our way back to the highway, but by nightfall had barely made it past Tikrit, birthplace of Saddam Hussein.

The next day all went smoothly and we pulled into our destination camp in Mosul, a former Iraqi Army base. Wandering through the littered compound next to the buildings we had occupied we found abandoned helmets, spent shells, and Arabic training manuals for gas mask use. In one room I found twisted hooks hanging from the ceiling next to an electronic control board and I shuddered at what my inner Hollywood pieced out of the scene.

But in the regular soldier's barracks I found a detail that irrationally moved me more. A black-bottomed coffee pot sat in the sill of a window, its spout pointing out the heavy bars on the windows toward the foothills in the distance. Here the poorly fed draftees of years past may have shared coffee and cigarettes, read letters from home, told each other the news of the families we knew they had not volunteered to leave. I sat there a long time, the door open behind me, finally moved to take myself back to the Army barracks I had freely chosen. Just outside the door I found a boy waiting for me. "Thank you" he said, his light brown eyes looking straight into mine, and then he smiled with what seemed years-worth of relief. Despite all my reservations about this war, I could not help but wonder if he was thanking me for freeing father, uncle, or brother from some cell like that I'd walked so easily out of.

Everywhere, from southern Iraq to this former garrison/prison of the Baathists, we have seen images of Saddam that have been literally de-faced, hacked out or painted over from hairline to chin, leaving his black hair, shoulders, and body intact. With Hussein still missing, the effect is ghoulish; the desecrations constantly remind us that the vengeful man still hides among the powerless that he has fed on for so many years.

I sit writing here among these ruins, looking out the unbarred window, thinking of you, missing you always.

With all my love,
Helen

NIGHT FLIGHT TO BAGHDAD

Personal Narrative

Master Sergeant Thomas W. Young

On April 9, 2003, Baghdad fell with relatively little bloodshed. The Iraqi military essentially disbanded itself, and Saddam Hussein and his senior commanders fled into hiding. Fears of a massive, catastrophic battle between U.S. and Iraqi ground troops in a final standoff around Baghdad were not realized, and the invasion was hailed as an extraordinary success. American troops focused much of their efforts in the weeks that followed on stabilizing the country's major towns and cities, particularly the Iraqi capital, which had disintegrated into chaos from looting and a wave of Shia versus Sunni revenge killings. On May 1, President George W. Bush announced from the USS Abraham Lincoln *that "major combat operations in Iraq have ended." The president then emphasized that there was still*

> *difficult work to do in Iraq. We're bringing order to parts of that country that remain dangerous. . . . The transition from dictatorship to democracy will take time, but it is worth every effort. Our coalition will stay until our work is done. . . .*

Forty-one-year-old U.S. Air Force Master Sergeant Thomas Young arrived at the Masirah Island Air Base in Oman just days before Operation Iraqi Freedom began. Young, who had become a pilot at the age of twenty-nine, joined the military in 1992 after watching young men and women sacrificing their lives in the Gulf War. He wanted to fly missions that would one day help American forces on the ground, and he got the chance eleven years later when he served as a flight engineer with the 167th Airlift Wing, West Virginia Air National Guard, which was mobilized to the Middle East in March 2003. Like most troops in the region, Young believed that by the beginning of May, the worst of the fighting in Iraq was over. But there were still sorties to be flown, and none of them was without risk.

"Baghdad tonight, fellas."

That word comes from pilot and aircraft commander Mike Langley as my crewmates and I emerge from our air-conditioned tent to board the crew bus. Our cold-soaked sunglasses fog up instantly in the 115-degree heat of outdoors. We stand around in butternut-colored desert flight suits, squinting against the harsh light of the desert afternoon, wiping our lenses with handkerchiefs and brown scarves.

Though war stories often focus on the youth of the warriors, we don't fit that mold. We're all around forty, with years of experience flying the C-130 Hercules, a four-engine turboprop transport aircraft. In addition to the boss, Langley, our six-man crew includes copilot Ed Bishop, navigator Kelly Washington, and loadmasters Roland Shambaugh and John Cox. I occupy the flight engineer seat.

Tonight's schedule calls for us to fly to Tallil Air Base in southern Iraq. There we'll pick up cargo and take it to the former Saddam International Airport, currently under new management thanks to the 3rd Infantry Division. Now we will build on their efforts by taking supplies and fresh troops into that airfield, newly renamed Baghdad International.

After taking on jet fuel, we gear up for the combat zone as night falls. My crewmates and I squirm into our flak jackets and tug at the fasteners. The flak vests are hot, heavy, and miserable, but they can spare you a lifetime in a wheelchair or worse. I've been known to nag my buddies about wearing them. "Yes, Dad," I've heard more than once.

Over our flak jackets, we also pull on survival vests, which contain flares, a knife, a first-aid kit, a Beretta 9mm, a signal mirror, and other things that might come in handy when you've had an airplane blown out from under you. There's also an item called a blood chit. It's a piece of cloth with a message in several languages that reads approximately like this: *I'm an American aviator, and I'm having a real bad day. I won't hurt you, and if you help me, my government will try to repay you.*

Finally, helmets adorned with night vision goggles take the place of our usual headsets. I fumble for the tiny switch, and the NVGs come alive with a faint, battery-powered whine. Night becomes full daylight, as if viewed through dark green sunglasses.

Throttles up and we're airborne. Practically as soon as we get the gear up, Washington, the navigator, informs us we're entering hostile territory.

"We're crossing the fence," he says, as if we're on some peaceful farm chore. A string of lights illuminates the Iraq-Kuwait border that stretches beneath us—a bright curving chain of white pearls. "Combat entry checklist," he adds.

Time to go to war. We begin configuring the airplane to make it harder to hit, and to minimize the damage if something does manage to nail us.

Lights off. Cabin pressure reduced. Fuel cross-feed off. I double-check the switches for external lights, touching each of them with a gloved index finger. I worry about forgetting something as simple as a light switch. I'd hate to get my crew killed because I let us fly into a combat zone with bright strobes flashing—a big, fat, stupid target visible to every jihadi on the Arabian peninsula.

The Herk levels off at cruising altitude, and we drone above a layer of scattered clouds. Above us, the Milky Way sparkles. Seen through night vision goggles, the stars appear as glittering dust, a scattering of crushed diamonds. A wondrous sight brought to us by the grim technology of war.

We have little time for stargazing. Too soon, approach control hands us off to Tallil tower.

"Cleared to land."

Throttles chopped, the nose comes down and we begin spiraling the big airplane toward the runway. The ground appears to rotate beneath us as we corkscrew lower and lower. Infrared runway lights, invisible except through NVGs, beckon us. This approach hardly compares to the landings we do in our civilian jobs as airline pilots, and I smile as I imagine pulling this off in a jetliner: "Ladies and gentlemen, please fasten your seat belts and lock your trays in the upright position. We'll be executing something called a random steep tactical approach for our arrival into Chicago this evening. If you feel any violent evasive maneuvering, please be advised that we are making every effort to avoid surface-to-air missiles."

Fortunately, we see none to avoid right now. We land and taxi to the ramp for an ERO, or engines running on-load. The loadmasters push several pallets of cargo into place in pitch darkness with the aid of NVGs.

We carry beans and bullets, as the saying goes, and just about everything else. On any given flight it could be ammunition, construction supplies, Meals Ready to Eat, medical equipment, blood plasma, or bomb-sniffing dogs. We also carry troops, soldiers rotating out, soldiers rotating in, we fly them all.

In just a few minutes we're airborne again, clawing for altitude at max continuous power. We want to get out of the threat range of missiles, small arms, and antiaircraft artillery, or AAA. Almost as soon as we level off, a green glow appears on the horizon like a Venusian dawn. The night vision goggles pick up the lights of Baghdad so far away that at first we seem to make no forward progress toward them.

However, the distance-measuring equipment on our instruments counts down the miles, and eventually when I peer under the goggles I can see the lights even with the naked eye. As we switch to the frequency for the command and control plane orbiting somewhere overhead, the AWACS bird, we catch a disturbing conversation:

"Say again that location."

The pilot of another C-130 reels off a sector designation for a spot near the airport.

"Copy that. Probable SA-7 missile launch. We'll relay."

Another aircraft checks in. "Burst of triple-A off our eleven o'clock. Maybe eight or nine tracers."

"That don't sound good," says one of our loadmasters on interphone.

"I'm thinking this is a good time to be wearing your flak vest."

"Yes, Dad."

Approach clears us for descent near the edge of the city. Although recent news stories have focused on electrical blackouts, Baghdad looks pretty well lit for a city in the midst of war. But we've never seen it before, so we don't know what normal looks like. And we know normal lights don't include tracers.

"Got some ground-to-ground fire off the left wing," calls Shambaugh.

I scan the ground urgently but find nothing.

"There it goes again."

This time I see it in the edge of my field of vision—tiny green needles of light, gone in an instant. They come in quick snaps, stabbing the night. You might call them pretty if you didn't know the light show results from tracer magnesium burning on high-velocity rounds. I'm glad to see them flashing right to left. The ones that don't appear to move are the ones coming right at you.

But now it's time to forget the tracers and just do the job. Tower clears us for a random steep.

Again the airport seems to rotate under us. I divide my attention between the unwinding altimeter and the tormented city below, watching for threats. To the north, the Tigris loops through the heart of Baghdad, reflected light shimmering on the water. The cradle of civilization, this land beneath our wings has witnessed some of the best and worst that human society has offered. Its sands contain the relics of Mesopotamia and the bones of mass graves. Its waters irrigated the beginnings of agriculture and carried bodies of Saddam's victims.

We want very much to help bring a change for the better, but that depends on many things far out of our control. All we can do is fly this aircraft to the best of our ability.

Bishop, the copilot, rolls the wings level onto a short final approach. Just a few hundred feet above Baghdad, I half-expect to hear the blaring of the missile warning tones. If that happens, our defensive system can launch flares to help confuse a heat-seeking missile. But down low and slow, we have little room and leverage for maneuver, like a knife fight in a phone booth.

No shoulder-launched knives for now, though, and the landing is normal. Or at least as normal as possible on night vision goggles, with firefights going on, after corkscrewing down like a falling leaf to land on a taxiway because the runways are pocked with bomb craters.

We park on a cargo ramp and off-load, again with engines running. I wipe my face with a handkerchief, double-check the takeoff speed and distance, then take a swig of water and a whiff of oxygen, just to clear the cobwebs. The loadmasters are almost too good. Before I can unbuckle my harness and stretch my legs, the guys have the cargo off the airplane.

"We're all closed up back here," calls Shambaugh. "Let's get the hell out of Dodge."

Works for me. As we taxi out, I briefly imagine Saddam himself boarding an aircraft on this ramp in his better days. No time to ponder that now, though. Throttles up, brakes released, and we're off again, lifting into the angry night over Baghdad.

Langley's flying now, and he wants what Air Force pilots call "smash." Smash is kinetic energy. Up high, it's altitude we can convert into speed by diving. Down low where we are now, it's velocity we can trade for altitude or a good, hard turn.

"I'm lowering the nose to get some speed," says Langley, thinking out loud. I'll remember that sentence for the rest of my life.

A tremendous flash lights up the cockpit like daylight. Magnified by night vision goggles, it blinds me.

For a tenth of a moment I think: *There's the fireball, it's all over.*

The missile warning tone screeches like a demon. Langley whips the airplane into a steep bank, and my arms grow heavy with the pull of g-forces.

I expect heat, pain, fire, eternity.

Instead comes speed, and speed brings life. I realize I felt no impact, my vision is restored, and this airplane is still flying.

Remaining among the living, I get back to work, calling altitudes and scanning instruments. The heading indicators spin through the turn, an unreadable flicker of numbers. The systems gauges show no signs of engine damage. That flash came from our antimissile flares firing off, the defensive system doing its job automatically. One for the textbooks, Langley's maneuver and the decoying flares have thwarted a little piece of heat-seeking hell.

"Anybody see anything?" he asks.

"Missile came up from the right," answers Cox.

"I saw it too, until I lost it in the flares," adds Bishop.

Cox explains that he saw a truck stop and turn off its lights, and the launch appeared to come from on or near the truck.

Away from the city, we climb through a sky as dark as a mineshaft. The night vision goggles don't help at the moment, because in the black emptiness of the desert, they can't find a speck of light to amplify. For perhaps twenty minutes, there is absolute silence on the interphone. Just a faint electronic hiss.

Finally someone speaks. "You guys all right?" asks Langley. "I need to know you're still in the game. Everybody check in." His tone is matter-of-fact, as if he's calling for any routine checklist.

"Copilot's good."

"Nav's okay."

"Engineer."

"Loadmaster one."

"Load two."

We fly home to Masirah weary and sobered, older and wiser. And damned lucky.

Back on our tent porch, I collapse into a deck chair and twist open a beer. The cap cuts my hand, but I don't care. The beer is cold and good, and if I can feel pain it means I'm still alive. The rest of the crew joins me, exhausted but not ready for sleep.

The enemy launched on us once before, but the missile missed by a much wider margin then, partly because the shooter didn't know how to use his weapon. After that first time, we even raised a lighthearted toast while having drinks back at base: "To bad guys too stupid to lead a moving target." We crack no jokes tonight. This time, the bastard knew what he was doing. Competence scares us more than fanaticism.

"That's the only time I have ever braced for impact," says Langley, shaking his head.

Everybody's first thought was a little different.

"I thought the loadmasters were dead," says Bishop.

"I just wondered what the hell was happening," adds Shambaugh, who'd been posted in the window opposite where the missile came up.

And I thought we'd all had our tickets punched. But I was wrong.

I was wrong by mere yards, by microseconds. I was wrong, but not by much.

In the dark on our dusty porch, I realize the distance between our aircraft and that warhead represents the life we have left to live. It is this moment and all that remain.

This war will alter many lives, and it will rip away some altogether. For now at least, it has handed ours back.

And as soon as we rest up, we'll fly into Iraq again.

Young returned to West Virginia two months later and remained on active duty for a year. While U.S. and Coalition forces had quelled some of the rioting that had exploded throughout the country in the immediate aftermath of the invasion, Iraq was far from secure. Violence against American troops was escalating, and by summer 2003, an organized and vicious insurgency seemed to be gaining in strength. The war, it appeared, was only just beginning.

CHAPTER TWO

HEARTS AND MINDS

INTERACTIONS WITH AFGHANS AND IRAQIS

Children in the Iraqi village of Jassan, near the Iranian border, see
Marines for the first time during the U.S. invasion, April 2003.

Photo by Major Benjamin Busch, USMC; used by permission.

A couple hours after we landed, we had a convoy to Kabul. It took about two hours, but I will never forget the trip. The scenery was incredible. I knew that there were mountains in Afghanistan, but there are so many that it is an unbelievable sight. It's hard to imagine that it can be 90 degrees on the ground, yet not generate enough heat on the mountaintops to melt the snow that is apparent. The native people are also a sight to see. These people are incredibly resourceful making shelter from clay and mud and using the minimal resources they have to work with. . . . On the trip, I saw many small children, some no older than 4 or 5, off by themselves in the middle of nowhere, waving and smiling as we passed by. The poverty level is so high. They have little food and little resource for potable water to drink. We were told not to give any of our food or water to the natives. However, I find it hard to see these cute children starving on the side of the road while I have a case of bottled water next to me in the cab. Needless to say, a half dozen of my waters were hurled from my window along the way. One kid really earned his; he saw our vehicles approaching and ran 150–200 meters across the land as fast as a deer. I couldn't believe how fast he was! As I approached him, it was evident that all he wanted to do was wave like a kid at a parade. He was 7 or 8 at best and wearing a cloth with no shoes. I couldn't resist tossing him a water. He picked it up as I saw in my rearview mirror and jumped up and down waving at my vehicle. It is so sad what kind of world these kids are born into.

> —Thirty-four-year-old U.S. Army Sergeant Andrew Simkewicz (210th
> Forward Support Battalion, 10th Mountain Division), e-mailing family
> back in Massachusetts from Afghanistan on May 30, 2003. Two days later,
> Simkewicz wrote: "One of the cute little Afghan kids that I had spoken
> about ran up to a soldier and knocked out six of his teeth with a slingshot."

ONE SMALL VILLAGE
Journal
Chief Warrant Officer Two Jared S. Jones

Culture shock does not even begin to describe the reaction that many young servicemen and women, especially those who have never been outside the United States before, experience when they arrive in a war-torn country like Iraq or Afghanistan. And even those who have traveled abroad are stunned by the poverty and destruction that greet them. "The majority of the people of Afghanistan are still living in the biblical times of Jesus," U.S. Army First Sergeant August C. Hohl, Jr., wrote in an account based on his deployment to the region. "Their mud villages, their homes covered by whatever tree branches and wood that they have salvaged, the caravans of shepherds—all these things are images I've only envisioned in my Bible readings or from a few books on ancient history." But as surprised as Hohl was by the conditions he saw, he was deeply affected by the people themselves and their perspective on life amid such adversity. "They don't take well to pity," Hohl observed about the Afghans he met, "but their personal and religious beliefs are not unlike ours in that everyone understands the importance of reaching out to and being charitable towards one another." Hohl was especially moved by his visits to rural schools, where he would bring pencils, paper, chalk, and other supplies provided by donors back home in Wisconsin.

The kids sit there and learn with old bullet holes and bomb-scarred walls around them. They are usually lucky if they even have wooden benches to sit on. Most of the time there's just the bare floor or a plastic tarp. But the children there are so proud to open up their book bags and show you their math, writing, or art books and what they can do. Then there are the teachers, all of whom talk about the needs of their students before even considering their own needs. Most of the teachers are two to three months behind in getting paid, but they believe very strongly in the importance of education for their people. Coming here has shown me that while we all might live differently due to environmental, geographical, and educational conditions, people are basically the same inside. Learning some of the history, social habits, and religion of this country has left me with a profound

*sense of hope that we can assist the people here. But we're not so
smart that we can't learn from them, too.*

*Service members are not unaware of the military value of fostering good-
will within Afghanistan and Iraq; civilians on friendly terms with American
forces are less likely to cause them harm, and they are more inclined to provide information about suspected insurgents, the location of stashed
weapons, rumors of possible ambushes or attacks, and other critical intelligence. But many troops, like Hohl, write with genuine emotion about their
desire to work with Afghans and Iraqis and help the neediest among them,
especially children. "You would not believe how different the world is over
here," twenty-three-year-old U.S. Army Chief Warrant Officer Two Jared S.
Jones wrote in his first e-mail home from the middle of Afghanistan. Jones
had left for Bagram in April 2004 with a sense of, in his words, "fear and
mistrust." But over time, not only did he begin to admire and appreciate
Afghanistan and its people, he fell in love with them. The deployment was
also special because one of his fellow AH-64A Apache pilots in the 1/211th
Aviation Attack Helicopter Battalion, Utah Army National Guard, happened to be his father. (It is not uncommon for parents and their grown children, spouses, or siblings to serve together in the same reserve unit.) In a
journal based primarily on his e-mails home, Jones chronicled his experiences flying both combat- and humanitarian-aid-related missions throughout Afghanistan, and the latter, particularly visits to the small village of
Jegdalek, were the ones that affected him the most. (The following entries
were written between early September 2004 and mid-March 2005.)*

Week Twenty-One

In recent news, our adopted village, Jekdelehek (uncertain of the spelling), is
one of the many war-ravaged villages from the days of the Soviet-Afghan war,
and we are trying to find medical supplies and raise money to establish some
sort of a medical clinic. Last Monday a little girl and her father were brought
to our U.S. Army hospital here in Bagram after we visited their village. The
little girl, Halima (pronounced Hah-lee-mah), is approximately five years old
and needed corrective eye surgery. I had the honor of attending the operation, wearing a medical hair cover, breathing mask, and all. There were two
surgeons: one U.S. and one Egyptian—it was a truly fascinating experience!
Don't worry, I won't share the gory details. . .

Week Twenty-Two

Last week, we returned the little girl and her father to their village, Jekdele-hek. What an unforgettable, truly amazing experience! Nearly thirty people reside in their humble, three-room abode. Most of the family are farmers of sorts, and possess a few livestock (a cow, a goat, and a family of chickens), which they share their residence with. During the Soviet-Afghan war, when the Soviet Army was first invading from the north, the family and the rest of the village took to the surrounding caves, hiding from Soviet aircraft that strafed and bombed most every village they came across, including theirs.

They told us that since America has come to Afghanistan, fighting for *their* freedom and way of life, the village has prospered like it never has before and they are very grateful for our presence. They hope that we (meaning U.S./U.N. support) can stay until the new democratic government, with the help of the Afghan National Army (ANA), is fully operational and their country has been rid of terrorist scum like Osama bin Laden. After we said goodbye, as I was riding on the CH-47 Chinook, I realized, even away from family, friends, and the luxuries of home, I had so very, very much to be thankful for.

Week Twenty-Nine

In Jegdalek we distributed more humanitarian aid, with donations ranging from personal hygiene to school supplies, shoes, and soccer balls. It is always a pleasure to see the difference we are making for these people, even if it is only one small village, whose people have next to nothing. I saw Halima again, who is doing incredibly well. Her eyes have healed completely and she continues to share her winning smile with us. Her father is now commuting to Kabul, working a regular job, where he is making significantly more than he did before. We continue to offer, as able, medical support to those who need it most. For example, we have been bringing antibiotics to a man who has lost an arm and a leg to infection and is about to lose another. Now he has a fighting chance of retaining this limb. There is a young boy, no older than twelve years old, who suffers from a heart condition involving a leaky valve. He can walk no further than a dozen yards before he must stop and catch his breath. If he does not receive medical care from a professional cardiologist, which we lack here in the country of Afghanistan, he will die shortly. We are now in the process of obtaining him a visa and passport. If we are successful we are going to use some of the funds we have received for humanitarian aid to fly him back to the U.S. where a former military doctor is more than willing to do the necessary surgery . . . for free. Please pray for this young boy.

Week Thirty-One

Combat is only one facet of the military, a necessary evil we must sometimes wage against evil people. There is much more happening in this country besides what you hear in the media. I want to share another amazing story with you. The young child with the poor heart condition has been brought here to Bagram Air Field. His name is Asedullah (the spelling may or may not be accurate). Everything to this point has fallen perfectly into place. Hospital administrative fees have already been waived. In Kabul, passports were granted in one day. Unfortunately, due to miscellaneous bureaucracies, it will be, at a minimum, thirty days before the visas are available. Therein lies another catch—Asedullah and his father, since he will be accompanying his boy to the States for the surgery, must pick them up, in person, at the nearest visa office . . . which is in Pakistan. What happens next? We wait.

Week Thirty-Four

As I continue to fly over Afghanistan, I have noticed that the people predominantly fly one of two colors—a green flag and a red flag. I have learned that the green flag signifies that that family has lost someone to the Taliban, whereas the red flag signifies that that family lost someone during the Soviet-Afghan conflict. Sadly, I have seen many, many of both colors. A black flag, however, is supposed to mark a home that supports the Taliban regime—I haven't seen many of this color anymore. Many of the graveyards, I have noticed, have fences around them. They are to keep out animals, specifically wild dogs and hogs that, if not for the fence, would dig up the dirt covering the fresh burial. I have seen entirely too many small fences, something I hope changes as this country continues to progress.

Week Forty-Five

The highlight of my week was something I have wanted to do for a very long time—observe Operation Shoe Fly. CW2 William Andrews, the driving, or rather, flying effort behind Operation Shoe Fly, invited me to come along. So how does it work? One or more CH-47 Chinooks are filled primarily with shoes, among other donations, such as blankets, clothing, and toys. As the pilots fly across the country, following the routes between forward operating bases (FOBs), they look for the desolate and more isolated communities. Flying near these, the crew chiefs wait for the best drop opportunity—typically beside homes and other prominent gathering locations, yet away from personnel. Once the shoes are flying, the children come running. Luckily, that we know of, no one has been hit by a falling shoe or any other gift from the sky.

One interesting story he shared with me—during one particular flight while dropping shoes, the villagers ran inside, scared. In all likelihood they were recalling the cruel tactic used by the Soviets, who dropped booby-trapped gifts. On the return flight, when they were flying over the same village, the villagers ran outside, proudly displaying their new shoes and waving their thanks.

Mr. Andrews estimates that Operation Shoe Fly has dropped more than ten thousand pairs of shoes over Afghanistan. Many of those come from one source—a resident of Hawaii who was in fact born in Afghanistan. She alone has donated nearly two thousand shoes! A few months ago she returned temporarily, and was flown aboard a Chinook, herself dropping shoes over her motherland, and even had the opportunity to visit Jegdalek, where she acted as interpreter on the trip.

Week Forty-Six

Asedullah and his father, who made it out of the country for Asedullah's operation, are scheduled to come back to Afghanistan soon. My father was finally able to set foot in their village yesterday. I wish I could have accompanied him, but I was flying. He had a wonderful time and I am glad he was able to see Afghanistan for what it really is.

Week Forty-Seven

This week we said goodbye to our adopted village, Jegdalek. I saw Halima and some of her family—our little Cinderella, as we have fondly dubbed her, is doing better than ever. I gave her some one-two-threes, a family tradition of tossing a child into the air, higher with each number. One of her brothers did something incredibly heart wrenching—he gave me a small ruby; a gift of friendship. By the way, the rubies of Jegdalek are world renowned. . . . Here is a boy, with almost nothing, giving me something, anything. I was so moved by this that I ended up giving away nearly everything I had on me . . . my gloves, my pen, my watch. Anything means everything to these people. And then, the time had come—hearing the Chinooks in the distance, we said our last goodbyes, never again to visit this small village in the middle of Afghanistan, that has come to mean so much to many of us. It was bitter-sweet, this finale.

Week Forty-Eight

Yesterday was a long flight—escorting one of the new CH-47 Big Windy Chinook aircraft, we visited nearly every FOB in our southern area of operations. It just so happened that our route of flight took us over Jegdalek. Flying with CW5 Layne Pace, we circled over the house of Halima and then Asedullah. I am not certain, but I think I could see them both, looking up at us looking down on them.

Speaking of Asedullah, at long last he and his father returned to the village earlier this week! He is doing very well and I learned that already he is running around with his brothers and the rest of the boys of Jegdalek. He will return to school shortly and resume the life that previously could not have been. What a happy ending to an amazing story.

These journeys to Jegdalek have been the highlight of my deployment—I will never forget the faces of this humble village. Looking back, I remember the first time we visited their village, the people reserved, uncertain. On our final visit I was struck at how so much had changed. Our friendship forever sealed, the people welcome us as family now. Afghanistan is changing, I have seen it with my own eyes. These children, this next generation, will one day be the next mullah or village elder, and they will teach their children how things were, and how things are, and how things can be.

Both Jones and his father returned to the States in April 2005, and Jones went back to school at the University of Utah to pursue a major in film.

LUNCH WITH PIRATES
Personal Narrative
Staff Sergeant Clint Douglas

Before embarking overseas, many U.S. troops receive cultural sensitivity briefings so that they do not inadvertently offend the civilians and allied military personnel they meet in Afghanistan and Iraq. Much of the infor-

mation is basic common sense and courtesy: Do not seem impatient or dis-
tracted during conversations, do not point a finger in someone's face, do not
use profanity, etc. But some rules are less obvious. One should not, for ex-
ample, compliment a host on any specific item in his home, as he will then
feel obliged to offer it as a gift. And it is extremely insulting to point the sole
of one's foot at another person, even if it is done unintentionally while sit-
ting and chatting informally. No matter how much preparation servicemen
and women are given, however, they will inevitably find themselves in situ-
ations for which there is simply no training manual or reference guide. In
March 2003, thirty-four-year-old U.S. Army Staff Sergeant Clint Douglas,
a former Peace Corps volunteer, was deployed to Afghanistan with the 20th
Special Forces Group (Airborne), Illinois National Guard, for more than
six months. Douglas quickly discovered that beneath the patina of social
niceties and expressions of mutual regard, some associations and alliances
with local leaders were considerably more complicated than they initially
appeared.

Overall we worked well with the provincial officials appointed by Afghan President Hamid Karzai. Like Karzai himself, they owed their positions and their continuing survival to the strength of our arms. Without us they were all dead men. But the most peculiar, if not spectacularly bizarre, of all of our relationships was that with Zia Audin, the local warlord in Gardez. It was one of distrust, conspiracy, and mutual antipathy. We endured a dysfunctional marriage of convenience, but divorce was difficult and we couldn't just get rid of him. The few men that he still controlled were encamped at several different bases around the city, but his real power emanated from the Bala Hissar, or Castle Greyskull as we called it, a massive fortification built by the British in the nineteenth century in the middle of Gardez. It dwarfed all of the other structures in town and dominated the entire mountain plain that surrounded the city.

Zia Audin, sorry, *General* Zia Audin, was responsible for many of the rocket attacks on our firebase and at least some of the IEDs that exploded around our patrols. All of the American and Afghan agencies around the region knew this, and most interestingly Zia Audin knew that we knew. But he didn't try to kill us out of a sense of either hatred or malice in his heart; he did it out of jealousy and pride, for Zia Audin was heartbroken. He suffered from an unrequited love of America, and this was awkward for all parties. So Zia Audin, in a fit of adolescent pique, did what came naturally—he tried to kill us.

Outright murder wasn't on his mind so much as grandiose posturing. What he wanted was attention and respect. What he wanted was to keep us frightened of the incomprehensibly alien and hostile Afghan countryside. By arranging the anonymous, nighttime rocket attacks that rained down on us as we slept in our bunks, he thought that he could reinforce the perceived necessity of his power and authority, if for no other reason than to protect us, and fortunately the rockets and mortars missed their mark. No one had been injured.

We were up to some not-so-subtle subterfuges of our own. In moving to the Gardez firebase, we had inherited from previous Special Forces teams a conspiracy to undermine and isolate Zia Audin, and it was something that we did with relish. Zia Audin was a bandit and a thug, and so, of course, he had been a close American ally. Although a Pashtun, he had been a member of the Tajik-dominated Northern Alliance. As a young man he had fought against the Soviets during the Jihad and then against the Taliban, who had imprisoned and tortured him for several years. When the Americans invaded, he joined the swelling ranks of unemployed warlords and reemerged from obscurity to fight the Taliban once again, along with their Arab allies. By all accounts he had been a brave and tenacious fighter. But he was now a petty warlord beholden to no one, and his rank of "general" was recognized due to his years of fealty and service against the Taliban.

The goal of the Americans was to provoke and humiliate Audin, and ultimately drive him from his castle in the city center. Stripped of the castle, which afforded him both symbolic and physical protection, he would only be safe in Kabul. He had many powerful enemies in Gardez, and the locals despised him. His men had terrorized the community, demanding protection money from the local shop owners and raping young boys on their way to school. They were highwaymen, who set up illegal checkpoints, charging "road taxes" from anyone unlucky enough to stumble upon one of their roadblocks. And they preyed on the local nomads, kidnapping prominent tribal elders until their families ransomed them from jail. Audin and his men had gone out of their way to alienate and piss off everyone in town. Rocketing our firebase didn't endear them to us either.

Special Forces teams, ANA (Afghan National Army) units, the Karzai-appointed provincial governor, and the new police chief all conspired to chip away at his power. First, Audin's men were forbidden from operating checkpoints along the roads, then they were banned from carrying weapons while out of uniform in the city, and finally they were prohibited from wearing their uniforms in the city limits as well. They were only authorized to travel from Castle Greyskull to their handful of crumbling encampments in the countryside, where they would languish in the desert. Failure to comply led to the emasculating spectacle of being publicly and roughly disarmed. Bandits stripped of their mystique and their weapons found themselves to be very vulnerable men, and their former victims suddenly saw them as the small-time criminals that they were.

And then there was the matter of the rapes. An old man stopped a patrol of ANA along a roadside and complained to the battalion commander about Zia Audin's men "touching the schoolboys, who were always crying when they passed his house." He'd seen Audin's soldiers taking boys into their barracks. The ANA battalion commander, an old communist who had fought with the Soviets and against our erstwhile mujahideen allies, was livid.

He marched a company of his men, along with two gun trucks of his American advisors, into the closest of Audin's compounds. His soldiers disarmed the men inside under gunpoint and surrounded them in the middle of a courtyard, then lined them up against one of the compound's walls. "If I hear about another crying schoolboy, I'll come back and execute the lot of you," he announced, his voice cracking with rage.

This was a threat that he made frequently and with solemn Stalinist sincerity, and it always worked. He could say things that we couldn't and we admired him greatly for it, although I couldn't help but wonder about a man who was so cavalier about firing squads and mass execution. How often had he delivered on this threat in the past? Or was I just being squeamish and weak? There were no more reports about crying schoolchildren. Audin's men were further restricted and forbidden from any contact with the Gardez shop owners. They would always push their luck, and after an armed confrontation they'd back down, losing more and more face in front of the locals.

This was the deteriorating situation. We'd whittled away at Zia Audin's power and his honor to the point where his men sat dispersed at their various barracks despised, unpaid, bored, and hungry. Because of their previous turns at bad behavior, the locals were enthusiastic about informing on them. Shame is a powerful force in Afghanistan, and we disgraced these sad pitiful fuckers without mercy. The consistency with which the Americans had dealt with

Zia Audin had also generated no small amount of goodwill among much of the local population. We were mostly tolerated as a necessary evil, and that was about as good as we could hope for.

I became obsessed with Audin and his gang of cutthroats. The Taliban were nebulous, as much rumor as reality, but I thought that we could actually do some real good if we could get these gangsters off the people's backs.

We were nearing the final act. Zia Audin was trapped and isolated. He was largely marginalized. We even treated the rocket attacks as more of a nuisance than anything else, the price of doing business in Afghanistan. But more sinister was his flirtation with the Taliban. We started to receive reports that he was assisting his old enemies, putting them up in the castle, and facilitating their activities in the area. He was trying to play both sides against the other in a last desperate bid to maintain some kind of relevance. It was the oldest game in Afghanistan, and a particularly dangerous one if all of the concerned parties found out what you were up to.

Out of desperation he had surrendered most of his heavy weapons as a goodwill gesture, but still we pushed. There would be no reconciliation. We would pressure him either until we could prove that he was working with the insurgents or until he just quit the city. And it was against this backdrop that Bill, our team sergeant, and I, along with our ANA battalion staff, called on Zia Audin for lunch.

Lunching with Zia Audin was a ritualistic courtesy, demanded by custom and protocol. The first time that I'd heard of such an absurdity was during a conversation with one of our predecessors at the Gardez firebase.

"You've actually had lunch with him?" I asked, shocked.

"Oh, yeah, sure. I've been up there a couple of times," he shrugged.

"Have I been reading the wrong intelligence reports or something? Did I miss a meeting? Are we talking about the same Zia Audin, *the* Zia Audin? The jackass who attacks our convoys, mortars our firebase, and who might be working with the Taliban?" I demanded, as I counted off his sins.

"That would be the one. It's just expected. You go up to Castle Greyskull occasionally and have lunch with him. You still have to talk to him, and anyway he puts on a nice spread of chow. If you get a chance to go up there, take it. You won't be disappointed," he said, obviously relishing the irony of the situation.

Now, I had never in my pitiful life knowingly exchanged pleasantries over lunch, or any other meal for that matter, with a man who was regularly trying to kill me. But when Bill invited me to escort him to the castle for his first meeting with Audin, I jumped at the opportunity. The idea seemed so elegant, like the medieval Spaniards and Moors retiring to each other's tents to play chess and exchange bons mots after a bloody day of battle and slaughter. Perhaps the metaphor was unnecessary; we would, after all, be departing from our own high-walled mud fortress to visit another, albeit grander one. We were literally making a kind of feudal social call. This situation, however, was less straightforward; Zia Audin was technically on our side. And anyway, I really wanted to see the inside of that castle.

Bill and I, along with one interpreter (or terp, as we called them), jumped into the old Mercedes jeep that served as our "get around town" car and followed two jeeploads of our Afghan officers up to the castle. Theoretically the purpose of this visit was to discuss ways to coordinate our efforts at stabilizing the area around Gardez, but the reality was that lunch provided us all an opportunity to size each other up.

At the bottom gate to the castle drive, Audin's men lined up for a slapdash review. They saluted and lowered the ridiculous cotton string that barred the road to the castle heights, which meandered up the hillside past the thick stone walls and into an immense central courtyard. The courtyard itself was littered with old Soviet antiaircraft guns and rusting howitzers under several ancient shade trees. All of this, in turn, was surrounded by decrepit barracks and administrative buildings that were missing doors and windows. The rooms themselves appeared to be ransacked, with rusting artillery shells, old rockets, and human feces strewn along the floor.

On the north side, a rocky outcrop ascended still higher and the crumbling stone marked an even older castle, whose origins appeared to have been lost in violent antiquity. And here atop the highest parapet stood two stone burial vaults decorated with the green flags of martyrdom. But to whom they belonged was also seemingly lost. Opposite the most ancient part of the castle was a two-story building that had seen at least some renovation during the twentieth century. There were no obvious holes in its corrugated tin roof and the window frames held actual glass.

Audin and his officers walked out from behind this building while his soldiers, wearing pressed uniforms rather than the normal mix of camouflage and civilian attire, assembled in two ranks. Then Audin and his entourage filed between them dressed in finery appropriate to their status as oriental despots. They wore a mixture of green and khaki ceremonial uniforms, accessorized by scarlet epaulettes and exaggerated peaked garrison caps that were a hangover from Russian military fashion sense. They formed a reception line for us to introduce ourselves, shaking hands gently in the Afghan custom, as we touched our hearts, mouthing, *"Salaam alaikum"* — Peace be with you. We left a couple of ANA privates to guard the vehicles in the courtyard. They were the only ones present who didn't feel the need to wear disingenuous smiles and instead eyed Audin's troops sternly, all business.

Audin's officers led us into what was the warlord's office and receiving room, with a large desk at one end and couches surrounding a low brass coffee table. The typical Afghan functionary would decorate his office with a bouquet of fake silk flowers, but Audin, the gaudy usurper, felt compelled to jam a dozen of them in every nook and cranny. The moldy brown carpet was covered by a cheap and threadbare burgundy-colored Afghan rug. The airless room stank of mildew, and body odor filled the space like a fog. Everyone settled into the couches, while Bill and I removed our body armor, piling it next to the door along with our carbines. We still had our pistols, and I chose to sit next to our gear, just in case this already awkward luncheon went horribly wrong. I calculated that Bill and I could shoot everyone in the room easily before any help could arrive for Audin, which I found reassuring.

Audin sat in front of his desk, and when he removed his pompous headgear, I could finally get a good look at him. Not surprisingly he was a small man, broad across the shoulders, but also handsome. His meticulously combed and pomaded beard merged into a full head of black hair. He had a fresh haircut and used a discreet amount of hair crème. His hands were soft for an Afghan, with long manicured fingernails, and they were no longer accustomed to physical labor. His face, the little that wasn't covered by his thick beard, seemed unaffected by his years of hardship and overexposure to the desert wind and sun. This coupled with his dark sensuous eyes and full lips gave him an effete quality. He looked younger than I'd expected, too young to be the potentate of Gardez. He did not smile, and when he spoke, he did so to the entire room and without looking at anyone directly, but taking in everything as his eyes shifted nervously from side to side. I knew right away that this was a man who had lost the taste for guerrilla fighting and living in caves. He was afraid.

Tea was served immediately and pleasantries were exchanged between Audin's staff and the ANA officers until the food was served. And it became glaringly apparent that Bill and I had made a serious error before we'd come to the castle—we'd brought only one terp, who was huddled next to Bill on the couch translating snatches of the conversation. I, however, was on the other side of the room and, being deaf as a stump, was having a difficult time hearing the translation.

This was just a tactical error; the strategic disaster was in our choice of interpreter. We'd brought Mohammed, who, while he claimed that he was twenty, didn't look a day older than fifteen and was fresh faced, pretty, and beardless. We'd brought a goddamn cherub to a meeting with a gang of pirates, pederasts, and rapists. Audin's henchmen couldn't stop gaping at him, their eyes bugging out of their heads. The young man shifted his slight frame nervously under the weight of their lewd stares, causing the couch to creak loudly and distracting everyone in the room. Beads of perspiration formed on his forehead, and he tapped his left foot incessantly.

He was also a lousy interpreter, one of our worst. All of his languages, English, Dari, and Pashtu, sounded like "moosh, moosh, moosh," and he had the affectation of pursing his lips when he spoke, giving the impression that he was blowing kisses to the listener. The suggestiveness of this unfortunate habit drove the assembled bandits mad with lust as they leaned forward in their seats devouring peaches and hanging on his every mooshy word.

But at least the captain had been right about the food; it was delicious— lamb and chicken kebabs with jasmine rice, followed by fresh melon, and ice-cold Pepsis. After the last plates had been cleared, we got down to the serious business of politics and war. I pulled out my notebook, if for no other reason than to look official and to write down my observations and the names of the men gathered. Bill began guiding the conversation where we wanted it.

"Attacks on Coalition forces have been increasing in the region for the last two months." He paused, looking directly at Audin. "Are you aware of this?"

"Moosh, moosh, moosh."

The bandit on my right crunched loudly into one of the last remaining peaches and juice dribbled down his long beard.

"Yes, yes, we are of course aware of this and we are concerned for the safety of our American friends. . . . We want to help, but our resources are sadly limited," Audin lied. "The people who are responsible for these attacks are not from this region. There are no Taliban here. All of the people are *against* the Taliban and bin Laden and the Al Qaeda. These people are foreigners, from Pakistan or maybe Kandahar."

"So you know nothing?" I said, staring directly at Audin, trying to be menacing and give my words weight by making eye contact, but failing.

He did not respond.

"Well, General, the only way that we'll be able to help you is if you join your forces with the Afghan National Army," Bill continued. He didn't have to threaten, he was a threat. The son of Norwegian farmers from Minnesota, he looked every bit the errant Viking that he was. His thick and muscled body always seemed to be straining to contain something explosive and volatile. His face was permanently locked in an angry scowl under a shaggy mane of sandy hair. I'd always had a nagging sense that Bill might feel the need to snap my neck someday, just to relieve tension, and I'd been his friend for six years.

"Yes, I'm very interested in this ANA. It is very good to build a new army for the peace, security, and stability of Afghanistan. Perhaps some of you Americans or some of these Afghan officers could share some of these new techniques with my men," Audin said, sweeping his hand toward the couch filled with our counterparts.

"No, I'm afraid that that is not possible. We only work with the ANA and the ANA do not train other militias. Respectfully, I don't think that you understand what the ANA is," said Bill, smiling. "Your men must eventually submit to ANA command and go to Kabul for training."

"Ah, yes, I see. Perhaps then I could send some of my men to Kabul for training and then they will return here to Gardez and share this new knowledge. Then together we will all work for peace, security, and stability here in Gardez. But after we have done this we will need new weapons and money for uniforms. Right now I do not even have the money to pay my soldiers." At this his men nodded in agreement, while our Afghans said nothing and betrayed neither emotion nor opinion.

"Again this is not possible. All of your men need to go to Kabul for training. We know that your men are good soldiers. There will always be a home for them in the ANA," replied Bill, speaking not to Audin this time, but to his lackeys, who were concerned about their personal fortunes as well. He was offering them a way out. He paused for dramatic effect. "But they will not return here under your command. They will become professional soldiers, and they will go where the army orders them, just as my army has sent me here to Afghanistan."

"Yes, I see. But my own men are from here. This is their home. Many of them must take care of their families, some even have sick relatives that they must tend to. Plus they know the city. The people of Gardez do not trust strangers. My men can provide information. They can recognize the people who come here to cause trouble. They can be a great contribution to the peace, security, and stability of Gardez."

I had had enough of the courtly circularity of the conversation and decided to force the issue. The empty cynical phrase "peace, security, and stability" was also giving me a headache. I looked at the terp, who I suspected had been doing a lousy job at the translation to begin with, and told him to pay close attention to my words, to which he responded with a peevish scowl.

"Who are the terrorists and where are they? If you and your men know the area and who the troublemakers are, then tell us. Give me their names and their addresses. We know that there are Taliban in Gardez. The firebase is attacked regularly, bombs are planted along the roads, and bandits set up illegal checkpoints to rob the people. You say that you can help us, then help us."

The room exploded into arm waving and excited jabbering, and the terp was overwhelmed.

"General Audin says that they do not know who these people are, but if they find them, then they would gladly torture them for you," the terp said affably, while trying to keep up with the six men who were all speaking to him at once. The mention of torture apparently brought all of the Afghan factions in the room together and now all of them were animated and jabbering and laughing and the tension eased. I lit a cigarette and waited for the room to quiet a bit.

"Now what are they talking about?" I asked the terp after the commotion seemed to die down.

"They're still talking about torturing their enemies," he replied with a shrug. I waited, but the Afghans seemed content to debate the nuances of abuse. Bill just smiled indulgently as he observed the scene.

"If you don't know who these people are, what use are you to us?" I interrupted over the din of the crowd. "They are the future," I said, pointing at the ANA officers, who were suddenly all quiet and stone faced. "If your men want to continue to soldier, then they will join the ANA. If they have to stay in Gardez, then they'll have to get civilian jobs. There's no way around it. It's inevitable."

The room grew silent and the tension returned, to my great malicious satisfaction. But Audin was a professional at these parlor games, whereas I was just an amateur. He was momentarily off balance, but recovered quickly. He made eye contact with me for the first time and only for a moment, before slowly reaching for his tea on the coffee table.

"Tell me more about this ANA of yours. My men and I very much want to help our American friends fight the wicked Taliban."

And around and around we went for another hour, just like the previous one. Audin was trying to find a way to hold on to some scrap of his power and prestige, while we tried to disabuse him of the notion that he had any future in Gardez. Finally, when everyone seemed exhausted from too much talking and jittery from too much tea, we left the castle after many florid pronouncements from all sides testifying as to the great productivity of the day and assurances to meet again soon.

During the drive back to the firebase, I found myself feeling oddly sorry for Audin. He was frozen in his own rhetoric, an anachronism, incapable of change. He was alone and justifiably terrified of the future, surrounded by enemies, a prisoner behind his own castle walls. Perhaps pity was a truer description of what I felt for him, however fleetingly. He was just a man after all and not the monster of my imagination. But the feeling faded as we passed the earthworks of our own fortifications and I saw the faces of my friends. He had made his own enemies, and I counted myself among them more than ever. It was his obvious position of weakness that I'd seen during lunch and it was this frailty that had spoken to my humanity, but it didn't last. I felt a clarifying rush of bloodlust instead.

We headed over to the Afghan officer tent when we got back to brief the ANA battalion commander and talk with our counterparts about their impressions of Audin and his cronies. We found the officers lounging around a long table drinking tea and smoking cigarettes. Two commanders from another Afghan militia unit had stopped by for a visit. They were from General Lodin's command and Zia Audin theoretically reported to them, although they exercised no real control over him. Everyone had been discussing how to remove him from Gardez before we even arrived. One of the guests, whose face remained shrouded behind aviator sunglasses, claimed that he was Audin's "best friend," and that while he remained loyal to his comrade in arms, he understood that his old friend needed to move on, perhaps to Kabul.

"He must learn that the world is changing," he explained, as he prattled on about the usual "peace, security, and stability" bullshit. They say never trust a man who says, "Trust me," and I decided while I sat there listening to this man pontificate that anyone in Afghanistan who talked at length about peace, security, and stability was probably working overtime to undermine all three. The general consensus among the Afghans was that Audin needed to be handled respectfully, if not gently. His mysterious friend promised to have a manly tête-à-tête with him while he was in town. It was impossible to tell whether he was there to spy for us or on us.

While all of this flowery discussion was taking place, I noticed that Bill seemed more explosive than usual, and then suddenly, he slammed his fist onto the table, spilling everyone's tea, and his face contorted into unmasked fury. "I *hate* that asshole!" he screamed to no one in particular. "I wanted to punch that no-good motherfucker in the face! Beat that motherfucker right in his own goddamn house! Beat him right in front of his men . . . mother-fucker. I'd love to shoot that bastard." And then he laughed like a maniac at his own bloody fantasy.

Audin's "best friend" literally winced in what looked like genuine pain, and the rest of the Afghans looked aghast and confused as they listened to the translation. "Oh shit," I thought, "so much for diplomacy." The ANA officers were laughing nervously and their insulted guests didn't bother to hide their irritation at this breach of protocol, both of them scowling and smoking in silent impotent rage.

Cultures everywhere celebrate their traditions, but they also chafe against them. Most Afghans were tired; tired of war, tired of fighting, and tired of meaningless talk. Bill embodied the unrestrained and unpredictable power of the United States, but his frustrated rage appeared to be honest, and honesty is a rare and precious thing. Stories of his impolitic explosion filtered through the terps, the ANA soldiers, the Afghan militias and mercenaries, into the city, and no doubt to our myriad enemies. Bill's reputation was made. That was the day that the Afghans named Bill *Shere Khan*, The Tiger. That was the day that the Afghans fell in love with him. Bill was a force of na-ture, and so it was impossible to tell whether his outburst was genuine or cal-culated drama, but it amounted to an earthquake. Here was Bill, heir to Iskander in all of his blond barbarous glory, equal parts courteous and cruel. My petulant badgering of Audin had been nothing more than second-rate theatrics, which no doubt all of the Afghans expected from an earnest and self-righteous American.

Up until that moment, the Audin situation was a local political problem, but Bill had made it personal, he'd made it tribal. And at that moment he'd crossed over and gone native. After that day there wasn't a thing that our Afghan troops wouldn't do for him; they trusted him completely. In a land fragmented by blood feuds, he'd transcended politics and had declared a personal vendetta. And in Afghanistan, it was considered a moral obligation to carry out one's revenge. Two weeks later Zia Audin quietly abandoned Castle Greyskull and fled to Kabul.

SIX WEEKS IN and KHOST-GARDEZ
Fiction
Specialist Ross Cohen

After graduating from Brown University in May 2001, twenty-two-year-old Ross Cohen immediately set out on what he expected would be a full year of backpacking throughout Asia. He spent two months in Mongolia working for an English-language newspaper and then traveled to Kashgar, a small city in western China. While checking e-mails late one night in the hostel where he was staying, Cohen learned of the September 11 terrorist attacks and decided to forgo his yearlong journey, return to the United States, and enlist in the Army. Cohen trained at Fort Benning and became an airborne infantryman, ultimately shipping off as a paratrooper to eastern Afghanistan with the 1st–501st Parachute Infantry Regiment, which was attached to the 10th Mountain Division's 1st Brigade. Cohen wrote several short works of fiction based on his experiences in-country, focusing primarily on the interactions between soldiers in a single unit. But he was also fascinated by the relationships between U.S. troops and local Afghans, including the misunderstandings and even confrontations that could flare up because of mutual suspicion and distrust. (Since Taliban and Al Qaeda troops did not wear uniforms and appeared, to most U.S. personnel, indistinguishable from innocent civilians, American forces had to approach almost every stranger, or "hajji" as they referred to them, as a potential threat.) In the following story, Cohen relates what happens when troops don't know for certain who is harmless and who is not.

I n the tent, 1730 Zulu — 2200 Afghan time. Today was exciting, sort of. We made our first contact with hajji in a small village near Khost. We killed four of them. Well, by we I don't mean "we," but Charlie Company. "We" were on base security, at the OP-6 tower, when the word came in over the radio. All the dead guys appeared to be foreign, not Afghani, so that meant Al Qaeda, not Taliban.

Now it was time to sleep, and that's all I cared about.

Our team leader walked in the tent. "Ginsburg. Peterman."

Goddammit. I had just taken my boots off.

"Sergeant."

"C Co. just brought some hajjis in. You've got PUC guard."

Fuck. "When?"

"Now."

"What's the uniform?"

"I don't fuckin' know. Take full battle rattle."

Team leader and I had been friends before the deployment. We used to watch football together at a sports bar in Anchorage, but now, a month and a half in-country, things had become strained. I asked too many questions, I guess.

"Really? Are they armed?"

"Jesus, Ginsburg. You can take your gear off when you get there, just bring it."

"Roger, Sarnt. What, uh, are we supposed to do, exactly?"

A deep sigh. This was . . . paining him. "They'll brief you when you fuckin' get there, okay?"

"Roger, Sarnt. Oh — and last thing — who's relieving us?"

Really paining him. "Benson and Nicholas. Two-hour shifts."

I smiled. "Gotcha, Sarnt. We're on it."

I pulled on and laced up my desert combat boots, something I hated to do more than once a day. Nothing — nothing felt better than taking them off. I grabbed my gear. Peterman grabbed his.

We walked out of the tent into the pitch black night. No lights at all. I never understood the need for light discipline on the base. They knew where we were. It wasn't as though some dude was up in the mountains, waiting only for someone nontactical to turn on his flashlight so that he could finally know . . . "Aha! *That's* where the American base is hiding!!" For a time I used the light from my iPod to get around, but that broke eventually.

We adjusted to the darkness.

"Do you know where this place is?" Peterman asked.

"I think so," I replied. I led the way, bumping into something every tenth or so step.

"This is pretty cool. Real fucking hajjis."

"Yeah it is. Too bad they had to come just before sleep." I paused, finding the opening in the gate that led to the PUC cages. "Well, we can always sleep on guard tomorrow."

"Yeah we can."

It was dark, but we both smiled. They had no idea. Though they would.

We neared the cages, and the silence bothered me. "You know what PUC stands for?" PUC—pronounced like a hockey puck.

"I dunno. Prisoner something?"

"Yeah. That makes sense."

A few meters away from the entry to the cages, we heard noises. Soldiers on the move, doing things. Unlike us, they had been outside the wire all day, and they deserved sleep more than we did. Whatever. They had guard last month. They'd have it again in a couple of months. Our turn now. Except tonight, we wouldn't sleep so much.

"Hey—you the guys from Alpha Company?" one of the soldiers asked me.

"Roger, Sergeant. Oh! Hey, Sarnt Greer, what's up?" Sergeant First Class Greer—a platoon sergeant—had been Staff Sergeant Greer, an Alpha Company squad leader, until just before the deployment. His promotion led to a transfer, and we hadn't seen him in a while.

"Oh, hey Ginsburg. We got two PUCs. You know what to do with 'em?"

"Umm . . . not really, Sarnt. No."

"Just make sure they don't sleep. Do whatever you have to do, but keep 'em awake."

"No worries, Sarnt. Were these guys part of the attack today?"

He was already walking off, heading to sleep or a briefing or whatever it was that platoon sergeants did at night. He hesitated for a second, and a second only. "Yeah. They were."

"Thanks, Sarnt. Have a good night."

His soldiers followed him out, looking at me, and Peterman and I were alone.

With the PUCs.

We walked into the cage area, and I leaned my weapon against a bench.

I glanced at the Afghans, but only for a second before I took off all of my gear. In three well-rehearsed motions, my back was free and I felt a shitload better.

I turned to Peterman. I nodded.

He extended his machine gun's bipod legs, and put it down. I picked up my weapon and slung it.

I moseyed over to the PUC cages. The Afghans were separated in different mesh-wire setups. They were two young boys. Not seventeen or eighteen young—twelve or thirteen young. But one was older than the other.

I walked up to the older-looking boy. "What the fuck, hajji. Why you tryin' to kill Americans?" Now I yelled. "Don't you know we're here to help you?!"

I wasn't so good at the shit-talk. I had been in one fight in my life, a fight I neither started nor ended. Though I did give him a bloody nose.

Peterman, five years younger than I, had been silent. Now he followed my lead.

"HEY FUCKIN' HAJJI WE'RE FUCKIN' TALKIN' TO YOU!!!"

He had removed from his weapon his ultrabright Surefire flashlight that we used for clearing caves and dark rooms. He shined it in the eyes of the one I was yelling at.

The Afghan didn't budge. He had a sandbag over his head, as they both did. His had slipped a little, though, and with his exposed left eye, he stared back at us. He was on his knees, with his hands flex-cuffed behind his back.

"Goddammit!! We're trying to fix your shithole of a country and all you can do is try to kill us!! That's FUCKED up, man. That—is—fucked—up!!"

He said nothing. He stared into the flashlight.

We heard a whimper from the next cage over. A mistake. I don't know why, but it was a mistake I felt the need to . . . do something about.

"Oh, is little hajji sad? Do you want to sleep, hajji? Well so the FUCK would I!!" I turned to Peterman. I was a specialist, he was a private first class. I was in charge. I nodded at the older one. "Keep your light on this fucker. Thinks he's a TOUGH guy!!"

As I walked to the younger Afghan, I heard Peterman shouting, "You think you're a fuckin' tough guy, huh! Huh, hajji!!" He ran up to the cage and threw his body against it. The whole structure shook. I looked over, and the Afghan was staring, unmoving.

Afghan the younger was openly crying now. "Oh, whatsamatter, hajji?

Sad 'cuz you tried to fuckin' kill our boys, and now you're gettin' what you deserve?! Oh, that sucks FUCKSTICK!!!" I repeated Peterman's body check to the door. The boy startled back and lost it. Big open tears.

"Don't fuckin' cry!! How old are you? *Tsu kelen ye?*" I had just started learning Pashtu.

No response. Just loud, painful bawling.

His older brother—I assumed it was his older brother—said something to him. I couldn't understand what.

"HEY SHUT THE FUCK UP!! NO ONE SAID YOU COULD FUCKIN' TALK!!" If Peterman hadn't said it, I would have, but maybe not so convincingly. He shook the bars again. Afghan the elder said nothing.

"So I asked you a question! *Tsu—kelen—ye?*" I was a little embarrassed that my accent might be off, or worse, my grammar.

He looked up, stifling his sniffles.

"*Tse?*"

"*Tsu—kelen—ye?*"

"*Yao-laas.*"

"*Yao-laas* . . . Ummm . . . you're eleven? *Yao-laas?*"

He nodded. His sandbag too had come loose.

"You're eleven years old, man. Why are you trying to kill us? Why? *Wali?*" He said nothing.

My Surefire was attached to the front of my weapon. The idea was for it to illuminate what you were going to shoot. I flashed it in his eye, and he flinched backwards.

We heard footsteps. Peterman and I looked over. It was team leader. He wanted to check out the action. He was smiling when he saw me with the flashlight.

"Havin' fun, Ginsburg?"

"These fucksticks, Sarnt. This one's all cryin' an' shit." I went back to the cage.

"IT'S NOT SO FUCKIN' FUN TO TRY TO KILL US NOW, HUH?!!"

Rattle rattle rattle! Team leader was pleased, and that made me feel good. "What'd they tell you guys to do with 'em?"

"Sarnt Greer was here. He said to keep 'em awake all night, but that's it. These are some of the guys who fired at C Co today."

He prowled the area. I wasn't in charge anymore. "I thought we killed all them?"

"I thought so, too, Sarnt. I guess not."

"What's this guy's deal?" He nodded at the elder.

Peterman. "He thinks he's pretty tough. Won't fuckin' CRY like his little fuckin' BROTHER!!" Speaking softly and then yelling, Peterman thought, would keep them on their toes. I thought so, too.

I broke into song. "Turn around . . . BRIGHT EYES . . . every now and then I fall apaaaart!!" On "bright eyes" I hit them both with the light from my Surefire. Team leader grinned at me.

He liked seeing me like this.

"All right, you two." He nodded. It was the closest to praise he came. "I'm goin' to rack out. You guys need anything?"

"Naw, we're good, Sarnt."

"All right. I'll see y'all in the morning." Kindness.

He walked off. I knew what team leaders did at night. They slept.

A moment later, we heard voices and steps from the opposite direction. It was Azizullah, the senior interpreter on base and an American citizen, followed by a couple of military intelligence guys I didn't recognize.

"Hey, Aziz, what's up?" I smiled.

He looked at me. He looked at the whimpering boy. He didn't smile. "They're in pain, you know."

"Uh . . ."

"Look at his hands. Open the gate."

I fiddled with the keys and the lock. I helped the boy to his feet. His wrists, zip-tied behind his back, were rubbed raw. I saw blood.

"Do you have a knife?"

I took out my Gerber that was attached to my belt loop. I swung it open and cut the zip-tie, with the MI guys looking on. I could feel his skin surging for air.

I told Peterman to do the same for the older one.

Aziz and the boys talked for a few minutes in Pashtu, while we looked on. This wasn't our show anymore, and I felt . . . not good. My upper lip curled up, and I was glad that Aziz hadn't come a few minutes earlier.

"Hey," Aziz said, "is there any water?"

I looked around. There was a case by the bench. I grabbed two bottles and handed them to Aziz. He gave one each to the boys. They talked in Pashtu a little more.

I asked, "So what did these guys do?"

He inhaled sharply. "They were lighting a fire in a field. Your guys saw them, so they panicked and started running. The running was suspicious, so they brought them in."

That sounded . . . reasonable.

"So they weren't part of the attack?"

"Look how old they are. Of course they weren't."

"Right. Could the smoke have been some kind of signal, though?"

"No. They lit the fire almost an hour after the attack. In a different village."

"So why'd they light it?"

"Kids like to play with fire."

"Oh."

Reasonable.

Aziz spoke with them a little while longer, and then he and the MI guys took off, telling us to keep a watch on them, but to let them sleep if they wanted to. I asked him what would happen to them, and he said that they'd be taken home in a day or two.

Both boys got back in the cages, but with their hands freed, they no longer had to sit on their knees. The elder sat Indian style, and watched us. The younger one crawled into the fetal position and slept. Every now and then Peterman would walk over to them out of boredom, and gently kick at the wire. I didn't say anything. I smoked a few cigarettes.

A little while later, after Benson and Nicholas had relieved us, Peterman and I walked back. Twenty-hundred Zulu now, a little after midnight Afghan time. In a few hours, we'd be awake again.

"So that was fucked up, huh?" I didn't want to go to bed without saying something, anything.

Peterman seemed okay. "Stupid fucking hajjis shouldn't have been lighting fires. What are we supposed to do?"

"Yeah . . ." The moon was out now, and we could see a little better. No stumbling anymore.

I pulled back the tent's canvas door and stepped inside. Everyone was asleep.

In a whisper. "Good night, man."

"Night."

I quietly took my gear off and sat down on my cot. I took my boots and socks off and massaged the balls of my feet.

I thought I might have trouble falling asleep that night. But I didn't.

In another story that was also inspired by a real incident, Cohen describes a brief but memorable encounter during a routine security check in the Khost-Gardez region of Afghanistan.

"Get off your ass, Ginsburg!"

Hooah, douchebag.

Using my left hand as a lever, and being sure to keep my weapon's two barrels out of the dirt, I worked my way off the boulder I had been sitting on. My back and shoulders pulled and sagged as eighty pounds of gear once more hung off them.

There was no reason to stand. I could see fine how I was. Either way, I didn't care. Whatever we were looking for on that roadblock on the Khost-Gardez Pass had long ago escaped me, if not us. My mission was to deny sanctuary to back pain.

I walked over to Benson, our team's light-machine-gunner. Team Leader Douchebag was too near to talk about, so we exchanged instead a lingering glance. Then, putting aside my M-4/203 (rifle with grenade launcher— fifteen pounds loaded), I pulled out a nearly empty pack of cigarettes from my cargo pocket.

"You have a lighter?"

"What happened to the last one I gave you?"

"Um . . . things. It's . . . around." I smiled apologetically, and looked down. My Kevlar helmet (4.2 pounds) weighed down my head and neck. Some guys looked good with helmets. Or at least they looked rugged and soldierly. Since Basic, though, I had always felt that the helmet made me look stupid. Worse, goofy. I could pass as a soldier with the rest of the uniform, but the K-Pot suggested that I was just playing at being a warrior in an oversized costume hat.

"Uh-huh. You guys are ridiculous with lighters. Here. But don't keep it."

"Thank you." On the third attempt, I lit the cigarette, inhaled and exhaled deeply. I placed my hands underneath the ammo pouches attached to my flak vest (total weight of M-4 and M-203 ammo: thirty pounds) and pulled up, taking the strain off my shoulders for a second.

"You want one?" I handed the lighter back.

"What kind are they?"

"Hajjis. But the good ones. With the Arabic writing."

"No thanks."

After my third drag, I spotted a jingle truck coming around the bend. "Goddammit." The Afghans loved their jingle, God bless 'em. These massive flatbed trucks that were affixed from bumper to tailgate with jingles and spangles and extravagantly painted mosaics were used to transport all goods up and down the narrow mountain pass. And yes, they jingled when they moved.

Someone had to search it.

"Fucking Bravo Team, man. Just waving it through to us."

Nicholas, my grenadier counterpart in Bravo Team, caught my eye as the jingle rumbled past his position. He waved and flashed a friendly smile. Your turn.

I walked up to the cab and used my best Pashtu. "*Motar tsecha kusha, meherabanee.*" Get out of the car, please.

The driver, a middle-aged Afghan (or Pakistani—I had no idea except that he was Pashtun), flashed an appreciative smile. "*Pashtu pohegey?*" You understand Pashtu? he asked.

"*Leg leg.*" A little bit. We need to search your vehicle, I told him. I asked if he had any explosives, bullets, weapons, Taliban, or Al Qaeda in his flatbed. He smiled again and said no. Without prompting, he spread his arms so that I could search him.

I considered putting the cigarette out. It would make the job easier, and I wasn't enjoying the tobacco. I was too hot and, at eight thousand feet, too high. But I held on to it. Why not smoke?

After Douchebag and Mormon (Alpha Team's M-14 gunner) finished the vehicle search and I had finished with the driver and the two passengers (Benson, with the biggest gun, pulled security), I thanked the driver for his patience and sent him on his way. The driver, part pleased and part bemused that this foreign soldier would be so polite and speak his language, thanked me and took off. Five minutes closer to calling it a day.

"Jesus, man"—I turned to Benson—"my back is killing me."

"I hear ya." He paused. "You wanna trade weapons?"

I knelt before the weighty supremacy of his shittier situation. Without question, his suck was worse than my suck. But then, he had been in the unit a good nine months less than I. "Eh, I'm good, thanks." I had carried his weapon, the squad automatic weapon (SAW) before: 15.5 pounds without ammo. An extra seven pounds per every two hundred rounds, with combat load being eight hundred. Plus spare barrel—seven pounds. Much like Afghanistan, it sucked, it was awkward, and it was a pain in the ass to clean.

Benson saw the stream of vehicles first. "Motherfucker." At least four jingles and three cars—invariably white Toyota Corollas—coming our way, with the sun showing no sign of abating. More bullshit searches. More tension all up and down the back as I bent down to check for explosives and sharp objects. (And what would I do if I found a sharp object? Were knives illegal?) Body armor with vest: twenty pounds.

"I wish one of them would blow up."

Bravo Team waved the first vehicle through, and then halted the second one. Neither team would be able to sham out of this one. (To sham: Army lingo for evading work. For example: "Hey man, I couldn't help but notice that while we were putting up barbed wire for two hours you were shamming in the latrine.")

Staff Sergeant Feiner, 2nd Squad—our squad's—squad leader, grabbed Ahmad and Zalmay, a couple of the Afghan Militia Forces (AMF) guys, and told us to wave the first car through to them.

As our vehicle—another jingle—pulled up, Feiner called over to us. "Ginsburg, I need some help with the translating."

I caught Douchebag's eye. "Hey Sarnt, Sarnt Feiner wants me over there." He glared at me, made me wait.

"Well then, I guess you better get over there, huh?"

"Hooah," I murmured, and got over there.

All smiles now. "What's up, Sarnt?" I took a drink from my CamelBak, the water-filled bladder that I carried on my back. (Five pounds full.)

In his good-natured Californian redneck drawl he said, "I need your Pashtu ex-per-tees, Ginsburg. Find out where these gentlemen are heading to, please."

The driver of the Corolla looked at me, wondering what I had to offer to our little group. I started off with a friendly "*Stalay mashe.*" Hello, and he relaxed and smiled broadly.

"Where are you coming from?"

"Kabul."

"Where are you going?"

"Khost."

"Why?"

Something that I couldn't quite get. I picked up a couple of words for relatives, though, and relayed to Sergeant Feiner that he was on his way to Khost to see family.

"Ask him if he's seen anything suspicious." This was always a fun game. I enjoyed learning Pashtu. It gave me something to do, and it made me feel special. I had a unique talent for a paratrooper with no rank. And it helped with building a rapport and communicating our intentions to the locals. But not once in seven months had I discovered any intel.

"Have you seen anything strange? Any explosives, bullets, weapons, Taliban, Al Qaeda . . ." I droned on in a playful monotone.

He smiled, getting the joke, and vigorously assured myself and Sergeant Feiner, whom he seemed to sense was the boss, that he had seen nothing whatsoever. Ever.

In the meantime, the AMF guys had searched him, his car, and his fellow passengers, who were all watching the exchange intently. In a land without television, Americans were high entertainment.

"Sa'eeshwa. Ta tlaay shay. Dera manana staala komak tsecha." Okay. You can go. Thank you very much for your help.

The AMF guys loved this. Children during the Soviet invasion, adolescents during the warlord years, and young men under the Taliban, they never grew tired of this spectacle of the polite soldier. I maneuvered my combat lifesaver bag (six pounds), slung around my torso, to a different place to readjust some of the weight.

Our Afghan friend stared at me, taking in my dark features and olive complexion. "Ta Afghani ye?"

"Nah. Ze Amrikayan yam," I teased him, pointing to the flag on my right shoulder. I'm not Afghan. I'm American.

"Ta Musulman ye?"

"Nah. Ze Yehud yam." I'm not Muslim. I'm Jewish.

Silence. My back spasmed, and I looked at my rucksack (forty-five pounds) attached to the grill of our Humvee, parked twenty meters away. Inside lay my three-part sleep system and MREs and extra T-shirts and socks and everything else from the packing list, down to never-used but always humped sunscreen and bug juice; all of it still hours and a long walk away from being of any use to me. Ahmad and Zalmay watched me and the driver.

Finally, from the driver. *"Sha Musulman!"* Be Muslim! Yes, of course. I smiled my most friendly of American smiles, the can-do smile that has been transforming the world for generations, and explained that I liked being Jewish. My dad was Jewish, my mom was Jewish, my sister was Jewish, my brother was Jewish.

He cut me off and told me that yes yes he understood.

"We are like cousins, then. We are all children of Ibrahim."

We shared a moment. Sergeant Feiner looked on, sensing and enjoying Douchebag's annoyance from a hundred meters away that we weren't moving the traffic along.

"Yes. We are cousins."

"Cousins."

"Cousins."

He reached out to shake my hand, and did the same with Sergeant Feiner. Thank-yous were exchanged between the driver, Feiner, and myself. Ahmad and Zalmay stayed quiet. He got back into his car and drove off.

Sergeant Feiner looked at me. "All right Ginsburg, you better get back to your team."

"Hooah, Sarnt."

He winked at me. "Thanks, Ginsburg."

"My pleasure, Sarnt."

A step away from Feiner's protective shield, I was barked at by Douchebag. "Ginsburg, get the fuck over here!!"

I glared at him, openly. "It's not like I was doing my own thing!" I had been accused of this crime in the past.

"You better watch your fuckin' attitude or you'll be doin' mountain climbers all up and down this fuckin' mountain." Benson and Mormon looked on. At least this would be more grist for later.

I stared back at him, not breaking eye contact.

"Don't be eye-fuckin' me, Ginsburg. I will fuck you up!"

I held eye contact but wouldn't push it any further. "What do you want me to do, Sarnt?"

I asked the question plaintively, not literally, but whether that illiterate fuck could sense that, after a pause he took it as an out.

"I want you to get over here and start searching these vehicles."

"Hooah," I mumbled, and with head down rejoined my team.

After being honorably discharged from the Army in January 2005, Cohen put on his backpack again and traveled through Europe, the Balkans, Israel, and Central America. He then returned to the United States and enrolled at Princeton University to earn a master's degree in public affairs.

RECLAMATION
Personal Narrative
Lieutenant Colonel John Berens

A veteran of the 1991 Gulf War, forty-seven-year-old Lieutenant Colonel John Berens was called out of the U.S. Marine Reserve in January 2003 to serve in Iraq with Task Force Tarawa, 2nd Marine Expeditionary Force. Growing up, Berens had never aspired to join the military; he wanted, in fact, to be a chef. But in November 1979, when he was twenty-four years old and studying at the Culinary Institute of America, Berens heard that Americans had been taken hostage in Iran. He immediately enlisted in the Marine Corps to, in his words, "make a difference in the world." In late April 2003, as he and his fellow Marines—along with a contingent of British and other Coalition troops—worked to secure Iraq in the early days of the war, Berens assumed that he would be employing his more than twenty years of infantry skills to assist with combat operations. Instead, he was assigned a task in the town of Al Kut that initially seemed to be of little value to the overall mission. Berens wrote the following narrative about the assignment shortly before his unit left Iraq in June 2003.

Brigadier General F. A. Houghton, in the gloom of his dirty tent, sat down to eat. It was early April and the temperatures often surpassed one hundred degrees. Heat, disease, starvation, and enemy assaults were devastating his men, and Houghton was trying his best to present a brave demeanor. He had witnessed men die following his orders, and it was weighing heavily on him. Food was also running dangerously low and today another rider had been forced to sacrifice his horse to provide as many men as possible a small taste of meat.

The siege of Al Kut had gone on much longer than he had expected, but Houghton was still hopeful that reinforcements would come north from Basrah and get his brigade out of this horrific stalemate. The general ate a bite of *saq*, called "spinach" by the troops, but it tasted particularly bitter. He asked one of the men who had prepared the meal if he was certain that he had picked *saq* and not the poisonous look-alike. The soldier assured him that the correct weed had been picked. Houghton slowly finished eating.

The soldier was wrong, and within a few hours the general was dead from accidental poisoning.

Eighty-eight years later in the one-hundred-degree heat of April 2003, Brigadier General Rich Natonski, the brigade commander for the U.S. Marines Task Force Tarawa, stood looking at General Houghton's gravestone in the ruins of a World War I British cemetery in Al Kut. General Natonski had just led his brigade through combat at An Nasiriyah, where, against fierce resistance, the task force had seized and held two vital bridges. It was the most brutal combat Marines had seen since Vietnam, and it cost the lives of nineteen of his men. The deaths of those nineteen Marines would remain with General Natonski for the rest of his life—a commander's burden shared with General Charles Townshend, who, almost ninety years ago in Al Kut, led the men of his British 6th Indian Division against the Turks. Townshend lost men in the thousands, including one of his brigade commanders, General Houghton.

General Natonski turned to me and asked, "I wonder how this general died?" He stood there and studied the grave of a fellow brigade commander and officer like himself, who had died doing his duty at this very place.

All who have ever gone to war carry with them the same burdens, regardless of when or where they have served. So when Task Force Tarawa fought on the same ground, under the same harsh conditions, with the same timeless burdens as British soldiers of World War I, the connection to those long-dead soldiers was close and visceral.

General Natonski assigned me to clean this cemetery, which was little more than a sunken acre of rotting garbage and donkey carcasses hidden under twelve-foot reed grass and dead, skeletal trees. Below the surface lay the remains of four hundred and twenty men.

On the face of it, the job was a nasty task that seemed to have no direct benefit to the Iraqi people. My personal misgivings, that we could be addressing more urgent needs, were irrelevant. My duty was to execute the mission I was given.

Al Kut is an ancient, crumbling place that would have died long ago, except that it sits on the banks of the Tigris River. Commerce still flows the eighty miles downriver from Baghdad. The site has made Al Kut a critical stopping point not only for supplies of grain and salt, but also for military units seeking a staging ground close to Baghdad. In 2003, Task Force Tarawa stopped its northern push at an abandoned Iraqi airfield just south of Al Kut. In 1915, the British 6th Indian Division stopped here as well and became trapped by Turkish forces. That siege resulted in thousands of deaths, including the bodies hidden here beneath garbage and grass.

"It is no problem for you to put up a cross here. We respect all religions." I turned to face a dark-skinned Iraqi, probably early thirties, very thin and smiling. He introduced himself as Hussein Zamboor, and he spoke with a clear British accent. "There are Christians who live in this neighborhood, and the only reason the cross was taken in the first place was so the metal could be used as reinforcement in cement—because of sanctions." We were looking at a truncated cement obelisk that was the base of a missing cross in the center of the devastated cemetery.

His English was very good. When I complimented him, there was something poignant about the way he looked down modestly and said, "Thank you." Hussein had learned his English by listening to the BBC. He became my translator but refused to be paid, saying that he wanted only to learn to speak better English.

Hussein and I were not alone in the cemetery. When we first arrived, there was a great buzz of excitement and barefoot children came from everywhere. Men moved about in large groups, some wearing traditional gowns, called *jellabas*, though most were in Western trousers and polyester shirts with colorful geometric designs. They were talking excitedly, with a fierce energy. They began to walk slowly around the site as if they too were evaluating the sanity of cleaning up this place.

After inspecting the cemetery, I was reeling from the magnitude of the project. I was about to return to the airfield to figure out a plan, when a large group of men pulled Hussein aside. With animated gestures they all seemed to be talking at once. Hussein then turned to me. When he spoke, all the men became quiet. "They want to know what you are going to do about the protesters," he said.

Driving through the town to the cemetery that morning, I had encountered about a hundred men in front of the town hall holding black banners and chanting over loudspeakers, "NO CHALABI! NO CHALABI!" They were protesting the possible insertion by the United States of Ahmed Chalabi, an Iraqi expatriate with a suspicious background, into power in Baghdad. There was no violence, but the chant was clearly directed toward us.

In Iraq, men guard their words like gems that might be stolen. They whisper their true thoughts only to those whom they know they can trust. The old regime had killed men for merely uttering words against it. Political protest had been a crime just weeks before. I answered that we would do nothing about the protest. "Those men are being peaceful. They're doing nothing wrong."

They asked: "Will anyone stop them?"

I said no. "Saddam is gone, and you are free to say anything you want to say. You can speak freely without fear."

The animated chattering stopped, and the faces of the men immediately changed. They looked hopeful, like a code they had been trying to decipher was beginning to make sense. These modest, hardworking men looked at me in wonder. They shook my hand, smiled big, mostly toothless, head-shaking grins.

The next day, we rolled in with every type of heavy equipment imaginable. Marine combat engineers and Seabees went to work with backhoes, bulldozers, and an assortment of smoke-belching, earth-moving machinery. We never made it past the front gate; the equipment sank in the soft soil, and the rest of the day was spent recovering the useless machines.

At the same time, the Seabees began to measure the obelisk so a new cross could be constructed. Another crew of Marines struggled to excavate an ornate gate, which was buried, half open, in a mound of dirt and garbage at the front of the cemetery.

Hussein came up and asked me, again with a group of men crowded around him, "Why are you doing this cleaning? Our most dire need is electricity. What are you doing for that problem? We do not understand why so much work is going on here when we cannot use the lights in our houses." Electricity had been off for many months.

"It is our biggest effort right now," I tried to console them. "We have helicopters flying from Al Kut to An Nasiriyah and to Baghdad to assess how many poles and electrical lines are down and to document any other problems."

They told me how Saddam used to punish the town by shutting off the electricity. Each day I kept hoping I would see lights come on in the houses. Still I offered no explanation as to why we were doing the cleanup.

General Natonski confided to me that he, too, was taking flak for spending the man-hours and resources for the reclamation, and he had thought hard about the justifications for the task. A student of history, a man of deep moral convictions, and a warrior-philosopher, he decided simply, "It's the right thing to do."

I inspected the grounds of the cemetery once again. Trash was everywhere, piled up against the perimeter wall, between the headstones, even stuck in the branches of the dead trees. I found a torn-out bit of notebook paper with an Iraqi child's English homework on it that, in shaky block letters, said, WHERE ARE YOU FROM?

This filth had been building up since 1991, when Saddam, angered by the Brits after the first Gulf War, ordered this place destroyed. Instead, the villagers just dumped their garbage here. When I poked around the putrid mounds of refuse, I realized that I would not be able to accomplish this mission without enlisting the help of the residents of Al Kut. That night I sought—and was given permission to hire—local Iraqis to help us with the garbage.

The next day Hussein introduced me to Methag Jabar Abdulla, a quiet, well-groomed man who owned a glass installation shop across the street from the cemetery. Methag said he could get the men to remove all the garbage. We needed to discuss terms of a contract, so he gestured to his shop and soon we were sitting in the damp coolness of the cement building. Methag drew water from a plastic cooler and offered the tin cup to me. Ignoring the sanitation risk, I drank the water, savoring my first cold drink in three months. The negotiation could now begin. I wrote on a piece of notebook paper exactly what needed to be done: In six days, remove all garbage down to ground level and haul it away. Hussein wrote the words in Arabic under my writing.

Methag consulted his brother and the other men in the room. He insisted that he must hire five trucks and at least fifty men. I said that this would be fine and asked him how much he expected to be paid. He said, "As you wish." It surprised me. As I wish . . . I wished I could pay him more, I wished I could bring in dentists, doctors, electricity . . . I wished this dignified man were not having to bargain to clean up garbage. We settled on $1,700, and he agreed to start the following day.

When I arrived in the morning, the Iraqis were already working. I was in awe of the simplicity of their approach. I counted only two tools. There was an old man standing on the highest pile of garbage with a shovel, the blade of which was broken in half along its length. Beside him was a younger man with a pickax that had a shaved tree branch for a handle. The younger man would plunge the pickax into the pile and loosen a small amount of the garbage that the older man could shovel. The rest of the crew carried sturdy vinyl bags as they climbed the mound and then leaned down to receive one shovelful of filth. One sack, one man, one shovelful, one trip to the sidewalk and back, over and over.

They began work at seven in the morning. In the course of the day, the heat rose to over one hundred degrees, but work never stopped. By seven that night, one small bagful at a time, the biggest garbage pile in the cemetery had been displaced to the sidewalk. In the process, the Iraqis uncovered four headstones.

As the work progressed, we learned more about the soldiers buried under our feet. The British had dug in with only two months' worth of food, and the Turks kept British reinforcements from breaching the siege. Hanny Tahir, a fifty-year-old general contractor who had come by seeking work, said that his grandfather once told him that many of the people of Al Kut had died along with the British. In fact, the reason the Brits' food did not last was that they fed the six thousand people of Al Kut during the fighting. He cursed the Turks.

The British soldiers were no longer anonymous. As their names and their struggles were slowly revealed, our work became more personal. The dates on the headstones related individual stories: Private J. H. Mitchell, of the 1st Battalion Durham Light Infantry, died along with fourteen other men buried here on December 10, the day the Turks launched multiple attacks on the 6th Division's first trench line. Two hundred and two men died that day.

The Iraqis continued their methodical work. One day I pulled aside a boy of about twelve who was carrying his sack to the sidewalk and, through Hussein, I asked him if he had yet been paid. He grinned widely and showed me a handful of dinars from all his work. I asked him how much he was being paid, and he said an amount that was equal to two dollars a day, twice the going rate. When I asked him what he was going to do with the money, he became serious.

"I will buy food for my family," he responded.

I asked him how many were in his family.

"My mother and my two sisters and me. I am the only man and I must work to feed them." He appeared to me then not like a boy, but like a very young man, full of decency and purpose. I asked Hussein what had happened to the boy's father, and he told me that Saddam's men had carried him away in 1998 and he had never been seen again.

The next day Methag shook my hand in the warm Arab greeting (clasp hands, then place your hand to your heart) and thanked me for asking the boy whether he had been paid. I told him he need not thank me, as I was just making sure that the contract was being adhered to. In fact, I was checking up on him. But for Methag, it was a new experience to have the people in charge give a damn about where the money was going. Under the last regime, no one cared where it went so long as certain officials got their share of it.

Most of the men hauling the garbage showed up each morning wearing the same shirts they had worn the day before. We did, too. But the striking difference was that while their clothes were always immaculate, ours were not. No matter how hard they worked and how dirty their clothes became, they washed them each night because they wanted to appear neat and clean the next day.

I looked at the men toting the sacks. There was a dignity about them, an innate bearing of nobility that, at least for today, they could hold their heads up because they were working. This was the first work they had been offered in nearly a year, and they were eager to earn the money. But it was more than money itself they were looking for; it was a sense of worth. Cleaning this cemetery was beginning to affect me. Amid a war, it was bolstering my faith in mankind.

Hussein and I were sitting in the shade one day when he felt comfortable enough to ask me about my family. Just a wife, I said, and I showed him her picture. He lowered his head and with a shy, charming grin said, "She is very beautiful."

I thanked him and asked him if he were married.

He said, wistfully, "No . . . no . . . I am not married. I am not wealthy enough to be married."

I asked him if there was a woman he liked.

He brightened, "Oh yes." He told me her name, and I asked, "Does she know you like her?"

"Oh, no. I think she does not."

Then I asked him why. He looked at me directly and said, "I am a professor of mathematics. I make a small salary. In our culture I must have enough

money so that I can take care of the woman I love. She does not know because I cannot tell her now."

Here was a noble man, an honest man with a tenderness and depth of
spirit rarely encountered. He had been caught in the grinding poverty brought
on by a mindless regime and the punishing effects of sanctions. It was not just
love unrequited; it was human ambition beaten to the ground and dreams ex-
tinguished. In conversation with one of the other translators, I learned that
Hussein made only enough money each week to buy one carton of eggs.

Hussein introduced me to a man who looked to be about forty and was
very handsome, but his hands were malformed. He explained, using Hussein
to translate, that two years ago he had been taken from his home and tortured.
The men responsible wanted him to incriminate his friends even though they
had done nothing wrong. This man needed to tell his story, and he wanted an
American to hear it. To torture him, the man continued, they tied him from a
rafter by his thumbs and shocked him with electrical wires all over his body.
He said he withstood their punishment, and when they finally believed he had
no useful information, they released him by swinging a machete right through
his thumbs, leaving them dangling in the air above his head.

The closer one comes to death, the more urgent it becomes to live genuinely. Military men know this simple openness. Men at war speak plainly,
make peace with their possible fate, and in moments of reflection they tell
one another what to do with their belongings if they die. There is no individual more honest than one who sees clearly the end of his life. The people of
Iraq have lived close to the edge of death since Saddam came to power, and
it has endowed most of them with an open, raw authenticity that strikes me as
honest and admirable.

Six days passed and, as promised, the garbage was removed. Methag said
that he was prepared for me to evaluate the quality of his work. I walked slowly
over each area where the piles of garbage had been, and the grounds were
spotless. A small group of Iraqis quietly followed as I made my inspection.

I told them the work was excellent.

Methag asked me when he would get paid, and I told him, "Now."

He was in shock. He seemed to be expecting some unforeseen complica-
tion, some official reason why he could not be paid. I had already gone to the
disburser and withdrawn the amount we had agreed on, and, with Hussein
helping me count, I placed the money in Methag's hand. His grin and barely

suppressed laugh told me that he was surprised to find it so easy and honest. I was proud to be the one that was giving the cash, knowing that this man would make sure it helped his community. I also believed, in the deepest recesses of my heart, that we had made a difference here. Despite my skepticism, the best thing we brought with our big machines, our loud talk, and our American money . . . was hope. I think now they believed we were truly here to help, and they were then free to hope for better lives for themselves.

While the work on the grounds was ongoing and the stones were being reset, the restoration work on the cross in the center of the cemetery began. Ali Jabar Abdulla, Methag's brother, had a 1982 picture of the cemetery in pristine condition. It clearly shows the cross. The intent was to make one that resembled, as closely as possible, the original. The Seabees constructed a three-hundred-pound cement cross and a flat, black metal cross that would be affixed to it, but offset by a couple of inches to create a shadow effect. It was creative metalwork on an industrial scale.

While I was busy supervising the reclamation, Brigadier General Natonski asked me to coordinate a ceremony to honor the British dead in Iraq, past and present. At this point in Operation Iraqi Freedom, British casualties almost equaled our own. Our goal was to hand off the cemetery in whatever improved condition we could achieve by May 8, 2003, with the hope that the British would undertake its continued improvement.

The Seabees were busy installing the cross on May 7. It was a beautifully rendered bit of ironwork, and I was admiring it when Hussein came to my side. We greeted each other as friends, "As Salaam alaikum," "Alaikum salaam." We shook hands and then put our hands to our hearts. We had been friends for only three weeks, but under such pressurized circumstances the bond seemed unusually strong. We had spoken honestly about our lives. We trusted and respected each other, and when I told him that day I would be leaving after the ceremony, I saw sadness in his eyes. I too felt acute sorrow because I loved this uncomplicated man, and I felt as if I were abandoning him.

When I got back to the airfield that night, I filled a small gift box with things I thought Hussein could use, along with one hundred dollars of my own money and a heartfelt note. I gave him the box after the ceremony but never got to see him open it.

His gift to me was a poem that I treasure:

You are a good human.
USA have honor that you belong to.
Your faithful face will not be forgotten.
Everything will pass away, gold, kingdoms,
But goodness will stay alive, engraved in hearts.
Here you are in front of a member of Saddam's victims,
An easy example for his misery,
But the perfume of freedom has opened silently the doors.
You and I were looking for life among the tombs.

The cemetery was as improved as we could make it. The reed grass was gone, the dead trees were removed, and the garbage had been hauled away. It certainly smelled better, and you could see every gravestone although some were still leaning and cracked.

The ceremony was meant to tie the past with the present, the dead to the living, Iraq to Britain, and to America. But it became a reflection on loss, a somber moment to honor both the men who had died recently and those who were buried in the cemetery. And, by extension, it became a gentle, dignified way of reflecting on the war, our grief, and the cost of this grim profession. It was the funeral we never got to attend for our nineteen Task Force Tarawa Marines. It provided a quiet moment to help the generals make peace with the fact that those deaths would be a part of them for the rest of their lives. I can only imagine the guilt, uncertainty, regret, and sorrow that plague the mind of someone whose decisions have cost the lives of his men, and this ceremony was a salve for those deeply personal wounds. It also tied our American grief at losing our young men to the honor paid to the British for their losses. Major General Brims, the commanding general of the 1st UK Armored Division, had lost thirty men. He was our guest of honor.

When the ceremony got under way, I staked out a little privacy for myself and stood alone behind the chairs. My mission was almost complete, and this was the first time I could begin to relax. Behind me stood most of the men of the neighborhood. Hussein, in a very subdued voice, translated throughout the ceremony for his countrymen.

At 3:00 p.m. Iraq time on May 8, the dignitaries arrived. Two bagpipes played "Amazing Grace" as everyone took their seats. General Natonski said this:

As the fighting men of Task Force Tarawa labored in the sun to clear the cemetery, to help restore its dignity and solemnity, they did it as brothers to those who lie herein. Just to the right of where I am standing, Private J. J. Jennings' headstone reads, "2nd Queens Own, Royal West Kent Regiment, Died March 22 1916. Age 21."

To the young Marine who sweated and strained to clear the site around his grave, Private Jennings is not a lost member of another generation, not just a soldier from the ranks of our closest ally, he is another twenty-one-year-old fighting man, a peer; his death is linked to the lives of those we lost. We mourn the passing of our young men with timeless, universal grief. Our bond to Private Jennings and to all the soldiers buried here is deep and spiritual. It transcends nationality and is rooted in the understanding that when we as soldiers and Marines go to foreign shores, our deepest hope is to see our homes and loved ones again.

As I thought about the work, the words, the men we had lost, and the men I had befriended, I was surprised by the deep emotion that surfaced. My biggest contribution to the war was, in the end, healing, not killing. But now I had to leave. I had been allowed to see into the lives of everyday Iraqis, and I knew there was so much more to be done. I would not be here to see the men make plans to marry, have children, regain their lives, or simply be able to flip on a light switch. I had, in three weeks, become close to these men. They, not the cemetery, had become my mission.

As General Natonski came to the heart of his speech, his voice faltered—and I began to cry. I just stood there and let my tears fall without moving and without shame. But I was not the only old warrior who had put his head down and let the wave of sorrow and relief wash over him.

JAG IN THE SANDBOX
Personal Narrative
Lieutenant Colonel Terry F. Moorer

During his one-year deployment in the Middle East as the staff judge advocate with the 226th Area Support Group, Alabama National Guard,

forty-two-year-old U.S. Army Lieutenant Colonel Terry F. Moorer ques-
tioned well over a hundred detainees and EPWs—enemy prisoners of war.
The detainees included Fedayeen militants who had sworn their allegiance
to Saddam Hussein, high-level members of the Saddam regime, regular
Iraqi soldiers who had been forced to fight under penalty of death, and
other potentially threatening individuals. (Some were civilians who had
been in the wrong place at the wrong time and, after being interviewed,
were released.) Moorer arrived in Iraq in April 2003, and the vast majority
of his time was spent in Baghdad and Um Qasr, where he adjudicated as a
magistrate in the former and conducted tribunals in the latter. Moorer kept
extensive notes detailing his experiences, and in the following excerpt he de-
scribes the challenges he faced trying to differentiate between the guilty and
the innocent.

My participation in the screenings began by working with and observing a British JAG captain named Margaret. After a brief handshake
with the prisoner, Margaret got right to the interview, interspersing her interrogation with questions whose answers she already knew. It was a method I
used as well back in Alabama, but I was surprised at how much more difficult
it was to seek the truth without reliable nonverbal cues. For instance, when
having a conversation with someone in English, I can focus on their inflec-
tion, demeanor, gestures, and eye contact to form an impression of how
truthful they are being. This was much harder to do when you didn't know
the language.

Tattoos and body marks were one nonverbal source of information. Strict
Muslims do not tattoo their bodies, so a physical inspection of the prisoners
was part of each interview. A tattoo raised a red flag for me if a prisoner, particularly one from a surrounding country, said he came into the country for a
religious purpose. A number of tattoos were depictions of girlfriends or, more
importantly, the Fedayeen Eagle. One sixteen-year-old boy had Fedayeen
marks on his arm, which he burned with cigarettes in an attempt to obscure
the tattoo. Unfortunately for him, he bragged to his cellmates about being a
Fedayeen and they relayed the information to the guards.

I also realized that some prisoners who could speak English would play
dumb. This enabled them to mask emotions or have additional time to prepare evasive answers. I chose to have my interpreters literally convey my ques-

tions, which I kept short and simple. When I started leading the screenings myself, I began every interview with the following sequence of questions, "What is your first name, your father's name, and your tribal name?" From a name alone, it's often possible to determine whether the person is Muslim, Christian, or some other faith. If I had been savvy enough to know more regional history, the names might have conveyed more subtle information.

An interpreter working with us, a Kurd, identified Saddam Hussein's cousin (Chemical Ali's son) when he was asked to give his full name. To my knowledge, no one was aware of the family relationship between the prisoner and Hussein prior to the interpreter asking the prisoner his full name. At lunch that afternoon, I asked the interpreter how he knew the prisoner was related to Hussein even though he had never met or seen this cousin. The interpreter told me, "You know who your enemies are if twenty-two of your close family members are killed somehow." The look on his face and the tone of his voice reminded me that when I was a child, certain names, such as George Wallace, held such a deep meaning to me as a black person that I knew who was in that camp, whether I had met them or not.

After ascertaining the names of the prisoners, their ages, and other basic information, I asked each prisoner to describe how he became a prisoner. The stories ran the gamut from the outrageous to the plausible. For instance, I interviewed a young Iraqi sergeant whom I will call Habib. Before I could ask substantive questions, Habib said that he did not want to go home under any circumstances. Habib had the misfortune of being drafted shortly before Desert Storm. In Iraq, as in most of the surrounding Arab countries, every male between eighteen and twenty-three serves a one- to two-year tour in the Army. Physical or mental disabilities are the only reasons for exemption.

The draft is different than one might expect. At least yearly, a "recruiter" goes into each town and stops every able-bodied male and demands to see his Red Book, which is a small, red book all Iraqi males over age eighteen must carry with them at all times and which verifies the person's military status. It is a serious crime for Iraqi males of draft age to be caught in public without a Red Book on their person. If they have not completed their mandatory military service, they are physically put in the Army that day. Some of the prisoners I interviewed had bought exemptions from corrupt recruiters.

Habib said he became a deserter in Desert Storm after several men died in their first aerial attack. Habib ran home to Baghdad and paid someone to make a convincing, forged Red Book. Habib worked and lived in Baghdad until the present war. One day, shortly before Operation Iraqi Freedom began, a sergeant in the Fedayeen shanghaied Habib into service. Habib knew that if he refused to serve he would summarily be shot. When U.S. forces went into Baghdad, the sergeant told Habib to cover him while he, the sergeant, fired a rocket-propelled grenade (RPG). When the sergeant took his firing position, Habib shot and killed him and then ran to an American checkpoint, promptly becoming a prisoner of war. Habib said that friends of the sergeant saw the killing, and therefore the sergeant's family would attempt to kill Habib as long as Habib was alive.

I also interviewed and actually felt great respect for several Iraqi officers who were prisoners of war. Most of the captured officers had surrendered their men with little or no resistance. Quit and surrender are *not* U.S. Army words. Officers in every military are responsible for accomplishing the mission first and seeing to the welfare of the command second. But when resistance is futile, the difficult but correct moral choice is surrender. Lee's capitulation at Appomattox is a prime example of such moral courage.

Unlike Lee, however, the Iraqi officers knew that surrender meant they were betting the lives of their families. During the early phases of the war, Saddam inserted Baath party officers into units to report the names of deserters. Family members of the deserters were killed or tortured by Fedayeen. According to the officers I talked to, a real fear existed among the Iraqi officers that their families would be tortured or killed because the officers chose to surrender their units rather than commit almost certain suicide by opposing a vastly superior force. In our Western eyes, family generally means the nuclear family. In Iraq, family includes the nuclear and extended family. The Iraqi officers at Camp Bucca made the difficult but correct moral choice to surrender rather than offer futile resistance.

I also had an opportunity to serve as the presiding tribune on a panel that heard a memorable case. A Syrian prisoner said he had come to Iraq with two other friends to visit Karbala, a holy city for the Shiite Muslims. According to the prisoner, he and his friends set out in their automobile with no particular destination in mind. Knowing that Syria was several hours from Karbala and many Syrians were coming to Iraq to fight Coalition troops, I suspected the story to be false. The sole matter left for the panel was to ascertain the motive behind the lie.

After the prisoner, whom I shall call Khalil, finished his story, we visually inspected him. Khalil had a tattoo that consisted of verses of the Koran and his girlfriend's name. A long surgical scar ran down the right side of his back. Khalil said he donated a kidney in Baghdad the year before and that he came to Iraq to have a follow-up examination. Coincidentally, his two friends were just about to appear before another Tribunal panel. After separately questioning the trio, we discerned that Khalil had sold his kidney the previous year and he had brought his two friends to sell their kidneys.

My assessment of the situation was, Khalil is desperately poor, has a family to feed, and has no real prospects for a better future. Under similar circumstances, many would be tempted to do the same because the $5,000 or $10,000 he and his friends would obtain from selling their organs is roughly equivalent to someone offering an American $2,000,000. We set Khalil free after we came to conclude he was not a physical threat to Coalition forces.

Another case exemplified the rampant evil in Iraq prior to the invasion. A prisoner whom I'll call Mahmed had the Fedayeen markings, but, more importantly, had been seen by several witnesses at work during the war. According to the testimony of these eyewitnesses, when Coalition forces invaded a certain town, Mahmed shot and killed persons leaving the city. Mahmed killed boys, girls, women, and men, old and young, as they fled toward safety. Mahmed had also threatened Iraqi soldiers by assuring them that if they didn't fight, the Fedayeen would kill the soldier and his family.

The serious cases were seemingly unending. One day, I literally had a foot-high stack of files, which represented the morning docket, including (I have changed the name of each prisoner):

Zaden—By his own admission, Zaden was an assistant to Chemical Ali. I found Zaden to be a security risk worthy of detention.

Sala—After the end of main combat operations, Sala killed two GIs near Tikrit (Saddam's hometown) by means of a bomb. Sala cut off the arm of one of the dead GIs, shook hands with it at various public places while saying, "Down Mr. Bush." I detained Sala as a security risk and identified him as a potential war criminal.

Mohammed—Mohammed slapped his wife during an argument and was promptly arrested by MPs. Mohammed was stupid enough to think he might be able to beat an MP. The MP quickly and painfully subdued Mohammed, dragged him out of the house, and dumped him into the back of a Humvee. MPs of the 800th Brigade have a technical term for this procedure:

"Carrying out the trash." I gave Mohammed eleven days, the max for simple assault, and another seven for attempting to assault the MP.

The next morning, I went into the House of Cards, where I met Tariq Aziz, the former deputy prime minister of Iraq, and other high-ranking members of the Hussein regime. Before the war, the U.S. military handed out decks of playing cards to the troops that had the faces of these "most wanted" Iraqis, which is why the facility that keeps them is called the House of Cards. Out of respect for their privacy and the regulations of Camp Cropper, our conversations with the "face cards" consisted of no more than a "Good morning" or a nod. Most of the prisoners wanted to talk and spoke fluent English with a British or American accent acquired from having lived in either or both countries. It was not appropriate to engage in substantive conversation or to gawk.

After the tour, I spoke with a guard who had worked in the Face Card section from its inception. The guard's impressions of the prisoners were that they were all extremely intelligent and well-educated individuals who had studied at the finer Western universities in the United States and Britain. The guard noted that there was a pecking order within the deck of face cards and that some of the prisoners were genuinely upset that their likeness did not rate a higher card than other inmates'.

WEDNESDAY 2/23/05
Personal Narrative
Specialist "Ski" Kolodziejski

Manning a .50-caliber machine gun mounted on top of a Humvee, twenty-one-year-old Specialist "Ski" Kolodziejski regularly patrolled the streets of Baghdad with the 617th Military Police Company (attached to the 18th Military Police Brigade) during a one-year deployment to Iraq. Kolodziejski was a member of the U.S. Army National Guard out of Kentucky and was called up in the fall of 2004. In February 2005, while driving through the eastern outskirts of Baghdad, Kolodziejski watched as a group of young Iraqis converged excitedly on a small convoy of American vehicles in hopes of getting candy. Kolodziejski's attention quickly turned to one child who was standing at a distance from the rambunctious crowd. What happened next prompted Kolodziejski to write the following short account after returning to base.

I remember pulling over on the side of the road in our squad's three Hummers. We were conducting a security halt to get out and stretch before continuing on with patrolling the routes. The sky was partly cloudy and the weather was warm, the way springtime feels at home in the States.

School must have just ended because a large number of Iraqi children were outside and then began approaching our vehicles to receive some free candy, which we often gave out to the kids. Some of them seemed just plain greedy, screaming, pushing, and swarming the vehicles like ducks feeding frantically on thrown bread crumbs.

A small girl of no more than eight or nine years old stood by herself in the rear of the wild youngsters, watching her peers scoop up all of the treats being handed out. She timidly folded her arms across her chest and observed quietly.

We finally made eye contact. As she was looking at me, I pointed to the blond hair pulled up into a small bun at the back of my head, trying to make her realize that I too was a girl. A smile suddenly came to her face. In that moment I remembered that females of this culture do not have the freedoms that we American women possess.

Once the noisy group of mostly boys descended on another truck, I watched as the small girl moved shyly towards me. I leaned down and smiled brightly at this beautiful child with dark hair and dark skin. I handed her a full bag of candy, a gift of gold to the girl, and she seemed overjoyed. The young child gazed at me appreciatively for a moment and then very politely said: "Thank you" in English. I nodded my head and replied "*Shukran*," which is "thank you" in her language.

Whether or not I made a real difference in that small girl's life I can't say for certain, but I know for a fact that she made one in mine.

Kristina "Ski" Kolodziejski returned to the United States in November 2005 and re-enrolled at Northern Kentucky University, where she had been studying as a freshman before enlisting in the Army.

AFTERMATH

Fiction

First Lieutenant Sangjoon Han

Since the March 2003 invasion of Iraq, tens of thousands of Iraqi men, women, and children have been killed as a result of both combat operations and insurgent attacks, and a substantially higher number have been permanently injured. (During a December 12, 2005, question-and-answer session following a speech, President Bush himself estimated the figure of war-related deaths at the time to be about "thirty thousand, more or less.") U.S. Army First Lieutenant Sangjoon Han, a twenty-four-year-old Korean-born soldier who served in Iraq from September 2003 through April 2004 with 1st Battalion, 12th Field Artillery, wrote the following story based on a real attack involving a roadside bomb. Han tried to portray the incident and its aftermath from many different angles, and while the American perspectives were based on his own experiences and conversations with other U.S. soldiers, the Iraqi point of view could, of course, only be imagined.

Specialist Bryon Chambers buried his face a bit further into the neck gaiter to protect himself from the cold air whipping past his skin. They had all scoffed at the idea of packing cold-weather gear to go to the desert. They hadn't realized they would be there through the winter.

The persistent itch at the top of his skull was returning, along with a vague sense of unease. He felt like he had missed something. The Humvee was doing just under sixty, which was entirely too slow as far as Chambers was concerned. The higher risk of fatal accidents was a perfectly acceptable price to pay for faster runs through the IED alleys that they traveled so regularly. Unfortunately, Sergeant McClintock didn't feel the same way, and he was the one in charge of the first of the two convoys in which their platoon was traveling.

Familiar sights and sounds surrounded him, from the decaying buildings and resentful people on the sides of the road to the belching of the overworked diesel engine under the dust-covered hood. It was the same depressing routine as every other day.

For a brief time right after the end of the invasion, they were greeted everywhere with smiles and cheers from Iraqis who were happy to be rid of

Saddam, but who, more important, were glad that the war had been relatively short. Now, Chambers felt harsh stares, even from toddlers barely old enough to walk. It seemed the whole country was spitting curses after them whenever they drove by, and as if that weren't enough, there were the select few who were actively trying to kill them.

That's why they were always on the lookout when they were running a convoy. The officers and NCOs told them that if something looked wrong, then it probably was. Chambers was pretty sure he'd seen something wrong, and it drove him crazy that he couldn't identify what it was. The ping of the radio speaker broke his concentration.

"We've been hit!" Sergeant Wilson's voice yelled on the speaker in almost a panic. It was only then, after the second convoy was attacked, that Chambers remembered the cracks in the road a few miles back where it looked like the pavement had been dug up. They hadn't been there before.

"Turn us around!"

Chambers had stepped on the brake even before Sergeant McClintock gave the order. He made a screeching U-turn and held the accelerator down to the floor.

"Hey!" Sergeant McClintock shouted up to the gunner. "Fire some rounds, get these idiots out of our way!"

The violent noise of the machine gun soon drowned out the sound of the engine, and Chambers watched as the traffic before him parted like the Red Sea.

Qasim was only about twenty paces from the road—almost at the ramshackle fence dividing his farm from his neighbor's—when he caught his first glimpse of the approaching vehicles. His heart jumped into his throat as he dropped the clump of soil he'd been examining. Something was about to happen. The town on the far side of the road was suddenly empty.

The three trucks drew steadily closer and were soon just a hundred meters away. Even with his weakening eyesight, from this distance Qasim could make out the faces of the individual soldiers. It was the closest that he'd ever come to them, he realized, and he was still studying their expressions when the explosion engulfed the last truck in the convoy.

The noise was deafening, and the old farmer felt the ground shake beneath his feet. A painful sensation started building deep inside his ears, but Qasim stood fixed in place, observing the aftermath. He wanted to see what the Americans would do. The answer was not long in coming. The Americans started shooting.

He turned to run.

Private First Class Roy Jackson could still feel the force of the blast when he heard Sergeant Wilson in the front seat yelling for Davies to turn them around. He was sure that they had taken casualties.

Jackson could see as he looked over the driver's shoulder that the second Humvee with Sergeant Price had pulled up right behind them. A hundred meters down the road, there was the outline of a crater and thick black smoke hanging over the pavement. The third and final Humvee in their convoy was nowhere to be seen.

A sick knot formed in Jackson's stomach as he realized that it was up to him to tend to the wounded. This was the reason the medics were there, and he was anxious to get to work. It was only when he saw Davies and Sergeant Wilson jumping out with their weapons at the ready that he remembered that their first priority was to secure the area.

Jackson climbed out of the truck and glanced nervously toward the town. There was hardly anyone visible, though the place was usually bustling. He wondered if the townspeople had gotten word of the attack in advance. The empty streets, at least, made the few who were inexplicably present that much more noticeable.

A young Iraqi, maybe about Jackson's own age, peeked out from a narrow alley toward the blast site. He didn't seem frightened or panicked, and if anything it looked like he was trying to assess the damage. In his hand, he clutched what might have been a weapon, but Jackson saw that it was even more damning—the means by which he had detonated the bombs in the road.

He was holding a cell phone.

"Over there!" Jackson shouted. "It was him!" The medic took aim and proceeded to empty his pistol. He reloaded his weapon while directing the machine gun toward the low wall behind where the Iraqi was hidden. The ground shook from the three- to five-round bursts capable of ripping a body in two, but Jackson could see that the young man had already escaped.

Jackson rose cautiously to his full height, still pointing the 9mm in the general direction of the town. His ears were ringing, the pavement under his feet was covered with spent casing, and he looked around nervously waiting for someone to tell him what to do next. The IED blast and the gunfire had taken its toll, but the medic was still able to hear the sharp crack of a rifle break the sudden silence. It was followed by an indistinct shout, and another shot rang out before Jackson could turn to look toward the source.

Sergeant Price was kneeling in the mud just a few meters away from his Humvee, taking aim with his rifle. Out in the field was an Iraqi man in a dirty white robe, running toward an earthen hut a few hundred meters from the road. But the medic could see that there was no way that he would make it. There was another shout, and then the warning shots came to an end.

"If they're running, they're guilty." The credo had been drilled into their heads over and over again, and it was what went through the sergeant's head as he knelt to take aim. He desperately wanted the man to stop running before he squeezed the trigger.

The rifle kicked back against his shoulder where it was braced, and Price could see a small puff of dirt rising a few meters ahead of the man. There was no way the Iraqi could have missed it, and yet he kept on running.

"Stop!" Price shouted at the man's back, though his voice was drowned out by the drone of the .50 cal firing from the next vehicle. He gave the man another second, then skipped another round in front of him.

It would be so simple for the man to stop, Price thought as a silent anger rose up inside of him. He took careful aim, fearing that his hands would start shaking from rage before he managed to get off the shot. *Just stop running*, his mind screamed at the man. The son of a bitch was going to make him shoot. Price hated the man at that moment. He wanted the man to die for the sin of forcing Price to kill him.

"STOP!" he shouted only a half second before he fired again, so that it was really no warning at all.

More dust kicked up in front of Qasim, who was now sure that the Americans were shooting at him. Relief mixed with terror as he realized they had missed again, but that the next bullet could easily find its mark. The world tunneled down to a shaky horizon and the roof of his house, which was just beyond a low mound of earth. *I'm going to make it*, he told himself. He only had to run a little further.

It was suddenly quiet, and the farmer wondered if the soldiers had given up. A morbid curiosity made him want to turn around and look, but another shot skipping past him was enough to make him run even harder. His legs burned and his lungs were ready to burst, and far away he heard someone shouting a word. It was a foreign word, an American word. A word he did not understand.

Qasim fell forward into the dirt. Three bullets had torn straight through him, piercing his back and the soft flesh of his stomach.

An unnerving silence followed the thunder of the guns, like clear skies in the wake of a hurricane. Private Jackson heard the blood pounding in his ears as he looked across the Humvee to Sergeant Wilson. The sergeant yelled, "Davies! Doc! We're moving!"

Jackson was still fumbling with the improvised latch of his steel door when Davies started the truck in the direction of the crater. Behind them, they left Sergeant Price and his driver moving out toward the fallen Iraqi. It was another moment before Jackson spotted the wreckage, crashed against a tree in the ditch by the road.

Specialist Sam Vargas took in short, shallow breaths as he lay on the ground, staring up at the Iraqi sky. A single white cloud floated toward the opposite horizon, but the interruption in the blue expanse hardly registered. The young soldier was consumed with terror.

The last thing that he remembered was thinking that he was too close behind the second Humvee. Now he didn't know where he was or what was going on, and he couldn't hear a thing except for a faint ringing in his ears. He tried to move but found that he couldn't summon a single muscle in his entire body. He had never been so scared in his life.

Doc Jackson hit the ground running before the truck was even close to a complete halt. Before him was the last Humvee, which had spun almost perpendicular to the road. Under its shattered fiberglass hood, the engine was venting a worrying amount of smoke. Two tan-clad figures were crawling out of the wreckage, but Jackson immediately knew that they were relatively unharmed.

On the ground were the scattered remains of the truck's provisions, mixed with broken pieces of the vehicle itself. Just beyond this debris field, a few meters from the driver's side door, a soldier lay on his back.

The medic knelt to get to work on Vargas, and at the same time shouted instructions back to Sergeant Wilson. "We need to call Vargas in as Urgent. I don't know what the other two look like, but they're probably both at least Priorities."

"Got it. What about the guy that Price tagged?"

"The Iraqi? At least an Urgent-Surgical. He's probably dead by now."

"All right, I'm gonna call in the medevac."

They were only a hundred meters from Sergeant Wilson's truck when Chambers slammed on the brake and brought an end to the wild adrenaline rush of the past three minutes. They had made it back with exhilarating speed, faster than he had ever imagined a Humvee could go, but he still couldn't escape the feeling that they were too late. There were already wounded on the ground. One of them was Vargas.

Chambers jumped out of the vehicle and rushed over to Vargas. He planted the butt of his rifle into the ground and dropped to one knee next to the medic.

"He's gonna be fine," Doc Jackson assured him, but the fear in Vargas's unblinking eyes told Chambers otherwise. Saliva started to foam around the young soldier's mouth, and Chambers saw a slight tremble go through his body. In Baghdad, Vargas slept on a squeaky green cot not five feet away from him, in the same leaky, rotting tent as the forty other people assigned to this mission. Now he was lying on his back in the Iraqi mud and descending into convulsions. Vargas was not going to be fine, and they all knew it.

Qasim kept his jaw clenched tightly shut as the Americans rolled him onto his back. Hot pain shot through his stomach, and he gripped still tighter the handfuls of dirt that he'd clawed out of the ground. He refused to look down at his abdomen for fear that the sight would fill him with horror and he would cry out or weep. He was less than two hundred meters from his house. Inside, his wife would be huddled in the far corner—the smallest children gathered around her while the older ones hid elsewhere in the field. He wouldn't let them hear him cry out. He would not die like some frightened animal.

In his mind, Qasim could hear the angry words spoken by the hotheaded young men every time they mentioned the Americans. Cowards! they cried. Murderers! That was how he wanted to feel now, as he lay dying in the wet, bloodstained earth. He wanted to hate them—to spit his anger and contempt in their faces before the last trace of life ebbed from his ruined body. But all he could feel was the searing pain of his wounds.

He saw their outlines when he opened his eyes, though the world had taken on a terrible brightness. The Americans were greater in stature than his sons had any hope of being, but there was something about them that made them soft, almost pudgy. They lived comfortably back home, he realized. They were people used to luxury, and soon they would go back to their old lives while he would be dead and his children left fatherless. At last, he could feel anger cutting through the pain.

Sergeant Price knew it was hopeless the moment he saw the ground under the man turning into dark, bloody mud. Still, the Iraqi was alive and conscious, and the only alternative to trying to save him was to return to their Humvee and watch him die from the side of the road. Since Price was the one who had shot him, it seemed only right that he try to keep him from death.

There wasn't much that could be done, especially with nothing more than the contents of a combat lifesaver bag. Price arranged the man's intestines over his abdomen as delicately as he could. The sickening warmth of the shredded entrails in his hands and the slickness of fluids were enough to make Price's stomach turn. He wiped the blood on his trousers before rummaging through his medical supplies.

About the only thing he could do was to give the man an IV to try to keep up his blood pressure. It was absurd, he thought to himself, that he was holding a little plastic bag over a man whose vital organs were sitting in a pile on top of him. But he simply didn't know what else to do.

Vargas was still on the ground in an unresponsive state. Waiting for the medevac was the worst part, Private Jackson thought. He remembered that the last time the chopper had taken forty-five minutes just to get to their position.

Jackson looked at the IV bag that Davies was holding up, then down at Vargas, who still had spittle around the edges of his mouth. The vacant expression bothered him. His eyes were almost unblinking but clearly not focused on anything. He could imagine Vargas at forty, still catatonic and sitting in a wheelchair in some VA hospital where a nurse spoon-fed him gray mush.

He tried to shake the images out of his mind; *Vargas will be fine*, he told himself. But looking down at the young man, who had once again started shaking just slightly, he couldn't help but wonder.

The low thumping noise was a welcome sound to Chambers, who had spent the better part of the past twenty minutes guarding the landing zone. He instinctively turned to watch the Black Hawk descend, though he knew he was supposed to keep an eye on his sector.

A cloud of dust kicked up over the demarcated area, partially obscuring the helicopter as it landed. The flight medic jumped out of the hold with his head bent low, carrying the litter they would use to transport Vargas.

Vargas struggled a bit as they moved him onto the stretcher, but it wasn't long before they had him secured and were running him into the belly of the chopper. The other soldiers from the destroyed Humvee followed behind, and the crew helped them into the hold. The litter team ran back out, and Chambers watched as they ran past him toward Sergeant Price, who was still kneeling next to the fallen Iraqi.

Price was amazed that the man lying on the muddy ground was still conscious, let alone alive. Up until the moment when they arrived with the litter, the Iraqi didn't make the slightest sound. He hadn't even looked scared as the blood drained out of his body. He had just continued to stare up at the sergeant with a coolness that Price found unsettling. It was as if he knew that Price had been the one who had shot him.

"Shit," the medic spat when he saw the extent of the damage. "This one's not going to make it."

"What do you want to do?"

"We'll load him up anyway. We can't just leave him here."

It wasn't until they were moving him onto the litter that the sergeant realized just how small the Iraqi was. He couldn't have been more than five foot two at most, and he was so rail-thin that he weighed almost nothing. But when they lifted him, for the first time he heard the man make the slightest of noises. A faint moan, a louder-than-usual exhalation was all that it was, and it didn't seem like anyone else heard it over the sound of the helicopter. But Price noticed it—maybe because he had been listening to the man's breathing for close to half an hour. He reached over and adjusted a coil of dirt-encrusted intestine that had slipped off the man's stomach while they were moving him.

Vargas had clenched his eyes shut when they came to get him. He kept them tightly closed even as he felt the blades beating faster and the bird beginning to move. Though more than half an hour had passed since he found himself lying on the side of the road, he still hadn't regained control over his body.

When the convulsions took hold once more, all he could do was pray again and again that when he finally reopened his eyes, he would be looking at the ceiling of a hospital in Kuwait or Germany, and not up at the great blue Iraqi sky.

The helicopter lurched forward, and the young soldier was on his way.

Sergeant Price was leaning against Sergeant Wilson's vehicle when Wilson himself walked up. He could tell that Price had something on his mind.

"What's up?" Wilson asked.

"Ah, just wondering if I did the right thing. I mean, I don't know if he's guilty or not."

"Hey, that motherfucker was running. There was no way for you to know."

"Yeah, I know. I just wish I could be sure. I mean, he's probably gonna die, right?"

"Don't drive yourself crazy about it, man. We've got enough to worry about."

Qasim could feel the American helicopter taking off. The physical pain had eased a bit, and overwhelmingly what he felt was anger and despair. *How will my wife and sons ever be able to bury me now?* he thought. He didn't even know where they were carrying him.

He was growing furious at himself as well. If he hadn't stood around to watch the convoy passing, he would still be out in his fields making preparations for the spring planting. He silently cursed his own stupidity. He also cursed the Americans for their guns and the young men who attacked them with their bombs. He almost cursed God, but just barely caught himself. He was going to die, and there was nothing he could do about it.

A sad sense of defeat came over him as his vision grew even blurrier. Anger gave way to another feeling. He wanted to hold on to life just a few moments longer.

He looked around the helicopter once more, trying to catch a few last glimpses of his surroundings. The inside was mostly black and burnished steel, covered with the same light dust that coated everything else. On the far wall was a window, the blue Iraqi sky beyond. He would have liked to have looked outside at the receding ground, but he knew he would never get that chance.

Across from him there was an American soldier clenching his eyes shut and shaking slightly. Qasim could see that for all the fabulous technology that his country had sent with him, the soldier was still filled with terror. *He is only a boy,* Qasim said to himself. *A scared young boy who looks like he just wants to go home.*

It will be over soon, Qasim thought as each breath grew more labored than the last. He took one final look at the soldier and closed his eyes.

ROAD WORK

Personal Narrative

Staff Sergeant Jack Lewis

Iraqi civilians are not only caught in the crossfire when hostilities erupt between American troops and insurgents, they are the victims of military-related accidents as well. In February 2005, forty-one-year-old U.S. Army Reserve Staff Sergeant Jack Lewis witnessed the aftermath of a late-night crash involving a nineteen-ton Stryker armored vehicle (call sign "Rattlesnake Six-Seven") and a small car. While Lewis had seen shocking acts of violence and bloodshed during his deployment with Tactical Psychological Operations Detachment 1290, 1-25 SBCT (Stryker Brigade Combat Team), nothing had struck him as hard emotionally as the suffering caused by this collision.

I never heard the boom-CRUNCH, only imagined it later. There was strong braking, followed by a great deal of shouting. Our Stryker moaned through its monstrous air brakes and then bumped, heaved, and finally ground itself to a halt.

"Six-Seven's in the ditch!"

"Did they roll it?"

"No, they're up. I think they're disabled."

"Where's the colonel? Is the colonel's vehicle okay?"

The colonel's vehicle was okay.

The major said that we would need a combat lifesaver. It wasn't combat. There were no lives left to save. But I dug out the CLS bag, because you never know, do you? And walked across a pitch dark highway.

Somebody was wailing in Arabic, hypnotically, repetitiously.

A single car headlight was burning, a single shaft of light beaming across the road like an accusing finger. When tactical spotlights suddenly illuminated the little car, we found the source of the wailing.

He was an older man with a silver beard, a monumental, red-veined nose, and a big, thick wool overcoat. He was hopping like a dervish, bowing rapidly from the waist and throwing his arms to the sky, then to his knees, over and over again in a kind of elaborate dance of grief.

Down the road a hundred meters or so, Six-Seven's vehicle commander and air guards had dismounted and were standing around in the ditch. Nobody had started smoking yet.

I walked to the car with an Air Force sergeant and moved the older man aside as gently as possible. He was built like a blacksmith, powerful through the neck and shoulders.

It's hard to describe what we found in the car. It had been a young man, only moments earlier that night. A cop or a fireman or a soldier would have simply said, "It's a mess in there." I used to be a fireman. I'm a soldier now. It was as bad a mess as I've seen.

I'm not a medic. We didn't have one with us. It's still my responsibility to preserve life. So I squeezed into the crumpled passenger area, sat on the shattered glass, and tried to take the pulse from his passenger-side arm (nothing) and his neck (nothing). I thought about CPR, but only for a moment. His left arm was mostly torn off, and the left side of his head was flattened.

Up on the highway, GIs walked around, gave and took orders. By the car, the victim's father still capered madly, throwing his arms around, crying out to God or anyone. I asked him, in my own language, to come with me, to calm down, to let me help him. I put my arm around him and guided the old Arab to the road. I sat him on the cold ramp of our Stryker and tried to assess his injuries. It seemed impossible that he could be only as superficially scratched up as he appeared. His hand was injured, bruised or possibly broken, and he had a cut on his left ear. I wrapped a head bandage onto him and tied it gently in back. It looked like a traditional headdress with a missing top. Every few seconds he would get animated, and I would put my hand firmly on his shoulder. He would not hold still long enough for me to splint his arm.

"Why can't he shut up?"

"You ever lose a kid?" This is a pointless question to ask a soldier who's practically a kid himself.

We moved him into the Stryker, assuring him that no, we weren't arresting him. But he didn't care. Whenever he started to calm down, he would look toward the car and break into wails. I sat next to him, put my arm around his shoulder, tried to keep him from jumping around enough to hurt himself or a soldier. I held him tightly with my right arm. By the next morning, my shoulder would be on fire.

Forty minutes later a medic arrived.

"What's his status, sergeant?"

"He has a cut on his left earlobe. I think his hand is broken." (I think his heart is broken.)

"Roger. Okay, I got this."

"Thanks." (Bless you for what you do every day, doc.)

I got out of the way, letting the old guy go for the first time in almost an hour. He started wailing again almost immediately. While the medic worked on him, the colonel's interpreter came over and fired a few questions at the man. It sounded like an interrogation.

They had been on their way back to Sinjar, just a few miles away. The younger man had been taking his father back from shopping. They were minutes from home.

We didn't find any weapons in the car—either piece of it. There was no propaganda, nor were there false IDs. If we had stopped these people at a checkpoint, we would have thanked them and let them go on.

The young man had been a student. Engineering. With honors. Pride of the family. What we like to think of as Iraq's future.

Finally, I had to ask, "What does he keep saying?"

The terp looked at me, disgusted, resigned, or maybe just plain tired. "He says to kill him now."

The colonel came over and asked the medic if he could sedate the man with morphine.

"No, sir. Morphine won't help."

"Well, can't you give him something to calm him down? I mean, this is unacceptable."

I walked away and lit a Gauloise. A sergeant came up next to me, smoking. I didn't say anything. After a few moments in the black quiet, I overheard him say, "It wasn't anyone's fault. It was just an accident."

"I know." Inhale. Cherry glow. Long exhale. "Why we gotta drive in blackout—here—I don't get."

"If Six-Seven had turned their lights on a couple of seconds earlier . . ."

"Yeah. I know." And he went to help carry the young man's remains into the sudden light show of ambulances and police jeeps, surrounded by young Arabic men with steely eyes.

The supersized staff sergeant who mans the .50 cal on our truck walked down the road to kick a little ass and get Six-Seven's recovery progress back on track. Within a few minutes, they had it hooked up. It would be two weeks before that Stryker would roll outside the wire again, this in an environment where trucks totaled by IEDs are welded back together and sent again into harm's way in mere hours.

I went and sat on the back gate of the Stryker. I felt the cold creep into me. The old man sat next to me, perhaps too tired to continue his tirade against cruel Fate, careless Americans, war and its accidents.

I haven't lost a full-grown son, just a little daughter. A baby. And she wasn't torn from me in a terror of rending steel, stamped out by a sudden monster roaring out of the night. She went so quietly that her passing never woke her mother. I like to think she kissed her on the way out, on her way home.

But still, sitting on the steel tail of the monster that killed his son, I think I knew exactly how one Iraqi man felt.

"Just kill me now."

We sat and looked straight into the lights.

MOORE THOUGHTS *and* GIRL INTERRUPTED
Personal Narratives
Captain James R. Sosnicky

For twenty-seven months beginning in May 2003, Captain James R. Sosnicky worked and traveled throughout the Middle East with the U.S. Army Reserve's 354th Civil Affairs Brigade. A graduate of both the U.S. Military Academy at West Point and Oxford University, Sosnicky first deployed to Iraq as an economic development officer to help reopen the banks and find reconstruction work for local contractors. To this end, he founded the Baghdad Business Center, which has assisted thousands of Iraqi small businesses. For the second part of his tour, he was assigned to an Iraq-focused civil affairs task force at the U.S. Embassy in Jordan. While overseas, Sos-

nicky wrote numerous essays and stories relating how the United States, its culture, and its citizens are often perceived in the Middle East. In mid-September 2004, Sosnicky had the opportunity to watch Michael Moore's documentary Fahrenheit 9/11 *when it opened in Amman. "Who knows how much of* Fahrenheit 9/11 *is true," Sosnicky wrote after viewing the movie. "It doesn't really matter, I guess."*

M r. Moore makes no secret of the fact that he doesn't like the current POTUS and that he'd like to see him thrown out of office. Half of our country apparently agrees with him. The other half thinks that Mr. Bush is doing a great job. It's not my place to say.

What is in my lane, and what did bother me very much about the film, was its depiction of the American soldier in Iraq. For the two of you who haven't seen the movie, there is one scene in which the American Fighting Man is portrayed as a callous idiot playing profanity-filled songs on his tank's internal radio as he goes blasting through the streets of Baghdad. There are a few other tableaux that reinforce the notion that every American in uniform is either a heartless ass or an embittered and sullen lost youth.

While it is true that most guys are tired and would love to go home, the idea that the typical soldier is a jerk, disconnected completely from the fate of the Iraqi people, is not true. To suggest otherwise is ignorant and offensive. In my job as a civil affairs officer in Iraq, I have worked and rubbed elbows with soldiers from nearly every division in the Army. I have seen their interactions with the local people. Every American soldier has Iraqi friends. Several, although they aren't supposed to, have Iraqi girlfriends.

In a violent, faraway land, where everything is unfamiliar, 99.9 percent of the American soldiers have behaved professionally, compassionately, and bravely. Of the hundreds of thousands of soldiers who have rotated into and out of Iraq, a handful have embarrassed us. The names of the a-holes of Abu Ghraib taste more bitter on the tongues of our troops in Baghdad than they do on those of the incensed-for-the-camera politicians who will sleep off cocktails tonight in their Georgetown abodes. And while the film showed a few conquering Americans talking about the rush of war, chanting "the roof is on fire," it did not show the faces of countless Americans rebuilding hospitals, delivering textbooks to schools, or providing Iraqis with clean water to drink. Those things, even I'll admit, do not make for interesting cinema.

Something else you didn't get to see is the Middle Eastern reaction to this film. As I said, I saw *Fahrenheit 9/11* in Amman, Jordan, sitting in the theater with an Arab audience. There was a lot in the movie to make an American uncomfortable in that crowd.

But while there was laughter in some parts, there were no shouts of anger from my fellow popcorn munchers. There was something else, however, something that took me by surprise. During the scene in which a grieving American mother named Lila Lipscomb doubles over in agony in front of the White House, crying, "I just want my son back, I just want my son back," every head-scarf-wearing Muslim Arab woman around me was sobbing. The pain of a mother grieving for her dead son cut through national and religious boundaries and touched on an emotion common to us all. That compassion, the compassion of the average Muslim Arab, is hardly ever put on display.

During his more than two years in the Middle East, Sosnicky also wrote profiles of the individuals he encountered personally and professionally. In the following story, he describes a young woman he befriended during his year in Iraq.

Mariam Maslawi worked as a dentist before the war. Since the American invasion, and the subsequent loss of reliable electricity at her clinic, she has not. The Iraqi Ministry of Health still requires her to show up to work six days a week. So she sits in the hot, dark waiting room with her fellow dentists doing nothing from 0800 to noon so as to collect their sixty dollars per month and to keep their names on the order-of-merit list, should things get better in the future.

Mariam's father is a pharmacist. He is an old man. His store was looted following the invasion. It has not reopened since. Her father has been a cripple all of his life. Now he is having prostate problems. Her mother takes care of him. Of her sisters, one escaped the country years ago, one is still in high school, and one is an unemployed recently graduated mechanical engineer. Mariam is the sole breadwinner for the family. She needs more than the sixty dollars per month from the government to take care of them.

Fortunately, Mariam taught herself English while attending the University of Baghdad. She keeps a notebook so that she can jot down unusual new words she learns. Though she is fluent, Mariam is not satisfied with her English. Her language skill allows her to work with the Americans. The first

Americans Mariam ever saw were those soldiers of the 3rd Infantry Division who came rumbling down her street in their Abrams tanks.

Like (presumably) the soldiers in those tanks, Mariam is a Christian. She told me she keeps a portrait of Jesus in her bedroom. When asked why, she replied simply, "I like Jesus." She then made a face and giggled at the absurdity of such a question.

Mariam looks like any young woman in America. She has light skin, brown eyes, and dark hair that she wears in a long ponytail. She likes to laugh and likes to dress as nicely as she can. She saw an advertisement for colored contact lenses in an American magazine and thought those would be nice to have. She likes popular Arab music, but also Shakira and Enrique Iglesias. "He is very nice." Like many Arabs, she believes in conspiracy theories. Without question, the war was fought for oil and Israel.

Every day, after her duties at the dental clinic, Mariam's mother drives her in the family's beat-up sedan to the eastern side of the Fourteenth of July Bridge. There is an American checkpoint there. After standing in line with the other workers, Mariam is searched for weapons by the soldiers. Most know her by face and/or name by now. When they go through her purse and wave their wands over her five-foot-tall petite body, they do so matter-of-factly, sometimes even smiling slightly. This familiarity will cease with the next rotation of soldiers. The new guys will be hard-asses for a while because they will be scared. And they should be. Mariam's cousin was killed at a similar checkpoint back in January, when a car bomb tore through the line of waiting Iraqis.

Mariam walks across the long steel bridge spanning the Tigris. Once on the other side, she is officially in the Green Zone or "International Zone" as they started calling it after the handover of power to the Iraqis. It is another mile walk to her store. All told, it takes an hour to get to her destination.

Though she has never smoked, Mariam sells cigarettes to the soldiers, embassy staff, and government contractors working in the International Zone. Her profits are small. One dollar per carton. She sells a few other trinkets, too, such as lighters and key chains with Saddam Hussein's face on them. Americans love these things. She got permission from the proper authorities in the International Zone to build this store. (The "proper authorities," however, vary depending on whom you ask, and they change every three or four months. There is a constant fear that one day someone will tell her to go away.)

Mariam went into debt to build her store from the ground up, using local contractors who charged her too much for material and labor because they could. In an attempt to save money, Mariam's mother came in one day and scooped up dirt in her hands that she put into a bucket for the builders to use. They looked at her and laughed. "What is this old woman?"

It is a simple structure, made of brick and concrete. There is no front, just three walls and a tin corrugated roof on top. The temperature gets up near 120 degrees Fahrenheit inside during the summertime. There is dust everywhere. The dust and leftover particles of building material cling to Mariam's hair and moist skin. She is careful to wipe the dust off the cartons of cigarettes before she hands them to her customers. She is very attentive to details like that. She is a professional. Much like she used to be as a dentist.

Shoplifting is a constant problem. Both the Americans and the Iraqis have stolen from her. The Americans call her a liar when they get caught, so she doesn't bother confronting them anymore. Once when she complained to the police about an Iraqi thief, his tribe threatened to kill her.

Mariam takes any threat of violence seriously. A couple of months ago, her house was bombed. The blast shattered the front windows and sent glass flying inside. Everyone hit the deck. By a miracle, no one got hurt. After a few minutes of huddling on the floor, Mariam cautiously stepped outside. The houses in front and on either side of her were fine. Only her house was battered and torn. Only her house contained a person working with the Americans.

Her house had been shaken by war before. When she was a young girl, Iranian missiles pounded the street. The Americans have bombed her three times since, in 1991, 1998, and 2003. Mariam is twenty-eight years old. She knows things women her age in the United States do not. A couple of weeks ago I was in Baghdad, visiting with Mariam. There was an explosion in the distance.

"What do you think," I asked, "car bomb or mortar round?"

"Definitely a mortar round," she replied.

Most girls in the U.S. have a tin ear for such things.

Mariam seldom complains. When I offered her a hundred dollars to help her get by, she got insulted and ordered me to put the money back into my pocket. Immediately she could tell she'd been too harsh. "Now, if you had a thousand, it would be a different story," she joked with a wink and a touch of my hand. Mariam never talks about wanting to move to the United States.

Her dream is to move to Jordan or, better yet, Beirut. "Someplace where the weather is nice and you can go outside without being afraid," she says.

The last time I saw Mariam, she had worked a long day. By then it was dark and her mother was waiting for her on the other side of the bridge to pick her up. At home, there would not be much relief. No electricity meant no air-conditioning. No air-conditioning in the murderous heat of Baghdad meant no sleep. Mariam hasn't slept much all summer.

I walked with Mariam in the darkness and told her how much I admired her strength.

"They won't beat me," she said. "They won't win. I won't let them."

"Who won't beat you?" I asked.

"The Iraqis, the Americans, all of them."

We walked on a bit longer. "Sometimes I get tired," she said quietly, tears filling her eyes. "Please forgive me. You are going back to Jordan tomorrow and I don't want you to remember me like this."

Unlike the Nile in Cairo, there are no well-lit, grand hotels or municipal buildings buttressing the Tigris in weary Baghdad. There is nothing to give people the feeling that they are standing in a city that was the sparkling jewel of the civilized world for five hundred years. There are just date palms and a general sorrow at night that manifests itself in the blacked-out houses, shuttered shops, empty streets, and lonely silence.

There were no other pedestrians on the bridge. No other sounds but those of our shoes moving over the span. A cool breeze blew away the stagnant hot air and lifted our spirits temporarily. "That is very nice," Mariam said gently. Directly below us the black Tigris flowed on into the India ink horizon. The moonlight reflected off of the peaks in its flow. At the far end of the bridge was the silhouette of a Bradley. Beyond that, I could not go.

As we got to the armored vehicle, we stopped and looked at each other in the moonlight for a moment. I could feel the eyes of the American soldiers in the Bradley on us. Mariam was sure that there were eyes of suspicious, hostile Iraqis on the other side of the checkpoint fixed on her. We both wanted to give each other a hug, but we could not. "I'll see you," I said awkwardly to the girl I'd known for over a year.

"*Insha'allah*," she replied. "God willing." We stood there for another moment.

Clutching her handbag, Mariam turned and walked away, disappearing finally into the darkness.

CHAPTER THREE

STUCK IN THIS SANDBOX

GRIPES, HUMOR, BOREDOM, AND THE DAILY GRIND

A few days before Christmas, Marines take a time-out from combat operations to play a
friendly game of baseball at Camp Ramadi, Iraq, in late December 2004.

Photo by Corporal Paul Leicht, USMC; used by permission.

Once a month, all soldiers must fill out a white index card like it's a postcard and write a message on the back of it. What happened was a lot of soldiers were failing to contact their parents and let them know that they were okay, and these worrywart parents were contacting the chain of command saying that their little Johnny wasn't writing to them enough. So to fix this problem, once a month we all had to form up and each of us was handed an index card to fill out to a parent or wife to tell them that we were okay, doing well, still alive, and hand it over to the squad leader who double-checks and makes sure that everybody fills one out, and he then personally goes over to S-1 and drops it off in the mailbox.

I was writing to my wife all the time, so the first postcard I filled out was to my parents, in the best kindergarten dyslexic letters I could:

DeAr mOM aNd dAd,
    I Am fInE, I aM 27 YeArS Old AnD ThEy ArE TrEAtiNg mE LiKe I aM 6. wEhAvE to fIlL tHeSe CaRdS OuT NoW bEcAuSe PeeplEZ ArNt wriITiNg tO MoMMY aNd DaDDiE EnUff, sO nOW thEy mAke uS. LoVe.CoLbY

My dad, who spent twenty years in the Army, fully understood that this was how the Army solves problems and laughed when he received the postcard. My mom on the other hand didn't quite get it and my dad had to explain it to her, and when my mom asked why I wrote all preschoolish, he said that I was just being a smart ass again, which she fully understood.

— Twenty-seven-year-old U.S. Army Specialist Colby Buzzell, writing from Mosul, Iraq, in July 2004.

CAMP MUCKAMUNGUS
Journal
Staff Sergeant Parker Gyokeres

"I'm going to kill my travel agent," thirty-year-old Staff Sergeant Parker Gyokeres (pronounced, appropriately enough, "jokers") wrote facetiously in one of his journal entries chronicling a five-month deployment to Tallil, Iraq. Officially, Gyokeres was an aircraft armament systems technician in the U.S. Air Force's 332nd Fighter Wing, but during Operation Iraqi Freedom he was tasked to serve with a force protection, or FP, unit that screened and escorted local civilians and foreign nationals working at the Tallil Air Base in the southern part of the country. (The primary responsibility of the FP airmen was to prevent insurgents from infiltrating the base by posing as contractors or day workers.) Gyokeres emphasized in his journals, which he also e-mailed to friends and family in the States, that his service was nothing compared to what other troops had to endure in more dangerous parts of the country. But he still relished pointing out the minor privations and absurdities of day-to-day life in the desert.

I know a number of you have been curious about what it's like over here, so we are going to take a small mental voyage. First off, we are going to prepare our living area. Go to your vacuum, open the canister, and pour it all over you, your bed, clothing, and your personal effects. Now roll in it until it's in your eyes, nose, ears, hair, and . . . well, you get the picture. You know it's just perfect when you slap your chest and cough from the dust cloud you kicked up. And, no, there is no escape, trust me. You just get used to it.

Okay, pitch a tent in your driveway, and mark off an area inside it along one wall about six feet by eight feet (including your bed). Now, pack everything you need to live for four months—without Wal-Mart—and move in. Tear down the three walls of your tent seen from the street and you have about as much privacy as I have. If you really want to make this accurate, bring in a kennel full of pugs; the smell, snoring, and social graces will be just like living with my nine tentmates. Also, you must never speak above a whisper because at all times at least four of your tentmates will be sleeping. That's where the flashlight comes in handy; you are going to use it to navigate a pitch dark tent, twenty-four hours a day.

Time for hygiene. Walk to the nearest bathroom. In my case, it's a thousand-foot trudge over loose gravel. Ever stagger to the john at 0400? Try it in a frozen rock garden. Given the urges that woke you at this hour, taking the time to put on your thermals and jacket might not be foremost in your mind. But halfway there, it's too late. So dress warmly. It gets really freakin' cold here at night.

I don't even feel like talking about the latrine experience. All I have to say is that, after the first time, I went back to the tent and felt like either crying or lighting myself on fire to remove the filth.

Time for the reason we are here in the first place. Work.

I am somewhat limited in my ability to say how, when, and why we do what we do, so I'll be vague at times. Overall the work is extremely interesting and different for an aircraft maintainer like myself. Essentially, my unit escorts third-country nationals (TCNs) and local nationals (LNs) who work on base. We handle their passes, and we also watch over areas in which they work and, in some cases, live. I currently work in the control center for those escorts and workers. I handle radio traffic and communication between the people coming in, patrols and posts controlling or containing escortees, and the police who search their vehicles. I am nearly always speaking through my Iraqi translator with Iraqis, Koreans, Italians, Dutch, and countless other nationalities while tending to multiple other duties.

In an average exchange I'll be speaking with an Arabic translator who is speaking pidgin Turkish who is trying to tell me he needs to get in touch with a person whose name he doesn't know, but whom I still need to contact, while some Pakistanis, Bangladeshis, and Filipinos are trying to steal back the knives I confiscated from them, as the Koreans bring fifteen kids into their hospital for medical attention. Meanwhile, the guy in the corner is making threats against my control team because he is sick of waiting for somebody on the base and the screaming kid just stopped screaming, because he puked on my weapons/contraband searcher who now wants to shoot the Korean escort for letting that sick kid loose. This goes on for twelve hours. Reminds me of a really stressed-out, low-budget version of ER—with automatic weapons—in Arabic.

Although things can get chaotic, there are rules that need to be followed. Many of them are ones we've made up on our own.

Rule #1: Not speaking English is no excuse for being stupid. I think I'm going to get a card that says that in Arabic and flash it to every person who attempts access to our facility. Don't even try "I don't understand" on me, all I asked you to do was sit down and stay there while I work on your issue. I then had to get the interpreter to tell you. Twice. I then had to post one of the troopers on you to babysit. If I have to tell you again, I'm going to kick your butt out and you might be barred entry permanently. And stop asking how long it will be. I told you twice we are waiting on your rep and he will be here when *he* feels like it. Ask me again and I'm going to start yelling.

Rule #2: Making me yell will get you in trouble. If you don't stop wandering slowly (like I didn't see you get out of our paddock) towards your truck, I'm going to yell. If you don't get off the cell phone in my yard, now, I'm going to yell. (No weapons, communication devices, cameras at all on base for TCNs or LNs, and we mean it.) If you don't tell me about the sharpened tire iron I just found under your floorboard (and don't worry, my guys will find it, I assure you), I won't yell when I take it, but I will yell loudly when you have the stones to ask for it back. You have got to be shitting me. What do you mean to tell me that your sharpened eighteen-inch piece of bent angle iron is a family heirloom? You go. Now.

Rule #3: If you don't stop after I tell you once, yell at you twice, and physically attempt to stop you from being terminally stupid or, more to the point, doing something that could be potentially threatening, I'll go the last step, and it always works, regardless of language, nationality, or IQ. We call it "the exclamation point" or "Shacking One." As in: "That damn idiot wouldn't stop, and when he started reaching into his bag again, after I had told him so many times not to, I had to Shack One on him."

Shacking One means you grab your rifle's charging handle and as quickly as possible (to make as much noise as possible) yank back till the handle stops and your fingers break free. As soon as your fingers clear the handle, the spring tension, from the pull, slams the bolt forward and chambers your first round. It sounds like a very quick sliding/slapping *SHLACK!* It's the loudest metallic noise in the world when it happens. And for at least three seconds, the only sound you hear, as the crowd unpuckers, is of your own heart trying to break out of its rib cage, one pounding thump at a time. Once you've heard both the noise, and its effect, you'll never forget it. I've never had to do it myself (except in training), and, again, it's really for cases when you believe there is a genuine security issue.

Shacking One is the international symbol for "Conversation over." Shacking One tells the individual that this is not a game and we are not going to allow it to continue. From that point, amazingly and without exception, people do what they are told, immediately. They suddenly understand everything we have been trying to tell them. Whaddaya know?

Please don't get the impression that all we do all day is run around and act like storm troopers. We all know our guns should never come off our shoulders, and if they do, that's the very second we need to be calling in the professionals to assist us. The guns are for our self-defense as an absolute last resort. Nothing more. Thankfully, events like these aren't common. Most days pass by smoothly with only funny stories to break up the monotony.

A week ago, for instance, Geraldo Rivera came to Tallil to do a report for Fox. As he was going into his shtick, just as the camera zoomed in on his face, a troop in the crowd, positioned just over Geraldo's shoulder and visible only in the midsection, "adjusted himself," on live, national television. In prime time. This is the same troop who got kidney stones, was shipped to Baghdad to have a CAT scan, and whose convoy was attacked while he was there. When he came back, the Army doctor informed him that he had two more stones, which he then painfully passed over the next two weeks. If there's a lightning storm, I'm running away from this kid, 'cause he's cursed.

Or blessed, as he's still here, still alive, and didn't lose a stripe after the *Pentagon* called the base commander the next day and wanted to know why reporters in the morning national press briefing were asking about an airman at Tallil AB being obscene, live, on prime-time Fox News. The kid had to scratch, for God's sake. He had no idea that the camera was zooming in at that exact moment. And, yes, he's one of my crew, God bless him.

I was just told that today he received a letter of reprimand for (and I quote directly) "an immature, childish, and obscene gesture that intentionally defamed the USAF." Was it bad timing? Yes. Was it bad manners? Probably. But was it, as the reprimand further stated, "a deliberate action, known as a 'package check?' " Ahh . . . no.

I'm still stuck on the very official usage of the words "package check," but I'm pretty sure that the troop's actions weren't deliberate. He's not an anarchist, attempting to bring disorder and chaos. He's an airman who worked hard all day, got pulled off of the dinner bus to be on TV, and was put directly behind a blowhard who likes a tight close-up. He was then left there, standing (and sweating) in the desert, for thirty minutes. Sooner or later you just gotta adjust, folks.

This place truly never ceases to trip me out. Last week I met a man who came through here to visit his wife who was in hospital. He spoke okay English and, it turns out, he was an American citizen from Dearborn, Michigan. His home was less than ten miles from where I lived before joining up. His driver's license was issued at the same office where I had gotten mine. What a head trip. I'm standing there in all my body armor, with a helmet and an assault rifle, looming at least a foot and a half taller and a hundred pounds heavier than he, talking about restaurants in Detroit like an old friend. He told me that eight of his friends from Dearborn have died in the service of the new Iraqi Army in the last few months. I had no idea that so many of those guys were U.S. citizens. He will be back to serve as an interpreter in a few months. He brought his kids in to meet me and they looked like American kids in their Spiderman jackets and Nikes. These kids go to American schools, they watch *SpongeBob,* and now they are swatting flies and getting the metal detector treatment for hidden weapons. I wonder often what they think about all of this.

Finally, and in the words of one of our tentmates: "Just when you think you have this place all figured out, it rains!" We assumed that, since this is the desert, it wouldn't rain forever, or because it's all sand it would just drain away. Well campers, it didn't stop, and this desert isn't sand. The dust and silt of which we are becoming such connoisseurs, is just that, silt. It is clay sediment from the Euphrates River that now flows a mile from us and, apparently, once flowed where we stand today. Add to that, all occupied ground was scraped to remove the bomblets and mines and this made the earth dense, fine, and impermeable to seepage. In short, our dry lake just became a very wet, muddy one.

The parking lots at each end of tent city have become chocolate reservoirs as a result of the huge hump in the center where the tents are. When Civil Engineering came out to appraise the situation, their expert estimate, based on size and depth, was that the biggest parking lot held over 110,000 gallons of water. There is nowhere for this water to go. The ground isn't absorbing it, and the six-foot walls of the compound contain its edges. The funny part of this is that some of the dirt wasn't as well compacted, and vehicle traffic has created huge holes that we like to call "sweet spots." Invisible from above, the only clue you have that you have hit one of these bathtub-size holes is when your vehicle frame slams to a stop, leaving you stranded inside a football field of water.

Sitting in the guard shack at the edge of the parking lot, we wish we had popcorn because the show is so good. We rate the hits and critique them. I have two favorites. The first was the driver of "Turdzilla," which is what we call the huge vacuum truck that sucks the poop out of porta-potties and field latrines. He nearly flipped his forty-foot rig in a hole the size of a Ford Ranger because he reasoned high speed was the way to beat the sweet spots. It wasn't.

The other guy figured, if you can't beat 'em, join 'em. This individual was driving an open-topped Army Hummer with no doors. His beast could ford thirty-six inches of water—if done sensibly. His was not, shall we say, a text-book demonstration of a sensible technique. He revved his huge diesel, dropped it into gear, and floored it. What happened next I will never forget. He hit the edge of the pool moving just a bit faster than the posted speed limit and was doing great, throwing huge fountains of thick, brown mud in gigan-tic arcs away from the truck. Then he hit the big one, the one we simply call "the hole." It's in the area of the highest traffic, created when the mud lake wasn't quite so full. It's the hole that all the other holes want to become. We have no idea how big it is, really, but I saw a mini pickup float across it two days ago. Anyway, he hit this hole and we just lost him. The front dipped down and immediately a huge brown wall shot straight up in front of his truck. He must have panicked a bit and taken his foot off the gas when his world went brown and wet. Bad idea.

Did I mention that this truck had an open roof? Yeah, the wall of mud fell on this brave chap and we lost him again. By this time his Hummer was start-ing to sink, and I found it amusing that it stopped one inch below the level of the doorsills. After hitting the wall, the wave of mud was on its way back, and in the time it took him to get the mud off his goggles, the wave crested over his feet and the entire truck was filled with slop. All I could see of him that wasn't brown was a set of white, grinning teeth. He eventually made it out of the pond, pulled up to us, and, over the sound of draining mud and a hissing engine, said: "God I love this job."

So do I, man, so do I.

VTC *and* HAPPY AUSTRALIA DAY
E-mails
Captain Steven A. Givler

Although danger is an ever-present reality to those serving in Iraq and Afghanistan, troops spend a significant portion of time performing mind-numbing bureaucratic tasks not unlike those found in a civilian corporation (e.g., ordering equipment and supplies, dealing with personnel issues, filling out paperwork). One of the most dreaded duties for those in uniform, regardless of where they're stationed, is attending seemingly endless meetings and briefings. Steven A. Givler, a forty-year-old U.S. Air Force captain who was on his second deployment to the Middle East and stationed at the Al Udeid Air Base in Qatar for five months, frequently wrote to his family back in Georgia about his experiences with the 116th Air Control Wing. Some days were clearly less dramatic than others. ("VTC," alluded to in the January 18, 2005, e-mail below, is the abbreviation for video teleconferencing. "RAF" refers to Great Britain's Royal Air Force.)

If you really want to break a man's spirit, subject him to several hours of VTC. The endless prattle of disembodied heads asking inane questions from thousands of miles away, the mind-numbing briefings of the office warriors who tell us the same thing time after time (the only difference being the exchanging of old cliches for newer ones)—to be spared this horrifying prospect, the captive terrorist would tell you everything he knows.

For us though, there is no escape, so we fashion what devices we can to get us through the misery. One favored pass-time is graphing the number of ums and uhs of one of the regular speakers. She is generally very consistent, but last week she made an exceptionally good showing, uttering 162 in just over five minutes. We are in tremendous suspense, waiting to see whether she will eclipse that record.

We also keep a list of odd sayings generated by another one of the regulars. Sometimes, if he comes up with a particularly good one, we make a poster of it and hang it where we work. That explains the sign over our door, which reads, "Apply here for granular answers to thorny issues."

Of course all this happens only during parts of the conference that don't pertain to us, and only when our microphone is turned off. Our spokesman, a very proper RAF squadron leader, always gives us the sign before his speaking part comes up, and then of course, we sit very straight for the camera, and act as if it would never cross our minds to do otherwise.

Today though, it was much harder than usual to pull that off. Just before our turn came around, we heard from a group not normally represented in our meetings. When they appeared on our screen it was obvious they hadn't looked at their own image before they transmitted. They were all slouched low in their seats, and, because of the angle of the camera, nothing showed above the table in front of them but their heads. "Holy cow!" one of us exclaimed, "They're leprechauns!" This brought the house down, and it was all the squadron leader could do to bring us under control before his time to speak.

I hope before I leave here to convince the squadron leader and the two officers who flank him to spend my final VTC beneath their table, using sock puppets to present their briefings. . . . Steven

Since the beginning of Operation Iraqi Freedom, thousands of Australian troops have served with U.S. and Coalition forces in the Middle East. On January 26, Givler e-mailed the following story about a raucous evening with a small group of Aussie soldiers.

In one stroke on 26 January, 1788, Captain Arthur Phillips claimed Australia as a British colony, and established a thriving industry (a penal colony) on its shores. Not bad for a day's work.

So impressive, in fact, that Australians have been celebrating the day ever since. Unaware of this, I was making my appointed rounds at work tonight, when I was collared by a couple Aussie colleagues (they refer to me as a "mate") and dragged to a party in a tent adjacent to where I work. Along the way, in order to compensate for the shocking gaps in my knowledge of History, I was apprised of the significance of this important date, said apprisings arriving on high-volume beer-scented blasts delivered directly into my ear, the loudness the result not so much of inebriation, as of a myth that has arisen about my being slightly deaf.

My hearing is perfectly fine, but I seem to have great difficulty with the Australian language. Some claim it's similar enough to our language that a native English speaker should be able to understand it, but this, of course, is completely silly. They are separate and distinct languages, and while they may share some curse words, they have little else in common. I know this to be true, but I seem to be in the minority. Because of this, I frequently find myself asking Australians to repeat themselves. As a result, my "mates" have formed the opinion that I am somewhat hard of hearing.

Far from causing them to shun me, this mythical handicap of mine seems to endear me to these kindhearted people, and they go out of their way to talk to me, asking, "How're ya goin' mate?" and—well I don't know what else they say, because I can't understand a word of it. I nod and smile and make what I hope are appropriate remarks from time to time, and I seem to be doing pretty well, because I'm often rewarded with a bone-crushing slap on the back, broad smiles and a stream of throaty vowels that sound as if I'm listening from under water.

Times like these make me miss (even more than usual) my wife. They remind me of my first year or so in South Carolina, where her ability to translate Gullah, or whatever people were speaking to me, saved me from several beatings, and impressed on me the certainty that my life would never again be complete without her in it.

She is not here though, so I get by as well as I can, which means I have become a master of reading body language, facial expression, and contextual elements of conversation too subtle even to be named. These clues provide me insights into the inscrutable utterings of my friends here, and allow me to "participate" in discussions that are completely beyond my understanding. An aside: How is it I can appreciate these modes of nonverbal communication when I cannot abide a mime?

My skills of interpretation failed me tonight in the tent though, when my hosts were playing an enthusiastic game of Australian trivia. Not only did I not know any answers, I could not ascertain the meaning of a single question. At one point in the heated competition, it was the turn of my "mates" to answer a question. Whether in the spirit of inclusiveness, or because they themselves were unsure of the answer, I'll never know, all I can say for certain is that, after the question was posed, they all turned to me, and beerily shouted things like, "Gowedan givatraymate!"

Well, there I was. A close-packed throng of inebriated amateur rugby players blocked the path to the door ahead of me, while all the men stood behind me. No way out. A quick survey of all my body language skills told me only that every ear in the bar was inclined in my direction, and that the fate of my team rested on my shoulders. A hush fell over the mob. Of such situations, international incidents are made. I raised my beer and shouted, "To Australia!" and, in the pandemonium that ensued, bought a brief respite, but it was over all too soon. Once again, the place fell silent, and I felt myself being crushed under the burden of the prestige of the United States. I ran through my small vocabulary of authentic Australian words and flung one out in desperation. "Dingo," I gasped. My team erupted in cheers, joined after a slight delay by our rivals, who were unhappy to lose a point, but glad to know that an American was so well informed about their country.

Later, when things died down, I happened to see the list of questions lying on the bar. Apparently the one they had put to me was, "What was the first non-native species introduced to Australia?"

Steven

Givler returned home in February 2005 and enrolled in the Naval Post-graduate School in Monterey, California, to earn a master's degree in Middle Eastern studies.

FORCE PROVIDER

Personal Narrative

Lieutenant Colonel Stephen McAllister

Among the numerous topics that inspire grumbling, controversy, and exasperation among troops, few are as beloved as the "portable, single-occupancy personal waste disposal comfort station," otherwise known as the port-o-john. Most complaints are about the seats (wet year-round, ice-cold in the winter); the smell, especially during broiling summers ("lethal," "not human," and "almost hallucinogenic" being just a few descriptions); the toilet paper ("AWOL"); and the fact that it sometimes requires a ten-minute hike, frequently in the dark, to get to one. U.S. Air Force Lieutenant Colonel Stephen McAllister, who had been stationed at the headquarters of the Combined Joint Task Force (CJTF-180) in Bagram, Afghanistan, wrote the following story in May 2003 about the barely civilized condition of their bathrooms—and the higher command's mind-boggling attempt to improve them.

Thanks to our friends in the Army we had flushing toilets, although they're actually called Force Providers, and they look essentially like a box trailer you might see on a flatbed railcar for hauling cargo. Inside the male Force Provider, along the back half of the right wall, there is a long, open urinal that vaguely resembles a feeding trough for cattle. The other half of the same wall has sinks and mirrors. The left wall is lined solely with toilets, which are elevated one foot from floor level on platforms that sit above the Force Provider's holding tanks. But there's a problem. Several, in fact.

First, these aren't typical flushing commodes. Each toilet has two pedals, one a little bigger than the other. The smaller pedal is pressed before you sit down, and it fills the basin with about four inches of water. Then after the toilet is used, you step on the larger pedal, which opens the flapper valve at the bottom and flushes out the waste. This also dispenses more water into the basin, theoretically washing it clean. The problem is that many of the flapper valves have lost their seal, which means that the four inches of water drains away prior to use. And the water released when you press the large pedal couldn't wash away dust let alone . . . well, you know.

Second, the majority of people here aren't experiencing regular movements due in part to the high-protein food we routinely eat. The unfortunate consequence of this incontinence is the explosive nature of the illness. This leaves a mess that a trickle of water simply can't handle.

Third, the headquarters is made up primarily of men—I'd say fifty-to-one. To no one's surprise, there are no problems with the women's Force Provider. But then the odds are in their favor.

So you're probably able to guess that the problem we have is one of cleanliness. And the Army leadership has had enough. The headquarters director, a brigadier general, got involved and issued the following decree:

MEMORANDUM FOR ALL CJTF-180 JOC PERSONNEL
SUBJECT: MALE FORCE PROVIDER GUARD ROSTER AND INSTRUCTIONS

1. Guard will immediately start on the Male Force Provider until further guidance is provided by the Director. This is a result of individual(s) trashing the latrine and other unethical acts. Each shift will be two hours long and both officers and enlisted are required to pull the duty.
2. Instructions. As an individual goes into the force provider, the guard

will take note who goes in and will be required to inspect the force provider prior to that individual leaving the facility. This is to ensure that the force provider is not trashed or vandalized during use. The purpose of the force providers was to improve the quality of life for CJTF-180 personnel.

We couldn't believe it.

The Army then decreed that each office in the headquarters would take their turn guarding the Force Provider. One of the guys in my work area suggested that we didn't have to because we were Air Force and not Army. "That'll endear us to everyone here," I said sarcastically.

A major said, "I'll go out there when I see the sergeant major out there." The Army sergeant that delivered the news replied that no rank was exempt. More rumbling and "Jesus Christ, I don't believe this" and "For crying out loud" and "There's typical Army leadership for you."

I thought to myself, *What will I tell my grandchildren when they want to know what I did during the war in Afghanistan? "I was in the thick of it, pulling CG duty." "What's CG duty, Grandpa?" "Crapper Guard."*

Our office drew a half-hour block just prior to sunset. I'd convinced myself that I would be the first to go pull our guard shift and had said as much but secretly hoped that someone, somewhere would realize the folly of this policy and cancel the shifts. But as we approached the hour, still no cancellation, and I resigned myself to the inevitable.

Only twenty-five minutes before I was due to take my post, Colonel Bledsoe, who goes by the call sign "Zipper," walked in and announced that he would take our shift. Zipper is a vice wing commander back in the States, and he fits the mold perfectly. He's a southern boy with a laid-back attitude, a common-sense guy who lets nothing fluster him. He's well liked and he's able to see the humor in virtually any situation. The CG duty was no exception.

Zipper decided that he would approach this duty with the decorum it deserved. He found a broom and a roll of toilet paper, and he gathered his book, water, and coat and asked Lovin, a popular, well-respected Army sergeant, to escort him to his duties and perform the guard mount. Zipper slid the roll of toilet paper down the handle of the broom, flipped the broom so the bristles were up and the roll of toilet paper rested on his hand, and marched out of our tent. Lovin marched in step behind, followed by a half-dozen giggling onlookers.

The small parade passed the headquarters' guards and moved out the door and on toward the Force Provider. Bewildered soldiers quickly moved out of the way of the duo and then, after a moment, decided to join the crowd. Zipper marched directly in front of the young sergeant currently standing guard, who instinctively came to attention but was obviously confused about what was happening. At that same instant someone started to come out of the Force Provider, looked wide-eyed at the procession, and promptly closed the door and retreated back inside.

"Sergeant Lovin, proceed with the mounting of the Guard."

"Yes sir."

Lovin stepped out from behind Zipper, who was now standing at attention with his broom and mirroring the outgoing crapper guard with his M-16, and then proceeded to flank both guards.

"Prepare for inspection!" Lovin commanded. The outgoing guard, still not sure what the hell was going on, looked helplessly at Lovin.

"Come on, prepare for inspection."

The guard came to attention again, unshouldered his M-16, and presented it for inspection. Lovin stepped in front of the guard, carefully looked over the rifle, proceeded to inspect the soldier's uniform, and reminded the soldier that, in the future when pulling crapper guard duty, he expected to see crisper creases on the sleeves and more attention to effective ironing. The crowd was laughing hysterically. Lovin then executed an about-face, as well as can be expected on loose rocks, and faced Zipper. Immediately, the broom and toilet paper came off the shoulder and Zipper stared straight ahead, over Lovin's hat, and into the eyes of Sergeant Woodin, the second guard.

"Colonel Bledsoe, your toilet paper's unraveling and the broom's in serious need of grooming," Lovin said with authority. "Can you explain this?"

"Sir, no excuse sir. It won't happen again sir."

"See that it doesn't." Approval from the crowd.

Lovin made a right-face, took two steps, performed an about-face, and yelled, "Attention to orders." Both guards brought their appointed weapons to shoulder and returned their left arm to their side.

"At twelve hundred hours Zulu, Sergeant Woodin is hereby relieved of his post. Let all who hear these orders beware. Dismissed."

And with that, Zipper and Woodin entered the Force Provider to inspect each toilet for cleanliness and serviceability. The soldier who had tried to get out during the changing of the guard made his escape. The crowd started to disperse and I joined them. Zipper was left to his guard duties.

Word got back to us that when someone approached the Force Provider, Zipper would snap to attention, broom and toilet paper at the ready, and bark, "Halt. Who goes there? State your business. Number one or number two?"

One young soldier turned around and went the other way, and Zipper had to chase him down to explain he was just kidding. The half hour came and went, and it was legendary. Pictures showed up on the Internet. People talked about it at the chow hall. Zipper had become a hero.

By the time I was getting into bed, no more than five hours later, word had spread that Crapper Guard duty had officially been ended.

LIFE ON THE USS *RAINIER*
Journal
Lieutenant Todd Vorenkamp

Troops on the ground are not the only ones, of course, who write about humorous incidents while serving abroad. During his seven months flying as a Sea Knight cargo helicopter aircraft commander, thirty-year-old Lieutenant Todd Vorenkamp kept a weekly journal that detailed the less serious moments he and his crewmates experienced aboard the USS Rainier, a supply, ammunition, and fuel ship. (The Rainier was part of the USS Constellation Battle Group stationed in the northern Arabian Gulf from November 2003 until June 2004.) Halfway through his deployment, Vorenkamp wrote the following entry. ("Air Det" is shorthand for the two-helicopter air detachment, Sideflare 64 and Sideflare 65, and "VERTREP" is short for vertical replenishment, which refers to the transfer of cargo using helicopters.)

There is a young sailor in the same berthing compartment as our Air Det sailors who allegedly walks around 24/7 with a 48-ounce coffee mug and he—allegedly—drinks two mugs a day while he works. Apparently he is never found without this coffee mug and it has become part of his identity.

This immediately becomes a joke to the Air Det guys, and they decide it will be great fun to steal this all-important coffee mug. So, they take it.

I hear the kid is beside himself—forced to drink out of coffee mugs that are only 25 percent of the capacity of his precious mug.

The guys then come up with a plan to torture the poor sailor by photographing his coffee mug all over the ship and printing the photos on a black-and-white laserjet printer. Within hours the mug has become our newest crew member.

There are photos of the mug waiting outside the command master chief's office, waiting for mail at the post office, sitting in the mouth of a dryer in the laundry room, on the shelf in the ship's armory with a shotgun and M-14 pointed at it, hanging out at the hazardous materials locker, running on the treadmill in the gym, welding in the hull technician's shop, sending messages from the signal bridge, answering nature's call on the toilet, getting a checkup in the dental chair, being defibrillated in medical, getting a trim at the barber shop, calling loved ones at the sailor phone, hanging from the rescue hoist of Sideflare 65, and finally resting on a shelf in the ship's store between the Q-tips and Tampax.

On Friday I got to fly a vertrep. We had to move about 300 pallets of ammunition from USNS *Shasta*—a Military Sealift Command ship. It was a pretty fun vertrep—very tight pattern when the ships were right next to each other—so it was pretty busy.

We were moving racks of three 1000-pound bombs. They are banded together—three abreast—in special racks. Well, we came over *Shasta* to pick up our 3000 lbs of bombs on one trip—and we attached the load and then lifted vertically for the trip over to *Rainier*, 180 feet away. Suddenly I hear from the *Shasta* tower, "Um, 65 . . . um, well, never mind."

I am perplexed for the half a second pause until my crewman in the back says, "HOLY SHIT, SIR! WE JUST DROPPED A BOMB ON *SHASTA*!"

Whoops.

Apparently the bombs were banded incorrectly and as we nosed over to go forward the middle bomb in the rack slid right out of its holder and fell about twenty feet to the deck of the *Shasta*. According to eyewitnesses it bounced four times before coming to rest on the flight deck of *Shasta*.

I talked to the *Rainier*'s gunner after the vertrep—he said there is no chance of the bomb exploding without the fuse unless it breaks apart when it hits the deck. Lucky for us, it stayed in one piece and we were able to finish the vertrep.

The captain of the *Rainier* likes to tell folks that I dropped the first bomb of the war.

On April 22, 2003, Vorenkamp had to endure the initiation "ceremony" commonly inflicted on all wogs (which is short for pollywogs or, literally, tadpoles, but in a maritime tradition refers to any sailor who has not crossed the equator). Vorenkamp argued that, as a former merchant mariner, he had crossed the equator multiple times, just not on a U.S. warship, and he should therefore be spared the customary hazing rituals. His superiors begged to differ.

Tuesday is Wog Day! The USS *Rainier* will be crossing the equator and King Neptune will be turning all of the slimy wogs into salty shellbacks. Somewhere during the cruise it was determined that I was a slimy pollywog even though I had been across the equator SIX times previous to this ship and even have a shellback card in my wallet. I am told that it does not count because I never went through the ceremony and merchant ships are not real ships.

I argue that merchant ships are real ships with real sailors and that I am a true shellback. After all, spending three months as slave labor on the M/V *Sea Fox* is much more difficult than a naval equator-crossing ceremony.

My resistance does not pay off, and I find myself up at 5 a.m. on Wog Day to undergo the torture.

I write the following on my T-shirt: I HAVE BEEN ACROSS THE EQUATOR OF THE PLANET EARTH 6 TIMES ON BOARD SHIPS. IF YOU HAVE CROSSED THE EQUATOR LESS THAN 6 TIMES PLEASE FIND SOMEONE WHO IS LESS SALTY THAN YOURSELF.

On the back: FROM "NAVAL TRADITIONS AND CEREMONIES": "THE CROSSING THE LINE CEREMONIES OF THE MODERN NAVY ARE MOST PICTURESQUE. IN MERCHANT SHIPS THE CEREMONY IS STILL REASONABLY SEVERE AND PHYSICAL DISCOMFORTS INFLICTED." ONCE AGAIN . . . THIS IS MY 7TH LINE CROSSING. THANK YOU FOR YOUR CONSIDERATION AND COMPASSION.

Wog Day wasn't too bad. It started in the wardroom where I was fed a saltine cracker while on my hands and knees. Yum. I love Vegemite on my saltines! I almost vomited.

I thought I would prove how tough us merchant mariners are by being one of the only fools on the ship not to make kneepads for the ceremony. After crawling over about 200 feet of nonskid I was completely regretting that decision. 1300 feet later—with bloody knees—I would be a "shellback."

The ceremony consisted of spending countless minutes with my head next to the bulwarks yelling for Flipper. Fun. Also, we were drenched in salt water the whole time. Fun. We crawled all over the place, sang "Row, Row, Row Your Boat" a hundred times, yelled for Flipper a bit more, got covered in sea-dye-stained water, swam in tubs of root beer, crawled over barrels and cargo nets, crawled through a plastic chute filled with lots of breakfast meals and some wog's vomit, was ordered to climb a steel pole covered with Crisco, and had to suck a cherry out of a portly Chief's buttered belly button. Fun.

Well, I did it, bloody knees and all, but I know that in my heart I became a shellback on 15 January 1994. I don't feel like I needed to do it—and my knees constantly remind me that I shouldn't have done it!

Two journal entries later, Vorenkamp related how some efforts by the sailors to entertain themselves were not appreciated by the senior command.

One thing that the morale folks on board do for fun before ports is Bingo Night. Saturday night was Bingo Night. I had not been a big bingo fan—I played for the first time the other week. After suffering through four hours of bingo before Perth I decided to volunteer to host the next Bingo Night. On Saturday I enlisted the help of Doc Quack and we were all set to do tag-team bingo!

Doc and I went down to the SITE (Ship Information, Training, and En- tertainment) TV studio fifteen minutes before show time. We chose the bingo patterns and planned our costumes. We would do a round in uniform. Round 2 would be in baseball jerseys—me in a Boston jersey and Doc in An- gels kit. Round 3 would be Hawaiian shirts and round 4 would be in hockey jerseys.

Round 5—the blackout round—was the shocker. As far as we know there has not been Naked Bingo since the Tailhook scandal of 1991. We thought it would be fun. (And, for the record, we weren't actually completely naked.) So, after round 4 the music videos start, we verify the winner from that round, and then the camera comes on with Doc and me shirtless on *Rainier* TV ready to do the blackout round! We were having a good laugh—and I hear that the people around the ship were laughing too. The whole night was rife with comedy—some good, some bad—all improv.

Meanwhile, approximately five minutes into the Naked Blackout Round the captain of the *Rainier* was channel-surfing the five channels on SITE TV in his stateroom when he came across a (seemingly) naked doctor and helicopter pilot drawing bingo balls. Apparently he was not amused and he called the executive officer, woke him up, and ordered him to call down to SITE TV to put an end to the shameless display.

The phone rang in SITE TV and we cut to "commercial" and returned with the Hawaiian shirts back on. Oh well.

Vorenkamp, who comes from a long line of servicemen (his father was in the U.S. Marine Corps during the war in Vietnam and his grandfather and great-grandfather served in the U.S. Navy), was later promoted to lieutenant commander and plans to stay in the military until retirement. Years after his experience on the Rainier, *Vorenkamp would write that his knees remain scarred from Wog Day and that the* Shasta *still has a sizable dent on it due to the thousand-pound bomb he dropped. Both were noted more with pride than embarrassment.*

IN THE HANGAR
Lyrics
Sergeant Sandi Austin

In a tradition dating back to the American Revolution, troops often sit around their campsites and sing of home, lost loves, and the hardships of soldiering. Although fiddles and fifes have been replaced by more sophisticated instruments and the words are undoubtedly edgier than those of the 1780s ("Lovely Nancy" and "The Willow Tree" being just two particular favorites of the times), music remains an integral part of military life in Iraq and Afghanistan. Rap, hip-hop, rock, heavy metal, punk, blues, jazz, and country are among the most popular, and many troops compose their own lyrics and melodies as well. In late December 2003, a twenty-six-year-old U.S. Army Reserve sergeant named Sandra "Sandi" Austin wrote and per-

formed the following song for her fellow soldiers in the 3-2 Stryker Brigade.
At the time, they were living on an old air base just outside of Samarra, Iraq.

Crazy thoughts running through my head
Making me think that silence is dead
In a world where your voice is seldom heard
Open your mouth but can't utter a word

Here we are searching for justification
In a nation searching for its salvation
Who's gonna take away my frustration?

Where is the music? Where is the praise?
Stuck in this sandbox for too many days

Back to the silence, where has it gone?
Surrounded by people who won't get along
Minds are all clashing, metal as well
We've all got our own views but none of us can tell

Here we are searching for justification
In a nation searching for its salvation
Who's gonna take away my frustration

Where is the music? Where is the praise?
Stuck in this sandbox for too many days

Dreams are our destiny in this waking life
No need for loneliness, worry, or strife

Where is the music? Where is the praise?
Stuck in this sandbox for too many days.

Austin wrote the song after having spent only six weeks in Iraq. She had al-
most ten more months to go.

COMBAT MUSICIAN, LOST IN TRANSLATION, *and* THE CIRCLE

Personal Narratives

Sergeant Sharon D. Allen

Bored with college and tired of working construction to pay the bills, Sharon D. Allen enlisted, at the age of twenty-two, in the U.S. Army. Along with wanting a challenge in life, she felt a sense of obligation. "It was my turn," she would later say of the decision; Allen's younger brother Luke was also in the military, and during World War II their grandfather had fought in Europe, where he had been wounded in battle and captured by the Germans. Allen joined the Ohio Army National Guard and became a fueler, or, more officially, a petroleum supply specialist, driving nineteen-ton trucks filled with diesel. Before she was mobilized to the Middle East, she concluded that being in a large vehicle with the word FLAMMABLE *written on the side "in eighty-million point font size" might not be such a great idea. Allen, who was shipped to Iraq in March 2004 with the 216th Engineer Battalion (Combat Heavy) as a sergeant, eventually received training to operate bulldozers, loaders, dump trucks, and other heavy equipment. As grueling as the labor was, Allen found humor and creative inspiration in the characters, both Iraqi and American, she met and worked with during her eleven-month tour of duty. While deployed, she wrote numerous short, nonfiction accounts based on these individuals, and in the following story, Allen profiles a soldier who was trying to teach himself how to be a musician. The instrument of choice was simply not one that she had expected, though it does prove that some things never go out of style.*

Most of my platoon is comprised of guys who work as prison guards in the civilian world. One of my best friends out here is Shannon Bear, a 240-pound, six-foot three-inch prison guard. When he got back from leave, he brought with him a new toy.

A fiddle.

In the middle of Iraq, Bear's learning how to play the fiddle. He's really, really happy because he's almost got two songs down. "Mary Had a Little

Lamb" and "Twinkle, Twinkle Little Star." You have to picture this grown man all excited because, as he said, he's "almost ready to turn the page!"

To "Little Brown Jug."

If you can't beat 'em, join 'em, so now I'm trying to pick it up. Got "Mary Had a Little Lamb" and "Twinkle, Twinkle Little Star" and a start at "Camptown Races." I am notorious for my lack of patience, however, so I convinced Bear to jump ahead to "Amazing Grace," which was in chapter twenty-six. Keep in mind, we were on chapter four.

He got the first two notes right off the bat, and we were really impressed with ourselves until we realized that we could not read sheet music.

"What's that little slashy-thingy?" I asked. "If we could figure out what that is, I can get it." Oh, yes, with the fiddle, as with most things, a little bit of knowledge is a dangerous thing.

Later we found a book with "Amazing Grace" without the little slashy-thingies. We are now unstoppable.

Music was more than just a diversion for Allen and her fellow soldiers, however. At times it was also a cultural icebreaker.

We work with a lot of Turks and Iraqis, especially Kurds. I wish that every deployed soldier had a chance to meet them because they are very different from the Arabs in the south. The Kurds love us.

I started to learn Kurdish to keep score in volleyball. Eventually I learned about two hundred words and phrases, but it wasn't so easy because they have sounds Americans can't pronounce. They can't say "left" or "six," for some reason, so I guess we're even.

One of our guys brought his guitar around to the guard shacks and played some American music for them. Note to Enrique Iglesias: Iraqis know you. For what it's worth, you rank right up there with Michael Jackson, Madonna, and Shakira.

Sometimes they'd try to join in. You haven't lived until you've seen a bunch of Iraqi soldiers, complete with AK-47s, sitting around and singing with gusto as they mangle the Beatles' "Let It Be."

"In times of trouble, mother Mary comes to me, speaking words of wisdom . . . Little Pea."

They really got into it.

"Little Pea, Little PEA! Little Pea, yeah, Little Pea . . . Whisper words of wisdom, Little Pea."

That was a good day.

More so than any generation of troops before them, servicemen and women overseas today have the ability to see and hear what the media are reporting back home and how the conflicts in which they are fighting are being portrayed. Allen and her platoon were well aware of the political debates being waged about whether American forces should or should not have been sent to Iraq, and they regularly discussed the subject themselves. In a longer, more serious piece written in June 2004, Allen describes how these conversations, which took place at their forward operating base near Kirkush, Iraq, became almost a nightly ritual.

The camp is under red-lens light discipline, which means we can't use an unfiltered flashlight. It severely lessens our evening entertainment options. So, soon after we arrived, we began our strange nightly gatherings. You won't find it on any schedule, but you can set your watch by it. As the sun nudges the horizon and the gravel cools, some of us give up our battle with the ambient light and surrender our reading until the morning. Others collect up their poker winnings or grumble about their losses. And we all drag our chairs and cigarettes and joylessly warm water out to the gravel and talk. We call it "the circle."

In the Army there is an incredibly varied cross section of society, and we are a diverse group. We have a couple kids straight out of high school, who'd either joined to get a little excitement out of life or to get a leg up on it so that they could go to college. We have older guys, who've already put in their time. They tend to be either jaded or genial, both in reaction to the accumulated bullshit slung at most soldiers who've been in the service for years. We have everyone from idealists to realists to fatalists, more than a few who began at one end of the spectrum and eventually meandered their way to the other.

I always find it amusing when people talk about "the military" vote, perspective, or whatever. My company has 170-some soldiers, and 170-some opinions. We might have more invested in foreign policy than people back home, but that doesn't mean we all agree on exactly what those policies should be. Two of the guys, Jeff and Sam, are brothers serving together here but in different platoons. They are both slightly to the left of extremely conservative, yet also very anti–Iraq war. Their father threatened to cut off his own head and send it in to Aljazeera if his sons aren't returned home soon.

Jake is one of my best friends out here, and one of the most infuriating people I've ever known. Jake's a former Marine who comes from a Marine family and whose biggest regret is that this isn't "a real war," something on the scale of World War II or Vietnam. I usually point out to him that we didn't lose many people in the first few years of Vietnam, either. And then I say something about how I'm really fucking sorry that not enough of us have died for him to consider this a real war. If I had met Jake in a bar in the States and he had said half the bullshit he says here, well, we definitely would not have become friends. But he's here, too, so I guess he's entitled to his opinion. His son, Joey, will be joining us when he gets out of Basic. I wonder if his opinion will change then.

In the circle, we talk for hours not only about the reasons for this war, but for the previous one, too, and if we were ever justified in coming to this part of the world in the first place. At least in Desert Storm, some members of the circle argue, Iraq was the aggressor. Also, the whole world seemed to support us. Several of the soldiers in my platoon are former Marines and more than a few had been in the Gulf War. Desert Storm, they say, was to keep Iraq from taking over Kuwait. Naked aggression that had to be stopped. Simple as that.

Others shoot back that even so, we have no right to get involved in a situation that was a fiscal, not physical, threat, to us. Now we're trying to change an entire culture? And aren't we being naive or arrogant to think that we will make any long-term difference here, anyway? Tempers can get heated, and on some days, it probably isn't a good idea that we are all armed. Unfortunately, two of the guys, Jeff and Jake, are too big for me to punch.

One night we started arguing the hierarchy of evil world leaders, and where Saddam stood on that list. There are obviously worse men, so why Iraq? Why now? For every Saddam, there are ten more vicious dictators, and we can't get rid of them all. Of course, then we had to delve into Saddam's motivations, and if he's really such a bad guy. For the record, I was on the "yes, he's an inexcusable piece of shit" side of this argument.

Jake, of course, wonders if the country is really less dangerous now than under Hussein. He doesn't think there would be suicide bombers and IEDs littering the roads without our impetus. Haven't we made everything worse? the question is inevitably asked.

You mean worse than when hundreds of thousands of people were executed, gassed, and tortured? the inevitable answer comes.

At least there wasn't so much random violence and bloodshed.

No, under Hussein it was all well-organized violence and bloodshed. People were scared to death to say the wrong thing.

Well, now they're scared to death to walk outside without getting blown up.

If we leave, this place will erupt into a civil war.

It probably will anyway. And it'll be our fault for lighting the fuse. . . .

And around and around we go.

I personally believe that living conditions are better now in Iraq than before we were here. I just don't know if they are safer. It seems to change from day to day. And even I wonder if one country can impose political stability and democracy on another.

Some point out that we did it in Japan and Germany. And technically, of course, the Iraqis can "vote out" a democracy if they prefer another system of rule. While I understand that most Americans believe democracy to be the best system of rule, we may also have to accept that it might not work for every culture. I sincerely want it to work, but Jeff and Jake hold out little hope.

Along with the whole question of mixing faith and politics, we're also dealing with a schismatic religion and people who loathe one another. A Sunni won't even use a toilet after a Shiite has. Now we want them to work together to create a new system of law? Then you throw in the Kurds, who are mainly Christian, of an entirely different culture, and whose claim to fame is that their mere existence is the one thing that brings the Sunnis and Shiites together. The Muslims and Kurds hate each other with a bloodthirsty passion most of us cannot even conceive. One member of the circle asked, "Jesus Christ himself couldn't get these people to get along. Do you really think Bush can?"

And where the hell are the weapons of mass destruction? (Here we go.)

Please, it's not like he didn't have them or use them before.

But did anyone think he was really going to use them on us?

He could have sold them to people who wanted to.

Some of the soldiers in my company, I'm told, still bear the scars of mustard gas from Desert Storm, and I've met Kurds whose family members were gassed to death. I don't know if Saddam shipped his stuff out to Syria or if he buried it, which, after being there and seeing the incredible expanse of nothingness that is Iraq, is in no way inconceivable. I don't know if Bush really thought we'd find any. He may have exaggerated the threat, but chemical warfare is nasty shit. Several of us have no problem if he was just staying on the safe side with this one.

Jeff and others don't think we're here to build a democracy or "make the world safer from terrorism." This led to a heated discussion about Bush's motivations. Halliburton, retribution (for Hussein's attempted assassination of Bush's dad), oil—they all came up. I refuse to believe that we're only here for oil. A logical, removed argument could outline the reality that Americans do consume oil and need a friendly government in charge of reserves. But Canada and Mexico have oil, and it'd be a hell of a lot easier to invade them.

If we're here for humanitarian reasons, Jeff asked, then why didn't we go into Rwanda?

Yeah, but there's no oil in Bosnia or Kosovo either, someone countered. And we went in there.

I cannot believe that Bush or Cheney are risking hundreds of thousands of American lives so they or their friends can make a little money. Rumor has it they're both pretty well off anyway. Jeff rarely allows any benefit of the doubt when it comes to Bush. I don't think Jeff could say a good word about Bush with a gun to his head—and some of us have, trust me, entertained the thought.

It gets pretty exhausting after a while. Things would be a lot less complicated if our government was totally innocent and Saddam's was totally guilty. Or if we hadn't been so buddy-buddy with him all those years before Desert Storm.

And speaking of old friends, someone asked if they thought we'd ever find Osama bin Laden. That was the whole point, right—9/11? There's hardly ever any mention in the news or by politicians about Afghanistan, and it's like the troops over there have been forgotten.

This last point we could all agree on. Maybe those of us in Iraq would be forgotten too, or worse. The public supported Vietnam for the first few years, too, then it changed. We don't know how we're going to be treated when we get home, but I think most people realize that you can be *for* the troops even if you're *against* the war.

Everyone says they are supporting us, but sometimes it seems that civilians have no idea about who soldiers really are. This, too, we all agreed on, that people back home have no concept of what troops go through. We're not robotic killing machines. We're regular Americans, just doing our jobs. This war has really tapped the National Guard, so the average soldier out here could be your mechanic or your plumber. Maybe your dentist. Or the girl at the cash register. I think we're all pretty proud of what we do, and, at heart, we're all patriotic. But we're not brainwashed, and we have differing opinions. And we realize that there wasn't only one reason for starting this war.

At least certainly not one obvious reason.

Because I honestly believe if there had been, in one of our endless discussions in the circle, we would have found it.

THE CAT
Poem
Ryan Alexander

Although it is against military regulations (primarily for health reasons), servicemen and women often adopt stray cats and dogs as unofficial mascots for their units or as personal pets. Surrounded by the harshness and frenzy of combat, many troops find it calming to care for something small and vulnerable, while others believe that the animals bring good luck. And for some, especially those grappling with homesickness, they are simply a reminder of a favorite pet back in the States. Before heading to Iraq in April 2004 with the U.S. Army's Stryker Brigade Combat Team (SBCT), twenty-eight-year-old Ryan Alexander gave his wife a cat to keep her company during his four-month deployment. (Alexander had served in the U.S. Marine Corps but was honorably discharged in 2001. When Operation Iraqi Freedom began, he volunteered to work with the SBCT as a civilian. The specifics of his job cannot be disclosed.) Alexander wrote the following poem about a cat he encountered soon after he arrived in Mosul.

> She came to me skittish, wild.
> The way you're meant to be,
> surrounded by cruelty.
> I did not blame her.
> I would do the same.

A pregnant cat, a happy distraction;
some sort of normal thing.
Calico and innocent.

The kittens in her belly said feed me.

And I did.

She crept with careful eye,
Body held low to the dirt,
Snagged a bite,
And carried it just far enough away.

She liked the MREs,
the beef stew, the chicken breast, the barbeque pork,
but she did not like canned sardines.
I do not blame her.
I would do the same.

She came around again and again
finally deciding that I was no threat,
that this big man wasn't so bad.

I was afraid to touch her as the docs warned us.
Iraqi animals were carriers of flesh-eating disease.
I donned a plastic glove and was the first to pet
this wild creature who may be

the one true heart and mind that America
had won over.

After a while I forgot the glove and enjoyed
the tactile softness of short fur,
flesh-eating bacteria be damned.

Her belly swelled for weeks
and she disappeared for some days
until her kittens were safely birthed

in the shallow of a rusted desk
in the ruins that lined the road behind us.

She came around again slim
with afterbirth still matted to her hind legs.

She would return, but not quite as often.
She came to eat and for attention,
but there was nursing to be done.

One day she crept up with a kitten in her mouth.
She dropped it at my foot and stared up at me;
she expected something, but there was nothing I could do.
The young black and white kitten was dead,
its eyes not yet opened.

It looked like some shriveled old wise thing,
completely still, mouth puckered,
small body curled and limp.

She let me take the baby without a fight.
She knew, but seemed unaffected.

She had fetched me a gift,
a lesson,
among the worried nights,
shot nerves from poorly aimed mortar rounds:

Everything dies.
The evil, the innocent,
her baby and
me.

I thought I should say a prayer and bury
this poor little thing,
but I did for it what will be done for me.

I laid it in the burn can amongst the ash
and said I'm sorry.

SPIN *and* FLIGHT
Personal Narratives
Major Richard Sater

Stripped of most, if not all, of the conveniences and luxuries of home, troops in Iraq and Afghanistan often discover that even the most ordinary moments can assume special meaning in the life-and-death context of war. For forty-three-year-old Richard Sater, a major in the U.S. Air Force Reserve who began his seven-month deployment to Afghanistan in September 2003, this realization came just a few days before Thanksgiving. Sater wrote the following after a visit to the makeshift laundry room in the Air Force village at Bagram Air Base.

One recent midnight finds me doing laundry, a necessity every eight or nine days, inside our plywood hut lined with dingy washers and exhausted dryers. The plumbing provides only hard, cold water, so sorting whites and colors and permanent press is pointless.

Usually I spend as little time as possible in the laundry room, stuffing things into two washers and then bolting for forty-five minutes. This night, as I measure soap powder and wait for the tubs to fill, a gentleman comes in — tall, lanky, generously mustached, with sad eyes the color of hazelnuts — with three bags of laundry. Small ones, with little in them.

He asks where he can get detergent around here. I hand him my box and watch, curious, as he dumps the laundry into three separate washers — odd, I think, as the few items of clothing would easily fit into one medium-sized load.

He wears a desert-tan flight suit, the two-piece kind, with no markings on it, identifying him by not identifying him as Special Forces aircrew. I introduce myself. He gives me a single name: Dash. I don't ask for more, not wanting to put him in a position of not wanting to say more.

His words faintly colored with British, he says he is an MH-53 gunner. Then I know why he's here. We lost a helicopter a couple of days ago, an Air Force MH-53 Pave Low. It crashed in the night soon after taking off from here. Five killed, Army passengers as well as Air Force crew. I extend my sympathies to him for the crash, and he shakes his head, disgusted.

"It was a resupply mission," he says. "Not even a combat sortie." Had the crash occurred during a combat mission—even if the helicopter had been forced down by enemy fire—he would not be as troubled. One can make peace with such things under war. But such cost for an ordinary resupply mission insults all who fly and fight.

Three colleagues lost. Friends, perhaps, at least brothers-in-arms. And somehow or other, the task has fallen to Dash of doing the laundry of these three, prior to sending their personal effects to their families. "Don't want to send them home dirty," he says.

I listen, since he seems to want someone to. He tells me a little about the deceased crew members. One was divorced, he says; one was a recent father and another had teenaged children. Through wash and rinse and spin and tumble dry, I stay with him, each of us sitting on the edge of a dryer, our feet hanging down. The air smells of fabric-softener sheets; the rhythmic click of buttons and the soft thud of damp clothes turning underneath us punctuate his story.

After he spends his quiet rage and grows silent, I ask about himself. I learn that his mother is English, that his dad served in the U.S. Navy. Dash tells me he has remained single himself because it is easier. He has twenty-eight years in the Air Force and has grown tired, he says. He's assigned to a base in the southeastern United States, and when his enlistment is up this time, he will get out.

And after retirement? He tells me he has bought himself a metal detector, the kind you see old guys using at the beach sometimes, looking for coins in the sand. And Dash plans to spend his own time on the beach to see what he can find.

Carefully, he folds his three bags of clothing, mundane socks and undershirts, some gym shorts, uncommon only because they're forced to bear the weight of wasted potential, of the price extracted for freedom to endure. Courteously, gravely, we shake hands. I would like to meet him again, I tell him before he departs, and he says the same.

And he goes.

Alone again, I fold. The water here contains enough cautionary bleach to kill the worst bacteria in it, but brown T-shirts turn pale purple and the desert-camouflage uniforms take on a salmon-pink tint over time. I count socks to make sure I have an even number.

In the cold dark of the early morning, I stumble through the empty compound, back to my tent, arms full of these clothes, baked hot and scented with boxed springtime.

Dash will find his treasure, buried. I am certain. He has earned his reward. And for my part, I will choose the important things and summon thanks.

Five months later, Sater wrote about another simple activity that had taken on greater significance in post-Taliban Afghanistan.

On the back road this sunny afternoon, I am flying a kite.

I arrived a couple of days ago at my old home, Bagram, gone for good from Kabul, in the status referred to as "awaiting transportation"—a seat on a flight heading in the direction I want to go, which is homeward. In the mean-time, I have a sunny, dusty afternoon free and a kite.

The kite is a gift from the International Security Assistance Force, which operates in Kabul, separate from Operation Enduring Freedom. ISAF is our opposite, a peacekeeping force, troops from approximately thirty nations serv-ing as police. Their kites are trisected into black and green and red, the shades of Afghanistan's flag. In the center of the kite, outlined in white, is a dove and (very small) the ISAF logo and a sentiment—I don't know what—written in Dari. Two bright yellow streamers make the kite's tail.

I'm accustomed to kites that are shaped like, well, kites, a paper diamond with crossed sticks and a long knotted-rag tail. But this kite is made of some kind of sturdy fabriclike plastic, and it's more or less square. It has no sticks, but it has pockets built into each side of it that catch air. I'm skeptical but de-termined to try it anyway.

I run a couple of miles down the perimeter road, past the power lines (which, I recall, tempt kites), and out to a deserted stretch. I unfold the kite and tie the string to it and, without ceremony, offer it to the wind, and up it goes. It is a good day for up.

Air Force pilots make much of slipping the surly bonds of earth. I am not a pilot, but attach your soul and imagination to a kite in the wind and blue sunny sky, and I believe you can accomplish the same result. A kite rising takes your spirit with it.

The wind—and it's a good, strong wind with mischief on its mind—likes this kite. I'm pleased and surprised at how easily it rises, tugging persistently and persuasively on the string as I unroll more and more.

Kite flying is hardly an everyday occurrence at Bagram. I wonder if I am violating airspace by sending this one skyward. Three helicopters take off, and I suppose it is possible that a high-enough kite could pose some sort of hazard, but our birds steer clear of me—or I of them.

Runners trot past. Most offer a grin or a thumbs-up.

The kite bobs and dips occasionally, but mostly it just aims higher. Sometimes it loops downward, catches itself and struggles back up, regaining lift.

I should say that the whole length of the road back here is fenced on both sides, barbed wire with ubiquitous red "minefield" triangles. Some of the land, of course, actually is mined. Some of it simply hasn't been cleared, so it's unknown whether there are explosive devices buried in it or not.

The Soviets mined the place years ago, and they thoughtfully put up posts, rows of them, in the ground to identify the path. Such a fence surely kept away anyone who might have attempted to infiltrate along its line. It's certainly kept us away.

After the kite goes down, I carefully begin rewinding the string. It's tangled in the concertina wire, and the kite itself appears to be tangled in a bush. With some coaxing and gentle tugging, I get the kite airborne again and it flies itself out of the minefield. I'm relieved.

My kite soars over the rusted hull of a MiG fighter, over piles of twisted, corrugated iron, skeletons of trucks, scattered scrap and ghosts. Even years later, quietly rusting under the harmless sun and blue sky, these tons of scrap metal suggest the cost of war.

On the other side of the road are the remains of mud-brick structures that were surely houses in the not-distant past, though their current condition makes them look like the ruins of an ancient civilization.

There is, not far from our road, a whole settlement that appears abandoned, broken and empty windows and no color. I've run by it numerous times and seen no signs of life until this evening. I can hear the call for prayer from within the settlement.

As I continue my kite flying, I also hear the voices of children playing. Their squealing and shrieking—only children can hit such pitches—carry across the coming dusk.

The Taliban outlawed kites. Too frivolous. Imagine. In town today, riding through Kabul, you can see children flying kites now because they can. We forget sometimes that genuine progress is measured in small increments.

Once the sun begins setting behind the mountains, I decide it's time to quit. The wind is reluctant to let go of my kite, but slowly, I rein it in and begin my jog back to the main camp. I round the corner at the closest point to the settlement and spot two young boys waiting there, probably not more than five or six years old. They point excitedly and chatter. I don't have to guess why they're so interested.

Three strands of concertina wire separate us. I fold the kite securely and toss it neatly over the barricade. The boys pounce, tussle; one of them triumphs and holds the prize aloft. They run off together and don't look back at me. I suspect they had the thing in the air within a couple of minutes, in the tail of daylight.

I hope the boys have as much luck as I did making it fly. Maybe they will know someone who can read the Dari passage on the kite and derive some encouragement from it. But if the dove depicted on the kite stands for nothing more than two Afghan boys having some fun for a day or two, perhaps no other significance is necessary.

A year and a half after returning from Afghanistan, Sater, who had also served in Operation Enduring Freedom-Phillippines in 2002, was mobilized for duty in Iraq. It would be his third overseas deployment in four years.

REFLECTIONS

Poem

Captain Michael Lang

Finding respite from the rigors and demands of warfare can be a challenge for troops in a combat zone. Some achieve it through everyday activities— playing cards, listening to music, watching DVDs, writing letters home, lifting weights—but many discover that their most cherished times are when they are alone. These private moments offer servicemen and women much-needed solace as well as an opportunity simply to think or process their emotions. U.S. Army Captain Michael Lang, an infantry officer with the 3rd Brigade, 2nd Infantry Division, wrote the following poem in July 2004 about an experience outside of Balad, Iraq. Lang had taken a short break to go off by himself and look out over a land that was both hostile and unexpectedly beautiful.

> In the desert, there is sand
> and space, filled up by wind
> and heat. It's black at night,
> lightless, aside from the stars.
> When the storms came one night,
> I smoked out in the sand
> and glowed within the world
> the lightning revealed.

SOLIDARITY *and* OUR WAR
Poems
First Lieutenant Stephanie Metzger Harper

Like Michael Lang, previous, twenty-six-year-old U.S. Air Force First Lieutenant Stephanie Metzger Harper wrote short, almost snapshotlike poems inspired by nature and the surrounding landscape. Harper, who served in Operation Enduring Freedom and flew over Afghanistan with the 12th Expeditionary Airborne Command and Control Squadron, penned the following lines of verse during her deployment, which began in November 2001.

> How strong the paper thin
> poppy stands against
> the sun and trampling wind

Harper, who was promoted to captain on New Year's Day 2002 and earned three Air Medals for flying thirty combat missions, was based primarily in the Middle East. She wrote most of her poetry in her tent, but occasionally she would jot down images in her flight notebook while working as an air battle manager aboard the E-8C Joint Surveillance Target Attack Radar System aircraft. In the following poem, Harper focuses on both the beauty of the physical environment around her and the people with whom she was serving. (A "saif," which Harper alludes to, is a curved Arabic sword.)

Another desert night
mercifully blacks out the miles and miles of flat,
                tan
                sand
stretching beyond the razor wire around our camp.

Off duty,
we've retreated to our tents.
—quiet and contemplative—

The first crew is up tonight . . .
Somewhere over the battlefield they are finding out,
for all of us,
what this war is going to be like.

A string of Christmas lights
glows above the center aisle of our tent
casting thick, black shadows into the corners of our new home.
We've dubbed it the "Chinese laundry" . . .
Flight suits, camouflage, and damp towels
            suspended everywhere
            from parachute cords.

Our cots are in line along each side of the tent,
most of us sleep with our feet towards the aisle.
            we drift off . . .
each of us just a few feet away from the next—
In musty beds that
            levitate us above the canvas floor
where sand is collecting in all the low spots.

The saif moon cuts an arc across the cool night sky.

And I,
waking just enough to check,
turn my head to see that my friend has made it back safely.
Wrapped in an olive drab sleeping bag—

the reassuring shape of her
rises up above the horizon of her cot,

In line with my own,
    and the next,
        and the next.

I breathe a little easier
    and sink back into sleep—
Until it is my turn
to disappear quickly
    into the dark,
        crescent-hung
          sky.

PVT. MURPHY

Cartoons

Master Sergeant Mark Baker

Along with recording their experiences—and simply passing the time—by writing poems, stories, and journals, some service members put pen to paper and express themselves through sketches, portraits, and other visual arts. In 1992, twenty-five-year-old Mark Baker began drawing a series of cartoons based on a character he named Pvt. Murphy. Baker joined the U.S. Army when he was eighteen and has served as a cavalry scout and intelligence analyst, and he is now an active-duty master sergeant assigned to Fort Huachuca, Arizona. The first Pvt. Murphy cartoon was published in 1993, and in November 2000 the series began running on a regular basis in the Army Times, where it is read by a quarter of a million people each week. Like the scruffy GIs Willie and Joe, created by the famed World War II artist Bill Mauldin (with whom Baker has often been compared), the cartoon's eponymous character offers the common grunt's perspective on military life. Although often running afoul of his commanding officers and frequently griping about Army rules and regulations, Murphy demonstrates a strong sense of pride in his fellow soldiers—especially those who have come before him. (In the first cartoon below, "B.C." stands for battalion commander.)

THE LAND OF ABRAHAM
Personal Narrative
Captain Donna Kohout

Many troops in Iraq and Afghanistan find comfort and strength in religious faith, and those who serve in the Middle East are especially awed by the biblical history that surrounds them. In the late winter of 2002 and through the early spring of 2003, Captain Donna Kohout was a fighter pilot with the 363rd F-16CJ Squadron, 363rd Operations Group, 363rd Wing, stationed in Saudi Arabia. In April 2003, Kohout shared the following observations with loved ones and members of the Dillon Community Church in Colorado, where Kohout was living before she joined the U.S. Air Force.

I'm still praising God for the opportunity to spend five months in the Middle East both to serve in the largest conflict of our day and to witness the wonders He was working at Prince Sultan Air Base in Saudi Arabia, where I lived. I don't know how to describe the feeling that there was a spiritual element to what we were doing. When I first arrived I did a double take when I looked at the maps in the back of my Bible and recognized the locations of the cities we were flying over. Tallil had been Ur of the Chaldeans, the birthplace of Abraham, who was the father of the Israelites. When God punished the Israelites with exile from the land He had given them, they were taken to Babylon, near present-day Al Hillah. This is also where Daniel survived his famed bout in the lions' den. During their years of exile in the Babylonian Empire, the Israelites camped out near Nippur, or the current Al Kut.

I wish I could describe the feeling of flying across what we called the TE Line in the months prior to "Night 1" of Operation Iraqi Freedom (OIF). The TE (Tigris-Euphrates) Line, which marks the edge of the settled area, is just south of the Euphrates River. South of the line is barren desert. At night, no lights are visible there, but to the north bright collections define the towns CNN made famous—Tallil, As Samawah, Basrah, Al Kut, Al Amarah, Karbala, and of course Baghdad. One clear day I looked down at the rich greens of the valley between the Tigris and Euphrates and pondered over the fact that these were the rivers that I'd learned about in church and school my whole life. Genesis describes the Garden of Eden standing at the headwaters of four rivers, two of which are the Tigris and Euphrates. That places the Garden just north of Basrah, within sight of where I flew almost daily.

Abraham, Daniel, Ezra, Nehemiah, the whole displaced Israelite nation, and perhaps even Adam and Eve all trod the ground I was looking down on day after day. And I was living in the same desert where the Israelites wandered. We complain about being there for three months—it's so flat, windy, hot, sandy, and dry, it's no wonder the Israelites complained during the FORTY YEARS that they followed God around the Sinai Peninsula between their exile from Egypt and their entrance into the "Promised Land" near Jerusalem.

In OIF, I flew only nights, except for the occasional late-evening or sunrise flight. At night a person can see every bullet and missile launched, near and far away, with the aid of night vision goggles. Thankfully, most of what the Iraqis shot was unguided and too small to reach the altitudes at which we fly. However, it is still nothing shy of a miracle that given the sheer number of airplanes in the sky, they didn't shoot down a single fighter, bomber, or tanker with all the projectiles they launched over those three weeks.

I may have officially been a part of OIF, and flown over Baghdad numerous times, but whenever we met for Officers' Christian Fellowship, Praise Band, or church, we agreed that we didn't really feel like we were a part of the war. We came back to base and slept in warm beds in air-conditioned rooms. Granted, three or four per room, and people even lived in the storage room down the hall, but that was hardly a sacrifice compared to what the Army troops and Marines had to endure. So, like many of you, we supported those guys the best way we could—in prayer. It really meant a lot to me to see the picture of a group of them, arms around each other, gathered in prayer. God really is everywhere. How amazing to meet in a chapel on a multinational base in Saudi Arabia to celebrate Easter, play Australian songs in a praise band led by a Scot, hear the sermon from an American while sitting next to a Brit, and write about it all to friends in Colorado. I'm overwhelmed just thinking about it.

Praise God for the safety He has provided to so many of us over the last several months. And please continue to pray for the Iraqi people and the soldiers over there now. There is a long and unconventional road ahead of them still.

Captain Kohout went on to become the first woman to fly the F-117A Nighthawk Stealth Fighter, one of the most technologically advanced warplanes of its time. Captain Kohout remains in the U.S. Air Force, and in the spring of 2006 she married a fellow fighter pilot, Lieutenant Colonel Richard J. Douglass.

THE MENORAH *and* DECEMBER 15
E-mail
Simone A. Ledeen

"For those of you who don't know—tonight was the first night of Hanukah," twenty-eight-year-old Simone A. Ledeen wrote from Iraq in December 2003. Ledeen was not a soldier but a civilian advisor with the Coalition Provisional Authority (CPA), which functioned as the country's governing body until control was transferred to Iraqi leadership in June 2004. Ledeen, who had been working for an economic consulting firm before the war, went to Baghdad in October 2003. (A close family friend had been aboard the airplane that was crashed into the Pentagon on September 11, and both Ledeen and her brother wanted to serve their country in some way. Ledeen's brother became an officer in the U.S. Marine Corps, and Ledeen joined the CPA to help with Iraq's economic redevelopment.) Ledeen regularly updated her family in Washington, D.C., via e-mail about life in a war zone. And, as a person of Jewish faith, few moments were as meaningful to her as celebrating Hanukah in the former palace of a brutal, anti-Semitic dictator. She continued her e-mail home:

So there were 6 of us—2 soldiers who led the service—two civilians in addition to me—and the chaplain here who is Christian but who wanted to witness this historic event: the first lighting of the menorah in Saddam's Republican Palace. As I was the only female they asked me to light the Shabbat candles. I actually got quite emotional and almost couldn't finish. Lighting the Sabbath candles in this place—in the seat of power of a man who tried so hard to destroy us. I thought about the Hanukah story—about how the Maccabees and their followers refused to compromise their beliefs—how they defeated Antiochus' army—and how they rededicated the Temple, making oil that should have lasted for only one day last for eight. I realized that in a way, now we are rededicating this place. What was once the seat of evil has been replaced by hope and praise to G–d.

The menorah we use is beautiful—it was a gift to the CPA from an Iraqi Jewish artist living in New York. All of the candle holders are shaped like pomegranates, a symbol of fertility—to bring growth and new life to this country.

I also thought about the miracle of Hanukah, of the lamp burning for eight whole days until they could find more oil. That is what this country needs—no, not oil (!!)—but a miracle of that kind. Even though there are limited resources . . . even though some people say it's hopeless . . . I couldn't help thinking maybe there's more to it than that. There are so many people here sacrificing so much—from the young soldiers to the translators who risk being recognized to the older men and women who retired from the military but still volunteered to come as civilians so this effort could have the benefit of their expertise. Then there are all the people back home who are praying for us and sending us good wishes . . . and food. . . . Basically what I am trying to say is there is a lot of good coming into this place—and I am not ready to give up on it.

It is late and I am going to sleep now. Love to all and Happy Holidays!!

"It's funny how quickly one gets used to the noises of war," Ledeen wrote about the constant bombings in the Iraqi capital just weeks after she arrived there. Even combat troops who put themselves in harm's way sometimes lament how repetitive and tedious the weeks and months at the front can seem, and when the monotony of wartime life is broken, it is often because of some terrible incident or attack. But every once in a while, a flash of good news surges through both the civilian and military communities like an electric current, infusing them with joy and excitement. On December 19, 2003, Simone Ledeen wrote home about just such a moment. (L. Paul Bremer, whom Ledeen refers to below, ran the Coalition Provisional Authority; Lieutenant General Ricardo Sanchez was the head of all U.S. and allied forces in Iraq; and Peggy Noonan was a speechwriter for presidents Ronald Reagan and George H. W. Bush.)

This morning started out like any other . . . got a wake up call from my mother (greatest mother on earth), and then promptly went back to sleep. Woke up 20 minutes later and rushed through the morning routine, and having missed breakfast walked straight over to my office. We are currently preparing a report to Congress regarding the supplemental spending bill so we are particularly crazed these days.

Anyway I was running around the palace with one of my colleagues today, making sure everyone was going to be ready with their parts of the document when in one office or other someone told us Saddam had been captured. We all said "oh, wouldn't that be great if it were true?! I hope it is!" and then we continued on to our next stop. Suddenly we heard a great cheer erupt from downstairs—we ran over to one of the balconies but didn't see anyone downstairs.

I had the distinct impression we were missing the party. But no matter—there was so much work to do! As we walked through the halls, I noticed everyone smiling—we passed a group of Iraqi electricians who were yelling excitedly and practically jumping off their ladders. We stopped in the DFAC to get some food where we learned that it was for real—that Bremer had told the Governing Council—and that there would be a press conference shortly.

We started hearing crazy amounts of gunfire outside. Our translators came over to say hello, just out of their minds with excitement. "For us this is better than the 9th of April!" one says. "It is really over now," added the other. After lunch we went back to the office—everyone had decided to go to the press conference so I joined the exodus to the parking lot. When we got outside I called my mother (woke her this time as it was 6am on the East Coast)—but she didn't seem to mind. As we walked down the street to the parking lot, I heard singing amid the sounds of automatic machine gun fire. I looked down the road and saw a large group of young Iraqi men, dancing down the street, waving their shirts over their heads. Keep in mind this is the famous Green Zone—not the downtown streets. As they got closer, I recognized the electricians I had seen earlier in the day. The men danced right past me and I held up the phone so my mother could hear. We all just stood there with big dumb grins on our faces, watching them and sharing in their happiness. One of the translators had also told me, "you cannot imagine what we have been through. Now we can really have a new Iraq." I remembered her words as the men passed by me singing and dancing. When I turned to get in the car I had tears in my eyes.

We zipped over to the convention center and found the room where the press conference was being held. Can't discuss security but there was plenty of it. We finally made it inside and I grabbed a spot in the back of the room against the wall where I had a perfect view in the space between two cameras. Bremer and Sanchez came out—Bremer said the words that are now famous and we all went nuts. The news reports I have read state that it was only the Iraqi journalists who got up and yelled and made a fuss—people I was there and let me tell you we in the back and on the sides were ALL yelling and screaming—soldiers, CPA, the security guys—don't let them make you believe it was only a few!

Then the video. When that image of Saddam all bearded and disheveled came up on the screen everyone gasped. I think I might have put my hand up to my mouth. It was so dramatic and shocking. I am sure you know of the Iraqi journalists who stood and screamed at the image, chanting "death to Saddam," and how one of them had been imprisoned and tortured for 2 years for the simple fact of writing for a Shiite newspaper. It was deeply moving. Everyone was transfixed. He finally sat down and began sobbing uncontrollably as General Sanchez continued with the briefing.

After the press conference was over, we all piled back in the car and came back to the palace. Celebratory fire could still be heard—actually it was pretty much nonstop. I still don't understand the whole shoot a gun in the air because you're happy thing. . . . My translator friend called me when she got home, saying the streets of Baghdad were crazy—people dancing, giving out candies, just general mayhem—but joyful mayhem. She couldn't stop talking she was so excited, and her excitement filled me with . . . a very good feeling that I am not sure I can describe. Happiness but something more profound—we really have done something good here. If we do every single other thing wrong, we still freed these people from Saddam Hussein. That is a legacy to be proud of. And unlike the Germans after WW2, the Iraqis get to put him on trial for his crimes. I'll bet the trial will be like Eichmann's in the 60s—with everyone disappointed to find the defendant just a pathetic, neurotic man with a complex or two. The banality of evil and all that.

Anyway tonight we have done a lot of work, but also broke for some Johnny Walker in honor of the day's events. There's a lot more to say—many things have happened in the time I haven't written so I vow to write again in the next couple of days and fill you all in.

In the meantime, we should all heed the words of Peggy Noonan and "not be boring people who Consider the Implications. Let's not talk about the domestic political impact. For just a day let's feel the pleasure history just handed us."

Much love

me

THE OUTSIDER
Personal Narrative
First Sergeant Richard Acevedo

Since October 2001, more than one million U.S. Marines, soldiers, airmen, and sailors have been mobilized to Afghanistan and Iraq, and a significant number have fought in both countries. If their wartime writings are any indication, these troops often find military service to be grueling, boring, terrifying, infuriating, and exhausting—but also the most memorable and fulfilling time of their lives. Many, if not the majority of them, will credit one reason above all for why the experience is so rewarding: the bonds of friendship they forge with their brothers- and sisters-in-arms. These relationships are not formed overnight, and it would be misleading to suggest that tensions and outright hostilities between service members do not exist. As in any community, some people just don't get along. Thirty-eight-year-old U.S. Army First Sergeant Richard Acevedo hadn't even left for Iraq when he was confronted with a problem that was proving to be, in his words, a serious "leadership challenge" relating to one of the men in his company. (Identifying information about the soldier has been changed to protect his identity.)

In the twenty years I've spent in the U.S. Army, I have always been in the company of infantrymen, a group of rough-and-tumble, physical individuals who are self-reliant, intelligent, and adventurous. They love bad food, adverse living conditions, sleep deprivation, constant physical abuse, and the lurking possibility that they might die in the execution of their sworn duties. It is not a life for everyone.

Manuel Ernesto was a soldier assigned to the infamous "Fighting 69th," a National Guard infantry battalion based out of New York, which is where I call home. The unit has a history of being one of the most decorated outfits in the Army, boasting a lineage that goes all the way back to the Revolutionary War and with a fair number of legends in its ranks. Men like the famed poet Joyce Kilmer; Father Duffy, the Army chaplain whose statue graces Times Square; and "Wild Bill" Donovan, who would go on to start the OSS (Office of Strategic Services), the predecessor to the present-day CIA. Today's members of the Fighting 69th are true New Yorkers and come from all walks of life. Manuel Ernesto probably represented that better than anyone.

Perhaps the best way to describe Ernesto is to say that he's a simple man. At the time, he looked to be in his late thirties, though it's hard to tell exactly. He was kind and had a childlike innocence about him, but he had difficulty understanding easy, straightforward tasks and directions. There was also something about him that seemed awkward and out of sync. My many years in the Army have taught me to be a quick study of men, and my initial impression of Ernesto led me to believe that he would not fit in very well within the Spartan, testosterone-driven world of the infantry.

Ernesto was shy and kept to himself, and since the Army is primarily a herd society, those who do not participate in the herd quickly get singled out. In the Army, it is never about the individual and always about the collective group. Men who don't contribute or carry their weight are considered a liability; anyone not fitting that mold gets ruthlessly ostracized. To his fellow infantrymen, Ernesto wasn't seen as one of them, and they labeled him a misfit. Despite what the other soldiers felt about Ernesto, I gave him the benefit of the doubt. Mainly for two reasons: one, I desperately needed bodies, since I didn't have the full complement of soldiers intended for my deployment; and two, Ernesto was extremely polite and sincere in everything he said and did.

We spent four months at Fort Hood, Texas, preparing for our deployment to Iraq. I figured that any soldier who couldn't handle the pressure of training for war would get weeded out during our train-up period. If Ernesto couldn't get his act together, I would handle it when the time came. Until then, I would monitor Ernesto's progress and hope for the best.

My first real observation of Ernesto in action was during one of our early morning PT sessions. I always started off the day's training with a grueling workout. I had to get these men in shape and help them shed the pounds that their comfortable civilian lives had packed on them. Combat in Iraq would be unforgiving on these citizen soldiers, and they would have to tote around as much as fifty pounds of gear every day in the brutal 120- to 130-degree summer heat. I often started the PT session with some stretching and light calisthenics in order to warm the guys up and prevent injuries before kicking off the real exercise. Usually I began with jumping jacks, and on this one morning as I was jumping along and leading the company, I could hear the men break out into a roar of laughter. I scanned the ranks looking for the reason. Lo and behold, there he was in the last row, rear left-hand corner of the formation. It was Ernesto jumping around in spasms of unsynchronized, discombobulated movement. He looked like a fish that just landed on the deck of a boat, flapping around waiting to be clubbed.

At first, I thought it was an act and began to get angry, thinking he was trying to get laughs during my PT session. I watched him for a couple of seconds more and came to the conclusion that this was no act. Men were laughing so hard they were losing their own rhythm. The harder Ernesto tried to get in sync with everyone else, the worse he looked. His body moved like a broken rag doll and the self-absorbed expression of concentration on his face caused the men to break up even more. One of the guys next to him started to mimic his movements, and instead of Ernesto catching on that he was being mocked, he looked at the prankster with a quizzical expression on his face and shouted to him between labored breaths: "Are you . . . having . . . a hard time . . . with this . . . too?" This caused the whole group to convulse in laughter. That was who Ernesto was. He tried his hardest, but he just couldn't understand basic concepts.

Ernesto's team leader, squad leader, and platoon sergeant began to complain to me on a daily basis that Ernesto was having a hard time grasping the fundamentals of being an infantryman. I would often tell them to try harder, that Ernesto was just a leadership challenge. All three sergeants looked at me as if I had lost my mind, but since I outranked them, they couldn't tell me that I was crazy. They left my office mumbling under their breath that Ernesto was hopeless.

Days turned to weeks and Ernesto wasn't making any progress. It was time to come up with a game plan for him or he would get himself or someone else killed. I decided one day to have a discussion with our battalion sergeant major in reference to Ernesto. I was going to explain all the things we tried in getting Ernesto trained up. If that got me nowhere, I would inform him that we needed to have Ernesto evaluated by a military psychologist for mental stability and have him released or discharged from the Army. I had the whole strategy worked out in my head.

As soon as the topic of Manuel Ernesto was broached, the sergeant major began to smile. Ernesto, it turns out, had been in his company some years back when he was a first sergeant. During training, Ernesto started to squirrel away food from the mess tent and keep it in his backpack in anticipation of some unknown impending famine. One day, he took three little containers of milk from that morning's breakfast. Most of the time, the Army's milk is processed in such a way that it has a very long shelf life. But on that day, the mess tent had served fresh milk, and Ernesto, not realizing the difference, stuck the containers of milk in his duffel bag. A few days later, people heard screaming in the middle of the night from somewhere inside the patrol base; Ernesto was on the ground writhing in pain and clutching his stomach in agony. The cause of his illness was consumption of spoiled milk.

After hearing the story, I became angry and asked the sergeant major, "If everyone knew this guy was so screwed up, why was he ever placed in my infantry company for this dangerous deployment?" I was upset, because I felt I was the only one in the whole damned battalion who didn't know how wacky this Ernesto guy was. The sergeant major assured me he would find Ernesto a job as a "gofer" somewhere safe within the battalion. But there was something else he said that stunned me: Ernesto, prior to this deployment, had been homeless and living in a city shelter. This was why he had been squirreling away the food, and this was why he had been saving the milk; these were habits he had cultivated from being homeless for so long.

A few days later, I was informed that Ernesto would be transferred to the headquarters company to work in their supply room. Essentially, Ernesto would get a job that would not require him to leave the camp to go out on missions. I informed Ernesto of the pending transfer to his new position. Up until that point, he had been teased relentlessly and was made the butt of many jokes within the company from all its resident alpha males. I figured he would be relieved to get out of this environment and move to a quieter arena. Instead, when I told him of the pending transfer, he seemed saddened by the news.

I told Ernesto that an opening in the headquarters company supply room had become available and that it was a hard decision for me to make with all the qualified men I had in the company. But I had to recommend somebody for this important position, and I felt he was the best man for the job. He cheered up a bit when I told him this and thanked me for my confidence in him. He said that he wouldn't let me or the company down in any way. I told him that I didn't doubt it. He quietly left my office and I was quite pleased with myself in how I had handled the whole situation. I would get a more fitting replacement for Ernesto, and he would get to work in a place where he wouldn't hurt himself or anybody else for that matter. Problem solved, case closed.

Some weeks went by and, one night while working late in my office, I heard a soft tap on my office door. I shouted, "Come in," at the same time wondering who was knocking at such a late hour. It was Ernesto.

He shuffled quietly into my office, shy and apologetic for disturbing me. I told him to come in, sit down, and tell me what was bothering him. I knew it wasn't a social visit at such a late hour. He sat down wringing his hands and looking all around my office, studying every nook and cranny and every object in the room. He looked at everything but me.

Ernesto attempted to make small talk and asked me about my family. I told them they were all well and in good health. When I saw this conversation wasn't getting anywhere, I gently asked him what was on his mind. He finally looked me in the face timidly and asked if he could come back to the company and be with the men. I was a little surprised by his comment, and I asked him if he was unhappy where he was. He said that the supply sergeant was taking very good care of him and that he liked the work he was doing and the hours he kept.

I told him I was a little confused about why he wanted to come back. It was evident that he had found his niche, and I had heard really good things about his work there. He had the hardest time looking me in the eye, and I finally told him as nicely as I could that I didn't think he was cut out to be an infantry soldier. I don't think Ernesto took this as a surprise, and I felt he knew the truth deep down inside. He quietly stated that he knew the men would be risking their lives soon in combat and that he wanted to be with the men and would do anything he could to help them—even if it meant picking up the dead and filling body bags.

Ernesto stayed quiet after that comment. We were weeks away from deploying to Iraq and the newspapers and cable channels were rife with stories about people getting their heads cut off, convoys being ambushed on a regular basis, and U.S. service members getting killed by the constant onslaught of bombs hidden on the roads. My soldiers were trading horror stories with one another and the rumors were causing quite a stir, and everyone was very tense.

I looked at Ernesto, and I realized that his comment about picking up the dead and filling the body bags was not just an idle or morbid statement. For all his awkwardness and childlike qualities, Manuel Ernesto was far more in tune with what was important than the rest of us. He understood the true ramifications of the dangers awaiting us, and he wanted to be a part of something important. Ernesto showed more compassion for his fellow soldiers than they ever showed him. I felt ashamed at that moment, especially considering that some men in my company were trying to do everything in their power to get out of going off to fight. Here was Ernesto, a guy who was homeless and shunned by the rest of civilized society, and, in the end, he turned out to have more heart and guts than most.

Ernesto sat quietly, waiting for my answer, and I knew that my response was important to him. I looked him in the eye and told him that if the day ever came when, God forbid, I had to pick up my fallen soldiers, it would be an honor for me if he could help in any way. He smiled and tears welled up in the corners of his eyes. He quietly got up and saluted me in an awkward manner, and I saluted back, not having the heart to tell him I was a sergeant and only officers get saluted.

He thanked me again as he left, and I thought to myself that I owed Ernesto a larger debt of gratitude. He had taught me a powerful lesson about humility and courage. I smiled as I watched him pass my window and disappear into the humid Texas night.

Both Acevedo and Ernesto deployed to Iraq for almost a full year, beginning in the fall of 2004, and both men returned alive and well.

PURPLE-HEARTED
Personal Narrative
Staff Sergeant Jack Lewis

The admiration that troops often express for one another cuts across race, ethnicity, religion, gender, and socioeconomic backgrounds. And generations. "Although I am, in fact, the same age as my driver's dad (which is to say precisely twice my driver's age)," U.S. Army Reserve Staff Sergeant Jack Lewis wrote in a December 2004 e-mail home about why he wanted to go to Iraq, "a country that sends only its young to war deserves to lose both its young, and its wars. Each one of us bears responsibility for every last soldier; this is my small contribution: to take care of the two kids on my little team." Several weeks later, and only days before the historic January 2005 elections in Iraq, Lewis wrote a story about one of these "kids," Specialist Joshua Yuse (pronounced yoo-see), a twenty-one-year-old soldier who provided Lewis with no end of grief—and pride. (The castle that Lewis alludes to is a thirteenth-century Ottoman building in Tall 'Afar being used as a police garrison.)

He's young enough to be my son. Annoying enough, too.

When I beat on his hooch door this morning to get him up for a mission, he was his typical floppy-jointed, addle-headed, eye-rolling self. It was pouring rain, I was standing out in the middle of it wearing PT shorts and a raincoat, and I was losing patience: "Get up, time to move. You're going down with Apache."

Long groan—but he had known what the mission was since last night.

"Quit your bitchin', Yuse," I told him. "You're lucky as hell—you get to hang out at the castle, and I have to ride the hatch in this shit."

Yuse was headed downtown to broadcast over the LRAD, i.e., long range acoustic device, a gizmo originally designed to warn boaters away from the exclusion zone surrounding naval vessels, while I was going to charge around town in one of Charger Troop's Stryker armored vehicles, broadcasting pro-election messages, prerecorded in Arabic, from a manpack loudspeaker system.

"Yeah . . . I guess," he said, rubbing the back of his head, sullen as a teenager, which, at twenty-one, he practically is.

"Be at the office no later than zero-seven-thirty," I told him before throwing on a uniform and four hundred bucks' worth of raingear to go there myself.

I was closing in on a peak experience of blood pressure when he slouched through the door at 0729.

"I took the trailer off."

"Oh," I said, surprised at his initiative. "How we doin' on fuel?"

"I filled it last night."

"All right, let's get your pack together."

"I already got it, sergeant—it's ready to go."

"Damn, Yuse. I hardly know you!"

Goofy grin from him. "I do what I can, sar'nt."

I dropped him down at Apache's hangar, ran to the chow hall to get him a box breakfast, and off he went into Tall 'Afar.

But I never went out on my mission. After I put together a briefing memo for the squadron commander and walked it over to the TOC, I ran into the battle captain, CPT Murphy.

He said, "Oh. It's good you're here. Yuse's your guy, right? We got a report he was shot in the neck—"

"WHAT?"

"—but apparently he was wounded in the hand. A fragment hit him in the chin, and it bled all over, and they thought he had a neck wound."

"Mortars or small arms?"

"We don't know yet."

"Are they bringing him in now?"

"We don't know yet."

I went to the aid station to wait. Yuse couldn't be evac'd immediately because all available combat power needed to stay on-site and fight. Then, after Apache's company commander rolled his own vehicle out to the castle to pick up my soldier, they hit an IED on the return trip.

Everything takes too long. It took twenty minutes for Apache 66 to move from the front gate across the FOB to the aid station, because a convoy of civilian fuel tankers was plugging up the roads. When A66 finally rolled in and dropped ramp, my kid soldier was sitting inside, holding up a bloody bulb of gauze the size of his head. He looked mighty uncomfortable.

The first words out of his mouth were "I'm all right, sergeant."

It seems that Yuse was running the LRAD when the castle came under fire, as it usually does when that bullet magnet is in operation. He put down his MP3, picked up his rifle, and took up a security position along the battlements. When the sniper found him, the neck-aimed bullet hit him in his forward hand, bounced off his rifle, and dug into his armored vest with a heavyweight punch. A fragment of the bullet jacket flew up and cut his chin to the bone. Infantry and commo soldiers gave him buddy aid. He wheezed pretty hard, but he stayed alert and responsive. And he never complained.

What Yuse did do, after he was shot: He trained up a commo sergeant on how to run the LRAD, so that while he waited for evac, he could keep his mission going. He secured, or caused to be secured, all of his sensitive items and equipment. He marveled at the bullet they dug out of his vest. He told everybody not to worry about him, and reminded them to keep their heads down.

Everything takes too long. At the aid station, one X-ray salvo wasn't enough; they had to go two rounds with that. The sleep-deprived lab tech who tried to start Yuse's IV failed five times on his right arm before someone else took it away and plugged it in properly, upstream of his bleeding left paw.

Through all that, nothing but some wincing and the occasional "Oww."

And this comment: "I'll tell you one thing. These elections better work. They better get democracy, and freedom, and their rights, and hot chicks in tight jeans. I hope I didn't take this bullet for nothing."

Specialist Josh Yuse was treated, given a bit of morphine, and then evac'd to the 67th Combat Support Hospital by a UH-60 Black Hawk helo.

I made sure he had his IBA with the souvenir slug in one pocket, along with his helmet, coat, and the bloody shirt with his name on it. They can wash it out at the hospital. They do it all the time.

I held on to his weapon, which caught the bullet as it exited through the meat of Yuse's left thumb. That weapon is NMC (non–mission capable) and irreparable; it won't ever cycle again without the bottom half of it being replaced.

I stood and watched him lift off, saluting Yuse in my way. I doubt he noticed. He was trying not to drop his IV bag, which sounds like a simple thing until you try it while juiced to the gills on morphine and battling the shaky shock of adrenaline withdrawal.

I'll miss Yuse here, and not just for the work he does, which is plenty if I remind him often enough. I'll miss his pulling dumb stunts, working so hard at *not* working that it exhausts him just to think about it, dropping to do push-ups just because I gave him a hard look, teaching me how to play Yahtzee (then beating the crap out of me), and schooling me at Ping-Pong until he gets impatient and starts hitting the ball too hard to spin it down onto the table.

He's a near-total dingbat with no sense of planning who still manages to get things done. A lazy sloth who works like a sled dog. A good kid with bad manners. A graceful athlete who trips over his own size twelves. This is the overgrown boy I have to kick out of the rack every morning, remind him to check the oil, bring his gloves on mission, and shower periodically.

Mostly, he's just too much of a goofy kid for me to have expected him to take this like a man.

Yuse didn't want to be deployed to Iraq. He wanted to chase women around Seattle, and go to college and find out what he wants to be. He wanted to play video games, drink beer, and buy a Mustang.

Guys my age are supposed to gripe about how kids today are letting the world go to hell in a handbasket, how there aren't any standards for behavior anymore. After all, we've taken such good care of things.

Maybe it's because guys my age usually work with guys my age. Guys Yuse's age are just parts for the big machine in civilian life: laborers, clerks, apprentices. Yuse went from busboy to combat soldier. Now he's WIA, and he doesn't even have the good sense to snivel about it.

He was subsequently evac'd to 67th CSH for surgery, then on to Landstuhl. As they loaded him onto the C-130, he was fretting about letting down my team and our detachment by flying out to Germany.

I don't want to hear any more about the passing of "The Greatest Generation." Ain't no generation better than his. Specialist Yuse didn't just take it like a man. He took it like his brothers across the generations, and earned his flagon of mead at Valhalla or at least his pint of Bud at the local VFW.

He took it like a soldier.

*After having surgery in Landstuhl, Germany, Yuse was sent back to the
United States to be treated at the military hospital in Fort Bragg, North
Carolina. Lewis returned to Washington in June 2005 after serving for al-
most ten months in Iraq. He and Yuse still keep in touch.*

BROTHERHOOD

Poem

Sergeant Dena Price Van den Bosch

*On August 5, 2003, thirty-two-year-old Sergeant Dena Price Van den Bosch
was waiting for a convoy with a group of GIs in 125-degree heat at an air
base in Doha, Qatar. Van den Bosch was serving with a military intelligence task force, and the others soldiers, although all part of the 10th
Mountain Division, were from various other units—infantry, transportation, signals, artillery—and barely knew one another. And yet, Van den
Bosch believed, the very fact they were all soldiers meant that they shared a
bond only fellow servicemen and women could truly understand.*

these same faces . . .

who share smokes
out of collective boredom

while offering
their own version of
sympathy
to stories of
unfaithful wives
over another game of Spades
will plot with
eager efficiency
to catch the mice
which terrorize their tent

transforming the moments
into something
almost bearable

these same faces . . .

may someday
crawl one hundred meters
under fire
to reach their brother
with no guarantee
they'll return

and people
wonder why

CHAPTER FOUR

WORLDS APART

LIFE ON THE HOME FRONT

PFC Noah Pincusoff, as a boy in 1992 wearing his father's Vietnam War helmet. *Photo by James Lois; used by permission.*

Dearest Son,

I don't know where to begin this first letter to you. I am so conflicted on your departure. On the one hand, I know you have trained very hard for this—everything you have done for the past 15 months was leading to this day. I know that you want and need to be there for your brothers. Not something I will ever fully understand or appreciate because I have never been or will ever go to war. So that intensifies my fears. Dad understands and fears all the more for you.

And he and I are indescribably proud of you for all you have endured and achieved. I know at times you don't understand why people thank you for your service, but I think someday you will. More than pride, however, is our love for you. You are the single most precious thing in our lives (as is each of our children). So, of course, we have spent our lives leading you, teaching you and protecting you. These fuel our fear. We have faith in you, your abilities, your skills—but there is nothing you can say or do that will alleviate that fear—a parent's fear—until you are home with us again.

I know that you will, in the next year or so, experience many, many things you have only heard about or imagined (and about which I am already having nightmares!). I believe your Dad and I love you more than you will ever know . . . but I also know we get that back from you ten-fold. Keep your eyes open and your head and ass down!

> All my love—always . . . until we are together again.
> Mom

—Carla Meyer Lois, writing to her nineteen-year-old son, Private First Class Noah Pincusoff, on January 16, 2005, the day before he deployed to Iraq. Seven months later, Pincusoff suffered severe neck and spinal injuries, as well as shrapnel wounds, from a car-bomb attack on the outskirts of Ramadi. After coming home to recuperate, he returned to active duty.

THE LIFE WE USED TO LIVE
E-mail
Kari Apted

"I miss you already and you're not even gone," Kari Apted lamented in a March 2003 letter to her husband, Sergeant Donnie Apted, as he was preparing to head to Iraq with the 878th Engineer Battalion, Georgia Army National Guard. Despite a two-hour drive each way, Donnie came home every night after training for ten hours with his unit in Augusta so that he could spend as much time as possible with Kari and their two sons, Zachary and Elias. "I'm glad you are still here," she wrote, "but in a way, it's hard. It's hard knowing you are so close by, yet so far away. I guess this time is allowing us to sort of wean ourselves from each other." No matter how much spouses on the home front brace themselves for the separation, many find that nothing can prepare them for how all-encompassing the sense of loss— emotionally, spiritually, and physically—can be. When Sergeant Apted left for Iraq in March 2003, no one knew how long the war would last. By that summer, however, it was clear that the fighting would be more protracted than expected. In early September, Kari Apted sent the following e-mail to her husband, who was stationed at the Tallil Air Base near An Nasiriyah.

My Dearest Donnie,

Man, I miss you. I seriously don't think a minute has passed since you left that a thought of you hasn't crossed my mind. I miss you, I miss us, I miss everything about the life we used to live together. I know that we are still together in spirit, but I miss the physical reality of you.

I know it sounds crazy, but I just now finished doing the last load of laundry in your clothes hamper. Four months after you left, I am finally wrapping up your laundry! I just couldn't bear to wash clean the last things I have that you touched. Or rather, that touched you. It has been so long since I've seen your things mixed in with mine. It was like every shirt of yours stood out like a red flag among the usual mix of my and the boys' clothing. I felt a tug in my heart with each piece I pulled from the dryer, and held a shirt or two to my chest as I folded them. I buried my face in the cloth, wishing your scent had remained but knowing it wouldn't have.

Did you know that your scent is still inside your armoire, though? As I opened it to put your clothes away, the familiar fragrance of wood and of you was so strong . . . it made my heart ache anew as I put away the last laundry I'll do for you for a very long time. It is so very lonely here without you. Yet it feels like I am never alone. Between the boys and our friends, I stay pretty busy. But as I know you are experiencing as well, you can feel totally alone even in the largest crowd. Sometimes I feel even more alone in those moments than in times that I truly am alone.

But what can we do, except keep plugging along, doing what we have to do, to get us to that wonderful day that we are back together again? It is so hard to resolve myself to that; that the best-laid plans I had for this year were all blown to bits by the plan that someone else had for us; leaving us with absolutely no choice but to submit to a situation we opposed with every ounce of our beings.

The struggle between my will and our reality has never been more apparent or more challenging than it has been this year. I want my family back together again. I want my soul mate by my side. I want to take you shopping with me, watch you bathe our sons, rub your back at the end of a hard day, and make love to you all night long. I want my life back, not this artificial, contrived happiness and acceptance that I have to conjure up daily, hourly, and force myself to believe. It's really not ok that you are gone. I am not complete without you here with me.

Everyone says to let God fill the newly empty places inside me and I try so hard to let him. But a nebulous concept like the presence of God doesn't fix the car when it breaks, doesn't hold sick children at 3:00 a.m. who miss their daddy, doesn't kiss the soft part of my neck when it literally aches for the touch of your lips. And there are those who would accuse me of being irreverent by saying that. I feel that the God I know understands what I'm trying to say. I think He understands the weariness I feel as I struggle to use Him as glue to hold everything together that you used to carry effortlessly for me. . . .

Trying to live in the "here and now" is so hard. I can't seem to help wishing the time away. Each time a Monday arrives and it feels like it came around again quickly, a little part of my soul leaps with joy as I think, "YES! Another week down!" and I want every week to pass as fast, or even faster. I tell myself platitudes like, enjoy the moment, seize the day, and I try, I really do try to be aware of the here and now and make the most of it. But the present time is so lonely and empty when devoid of your presence, that I cannot help anticipating with every part of my being the day that we are together again. I'm ready to stop missing you, and start living with you again. If it could begin in this moment, I could not be happier. But for whatever reason, we wait, and wait and have to wait some more.

Just know that I miss you, every part of you, and these ramblings are a poor attempt to express to you how much. I pray so hard that you are home soon.

Sending big hugs and soft kisses, as always . . .

Kari

Sergeant Donnie Apted returned to his family in May 2004 after a fifteen-month deployment.

TOO MUCH REALITY
Letter
Pamela J. Clemens

Before Operation Desert Storm in January 1991, when the opening air strike against Baghdad was captured live on television, it could take anywhere from a few days to more than a year before combat images from a war were shown on the home front. The ground invasion of Operation Iraqi Freedom was the first such assault ever broadcast in real time, and for the loved ones of troops watching at home, the experience was agonizing. When U.S. Army Staff Sergeant Jason R. Clemens embarked for Iraq in February 2003 with the 54th Engineer Battalion, 130th Engineer Brigade, his wife, Pam, found it nerve-racking to follow the news. But she also found it impossible to ignore. On March 23, 2003, Clemens wrote a letter to her husband the day after seeing one particularly horrendous update.

Jason, I miss you so much!!!

Please forgive me, as I need to tell you about yesterday. I pray with all my heart that this does not upset you, but I need to tell you. Yesterday was the worst day of my life. The TV reported that there were POW's and then all of a sudden the reporter said that they had come from a maintenance unit that was traveling with the 3rd ID and took a wrong turn and was all of a sudden staring down the barrel of an Iraqi tank.

He said that they were showing a tape of the POW's being interrogated on Iraq state-run TV and being played on Aljazeera. Then he said that they showed a room full of bodies that appeared to have been shot in the forehead. I thought I was going to die. I thought it was you. I was so scared. I did not know what to do, what to think. I just stood there not knowing what to do. Jason, it was horrible. I was so scared. I can't even begin to describe what I felt to you in words. My whole body was screaming on the inside. I don't ever want to relive those feelings again. It was awful.

Then the phone rang and it was your dad. Jason, he broke down on the phone. We both sat on the phone and cried, neither of us knowing if it was you or not. He kept asking me if anyone had contacted me. I did my best to reassure him that no one had come to the house to tell me anything. I think that was the only comfort we had. Your mom was on her way back from the coast and I was worried for him, but we cried and talked and by the time we hung up, he seemed to be better. He loves you so much. . . .

I took Jake for a walk and cried the whole time. I just don't know what I would do if anything happened to you. When I got back from the walk, I was pouring the dog food into the bin when the phone rang. I answered it and the person on the other end hung up. I was scared that it was someone calling to see if I was home so they could come tell me that you were a POW. Well I went back to pouring the dog food and since I cut the bag at an angle, it spilled all over the floor. I was bent down picking up the food and I began to cry. Then the phone rang again. As I was getting up, I banged my head on the corner of the cabinet.

I answered the phone and it was my dad. Jason I broke down like a baby. I think my dad must have seen the news too as he kept assuring me that it was not you who was captured. He just let me cry and told me everything was going to be okay. He promised. I felt better after I had cried to him and he let me cry just like when I was growing up and needed to cry to my daddy. Migi came over after that phone call and would not let me cry for the rest of the night. I had went earlier yesterday and bought three new DVD's. I am sorry to buy so many, but I just can't watch the TV. I am so sorry, but it is just too hard for me. I watch some, but the majority of it, I just can't take. It is too much reality for me. . . .

I was watching Tom Brokaw right before I was going to go to bed when he said that the maintenance unit came from the 3rd ID 507th out of Ft. Bliss TX. They even have an African American female. Jason, I can't tell you what went through my mind. I was so relieved, but my chest still hurt for the families of those who were captured. I feel so guilty because I was glad it was not you. I immediately called your dad and your mom answered the phone. I was so glad she was there. She said that your dad was doing a bit better. I told them what I had heard and they were relieved.

We kept talking and they said that they found comfort talking to me since we were all in this together. Then your dad got on the phone and said he was sorry if he upset me and I told him that he could call me anytime day or night, as I would do the same for them. Then he told me he loved me and to come and see them. When your mom got back on the phone, she told me that people forget to say the things they should say and she told me that she loved me and that I was a good daughter-in-law and she was glad I was married to you. I was so touched and did not know what to say. I was glad when she broke the emotion by saying that when she was talking to your dad that they both agreed that they were glad that you were not married to anyone else. That helped to lighten the mood. I told them I loved them too and that I was also glad that you weren't married to anyone else either. . . .

I will write more later and fill in the gaps in this letter that I forgot to write. Love You!

Staff Sergeant Jason Clemens returned to Pam in December 2003.

BUZZ SAW

Poem

Billie Hill-Hunt

Some spouses go to creative lengths to ease the pain of separation. A month before Billie Hill-Hunt's husband, U.S. Army Specialist Corey T. Hunt, left for Iraq in January 2005, she secretly made an audiotape of him sleeping.

> I used to say
> "You are cutting down an entire forest with your snoring."
> Now without it
> Bedtime seems boring
>
> I recorded you
> The last time you were here

Call me crazy
But I play it from time to time
Just to keep you near

Specialist Hunt returned to Billie in December 2005, and while she is thrilled to have her husband home, she now finds his snoring annoying once again.

ALBUM
Personal Narrative
Kathleen Furin

Spouses and parents are not alone in their heartache when a soldier, Marine, airman, or sailor embarks for Iraq or Afghanistan; siblings, too, worry about their brother or sister heading into harm's way. In January 2005, Kathleen Furin watched as her younger brother, a U.S. Army captain, left their home in Pennsylvania to fight in a war she did not support. His deployment—and the photo album she often looked through to remind her of the times they had been together—prompted Furin to write the following account while he was gone.

We are flipping through photos one evening, my daughter Aya and I, something she loves to do lately. A friend who is a teacher tells me how children learn about the world; first themselves, their own bodies; then their families, their neighborhood; later the larger city, state, country, world. I show her Iraq on the globe. "It's a far way, Mama," Aya says, "almost as far as you can get." "It is, baby," I say. I don't know what Iraq means to her; she knows only that her uncle, my younger brother, is working there for a while. I know through my travels that no place has meaning until you experience it, its sounds, its smells, the quality of light, the way people's faces express emotion. She goes back to the album, studying the pictures with a look of contentment.

In this one you are leaning away from the others, from us, as if you have already left. Of course at that time we could never have imagined a life without you. Not on this day, even though you are in your dress blues. Today is a happy occasion, a baptism, a welcoming into family of a sweet new little soul—your daughter, Lilly.

Although the gathering is because of her, in this one you can barely see her. She is swaddled in blankets, despite the summer heat, and tucked carefully into Kim's arms. I am next to Kim, smiling broadly, one arm around her. It strikes me, looking back at this photo, that I didn't know how close we would become, how the events of the world would shape our own lives, how 9/11 would change everything.

We were afraid that you would be sent then. I worried for you even though we still weren't close, not close in any real way. I loved you through loving your family: your wife, your daughter, later your son. We had always had our differences, and I remember thinking you were a total asshole because you stopped getting pizza from our usual place; it was owned by Arabs. "A-rabs," as you would say. For some reason you developed a strong hick accent in the military. "It's probably a sleeper cell," you'd say, and sometimes I would almost believe you. Maybe military people knew more than regular people, at least about things like that.

But then I would remember how the delivery guy had hugged my husband, given us our pizza free when he saw the pink stork and drooping balloons after Aya's birth. A few weeks after 9/11 they changed their pizza boxes so they had huge American flags and the words "God Bless America" on them. I preferred their old boxes, the ones that said "We use only the finest ingredients." But you only ate Sal's pizza then, and you *guaranteed* me that there would definitely be another terrorist attack on U.S. soil, which did nothing to ease my fears. You have this way of speaking, probably honed in the military, as if you are the absolute authority on any subject. "But what if you have to go over there?" I asked—there, at that time, being Afghanistan. "You can't leave Lilly," I said. But you shrugged, the perfect American soldier, bound to do his duty no matter what. "If I go, I go," you said. "Just tell Lilly how much I loved her. Make sure she knows I was a good dad." I could do that, I thought, if the worst happened, I could do that.

In this photograph the girls are all excitement, sweet summer dresses, grinning and fighting over the new baby. Aya holds him; you can't see her face as she gazes down at him. She is dwarfed by the pink of the hospital chair, a chair not made for children. Lilly wraps loose limbs around her, looks up, grins. Your son, A.C., is a big baby, but in these he is overshadowed

by the girls. I think he will always be overshadowed by the girls, especially
after my own new daughter, Chaundra, is born three months later.

In this one you are standing with Kim, one arm around her, formal. By
then I loved Kim like a sister, loved her quiet strength, her humor, her devo-
tion to the kids. But I hated that she wouldn't stand up to you. She wanted
you to make a DVD of yourself reading to the kids before you left. She
wanted a piece of you, something to show them when they asked about
Daddy. But you refused. "I'm not making a death video," you said. I saw her
tears that she tried to keep in, saw her tight, tense jaw. So I pulled Mom and
Dad into it, which maybe wasn't fair. But that's your wife and kids that you're
leaving for God knows how long. In the end you did it. I haven't watched it,
but I can imagine how you look: loving, reassuring, tight triangles of stress at
the edges of your lips, triangles that only the adults can see.

I started having war dreams about a month before you left. Constant,
vivid nightmares; the baby would wake me up to nurse and I would fall right
back into the same dream. Bombs, bodies, body parts, dead children. In some
ways the anticipation was worse than the leaving. We lie to Lilly and Aya; you
have a job that requires you to be far away for a long time. How old are kids
when they learn about bombs, guns, war? Are we wrong for wanting to protect them from the knowledge of these things?

And what do we do now, other than wait? I was vehemently opposed to
the war in Iraq, still think it was a huge mistake. I can't watch the news, and
when it comes up on AOL or whatever, one hundred dead in car bomb in
Baghdad, I can't read it. I just shut my eyes and hope. What frightens me is
that I feel like I'm not the only one who is not paying attention. I remember
hearing Grandma talk about World War II, how hard it was, how much everyone was willing to sacrifice. Grandma told me about folding foil up into little
balls, getting ration tickets for butter and meat and gasoline; nothing was
wasted. I was too little to remember Vietnam, but it seems as if it was huge in
the consciousness of the nation. People were watching their TVs every night,
following each and every battle. The depth of the protests, the unrest; it spoke
volumes about people's engagement with the war, with their country. This
war hasn't *gripped* us, hasn't absorbed us like the other conflicts did.

Recently, I went to the protests. When the one-thousandth soldier was
killed in Iraq we took the girls to the candlelight vigil. We were interviewed
by a news team. "It's not just the one thousand American soldiers who have

died," I said. "It's all the Iraqis as well. This is about everyone who has suffered." Then I speak of you, my connection to the war, and I begin to cry. Of course this is what they show later on the eleven o'clock news, me crying.

I don't know many others who are touched personally, and this is what bothers me. We are at war. We are spending inordinate amounts of our resources, yet we are not being asked to conserve, to cut back, here at home. The forty-five-million-dollar inaugural ball went on as scheduled. The Oscars, the Super Bowl; we are a country out of touch. It is this, I fear, this lack of consciousness, this unwillingness to see the ugly things, to make the hard choices; this will destroy us faster than any terrorist could. I want some kind of recognition; hey, our people are dying over there. Our national dialogue should be loud and inflamed, we should be working day and night to figure out a way to handle this mess, not tuning in to *American Idol*.

I have gotten only two e-mails from you. It blows my mind that I can receive your e-mails, you, in the middle of a war zone, on a base in one of Saddam's old palaces. They were group e-mails, to all of us in the family; somewhat cheerful, describing your residence, the weather. When I asked Kim why we haven't heard from you, she says you can't always get online, but I know that's not true, because you pop up sometimes on my buddy list. You must have your reasons for wanting this distance. What would I do if I were there, in your position? Would I want to be reminded of my old life or would I just focus every little piece of my being on getting through the next moment, the next day, making it home as whole as I could be?

I picture what you are doing as a kind of death, a folding in of the soul, so that only the essential, survivalist parts peek out from thick cloth that hides everything else. A friend whose brother just came back described it—being there, the whole experience—as a suffocation. "He was stuck in a building most of the time and now he can't even go to the grocery store," she says. "The frickin' grocery store scares him speechless. It *overwhelms* him." She sighs. How do you come back from that, start chipping away at your life again?

And what if you don't come back at all? When I allow myself to imagine the unimaginable, I think of a life without you. I imagine that your absence would fill even greater spaces than your presence. Your death is like a TV screen at three a.m., all gray and white and static. Quiet, really, but disturbing nonetheless, something that jolts us all awake.

Here are the pictures of our last holiday together. Lilly and Aya look like two little flowers about to bloom, their bright faces upturned, towards the sun.

They are wearing identical outfits like they insist on and each is wearing one of her own shoes and one of the other's. Their arms are wrapped tight around each other; Aya's curls boing up and away, Lilly's golden hair falls over both of their shoulders. They remind me of two strong trees. In the next one Chaundra is curled in the middle of them, a wild look on her face. All three are laughing, all in red and black and patent leather for Christmas.

In this photograph you are laughing, head tilted back just a little, warmth in your eyes. Is this the one we will treasure, the one that will be passed down generation to generation? You are the keeper of the family lore; it is you who know all the cousins and second cousins and who doesn't talk to who and why. You have all the old photographs, the ones of Grandma Lola and Papa, of great-grandparents and uncles and everybody else. In this one Grandma Lola sits just so, Papa's hand on her shoulder. You cannot tell that they have known each other since childhood, loved each other almost as long. Is this what they dreamed of? That they would bear a son would who bear a son who would be sent to fight and maybe die in a country they have never even heard of? You always envision a better future for your children; otherwise, why have them? You don't envision death in a desert: bloody, gory, loud.

A friend suggested that I give you something before you go, something spiritual, something sentimental, and at first I rejected the idea. I'd already given you something practical; the Leatherman Super Tool 200, which just made me cringe, knowing why you needed it, knowing where you'd be. "Not a knife, Kathy," she said. "Something *real*." "He'd laugh at me," I said, but the idea stayed with me. It gave me a kind of power, that I could offer you a small gift and you would know how much I cared. In fact, I began to realize that expression of love is the only true power there is.

So I did it. I bought a small green crystal. I don't know why I chose green; perhaps it reminded me of the earth, it reminded me of a feeling of safety. I waited until late one night to shove it into your hand. "Here," I said. "Take this with you, it's small enough." You had had a beer or two and the feeling was warm, light. You laughed, but it was a kind laugh, and I could tell that you appreciated it even if you didn't understand it. I could tell that I had done the right thing.

"Kim gave me a cross blessed by the Pope, Mom gave me a rosary, and now this," you said.

"Well, shit, if all that doesn't keep you safe I don't know what will," I joked.

I would not cry. I did not cry. We went back to watching the movie we'd rented and I stopped thinking about what the future would hold, if, when I would see you again. One by one we peeled ourselves off the couch, tumbled into beds or sleeping bags throughout the house, so that I was alone, startled by loud static at four a.m. I turned off the TV and crawled onto the air mattress. I listened to everybody breathing around me; in, out, in, out. Aya moaned a little in her sleep then rolled away, one chubby arm flung over her smooth eyebrow. How many breaths would you be away?

In, out, in, the most basic physiological function, what keeps us together. I fell asleep counting breaths instead of sheep, counting the minutes hours days until we could stop holding ours and have you with us, here, safe again. In, out, in. Safely now, almost there, one breath at a time.

Furin's brother returned to the States in January 2006.

TO COLONEL LISAGOR
Poem
Sara Lisagor

More than one third of the troops in Iraq and Afghanistan are "civilian soldiers"—members of the National Guard or reserve who, in many cases, have families and full-time jobs but can be called up for long periods of time if there is a war or national emergency. Most are in their early to mid-thirties. Dr. Philip Lisagor was fifty-eight when he left his wife, their two daughters, Sara and Jessica, and their home in Nevada to serve as deputy commander for clinical services of the U.S. Army's Second Medical Brigade in Iraq. Colonel Lisagor's almost seven-month tour of duty began in June 2004 and his responsibilities included everything from overseeing the creation of field hospitals (which meant he had to travel frequently through dangerous regions of Iraq) to performing trauma surgeries. Lisagor and his daughter Sara had actually become somewhat distant while she was in college, but after he deployed overseas, Sara developed a greater appreciation for the sacrifices he was making. In the fall of 2004, she wrote the following poem for her father.

Dirt, road salt, snow and oil
smother the underbelly of our
dinosaur Suburban. Daisy
paws her ball under the steel
carcass one more time. Shit.
The frost gnaws through
the knees of my jeans
while I jab with a shovel
at the tooth-rotten toy
that soaks in a soup of slush
between mud-drenched hubcaps
on the snow tires you bought.
I see you, eleven hours
away, hunched over just like me.
You curse under your breath,
scanning beneath your Humvee
for traces of a car bomb.

In December 2004, Colonel Lisagor returned home and went back to his job as the chairman of surgery at the Veterans Administration Hospital in Reno, Nevada.

DOWN THE ROAD
Personal Narrative
Anne Miren Berry

Focusing on the future helps many family members on the home front cope with the anxiety of waiting for a loved one serving abroad. They often visualize and plan for everything from the joyful "Welcome Back!" celebration to larger, more long-term matters such as whether or not they will move to a new town or city, have (more) children, further their education, or start a different career. Anne Miren Berry and her husband, Lieutenant Colonel Joel Berry, were living in North Carolina when he was shipped off to Iraq for six months in January 2003 — three months before the invasion began —

with the 2nd Marine Expeditionary Brigade, 1st Marine Expeditionary
Force. During her husband's deployment, Berry looked for coastal property
where she and Joel would build their retirement house one day. In the fol-
lowing piece, Berry reflects on the life that she envisioned the two of them
sharing once he came home—and the jarring realization that, in the con-
text of a war, even the hope of having such dreams can often seem futile.

I didn't have a box for that first care package. All I had was a jumble of baby
wipes, Gatorade bottles, and a Valentine's Day card, which was hard to
find in early January, but the package could take weeks to reach my Joel, who
was steaming on a ship toward the Middle East. I knew exactly where he was
going, and so did everybody else, but the official word we families had was
that his ship would be standing by in the Arabian Gulf.

I didn't wait to send a care package, because I couldn't stand the thought
of Joel unable to bathe under a fierce sun and sinking into the relentless itch-
ing, thick, filth of his cammies. I worried that he would be thirsty, lips cracking and throat ragged, but have nothing he actually enjoyed drinking. I knew
that regardless of the timeless, day-in and day-out rhythm of war, he would
pause on February 14 and wonder why I hadn't sent a sentimental card.

So I stood in the post office line, watching the backs of people's heads as
they muttered and sighed. After twenty minutes, I stepped out of that line and
drove a few blocks to the Mail It store.

There was a chime on the door, but I didn't need it to announce my entrance. The Mail It shop was empty except for the woman behind the
counter, tan and sturdy and with curly brown hair in a bouffant bubble. She
looked at my bag.

"You're gonna need a number nine for that," she said, sizing me up. I
dumped my bag on the counter as she plucked a flat box off the shelf.
"Where's this going, sugar?"

I wasn't sure, exactly, how the mail would make it to his ship, when its location changed with every knot left in its wake, but I dug around my purse for
the scrap paper with the address he'd left me. I flattened it on the counter, a
mess of numbers that made no sense. The only human touch was Joel's full
name and rank, a lieutenant colonel in the U.S. Marine Corps.

"Oh, you poor thing," the Mail It lady said, lining the box with crumpled
newspaper. "You'll need to fill out a customs form, just tell 'em what you're

sending. Only don't write down the coffee, they don't like to see that. They'll open this box as sure as I'm standin' here."

"What about these?" My voice rose as I pulled out a pack of photographs. "These have no value. I don't know what to write on the form."

"Now, sugar, don't worry," the Mail It lady said, putting a wrinkled hand over mine. Her fingernails were a cotton candy pink. I read the name pinned to her green polo shirt.

"It's just—well, these pictures, Sandy, I took them last week," I babbled. "I took pictures of the waterfront property we're going to buy when he gets back." Sandy's was the first kind face I'd seen all day, and I had the urge to run behind the counter and lay my head on her shoulder and have her stroke my hair.

"Let's see what we've got here," Sandy said, prying open the sleeve of prints. "Aren't these pretty."

They were landscapes, void of all people except for a man in the back corner of one shot. I told her that was Esley Brown, the first realtor who'd returned my call.

His office was in Oriental, a sleepy waterside resort town at the far end of a country road.

I got lost driving to his office, so it was nearly lunchtime when I first met him. I shook his hand and passed him a carton of fried chicken. It was a breezy January day, but I also brought iced sodas.

"Well, isn't this a hoot!" he said, steering his car with one hand while waving drumsticks with the other, pointing out the marina and the restaurants and the schools. "You have kids?" he asked.

"No," I said, not knowing how to explain that, although I was thirty-five years old and had been married nearly a decade, Joel and I couldn't commit to a baby. We sometimes played roulette in the dark, exuberantly taking up the dare, but really it was something we kept postponing. Even Joel's deployment for war didn't make us want to try harder.

"I won't be here if you freak out," Joel had told me.

"Maybe we should try, just in case," I'd said, and the "in case" immediately soured on my tongue, because I always felt he was coming back to me. He'd come back, and life would be good again; better, in fact, because Esley Brown was going to find for me a dream property on the Pamlico Sound, and that's a future I saw clearly, Joel and me and a house overlooking the water.

I would be a history professor with slack hours and an office in our sunroom. I'd grade exams and watch Joel sit on the dock with a fishing pole, and he'd wave to me whenever he got a bite. Our house would be white, or maybe it would be brick, and it would for sure have a wraparound porch, and we'd entertain family in the summer with barbecues and poolside picnics. His parents and my parents would drive down together and argue over who got which guest room, but it wouldn't matter because each would have a suite with its own bathroom and a view of the water. And while I was baking biscuits and tossing German potato salad, Joel would hug me from behind, and we'd fit together with warm perfection.

Sometimes there was a little girl in our picture; never a baby or older than a toddler, but sometimes she didn't exist either.

"How much can you spend?" Esley Brown had asked me. I told him about Joel's war pay, which wouldn't be taxed and which, if I saved it carefully, would be enough for a down payment on some fine waterside Carolina dirt.

Esley Brown winked and stepped on the gas, hurtling down gravel roads to raw neighborhoods, tracts of land marked off with tiny red flags, some with signs that read SOLD or UNDER CONTRACT and next to sweeping views of the wide-open Pamlico Sound. Those prices stunned me, much more than we could afford, even if all we ever did was park a trailer on that waterfront.

So Esley Brown downshifted, driving me to property along the less expansive Intracoastal Waterway, and that's when I took out the camera. I stepped to the back of the property line for the wide angle and then walked to the edge and snapped the waterline.

Esley Brown watched me and smoked. Even these lots were overpriced, and bigger than our budget allowed, but just barely.

As the bucket of chicken emptied, Esley Brown took me to pockets of marsh property, tiny lots that were cut into weird angles with only a foot or two along the waterfront, or that had a half mile of wetlands to be crossed. I reluctantly took pictures here, as Esley Brown remarked that these lots flooded during hurricanes—we could be trapped for days—but these were the properties we could definitely afford, or at least we could once six months' hazardous duty pay made it into our bank account. Six months. That's what I was counting on, though Joel had told me not to count on anything.

"We don't even know if there will be a war," Joel had said, though I knew he didn't really mean that, not with the posturing and threats and deadlines to meet.

"Before he left, we promised to think of each other every day, at the same time," I told Sandy as she fit the photos into the box and began to bind it shut. "Do you know what the time difference is over there?"

She looked at me. "Eight hours. My son is there, too."

I promised to ask Joel if he knew Sandy's son, Corporal Tom, whenever we spoke next, but I lied. I would get only two phone calls in the month before Joel's ship pulled up to Kuwait, and each call was crackled and full of mysterious clicks and awful feedback that made it impossible to be spontaneous, our voices tripping over each other before he disappeared for good, in midsentence.

Sandy told me about her son. He was twenty years old and was born with so much thick black hair he'd needed his first haircut only a month later. Now in the U.S. Army, he shaved down to his scalp every other week.

He was tall and loved to tell jokes to make his mama blush. His favorite home-cooked meal was rib-eye steak on the grill, so when Sandy sent him care packages, her boxes were filled with next-best beef jerky and pepperoni sticks. She was working on a way to send him homemade biscuits.

"Mm boy, Mama, please send more," Corporal Tom wrote to her on the side of an MRE box, which told her he'd eaten Mexican rice that day.

I finally began getting letters, too; short messages in envelopes that had traces of Iraqi sand in them.

"Great!" Joel had underlined three times, about my pictures. Some wives sent their husbands photos of themselves, glamorous studio shots that overlooked their everyday crooked-buttoned shirts and worn-down fingernails. Sometimes soldiers got pictures of children taking a first step, or dogs with a new litter, but Joel liked mine very well.

He asked me for more details about the bridge-side property in Oriental, across from the marina, where he could see our lives unfold together, could see the rocking chairs, side by side on that front porch. If he saw our little girl, too, he never let me know.

He also didn't tell me about the things he saw on his ride to Baghdad. I watched the news while I packed each box, one eye on the sandstorms and ambushes and prisoners, ours and theirs; the children clamoring for candy as American tanks rumbled past.

"You might say this is the highlight of my military career," he wrote wryly. "Keep the pictures coming." So I did, color pages I ripped out of realtor websites and magazines.

Esley Brown called me one day to tell me that the bridge lot had gone off the market. The buyer had paid twenty-five thousand dollars over the asking price. He said he'd find me another property, and made me swear I would call him when Joel returned.

I didn't know when that would be, until the families were told to stop sending letters and boxes. Our Marines were coming home. I'd miss placing my tokens of love into that plain cardboard box, size No. 9, but soon I'd have the real thing in my arms.

Even without the care packages, I found a reason to go back to Mail It. I wanted them to print two banners, one for me and one for Joel's parents to wave on the day of his homecoming. I wanted OUR HERO and WELCOME HOME to be big enough to see from the helicopter as it neared the families.

I blew into the Mail It store, full of plans for the Saturday of Joel's return, but behind the counter stood another woman, a younger woman who looked politely but coolly at me.

"Where's Sandy?" I asked.

"Delaware," she said.

And that's when I knew.

Sandy was headed to Dover Air Force Base to meet the flag-draped casket of her only son, killed the week before, I would later learn, when his Hummer came under enemy fire. Corporal Tom and three other soldiers died that day.

I returned to Mail It to pick up my banners, but Sandy wasn't coming back. She was moving, the new woman told me, going to live with her daughter in Florida.

I foolishly clutched the banner poles. How could I have presumed a happy ending for any of us? Why hadn't I been more aware that my story could have ended just as badly as Sandy's?

I wondered how we had handled the silence in our homes, waiting for our lives to resume, hoping when they did that they would somehow be the same as we remembered. I wondered how any of us had let these men go.

After leaving Mail It with my banners, I came home to a message from Esley Brown. His voice was excited for me. He'd found property he was sure we'd like, but I'd have to come right away and see for myself.

I stared at the answering machine, its light no longer blinking. I deleted his message that day, and the one he left me the following week. I swept the real estate brochures into the trash. I kept my copies of the pictures in an envelope inside the third drawer of my rolltop desk, under the take-out menus, just in case.

Joel did come back to me, in a flurry of chopper blades on a hot June day, and I handed off my banner to a friend as I ran across the landing field to greet my Marine.

As we embraced, I cried, "It's you. Oh, it's you!"

And I knew then that the sustenance of our time apart, the pictures of our waterfront property, were mirages as surely as if he'd seen them in the desert. The only future I needed was in my arms, clinging to me in rough cammies that now outsized him, and wherever our future home was, it only mattered that he was the one to hold my hand as we sat on the front porch, our rockers going in perfect rhythm.

SAFEKEEPING

Fiction

Commander Kathleen Toomey Jabs

Kathleen Toomey Jabs entered the U.S. Naval Academy in July 1984 at age eighteen (she graduated, with honors, in the top fifty of her class) and was commissioned as an officer in 1988. Jabs is currently a commander in the Navy Reserve and assigned to the office of the Chairman of the Joint Chiefs of Staff. In the spring of 2003, Jabs was rushing through the Baltimore/ Washington International Airport on her way to report for reserve duty, when an incident occurred that inspired her to write a story about a female sailor heading off to the Middle East. Although this is a work of fiction, the sentiments expressed are ones that, for Jabs and her husband (a Navy commander who deployed to Iraq in the fall of 2004), strike very close to home.

Five days after the notification, Brenda Croce, wearing fresh-pressed Navy summer whites, urged her four-year-old son, Tommy, through the rain and into the revolving airport doors. She was a long-legged, sinewy woman with short-clipped hair and dark purple crescents under her eyes. For the past week, she had been living on pots of coffee and sleeping only three or four hours a night. In her arms she carried two green duffel bags, a binder of official papers, orders, and tickets, and a wooden, two-foot-long, half-bald hobbyhorse. Rain glazed her uniform. She shook herself off in the doorway and removed Tommy's jacket, tucking it under a duffel-bag strap. In the distance a disembodied voice made announcements, calling out departures and reminding passengers not to leave their bags unattended. Brenda checked her watch.

"Hey buddy, we gotta catch your flight. You ready? Can you run?" she asked.

Tommy stood rooted, brown eyes wide, fists pressed under his chin. Brenda handed him the horse and told him to ride it. He pulled the horse in close and whispered something before he started off in a slow shuffle. Brenda smiled at him, and, after shifting the bags on her shoulders, they trotted past food stalls and down the long corridor of vendors and ticket counters. At the security check-through, the line snaked down the corridor past the restrooms about fifty people deep. So much for advance planning, she thought. She found the end of the line and glanced at the clock on the wall. First the late cab, then the traffic, now this. She slung her bag to the floor and began to tap her foot. It was Tommy's first flight alone and she was supposed to have him in place ninety minutes early. The departure monitor showed the plane would begin boarding in less than half an hour. Knowing her parents, Brenda thought they were probably already waiting at the arrival gate on their end.

When she received the recall orders, she had phoned them first. Tommy's father was out of the country, out of money, and out of their lives as far as she was concerned. Her father had assured her yes, of course, Tommy could stay with them, they'd love to have him, and then her mother had added in a mournful drawl, I told you this would happen. Brenda had recited the lines she'd rehearsed, her own rationalization cloaked in duty. My number's up. At least Tommy has health care. If I go AWOL, I'll be "away" a lot longer. Her mother had held her tongue after that and Brenda had excused herself and hung up the phone. She continued working her way down the check-off sheet: bills to prepay, notices to give, copies of orders for her employer, forms and more forms to fill out. The orders activated her for a year, but the stay could be extended.

The line for baggage check inched forward. Brenda strained to see what the holdup was. She had no idea what she would do if Tommy missed his flight. He had to make it, she thought. He just had to.

Finally, it was her turn. Brenda showed her military ID to the first security guard, who nodded for her to go on, calling out, "Line five," in a bored voice. She led Tommy to the scanner and stacked her bags in plastic bins. Security guards stood at both ends of the conveyor belt. As she approached the checkpoint, the first guard called her back. "You need to remove your shoes and belt," he said.

"My belt?" She pointed at the anodized silver buckle.

He nodded.

"What about all this?" She gestured towards the silver chief petty officer insignia on her collar and the warfare pin and rows of ribbons over her left pocket. "I'm a metal detector's dream. I don't see what difference the belt is going to make." She unfastened the silver buckle and placed the belt in a bin on top of her shoes and purse. "Go on, Tommy. Put the horse on the machine and walk toward the man. Mommy will be right behind you."

Tommy walked through the scanner and looked back to watch her. As she expected, the detector beeped as she walked through it.

"Over here please," a guard said. He pointed for her to step behind a clear screen and called out "Female." Brenda motioned for Tommy to follow. A short woman in a blue uniform with a gold star approached. She told Brenda to spread her legs as if she were taking a step forward and then she ran a metal wand along Brenda's inner and outer thighs and squatted down to pat the legs of her trousers. The guard stood up and waved the wand across Brenda's back. The wand made a dinging noise and the woman said, "I'm going to touch you. I have to verify your bra has an underwire."

"Fine," Brenda said.

She felt a nudge along her spine and then the warm pressure of the guard's fingers along her ribs. She knew she should act agreeable; it wasn't the woman's fault. It was all standard operating procedure. Brenda knew the drill. She suspected she would be doing something similar by the end of the week. Her orders were to fly to Fort Bliss, join the other Navy stragglers, pick up body armor, cammies, and an M-16, and then catch a hop into Kuwait. She was an electronics technician, but rumor had it that everyone without a hard billet was pulling security duty.

While the woman finished patting up and down her arms, Brenda noticed Tommy staring at them. His hands were clenched into fists and balled under his chin so that his face seemed contorted. When had that started? she wondered, or had Tommy been doing it all along and now that she was leaving she was more aware of it? She tried to shake off her worry. It was probably nothing. By nature, Tommy was a quiet child, timid even. She thought of him as an old soul, gentle and resigned to the constant shuffling of their life. "It's okay, bud," she said. "I'll be done in a minute."

The female guard handed Brenda her shoes and Brenda slipped them on and walked over to the conveyor belt to claim the bags. The hobbyhorse was leaning against a felt partition, off to the side. When she went to pick it up, another security guard stopped her. "You can't take that," he said.

She assumed he was joking. "Don't worry, I'm a sailor. I ride ships, not horses," she said. "It's my son's. It plays music." She pressed the head of the hobbyhorse and a canned version of the *Lone Ranger* theme music crackled around them.

"You can't carry it on. You'll have to check it in."

Brenda looked at her watch and then at the line of people waiting behind the security checkpoint. Fifteen minutes until boarding. "I don't have time to go back through this line."

"I'm sorry but you can't take the horse."

"What do they think my son's going to do?" she asked. "Ride it in the aisles? It's not like it's some secret rifle. You have my word of honor." She held up her hand like a scout.

"Step over here please, ma'am," the guard told her.

"What'd I do?" Her heart started to pound and her cheeks flushed.

"What's wrong, Mommy?" Tommy asked. His fists were pressing against his chin so hard she could see the whites of his knuckles.

"The man wants Blackie." She bit her lip. "He doesn't think you should take Blackie on the plane."

"Why?"

"He's . . ."

"What's the problem here?" asked the new guard. She assumed he was the supervisor; he wore gold bars on his collar.

She shot a look at the first guard and twirled the stick horse in her hand like a baton. "My son's horse."

The supervisor picked up the horse and shook it. He batted the handle against his arm and smacked it into his palm. "I'm sorry, ma'am, this can't go."

"There's nothing on the sign about hobbyhorses," she said. She pointed at the posted list of banned items, which showed pictures of scissors, golf clubs, box cutters, nail files, razors, knitting needles, but no horses.

"The handle is wood," the guard said.

"My son's four. I don't think he's planning to pound down the cockpit door. I doubt it would work anyway. He'd have to bat a stewardess first."

The guard's eyes were flat. He squinted at her a little, and she saw that he was young and unschooled. He lifted a walkie-talkie to his mouth. She was seized with a sudden panic. "I'm sorry. I didn't mean anything," she said. "Bad joke. Forget it."

She squatted down so she could look Tommy in the eye and spoke in a voice of forced calmness. "Tommy, can you be brave? We can't take Blackie. I'll ask Nana and Grampa to get you a new horse. A better one. Okay?"

"I want Blackie," Tommy said. His eyes widened and she saw that he was going to cry. Not here. Not now, she thought. The time for tears had passed. Now she was in the groove, executing the plan. Put Tommy on the plane. Catch her own flight. Report for indoc. Deploy. She had ten minutes to find Tommy's gate. Her own flight left in an hour.

She took a deep breath. "They'll feed Blackie here," she said. "I think it would be too hot for him in Atlanta. You know how humid it gets in the summer. Blackie's not used to that."

"Really?" Tommy asked.

"Blackie is a special horse," she said quickly. "He has secret special powers. Like the way he talks to you and the way he listens. If he stays here, they'll put him in a paddock with all the other confiscated toys and keep him safe."

"What's confiscated?"

It was the wrong word, Brenda thought. It sounded too negative, and Tommy couldn't possibly understand it. The refrain "Ask me no questions and I'll tell you no lies" flashed through her mind. She had told Tommy only the barest facts about an important Navy job Mommy needed to do, and all disguised in a story about a wonderful visit to Nana and Grampa. It was the same thing the Navy was doing with her. Who knew what anyone really believed; nothing was happening as expected, but the orders were valid and needed to be obeyed. At some level she believed the stories and all the talk saved you; you had to fall back on them or you would go mad. She leaned in towards Tommy and spoke in a soft voice. "I meant special. Very special.

Blackie's going to make new friends. Bears and lions and tigers. Maybe some dolls."

"Oh." His eyes brightened.

"They have lots of good food here. They'll keep him safe and maybe, when we come back, we can get him. He'll be all fattened up. How about it?"

Tommy glanced at the horse and then back at her. His voice shook a little. "When can we get him?"

"When we come back."

"When?"

"It won't be too long. Just long enough for Blackie to have a good adventure. And for you, too. A little time apart . . ." She stopped abruptly. She bit her lip and pressed her eyes shut; she felt dizzy and a little woozy. Her whole insides seemed to be churning. When she opened her eyes, Tommy was staring at her.

"What's wrong, Mommy?"

She gripped the orders and stood and shook out her legs. She had no idea how long she would be gone or if she would be back at all. "I'm okay, bud. I can't bend like I used to." She felt her heart quiver and tighten. The din around her was almost overwhelming: suitcases slapping the belt, guards calling for IDs, radios buzzing, and overhead the announcements kept coming. In the midst of all the noise, she heard a slight rustle and saw Tommy move towards Blackie. He patted the horse on the neck and pressed its ear and the scratchy familiar music floated out. He whispered something in the horse's ear and then he turned away and walked towards her without looking back at the horse.

"What'd you tell him?" she asked.

"Goodbye," he said.

"That's it?"

"I said he has to be brave."

Her eyes started to burn. Everything was loud and bright. Tommy slipped his hand into hers, and she clasped the small fingers and squeezed them hard. Her heart, she thought, had seized; she couldn't think up any lie to numb the pain. She stood immobile until Tommy tugged on her arm. "Okay, Mommy, time to go," he said. He pulled her forward and led her into the crowd heading for the gate.

DEAR BABY

Letter

Staff Sergeant Sharon McBride

The daughter of a Vietnam veteran who was killed on active duty, Sharon McBride joined the U.S. Army herself to—in her words—"repay" the military for covering her college expenses and taking care of her. (McBride was three when her father died.) After spending fourteen months in the Middle East in support of both Operation Enduring Freedom and Operation Iraqi Freedom, Staff Sergeant McBride returned to the United States in the summer of 2003 and was assigned to Fort Richardson, Alaska. Although her sense of pride was undiminished, McBride did not romanticize military life and recognized full well how arduous it could be. Months after she moved to Alaska, McBride, thirty-four years old at the time, knew it was about to get even more difficult; she was pregnant and would probably have to raise the child on her own. (McBride and the child's father had separated.) Two months before her daughter was born, McBride wrote the following letter.

Dear baby:

As you grow inside me, I have been thinking more and more of what it means to be a mommy in the U.S. Army.

Let me be the first to tell you, though, that we have a rough road ahead of us, kiddo. The life of a soldier isn't an easy one.

Already in the seven years that I've been in the Army, I've spent a lot of time away from home. It's very rare that I get to spend holidays with my family. And more and more I see my friends and comrades departing on deployments that send them far away from their families for extended lengths of time. And I have a feeling that life isn't going to get any easier, sweetie.

And, although we have been given a reprieve of sorts, I have a feeling it won't be too long after you are born that I, too, will be asked to go away—again.

It seems, my dear, that there are too many nasty people in this world that feel like they need to oppress, suffocate and stamp out human pride and freedom among their fellow man.

Why, sweetie? I don't know. But these men seem to be everywhere. Every day when I turn on the news, there's a different man in a different part of the world that's making life unbearable for others.

As a soldier, I have given my word that if the call comes for me to do my part in making the world a better place to live, I'll go. No hesitation. No questions asked.

That call was a lot easier to answer when I didn't have you—when I just had myself to think about. Now, as a future parent, I can see why some single mommies choose to get out of the Army, but my resolve is true.

I know baby, this is going to be hard for you to understand. You're going to want your mommy and she'll be far, far away.

I'm going to miss a lot of important things—perhaps many of your firsts: birthdays, holidays, you know, all the good stuff. But, I am a soldier. It's a profession that few choose, but one that the many don't hesitate to call when there's trouble to be fixed. That's our job; our mission in life: to help others that can't seem to help themselves.

But, take comfort in the fact that there are going to be other children that will not only be missing their mommies but daddies too.

Many families have gone down this road before us. We won't be the first.

And we certainly won't be the last. So, if they can do it, surely we can do it too.

While we are together, though, I promise to hold you a bit longer than necessary, read the story about the purple dinosaur as many times as you want, fix your favorite food for dinner, kiss you a lot, hold your hand and take as many photos of you as possible. Memories of these things will have to sustain us while we are apart.

Just take heart that being an Army baby won't be all bad. There will be sweets to go with the sour. You'll get to travel and see other cultures that other kids won't get to see. There will always be food on the table and clothes on your back. If you get sick, you will always have medicine to make you feel better.

Some children in the world don't even have shoes. I know, because I've seen them.

So, as you grow stronger and bigger inside me, I can only hope and pray that you remember the lessons I will teach while we are together and that they will help you when we are apart: Always share your cookies, never call names, remember to say "I'm sorry" if you are wrong, wash behind your ears and brush your teeth, and say "I love you" every chance you get.

heard so much about since "the pictures" came out, and she provides medical care and comfort to the prisoners. Some of them are Iraqis who have been caught up in the maelstrom of war and it's not clear how dangerous they are, but others are bombers and killers. I smile less when I think of my wife in the company of these individuals. I am a civilian now but I was an officer and Army aviator, and I know what war does to people. I know my wife's suffering. I hear it on the phone and see it in her letters.

We were a typical American family until Juliet went back on active duty in hopes of entering the Army's Physician's Assistant Program. I supported her quest then and I still do today. She is a very beautiful woman, an excellent student (3.98 GPA and National Honor Society member), a fabulous mother, and the love of my life. I will support her in anything that she wants to do. I had my turn and now it is hers.

She was in North Carolina, and I was at home in New York, sick in bed, when she called me with the news of her impending deployment to Iraq. I have made those calls to her before and yet, despite that and a daily dose of CNN, I was stunned. We agreed not to tell the kids until I brought them to her in North Carolina. We hoped the closeness would somehow minimize the reality of the message.

We decided to move to Fort Bragg so the kids and I would be surrounded by other military families. It had helped when I had been deployed, and we assumed it would be the same when my wife was gone.

Lesson #1: Just because they have changed the name to "Spouses' Club" from "Wives' Club" does not mean that men are welcome.

Lesson #2: If I were deployed, I'm not sure that I would feel comfortable with my wife hanging out with the husbands of other soldiers.

Ultimately, I felt totally alone.

When Juliet first left for Iraq, I didn't do as well as I thought I might. I sat in bed telling myself over and over that I could do this. Then the panic set in, and I cried. I had no idea how to get the kids to school on time let alone how to feed them on a daily basis. I was simply not prepared for this. Apparently our wives do more than sit around eating bonbons and watching the Home Shopping Network. The list of things that keep a house in running order doesn't just get done by itself, and that was pretty apparent in our home within days of Juliet's departure.

The house was a mess, the laundry pile grew daily, and the kids were becoming rather unimpressed by the menu selection. I was lying on the couch

Lastly, don't forget to pray for Mommy and the other parents that oft
have to be so far away from their little ones. We don't want to leave, but som
times duty calls.

Love Foreve

Mommy

*On February 6, 2004, McBride gave birth to a healthy eight-pound, twelve-
ounce baby girl, whom she named Lyssa Bree. Two years later, McBride received orders to deploy overseas once again.*

MANNING THE HOME FRONT

Personal Narrative

Peter Madsen

*"I am a single father of three, a sometimes retail and distribution manager,
and a husband," Peter Madsen wrote in the summer of 2004 from Fort
Bragg, North Carolina. "My wife, Specialist Juliet C. Madsen, is an Army
Medic stationed in Iraq." The high number of female troops heading off to
war has created a relatively new social phenomenon: the single-parent,
home-front husband. Madsen himself had been in the military for nine
years before retiring in 1999 after breaking his back in an accident. His wife,
Juliet, was in the Army Reserve before the launch of Operation Iraqi Freedom and went back on active duty March 30, 2004. She deployed two
months later, leaving Peter and their three children—Tyler (age eleven),
Joshua (ten), and Erin (seven)—behind in North Carolina.*

When I first thought about my wife going over there, in the desert, I
had to smile; even she will admit that she looks a little funny with all
her gear on. Juliet is tiny and childlike buried beneath a mound of fatigues
and body armor. Blond wisps of hair escape from under her Kevlar helmet. I
could never have imagined this very attractive, blond waif of a girl going to
war, but there she is.

She works at one of the Theater Internment Facilities (TIF) we have watching Oprah on TiVo one evening after work when they gathered around me. The eldest cleared her throat. "Dad," she said, then paused for a moment to gather her thoughts. "Dad, we don't really like pizza that much anymore."

I looked at the younger two, and they were nodding rather emphatically. Being a good father, I realized we needed to make a change.

Two weeks later, they came back. This time Joshua, my middle child, spoke. "Dad, we don't like Chinese either."

My wife had made me a list of all the important things that I should remember while she was away. It was long but it could not be all-inclusive. She was pressed for time as she was getting ready to leave and most of it represents the expected. Bills, vet appointments, and school records were there. A reminder to transfer medical records and set up school physicals was on the list too. Daughter's hair appointment was not.

It isn't like I hadn't been a parent before (just not a single one), so I was pretty confident that I could successfully add one or two things to the list on my own. Well, I was wrong. Tyler is eleven and was starting the seventh grade. Like her mother, she is a tiny thing. She was nervous about going to a new school where she knows no one, so I was determined to make it a good beginning.

Knowing she wanted to look nice on her first day, I offered to take her to the barbershop just off post. She provided me with a resounding "NO!"

Lesson #3: Girls do not go to barbershops.

Several days later, after some serious thought, I hoped to make the situation right. I announced that we could go and get her hair done at a beauty salon. She threw her arms around me and kissed me, thanked me, and told me that she loved me. I have rarely felt so alive as I did just then. At moments like that, I realized that I could do this. My children have a deep connection with their mother, and I have watched them grieve over this loss of her. They are good to me and we are building a wonderful new relationship, but I cannot light them up the way that she does. Watching my daughter smile, I began to think I might have mommy magic too.

The big day came and Tyler and I went to the mall to find a hair salon.

Lesson #4: Apparently, you are supposed to make an appointment before going to these places.

We went blindly in search of a salon that would trim her hair and add some highlights. I'm told that is the "in" thing to do, and I wanted to help my little girl be cool. After an intensive search, we found a salon that would take her right away and, after several minutes of conversation, we agreed on a trim with blond and honey highlights. Proud of my success with Tyler, I set off to find a good coffee and a quiet bench to sit on while I waited.

I returned to see Tyler under the dryer. She was smiling and laughing with the girl next to her. I felt a connection with her and was so proud of myself for adding this special item to our list. After twenty more minutes she came out smiling, twirled around, and asked me what I thought.

I can only imagine what I looked like standing there with my mouth hanging open. My daughter has long, beautiful, strawberry blond hair with the natural wave that most women pay for. She has sparkling blue eyes, and I am terrified of the boys who will surely come calling over the next few years. I did not expect the red, almost burgundy, streaks running through her hair.

Whatever my expression looked like, it was enough to make her face go ashen. Then, I really blew it. "What did you do to your hair? What *on heaven and earth* did you do to your hair?"

I paid the stylist, grabbed my daughter's hand, and almost ran towards the car. I muttered and grumbled to myself along the way. As we pulled out of the mall parking lot, I raged on and on about her hair and her mother and what kind of trouble I was in. I did not notice Tyler's silence until we hit the first stoplight, a mile down the road. She was lying on the back seat of the mini-van crying quietly so as not to interrupt my diatribe.

I have never felt so small or so inadequate.

Realizing my mistake, I apologized to her. I told her how much I loved her and that I was sorry for being a boob. Once her hair dried more, the highlights really did look good, bringing out the natural color of her hair. We went home to take pictures for her mom of her cool new haircut. We e-mailed them to her and surprisingly, given the eight-hour time difference between North Carolina and Nasiriyah, Iraq, Juliet e-mailed back almost immediately. She wrote that she loved the new haircut, and Tyler beamed.

Over time, I learned how to be a father and a mother. It does not always go well. Sociologists and psychologists would have an absolute blast in my home. I could write a book about what *not* to say to young children. I've said them all in just a few weeks. The good news is that I don't think that I have scarred them permanently. I start each day with "I love you" and end it the same way. At night they sneak into my bed, kiss me quietly, and whisper, "I love you, Daddy." This is a new world where our mothers, sisters, daughters, and wives go to war. Gentlemen, we had better get prepared.

I'm not sure when it happened, but one day I walked into my house and looked at the dirty dishes, the dirty clothes, the dirty kids, and the light came on. I cleaned up and did the laundry. I sent three grumbling maniacs to the bathtub and I made dinner. Joshua, my ten-year-old, said it still sucked but he ate it. (Lesson #5: Hunger makes anything palatable.) The next morning, Erin, my seven-year-old daughter, said I didn't kiss as good as Mommy. She kissed me twice so I could practice. Tyler cleaned the house for me while I was out the next day. It was spotless. An amazing transformation was taking place. Life was perfect! Our lives were running smoothly.

And then we hit a rough patch. No one liked my spaghetti and, on one particular evening, no one wanted to be tucked in. My wife had recently figured out how to instant-message online with her friends and really didn't have time for me that night. It takes hours to get a chance at fifteen minutes on the computer or phone, so it's not always fun to hear a broken husband whining on the other end, and I was whining long and hard.

I can't say that it was an easy day. I can't say that it was an easy week, and I can't say that this has been an easy month. I can say that we are making it one day at a time. I have killed two goldfish and a hamster, and I have ruined at least three loads of laundry. The good news is that once you turn everything pink, it stays pink. The fish went to the porcelain graveyard with snickers from the older kids and a somber eulogy from the youngest. The hamster has a place of honor and a cross in the backyard.

I have learned what our soldier's wives have lived for generations: hope and grief and perseverance. I find humor with my children every day. When you are seven, two wrongs really do make a right. Seventh-graders can be cruel to one another, but fathers can make it better. Why would you wash the minivan with a steel-wool brush? I don't know, but her heart was in the right place.

Each morning when I wake up, I kiss my children and hold them close. We talk about Mom and the war, but we leave CNN off. We go to bed each night and all say one prayer: "God, please bring our mommy home safe. She is always in our hearts and in our thoughts and we can hardly wait to have her home with us." I say an extra prayer, too, just for me: "Thank you, God, for giving me this time with my children."

I don't know where our story will end. I just know that we make it through each day with love and laughter, and that is good enough for now.

In September 2004, Madsen received a distressing phone call informing him that his wife had been rushed to the Landstuhl Regional Medical Facility Center in Germany. Specialist Juliet Madsen had suffered massive and prolonged heat-related injuries that had damaged both her brain and central nervous system, and she was eventually flown back to Fort Bragg to recuperate. Juliet was medically retired from the Army in January 2006, and the long-term impact of her injuries is not known.

HURTFUL WORDS
Journal
Ruth Mostek

They know that the troops in Afghanistan and Iraq have it worse. But for the family members burdened with added responsibilities and pressures on the home front when their loved ones deploy overseas, bitterness and anger can begin to fester. "I finally feel that I'm getting the hang of this single parent thing but I keep getting mad at my husband," one military wife wrote after her husband, a staff sergeant in the U.S. Army, left for Afghanistan in April 2004. "I'm mad when I have to care for sick children myself." She went on,

> *I'm mad at him for not being here when I've totally lost my patience and there is no one to rescue the kids from my yelling. I'm mad because if something goes wrong, it's all my fault . . . there's no one to share the blame. Although I know he's not on vacation over there, I resent that he doesn't have to pick up after anyone else. I resent that he can sit and read a book in private. But under all this resentment is something worse . . . fear. I'm afraid that I'll say something out of frustration on one of those infrequent calls and that will be the last thing he hears from me. I'm afraid that this loneliness will be mine alone forever. I resent him for making me worry.*

Few issues have as much potential to cause strife among family members as concerns over money. In December 2003, twenty-three-year-old U.S. Army Sergeant Hiram Zayas was mobilized for duty in Iraq as an MP with the 800th Military Police reserve unit out of Michigan. (Zayas's unit did not arrive in the Middle East until February 2004.) Zayas had started a small used car business before he left, and he asked his mother, Ruth Mostek, in Indiana to help manage his finances while he was gone. The following journal entries, which were written by Mostek, record how rapidly tensions can escalate even between people who love each other.

March 11

After Hiram left for Iraq there were still loose ends with his financial affairs. He made phone calls from wherever he was stationed to handle most of it. It was unclear to me whether or not he wanted to keep his small business going. I had paid his business insurance that was in danger of being cancelled. He said if I had not done that he would have enough money in his account. We started blaming each other. Hiram was very conscientious about wanting his credit cards paid off as quickly as possible. I tried to pay them off but there was never enough money. I began to think perhaps "going off to war" should be a total break from parents, like in the old days. A son would tip his hat and say, "Maybe you will hear from me in two to four years." It didn't seem like such a bad idea now. He was aggravating me, his mother, half to death—from across the ocean and an entire continent! I confronted him in an e-mail. He wrote back. The words exchanged on both sides are too hurtful to include.

March 30

I deeply regret arguing with Hiram earlier—and here it is the worst month of attacks upon them so far. His tension over his situation, loss of innocence, loss of closeness to loved ones, the strain of having to figure out what to do in new untenable situations—were somewhat taken out on me. (The e-mail I shredded began, "Mom, you have really managed to piss me off!!" He had never spoken to me that way in his life before.) That's o.k. I understand, as my sister reminded me, people lash out at their loved ones because they are the closest ones to them. I e-mailed him that I was sorry, sent him a magazine. But how could these little things put a dent in the tremendous pressure he is under now? How do you reach someone in the middle of an honest to goodness battle?

April 4

My son & I continue the argument. I think he is a pompous arrogant 23-year-old male mass of conceit—who absolutely cannot see something from someone else's point of view. He probably thinks I'm stupid & incompetent. He thinks I have a chip on my shoulder & whine over nothing. I am now to blame for all that is wrong: for his difficult adjustment to the war, for his shock at man's inhumanity to man, for the fact he has to work hard for his money & never get ahead. Good—if that's how he feels about it. Meantime he is the epitome of selfishness. I have failed. This hurts me most of all. Well, there is one clue he may have some compassion. He has noticed how the poor Iraqis suffer & have little. Good for him.

June 8

My son & I made up last week. His girlfriend called to tell me to get online with him. So I did & he and I "talked" pleasantly. It was a big step & one I'm grateful for. I think each of us both knows now how quickly tempers can flare & so I consider it a temporary truce until we can talk more honestly in person. But I'm still kept in the dark because I didn't expect to see him until January, then I find out he's just come back briefly for a funeral, on his dad's side.

June 9

Today Hiram finally came by to visit while he's on leave. After he'd had hours visiting with his father, I went ahead and called his girlfriend's cell phone to reach him. She told me (which I'm sure she's lived to regret) that he was out looking at car lots to buy with his dad. Buying a car lot?! With what? When he hasn't filed taxes?! (Later I realized he just wanted to go out alone with his father for a while.) I snapped. I bitched at his girlfriend about it & had her have him call me (poor girl in the middle). I harangued at him when he called me back.

In spite of our phone argument & me saying it was absolutely no problem for me to drive up there to see him, he and his girlfriend came by anyway. Neither of them hugged me back. I admit it was phony of me to try and greet them smiling but what else was I to do than try to squelch my temper? We did talk some on other subjects. His girlfriend wanted nothing, not even water which I finally gave her anyway as she looked so sad & miserable. He wanted only coffee & I offered him a bowl of chips but I didn't see him eat any.

As they were leaving she went to the car, he lingered in the doorway & we started to argue. I laid out everything that's been bothering me about his asking me to pay his bills, then demanding when & how they be paid & the many overdraft fees.—The first thing he said was, "Maybe it's because I'm in a *war*, you know?!" and "All of the financial stuff is unimportant. What does it matter? I might not come back—this may be the last time you ever see me. What is your problem? You are upset over nothing & always make a big deal out of little things. Haven't I always treated you nice?" I had to agree, but gracious & humble I am not—especially when I have a point to make.

There was no bringing the argument to a loving close. How do you wrap up the sparking ends? The wires were still too hot to touch for an embrace.

Mid-November

Hiram came back to the United States after serving for nine months in Iraq. I heard about his return from his sisters.

Dec. 15

Hiram got married today. I wasn't invited to the wedding. Hiram and I have spoken on the phone only twice (briefly) since he got back. Once he called to ask me a question regarding his business, thinking I would have certain papers. There were no apologies between us. Another time I called him. He was fairly cheerful that time. He was proud that he had gone into partnership with someone, and they've opened up a car lot. I said, "You know I love you Hiram." He said, "I know." I tried to apologize to him in writing several times but he didn't reply.

March 7, 2005

I'm just remembering the excited, happy look on Hiram's face the day his unit was leaving for Iraq more than a year ago. We had left the unit's building to go to the bank in South Bend. He was coming up to the car on the passenger side as I was sliding into the driver's seat. I looked out the car window to see him bend a little to open his door & I wanted to freeze that look in my mind. His face was lean—such smooth features—and he had a humongous, happy proud grin on his face. I just thought my son looked so handsome. Of course I was aware he wouldn't be the same when he returned from war. I've heard it changes boys into men. I was also acutely (and painfully) aware of my role as mother. I didn't want to baby him so I gave him advice instead.

April 15, 2005

My son and his new wife have moved to an apartment close to where he has his business, which is operating successfully from what his sisters tell me. Apparently he lives less than two hours from me. There is still no communication between us. Last week I called him twice requesting an address to forward a personal letter someone mailed to my home. He did not call back.

Although Mostek and her son did not see each other for almost a year after his return to the States, in October 2005 they reconciled and now write, phone, and spend time together regularly.

REGARDING TIGGER

E-mail

Jennifer Huch-Gambichler

Humor, for many family members of deployed troops, becomes an emotional necessity when life on the home front reaches a point of seeming unbearable. Caring for two boys, five-year-old Sam and fifteen-month-old Max, by herself in Fort Hood, Texas, Jennifer Huch-Gambichler received terrible news one day about a beloved pet. (Her husband, U.S. Army Captain Steven R. Gambichler, had recently left for Kuwait and would not return for another ten months, in October 2003.) Although the incident was devastating to everyone involved, especially little Sam, Huch-Gambichler sent an e-mail to relatives that recounted some of the day's lighter moments.

Dear Family,

So sorry to depress each of you today with this unfortunate group email, but I just can't face the 20 or so phone calls it would take to put the word out, so here goes . . .

It's not about Steven, first of all. He's gone, which still completely sucks, but we had a phone call a few days ago & all seems well so far. It's just that tomorrow I have to call our rear detachment commander & get word to the hubby that Tigger died today.

Our beloved doggie somehow escaped & was hit by a car on the horrible road behind our house. In fact, he was directly behind our back fence when we finally got to him, thanks only to a benevolent lady caller who took it upon herself to deliver the bad news. She wasn't the one who did him in but she was gracious enough to pull over when she spotted him lying on the street, &

even carried his body to a grassy stretch that lines the sidewalk of our notorious road from hell. . . .

We think he was gone maybe 30 minutes before he was hit & instantly
killed, of course by some bastard who didn't bother to stop. It all happened so
fast that my four legged baby was still warm when I found him.

Poor Sam. He gave Tig his usual kiss before we walked to school this
morning & 8 hours later the kid came home to a frazzled mess of a mother
who had to explain why his best friend in the whole world was gone for good.
He spent the entire afternoon crying on the couch with his back to the room
& his head under Tigger's favorite pillow, wailing "GO AWAY!" every time I
tried to comfort him.

He finally ran out of steam late this evening & wandered into the kitchen
looking for juice, demanding to know if heaven was real & if Tigger had
"passed the test to get in" (no earthly clue where that came from). I hemmed
& hawed & bullshitted for a few minutes until I remembered a story another
Army wife told me, something she made up for her own kids. I assured Sam
that all animals go to a paradise called "The Rainbow Bridge" & that Tig was
in a happy place where smoked pig ears grew right up through the ground &
he could chase rabbits all day & poop in dad's favorite shoes anytime he
wanted without getting yelled at. I got the tiniest smile from him with that,
but it was still another 3 hours of crying before he finally passed out face
down on his Batman comforter with Tig's leopard print dog collar grasped
tightly in his chunky little fist.

Thank God for my beloved friend Judy. She's our Executive Officer's wife
& lives right around the corner, so she was there in a flash when I called sobbing incoherently into the phone. We went together to the spot described by
the lady caller & found my sweet baby in the grass. He looked so completely
undamaged, only a little blood around his nose & mouth, & we held him &
wept over him there on the side of that stupid road. . . .

But, as is the custom with tragic events in this family, the day wasn't totally
without humor. Tigger, well known in the neighborhood for his perpetual
"display of manhood" despite an early neutering, chose to die as he had
lived . . . sporting his usual mondo erection. After we had said our farewells
& prepared to load him into the van, Judy & I rolled him onto his back &
there it was, the most enormous doggie boner you can imagine. We both saw
it at exactly the same instant & busted out laughing, tears streaming down our

faces, Tigger's hind legs wide open & Mr. Happy flapping joyfully in the breeze. . . .

Steven is never here for this! I know an Army wife has to be a tough broad and I love a challenge as much as the next girl, but Jesus! They don't exactly cover this territory in the Army Wife's Handbook. It's loaded with all that 1950's Donna Reed crap about party etiquette & how to practice tying your husband's bowtie on a bedpost (no lie, it actually says that—my feminist mother nearly had an aneurism). I'd sure like to add a few chapters of my own, maybe "Absent Spouses, Pet Crises & Navigating Your Neighborhood Crematorium," or "Grief Reactions in Pissed-Off Five-Year Olds." Now I have to tell our soldier his dog is dead & our son is devastated. He tried to tell me (warn me, really) exactly what to expect as a military wife the night we got engaged. Above all things he promised I'd never be bored. Well, he sure delivered!

* Dogs Rule *

Love you all so much,
Jen

WORLDS APART

E-mail

Petty Officer Second Class Edwin Garcia-Lopez

Military personnel serving abroad are not unaware of or unsympathetic to the strain that their absence might be causing back home. Many try, as best they can, to remind their loved ones how much they long for the moment when they will be reunited. Forty-seven-year-old Petty Officer Second Class Edwin Garcia-Lopez was shipped to the Middle East in August 2004 with the Naval Coastal Warfare Group Two's Mobile Inshore Undersea Warfare Unit 204. Garcia-Lopez guarded an Iraqi oil platform in the middle of the ocean for almost a month, and, after one restless night, he walked out on the platform deck to watch the dawn break over the water.

Desperately missing the woman he loved, Garcia-Lopez handwrote the fol-
lowing letter to his wife back in New Jersey. (He later typed it out and sent
it to her via e-mail.)

September 12, 2004

Debra,

It is zero four thirty. I again awoke thinking of you. It makes me smile when the first thought I have when I awake is of you. My love, I try not to count the days until I see you again. . . .

Debra, I miss the parting of your lips as we kiss. I miss sleeping with you, our bodies entwined into each other as a soft whisper.

And I miss our home built of work, sweat and years of sacrifice. I miss my vegetable garden; kneeling in the damp ground and sinking my hands into the dark soil of our back yard and with brief fertility prayers bury seeds, lovingly I hope. To watch with delight and much surprise as slowly, fragile sprouts break through the ground searching the sun and warmth. Later, to bring to our mouths a little piece of heaven from our blessed earth. These and many other small miracles are pleasant victories to my heart that I miss dearly. . . . Worlds apart and yet together . . .

As I now gaze out across the sea, the horizon has become thin strands from sea to sky of dark haze, a shy red, a yellow gold and finally a light blue. I look behind my shoulder and the coast of Iraq is still dark. I turn forward as the haze succumbs to a soft orange rising Sun. Behind me, as minutes grow; the Iraqi coast turns a quiet blue with the increasing light. And once again, slowly, another cloudless day awakens. I have watched dawn not break, but blossom.

And with that, I must get myself ready for another day. With a longing for you, this lonely American stands and lives with hope of a great future for our country and the good people of a new Iraq. We all here will do our best to serve as promised.

Still, I can't resist telling you a dream I had some nights ago. I am walking alone on a beach and I feel as if I am searching my heart for something to give you. I sense the distance and am angry at the expansive Oceans and Continents that separate us. In the dream I remember cursing in two languages on why I could not lift and carry myself to you, to offer you something that would make all things right and happy. Later that day as I remembered the dream, I promised myself that given the opportunity I intend for you and me to accumulate many pleasant memories that in retelling, will keep us warm in our old age.

My love, I wish I could offer you more.

Yours always,
Edwin

Garcia-Lopez returned home in May 2005.

ANOTHER BUMP IN THE ROAD
E-mail
Specialist Michael A. Vivirito

Twenty-two years old when he joined the National Guard in 1997, Michael A. Vivirito was a specialist in the U.S. Army's Individual Ready Reserve, or IRR, when the war in Iraq began in March 2003. IRR reservists are rarely called up (they are essentially in the inactive phase of their military service), but in August 2004 Vivirito was mobilized and sent to Kuwait to drive supply trucks into Iraq. The timing could hardly have been worse. Just before he left for the Middle East, his infant son, Charlie, had to undergo open-heart surgery, and his wife, Jessy, was expecting their second child. Vivirito's job was a dangerous one — many drivers have been shot, kidnapped, or killed by roadside explosives — but what was foremost in Vivirito's mind was that his wife had to confront so many problems on her own. On April 6, 2005, Vivirito downplayed his own situation and e-mailed his wife, whose pregnancy was turning out to be a difficult one, to keep her spirits high.

Jessy,

Baby, I miss you so much, I think about you constantly. We are still here at Anaconda, I feel much better today. No more blood or nausea. I guess it was just the settling of my stomach. Bull and I went to the movie theater here. It was weird. It is an actual movie theater, with a balcony and concession stands and all. We watched some crazy movie with Lawrence Fishborne and Ethan Hawk. When we left and walked outside we had totally forgotten where we were. It felt like home for about 30 seconds. I said to Bull, "you know 6 months ago, I did not know you, and there wasn't a chance in HELL I ever would have met you. Now, I know you better than some people I have known my whole life." It is really amazing. But, I would trade it all for one good nights sleep next to you. Jessy, I can't imagine what you are going through there with our new baby growing inside of you, and Charlie at your knees.

All I can think and dream is that deep inside you is a paradise where this baby is growing and when he or she comes out we will make our life the same kind of place of warmth and love. I am so sorry I am not there for you. But I am Jessy, I am right there with you all day, everyday. Because every-day you are all I see when I close my eyes. I hold my breath and I reach for you and I can almost grab you. I can almost touch your cheek. I reach for your hand and another bump in the road jerks me back into this truck. An-other bump in the road, that's all this is, right? That is what they all say, those who do not have to go through this. "Ah, just a bump in the road, and everything will be fine." More like a pothole if you ask me. It's just like that Italian movie, "Everybody's Fine," just as long as you don't ask too many questions. Your Dad was right; heaven must be a bar with a jukebox and a cold beer.

Baby, someday, I don't know when and I don't know how, but we will be together and there will not be anything or anyone who will pull me away from you again. I need you to breathe; I'll hold my breath for both of us. I'll take it all. Will you dance around the world with me . . . ?

Love you forever,
Michael

Due to complications during the birth of their second child, Isabella, Vivi-rito was allowed to return to the States early, but he ultimately served more than eleven months overseas. Charlie and Isabella are both fully recovered and doing well.

DEAR BOYS

E-mails

Lieutenant Colonel Chris Cohoes

Parents serving abroad are especially sensitive to how difficult it can be for a young child to comprehend why Mom or Dad is away for such a long period of time. A veteran of the 1991 Desert Storm campaign, thirty-nine-year-old U.S. Air Force Lieutenant Colonel Chris Cohoes deployed to the Middle East in the summer of 2004, leaving behind his wife and their two sons, Cavan, who was eleven at the time, and Crew, age five. Cohoes frequently e-mailed his boys to encourage them to be good to each other and to their mother, but mostly to emphasize that as much as he wished he could be home with them in Nebraska, he felt strongly about his missions over Afghanistan and Iraq. Other troops, he reminded his sons, were sacrificing even more.

13 Aug 04

Boys,

I was walking outside today and made a big mistake. I grabbed a hand rail when I walked down the stairs. I have some nasty red marks from where it burned me. That's how hot it is. You just can't believe it.

Trust me, I'm not complaining. I flew a mission yesterday. A squad of Marines was in the mountains way up above 10,000 feet, and they were attacked by some bad guys. These bad guys fired six big rockets at the Marines' position. I saw the explosions. Don't worry, they can't reach me with anything they have. Some of those Marines are only seven years older than you are, Cavan. All I could think about was you two hunkering down in the mountains with rockets landing all around. I have no fear for my own safety, but I'd be petrified if you were in my shoes—or worse yet, theirs.

Thinking about that stuff wasn't helping me or the Marines, so I had to box up that feeling and store it away for another time. Hope you guys learn how to do that because it can get you through the rough spots with a clear head. Trick is that you have to remember to find the box again later. Keep them stuffed away, and eventually you'll run out of storage space when you need it.

We helped get those guys out of their mess, and none of them got hurt. It felt great to help Americans in trouble. More than great. We did roughly the same thing three days ago, and after that one, I sent an e-mail to a Marine Major who is a friend of mine. Here's part of what he wrote back.

". . . . As you well know, we are a family, we're tight—very tight, we don't ask for much: honor, courage and commitment are truly what we live by—and when somebody gives us a hand, we consider it a pretty big honor. You've earned a place in our family as a result. I can't even describe what it means to us as a whole. Thanks brother, for all that you do, and for keeping our brothers on the pointy end of the spear out of harm's way. Please pass back to your crew and squadron as well, **we all** say thank you."

Maybe that sounds like dialogue from a mediocre movie you've seen, but it actually brought a tear to my eye. I told you in the last letter that certain experiences change you forever and cause you to see things differently. The message above might seem a little sappy for most people, but it meant a great deal to me.

Tell Mom I love her. Tell Mom you love her too.

Love you both, Dad

Just over two weeks later, Cohoes sent the following e-mail after flying over Iraq:

29 Aug 04

Boys,

I flew in a pretty amazing area of the world today. Have you ever heard of Mesopotamia? Probably not, but you will. This is where civilization began on earth (the Sumarians)! Two great rivers of the world, the Tigris and the Euphrates, flow together here then empty into the Persian Gulf. Mesopotamia was the area between the two rivers (in Greek, Mesopotamia means "between the rivers"). The Bible talks a lot about it. It says that the Euphrates River flowed from the Garden of Eden. You've heard of "the Promised Land"? It's right here. Heard of Babylon? Here, about 30 miles south of Baghdad. The city was built about 3,800 years ago by King Hammurabi. King Nebuchadnezzar (I can't say it either) built the Hanging Gardens of Babylon about 2,600 years ago. It is one of the Seven Ancient Wonders of the World.

This is where many great battles took place. The Romans fought here. One of the Egyptian Pharaohs fought here. Now I'm fighting here. Doesn't seem like a "great" battle to me, and I'll bet you the Egyptians and Babylonians didn't think fighting was great then either.

It is sad to see what history has done to this area. It was the beginning of everything we have now. It was beautiful, there were forests nearby, the people were proud. Now it is a disaster. Now it is called Iraq. Lots of people from other countries are going there and setting off bombs to try to scare the Iraqi people, and it is working. I wish they would stop, but they won't. Too bad Hammurabi isn't here now—he was amazing, and he could get his country under control once again.

It was nighttime when I was flying around thinking about these things, then every single light in my plane went out. It is a full moon tonight, but I still needed a flashlight to see in the cockpit. The first thing I thought after making sure the engines still worked was what you would've said, Cavan, had you been there. "Hey Dad. The lights went out." I started laughing. Then I got most of my lights back and came back to base.

Cavan, remember this: Babe Ruth struck out 1,330 times. Crew, I think that you and Mark Twain would've been great friends. Here's something he said about boys that makes me think of you: "Now and then we had a hope that if we lived and were good, God would permit us to be pirates."

Love,
Dad

Cohoes came home in October 2004 and then redeployed to the Middle East with the Air Combat Command less than a year later.

MY SON
Poem
Sergeant First Class Paul D. Adkins

As much as troops on the front lines and their families back home try to remain optimistic, it is impossible for them to disregard war's perils and the obvious fact that they might never see one another again. And the delicate equilibrium they struggle to maintain, with each side trying to concentrate on the positives and minimize the negatives in their e-mails and cell phone conversations, can easily be shattered by a stray remark or offhand comment. Soon after he arrived in Baghdad with the 10th Mountain Division's 110th Military Intelligence Battalion, 2nd Brigade Combat Team, U.S. Army Sergeant First Class Paul Adkins learned from his wife that their two-year-old son was suffering from sudden, uncontrollable crying fits. The news prompted Adkins to write the following poem.

> Gone three weeks, we were driving somewhere in Iraq
> on a convoy, the desert gritting in the sun,
> that torch of sand and wind. But my son
>   back home, age two, cried
> and cried; he knew
> that I was dead.
>   I had left him forever
> like a balloon which slipped
> from his fingers. I was floating off somewhere
> alone. And he was finally
>   turning and walking away
> from the spot he had lost me, finally
> not looking at the patch of sky
> where he had last seen me wave
> and pull away from his hand.

Adkins survived his one-year deployment to Iraq and returned to his wife, son, and three daughters in New York in May 2005.

NO TIME FOR SNOWMEN
Letter
Captain Zoltan Krompecher

Convinced that the letters tempt fate and may be self-fulfilling, some military personnel refuse to write them. Others simply prefer not to dwell on the subject at all. But the servicemen and women who do compose a "last let-

ter" before going into harm's way believe that, in the event of their death, their letter will offer words of love and comfort to grieving family members. And in an age of instant messaging, quick cell-phone calls, and e-mails dashed off in haste, many troops feel that these final messages should be crafted with great care and, ideally, written by hand. One month before leaving his home in New York to link up with a special operations unit in Iraq, thirty-seven-year-old U.S. Army Captain Zoltan Krompecher penned (and also typed) the following letter to his two little girls, Leah, age four, and Annie, age two. (Krompecher had a two-month-old son named Jack as well.) Although he focuses on his regret for not spending more time with them because of his obligations as a soldier, Krompecher specifically wrote the letter in the event that he did not return.

Spring 2004

Dear Leah and Annie,

My precious little girls. I write this letter to you because soon I will leave for Iraq. Your mommy and I just tucked you both into bed, read your books, and said our prayers together. I've been watching the news and am worried that there could be the off-chance that I might never get to watch you board the school bus for the first time, place a Band Aid on a scraped knee, or walk you down the aisle of your wedding. So if you are reading this years from now, I want you to know how very much your daddy loved you and that I am also watching over you and protecting you. You are my everything, and now I must say goodbye to you. I cannot express adequately how much you mean to me, but I will try.

While I was your father, I was not always a good daddy. I failed in balancing the life of a soldier with the awesome responsibility of being a daddy. Even now I talk about, almost brag, to my fellow soldiers about going over—many of them are not deploying—but I suppose I do this to convince myself that I'll be fine and to hide my fear and worry about what could happen. I am a soldier, and going to war is something few American soldiers, at least those I know, want to miss. Fighting our nation's war is what we train, sweat, and prepare for our whole careers.

Still, I am worried. When I was a young, single Green Beret, I was so full of bravado that little would faze me. But now, I have you two, my little princesses, and your brother and mother to think of. I don't want this to be our last goodbye, but I realize thousands of others have left their families to go to the sound of the guns: I am going too, and I am proud of the men (fine men who give much of themselves) I'll be serving with over there, but I am scared about not coming home alive. I worry that the next time you see me will be when you stand in front of my coffin wearing your Sunday best to say goodbye to a daddy you hardly knew. I'm scared, but I'm a soldier. . . . I can't make sense of it either.

Leah, when you were two, we went sledding for the first time, just the two of us—daddy and daughter—out enjoying the snow. After each ride down the hill, I would tow you back up while you sat on the sled. During one of our treks up, I overheard you crying and looked back to see that one of your snow boots had fallen off at the bottom of the hill. I picked you up, placed your foot in my jacket and headed down the hill to retrieve the missing boot. Little did I know that you would forever remember that incident as a pleasurable one because it was a moment in which we bonded. Now, any mention of snow and you respond happily with, "Daddy, remember when we went sledding and my boot 'felled' off?" quickly following with, "Daddy, when can we go sledding again?" That was two years ago, and you still remember it as if it were yesterday.

One night during this past December, I read you girls *The Snowy Day* before bedtime. The next morning revealed three inches of fresh powder. That morning you greeted me with the plea, "Daddy, can we go outside and play like Peter did in his book?" Sadly, I replied that I had to get to work but maybe we could build a snowman after I returned home. Unfortunately, it was so dark by the time I returned from work that there was no time for snowmen, or anything else.

Every morning, I walked outside to kick the icicles hanging off my jeep before driving to work through the slush-covered roads. In January, it snowed again, and you (Leah) came running up to me with your pull-on boots on the wrong feet, wearing an unzipped jacket and mittens. At the same time you, Annie, pointed excitedly at the blanket of snow that covered our backyard. Both of you smiled eagerly in hopes of playing outside. Sadly, I felt that I had no time to play games in the snow. I had received orders for Iraq and was preparing for war. Eventually, you both stopped asking me to play in the snow and would instead sit quietly in your reading chairs while I made important phone calls and dealt with other business.

During one of the unseasonably warm days we had just weeks ago, I pulled up in our driveway and looked out the car window just in time to witness you (Leah) attempting to play kickball with the neighborhood children while Annie looked on from your picnic table in our front yard. In the middle of the field was another father from across the street. He moved towards you (Leah) and gently rolled the ball as you stood uncertainly at home plate. You responded with a kick and laughed hysterically while running the bases. Annie clapped and cheered you on.

Then "it" hit me. Sitting in my car wearing my uniform, the thought of how I had wasted enjoying so many precious moments with my little darlings slammed into me. I realized then that that should be me out on that plate. That should be *me* guiding my daughter to first base and then deliberately miss tagging her out as you rounded third for a homerun. That should be *me* enjoying a tea party with my daughter on her plastic picnic table. I suddenly understood how I should have taken you both sledding to see if perhaps we could make it down a hill without a boot falling off. Later that week, I saw you (Leah) ride your bike by yourself for the very first time. I asked mommy who had fastened your bicycle helmet and helped you move the bike to the front of the house. Mommy responded that you had found your helmet, dragged your bike to the front of the house, and proceeded to ride (with no one walking at your side). I knew then that you were both growing up and would not always need me.

When I was stationed in Georgia, my friend SFC (Ret) James Smith sent me an e-mail that ended with the quotation, "To the world I am an individual. To an individual, I am the world." Unfortunately, I never understood that line until recently receiving orders for this deployment.

Last night, as I was putting you both to bed, Leah looked up at me and said, "Daddy, I have tears in my eyes because you will be leaving." Annie, you must have realized something was wrong because you started crying, too. With that statement, I resolved to take SFC Smith's advice to heart and decided to "be the world" to you all. Years from now, I do not want to be the guy who sits alone sifting through a box of pictures trying to recapture fading memories because he left his children clinging to unfulfilled promises.

April has arrived, and there is little evidence of the long winter. I have put the sled away until next year. Winter is over, and I leave for Iraq next month. You are growing. All I can hope for is that it will snow just one more time.

Love,
Your Daddy

Ten days after he wrote this letter, it snowed, and Krompecher and his children spent the afternoon sledding and drinking hot chocolate. After

*serving in Iraq, Krompecher came back alive and well to his wife, Tina,
and their three children.*

TIMELESS
Personal Narrative
Christy De'on Miller

*Every parent or spouse reacts differently. Many, upon seeing the uniformed
military personnel walk up their front steps, begin screaming right away.
Others refuse to let the casualty notification officers inside, believing that if
they do not hear the message the officers have come to convey, their loved one
will still be alive. Some lash out in despair, even slapping the officers in the
face. And in the most extreme example to date, a father in Florida attempted
suicide immediately after being told that his twenty-year-old son had been
killed in Iraq. Like other parents with a child fighting overseas, Christy
De'on Miller visualized how the news of her son's death might come to her.
It was not something she, or anyone for that matter, wanted to think about,
but it was unavoidable. Lance Corporal Aaron C. Austin was a U.S. Marine
on his second tour of duty in Iraq, and he had already had numerous close
calls. Miller herself had served in the armed forces and, at the age of thirty-
five, was a U.S. Army specialist running support missions during the 1989 invasion of Panama. During her son's deployment fifteen years later, Miller,
who goes by the name De'on, wrote constantly—poetry, short stories, letters
to Aaron and other friends and family members, as well as journal entries—
to help her express the range of emotions she felt while waiting for her only
child to return to their home in New Mexico. (Aaron also lived with his father in Texas.) In October 2004, Miller began writing about the morning she
first heard that a firefight had erupted in Iraq between insurgents and a
group of Marines, with possibly one American fatality. The following account, based primarily on her letters and journals, chronicles the many
thoughts that went through her mind that day—and in those that followed.*

On April 26, 2004, I woke up around 4:00 in the morning and turned on
the television in my bedroom. At least twelve Marines had been in-

jured, and by 6:00 a.m., reporters were saying that one had died. I typed Aaron a letter, as I'd been doing daily for several weeks, trying to sound positive, and finally landing on an effortless subject concerning how much I'd paid on each of his bills, what was left in his checking account, and how much I'd pay next time. Mundane stuff, safe, easy, factual. Outside of mentioning that we had one Marine down, I avoided the hard news of the day. He would have already known about the Marine, and of course, I knew it would take three weeks for him to get the letter. But communication is so important to moms and their Marines.

I took Aaron's dog, Hennessy, for his morning walk, and, as was the norm, I was relieved to round the corner and view my home—void of an unfamiliar government vehicle parked in front of it. No one had brought me any bad news.

Some believe that a mother knows immediately, somewhere deep within her nurturing nature, the moment that her child has suffered harm. It had been a restless night, but there was no sense of foreboding. At least no different than any other time. I knew Aaron was always in danger.

It was around 4:00 or 5:00 p.m. when the two Marines drove up to my house. Aaron would have appreciated the almost limolike tinted windows on their silver minivan. At first, I thought it must be a friend coming to visit, but after mere moments, my eyes made the adjustment.

My mind wasn't far behind.

The noncommissioned officer began to approach me. It seemed to take an eternity for him to cross my lawn—I think I must have walked some, gone to meet him halfway.

He began, "Ma'am, are you Christy Miller?"

The Christy has always thrown me. Only government agencies, debtors, or new teachers have ever called me by my first name. It's rarely been used to bless me with good news.

"What? What did you ask me?" I think I was hollering. I thought he'd said Kristen Miller.

No, no, I wasn't that person.

I saw sympathy.

He asked me again. Time and space and neighbors and dogs, all—everything—grew into a blazing, buzzing blur.

I couldn't let the Marines in my home because I'd just put my two dogs in there and Hennessy is a pit bull.

"Can we go inside? We need to talk to you." His wasn't an easy job.

"No, we've got to do this outside." Mine, still the harder.

After a muddled exchange regarding the dog situation, the other Marine, the officer, finally said, "Ma'am, your son was killed in action today in Al Anbar province."

I said, "My son was killed in the firefight that's on the television right now. He was killed in Fallujah. There's been one Marine killed today."

There, in that moment, that tiniest and longest length of time, there must've been a mechanical failure, an embodiment of someone's (it couldn't have been mine) heart and brain colliding.

"Mine," I finished. Yes, the Marine was mine.

Aaron Cole Austin was born on July 1, 1982, at 8:53 p.m. central daylight savings time in Amherst, Texas. Circumcised and sent home on the Fourth of July, he was my breast-fed, blanket-sucking baby boy, a little Linus look-alike. He threw his blanket away when he was ten. God, how I wish for that blanket now. It surely would have carried some scent. You couldn't even bleach it out.

Lance Corporal Aaron C. Austin, USMC. Machine gunner. Team leader. Echo Company, 2nd Battalion, 1st Marine Regiment, 1st Marine Division. KIA on April 26, 2004, in Fallujah, Iraq.

For a period of time, I thought he must have been killed on April 25, 2004, New Mexico time. I almost had the twenty-fifth etched on his headstone.

Almost. Facts and times were very important. Are very important. I kept checking his social security number on everything I signed, just in case there was some inaccuracy in this news. Some tragic fact overlooked or flawed. Then I got his watch back, the one he was wearing that awful day, and after I took some time to count the hours, to do some real figuring, I realized that we shared a few hours of the day. It was definitely the twenty-sixth that he was killed. Around 2:00 a.m. My time.

Aaron's company commander, Captain Zembiec, wrote me right after it happened.

040426

De'on,

Your son was killed in action today. He was conducting a security patrol with his company this morning, in enemy territory. His company had halted in two buildings, strongpointing them and looking for insurgents.

A large number of enemy personnel attacked Aaron and his platoon at around 1100. Despite intense enemy machine gun and rocket propelled grenade fire, your son fought like a lion. He remained in his fighting position until all his wounded comrades could be evacuated from the rooftop they were defending. It was during his courageous defense of his comrades that Aaron was hit by enemy fire, enemy machine gun fire.

We held a memorial service this afternoon in honor of your son. With the exception of the Marines on Security, every man in the company attended the service. Aaron was respected and admired by every Marine in his company. His death brought tears to my eyes, tears that fell in front of my Marines. I am unashamed of that fact.

Your son died a warrior's death, in battle, in a fight as tough as any battle that Marines who have gone before us fought. Your son died a hero, killing enemy soldiers in order to defend his fellow Marines.

Captain Teague and Gunny Sergeant Velasquez brought Aaron's things to me on June 30, 2004. From the men who first told me the news, who had stood outside my home, compassionate Marines in dress blues, to those who entered my living room and placed before me the one remaining box of my son's life, and then, on bent knee, took out a smaller box from within the larger, and handed over to me Aaron's watch, the one removed from his body at the time of death—it is to these men that I owe so much.

June 30 also just happened to be the day that Lea County unveiled the granite stone with his name etched there. Thus far, Aaron's name remains singular on that stone. He also holds the distinction of Texas as well as New Mexico both claiming him as their own. Since the tender age of nine, Aaron has always had at least two places to call home.

I began to wear Aaron's watch, which was still on Baghdad time. His alarm would go off at 3:28:24. Then again at 3:33:20. Aaron was always, "Give me five more minutes, Mom."

This early alarm, its hidden meaning, meant only for him, for duty on a rooftop possibly, is 5:30 p.m. (the evening before) my time.

His watch became my watch. And this is the way my mind works now, as I watch out my window, watch up in the sky or into a sunset.

It will be almost eight months before I'll sit and purposefully watch a sunset. Oh, I've witnessed them since April 26, but I've not really looked at them, not regarded them. There are the times I've glimpsed one, almost accidentally, outside the small window in my entryway that faces the east, a window more inclined toward sunrises, not sunsets. This window welcomes the sun as it catches on the crystal suspended there, splashing purples, blues, oranges and hope, early, very early in the morning. By sunset, the parade of color has long marched past.

But one night I'll realize how much more beautiful it is to go out my front door, cross the street, sit on a familiar but lonely park bench, and observe the real thing facing west. It doesn't explode into sudden bursts of color, but eases into a full palette of shade, form, and light. I watch as the same colors I sometimes noticed in the morning are given back to me in the evening, in full. Purple, blue, orange. I'm not filled with the same hope I carry in the morning, but rather, burdened by memory.

I could just about hear his voice as I sat there. As other teenagers and youngsters gravitated toward each other in the street, strolled toward their homes, or drove by me without really looking, the bass beating in their cars, cruising, their voices triggered an image of my own young teen, then sixteen, laughing, full of hope, a very temporal hope—mostly, a mind busy with a new strategy on how to con Mom out of something tangible, name-brand shoes, or jeans, or something else costly, cool, sweet.

My mom once told me that my parenting skills bordered on contributing to the delinquency of a minor. Because he always knew how to charm me, how to make me smile, I was always "The Rescuer." He used to call me Momma when he wanted something. I got called Momma a lot.

Parents spend a great deal of effort teaching their young how to use time well, how to manage it, how to spend it economically. But maybe, sometimes, they should just go fishing, boating, or to a movie, something that means little more than killing time together. Sometimes. Aaron and I went fishing and boating a lot. We watched many movies together. Military, usually.

On December 20, 2003, at age forty-eight, I graduated with a Bachelor of Arts in English. My very proud son flew in from Camp Pendleton to attend the ceremony and to celebrate Christmas with family.

Aaron had returned from overseas duty in July 2003. He'd been with the Marines, some of the first ground troops to cross the border between Kuwait and Iraq, and he was due to go back in February 2004.

At my graduation ceremony, Aaron sat through the many speeches. He struggled through as each of the PhD candidates received their just dues, made it through the many master's degrees, a fraction of the bachelor's degrees, and then right before his mother's name was called, right before I walked, my son had to go to the bathroom. I graduated while Aaron was in the head.

I kind of smiled when I first heard. I would have been disappointed had it been any other way.

When we were leaving the building, Aaron stopped at one of the concessions there in the United Spirit Arena and used his last few bucks to bless me with a bouquet of white roses. He always knew how to charm me. How to make me smile.

Aaron and I used to joust with each other when we were alone, when he could finally be still.

"I love you," I'd say.

"I love you more," he'd respond.

"No, I love you the very most."

"No, I love you the mostest of the most."

"I love you more than all the eyelashes in the world."

On and on we'd go.

When Aaron was back on the USS *Rushmore*, he e-mailed me. "I love you more than all the sand in Iraq." He always one-upped me.

After Aaron was killed, his platoon leader sent me twelve white roses laced with ribbon and tiny dried petals of baby's breath. One rose, from Lance Corporal Austin, is pressed in waxed paper. Another rose, from First Lieutenant McCoy, is pressed in tissue. The two white roses stand together, pressed between two small panes of glass in my "Girl's Bathroom."

They both bless and break my heart today.

At times, I try to go back in my head before there was an Aaron. I'll listen to music from the sixties or seventies. I'll try to recall that I had a life before Aaron. But in the end, this does nothing.

Words like Forever and Eternity really mean something to me now. Before, when I would read these words, I wouldn't really concentrate on their true definition, on their real essence. I guess I thought they were for later. Now, I have a real need, a down to the white sand of my bones aching need, to know that forever and eternity started long before my time, way before Aaron, before the Marines came to my home That Day, and then later, brought me his watch. Every day there are gifts. And every day, things are taken away.

Aaron's watch stopped somewhere between late afternoon on the twenty-eighth of November and noon on the thirtieth. I learned that when the battery goes dead on a digital watch—it's gone. Blank. Not even a zero. The watch now rests in an Americana chest in his bedroom.

Since Aaron's death, I've experienced the first Mother's Day without my son, his would-be twenty-second birthday without him, and the homecoming of his unit without him. Right around the corner are his unit's Marine Ball (their 229th Birthday) and our first Thanksgiving and Christmas without him. Many of the "firsts" will then be behind me. I don't know if the seconds, thirds, and fourths get any better. I imagine they become more manageable.

At times I believe I can learn to live a life without my son. After all, I must. I am certain there are other mothers who have lost their boys—car accidents, war, illness—who can shop for dinner at the local grocer's without the macaroni-and-cheese boxes suddenly causing them grief. Moms who can roll sausage balls without tears; perhaps the festive food would even cause a smile. But the memory of him is planted in everything around me. Inside of me. So much is gone. Him, of course. But so much of him has been lost, is fading, breaking down. His blanket, his watch, his uniform. The military uses commercial washers to clean personal items before they are handed over to the families. Understandable, but it leaves a synthetic laundry smell. Aaron's scent was gone. These were the realizations, the moments I most dreaded. And they came out of nowhere.

My faith doesn't equal that of Job's. I question. Why has God cut the fruit from my vine? Taken the only child that remained? Left me with no hope for a grandchild? I'm certain there can be no more. No more children.

And yet I have no particular animosity for my son's killer. He's a nameless and faceless combatant to me. Should I ever have the opportunity to meet him, I hope that I'd forgive him. To me, the buck stops with the Father. His power stings at times. But He's listened to me; perhaps He's even cried with me. And yes, I *do* know what I'm talking about here. *It's a belief, man.* Aaron's words. *You either believe in God or you don't.* Yes, I'd forgive. I do forgive. There is absolutely nothing I'd do to keep myself from spending eternity with God and Aaron.

The moments pass. I can't say how. It's not of my doing. I find comfort in the late-night phone calls from Jerrod, Aaron's best friend, or Tiffany, the broken and faithful fiancée Aaron left behind. Those trusted ones who've seen fit to adopt me. Here, with these people, within this grafting, He gives back to me not only a part of Aaron, but also a stronger ear to hear them, to listen to who they really are, an eye, no longer singular, now that my son does not soak up all the light. They become more than an extension of him. Perhaps I'm beginning to know them in the way Aaron took the time to.

He proposed to Tiffany on March 18. They sent catalogs back and forth with circles around the engagement rings each liked. She bought her wedding dress on April 26, 2004. That Day. Two days before they were to get married, on December 11, 2004, I wrote her a letter.

To my Darling Daughter, one not given to me by birth, but by God all the same.

This ring cannot replace the ring you hoped for. I cannot replace Aaron, but I will be here for as long as you should ever need me, in whatever capacity that life and grace both grant us.

It is the color purple: your favorite color and my favorite color.

It is the color of his Purple Heart.

It is the birthstone of the last month you physically touched him.

Amethyst is your birthstone.

The color purple is associated with royalty. Don't ever settle for being loved less than a Princess, less than the Bride of Christ, which is who you are.

I love you. Aaron loved you before, and I feel his love for all of us now. It has been perfected in a way that we cannot even understand while we are here. Just trust The One Who gave Aaron to us. Just trust.

Thank you for loving my son, Tiffany. Thank you for giving him all that hope and all those dreams while he was there in Iraq. Thank you for loving me.

God bless you; give you strength and peace. Hold you in His merciful arms. Show you new and beautiful, deep, rich and royal color in your life.

Always,
De'on

On a day in which I felt pretty bruised, I went over to my mom's house. She was sitting out in her backyard, a yard that at times I feel she must have designed with the Garden of Eden in mind, but anyway, it's relaxing. Habitat is well and alive. I sat down at one of the sitting areas and looked up at her. I guess my eyes must have said everything. I began, "Mom, how long before the bad . . ."

She stopped me in midsentence and held up her index and middle finger. "De'on, I asked Dr. Chatwell"—a family doctor since I was a babe—"that very same question. I knew that he'd witnessed many deaths, and dealt with the survivors' grief later, and when I asked him, he said two summers." She continued, "The Indians also say two summers, so if you lose someone in the winter, then it takes longer. By the third summer, there are more smiles than tears."

I sat there for a moment and then thought, okay, then there is some end to this.

And for my benefit, she added, "We lost Aaron in the spring, so we won't have to wait as long."

I really don't know how to describe that moment of finding those house shoes. First of all, there was a history to them. For several years in a row, at Christmas, one of Aaron's Santa gifts was a pair of Dollar Store house shoes. It was kind of a joke, in a way, because Aaron loved the name-brand things. I'd always get these house shoes because we liked to slouch around in our comfies on Christmas and weekends. They were comfortable, cost about four bucks, kind of cheap suede things, beige. Each year, Aaron would rework the house shoes by taking a Nike tab off of an old pair of tennis shoes and affixing it to the back; or, on this particular pair, he'd taken a Sharpie pen and drawn zebra stripes all up and down on them. These shoes were stuffed into a closet for things we didn't really need. At least, thought we didn't really need.

I'd already been through several rounds of "looking for him." Articles, pictures, his voice, things like that. He used to chew on the caps of pens, his dog tags, everything, so I'd already saved a few things I'd found like that. You're not ever preparing for this day, so everything had pretty much been washed, given away, or thrown out when Aaron deployed. I did find his voice on a couple of tapes, including when he was in the third grade, and he was studying for a spelling test, spelling dinosaur words over and over. Then his voice for a few minutes back in '98, I think, and then, after his first trip to Iraq when a news station interviewed him. Each and every new little discovery is uplifting for a while, it lends hope, and then you remember why you're even doing this, and so it goes.

Then one day, I was in that closet, and I looked down and saw that pair of house shoes, the lizard-striped ones. They brought a smile and tears and when I grabbed them up, noticed a kind of grimy stain in the bottom, I sniffed, over and over. I cried, of course, but I was still so happy. It was the smell of his feet. No one ever expects that kind of smell to be a gift, but to me, that day, it was, and still every once in a while, I go and get them out of his room. Now they sit by his bed, close to our two pairs of boots: the jungle boots I wore in Panama, and his pair, from Iraq. I can smell him better in the house shoes than the boots.

Hennessy once went to Aaron's bedroom door (it was shut), scratched on it, whined, went to the front door, did the same, and then just laid down, sort of depressed. (He's by nature a depressed dog, anyway.) My animals are the ones who witness my grief the most. They see me in the day, crying. And I wonder how much they know. I can't talk to Hennessy in any real way. I wish I could. I don't want him to feel deserted. The other night, he went into Aaron's room at least three or four times, and whined. I keep the door opened most of the time, now. It just seems easier that way. That's the only time he's done that. Hennessy, however, has no reaction to the house shoes. I've wondered about it over and over. It's strange how these things are.

The days have become different. Sorrow is a tiny tile in the mosaic, which doesn't lessen the sadness, and flashes of grief still come. But I believe that time does heal. I think it teaches. I now belong to organizations and support groups of which a mother never imagines becoming a member. While others may recognize the scar of sorrow and ask about it, or perhaps because of their own scar, they will turn their head away, we share in the sorrow, and in the hope—a new hope, one that has been bought with tears and prayers, not just day by day, but minute by minute. I do think that time is on our side. It's easy to talk and write about sacrifice, it's quite another to live it. But like the sons and daughters we buried, we want to be strong. We hope they are proud of us, because God knows how very proud we are of them.

We aren't always sure in this life if the words we speak or those we write will be our last. Long after the day Aaron died, I found a letter I wrote to Aaron that he never received. It's dated April 26, 2004. Aaron was already dead. But he was alive when I wrote it. To me, at the time.

Hi Son,

Well, the news is bad. Another Marine killed, and it sounds like your unit was the one in the firefight. Ten others wounded. I am just about as heartsick as I care to get. Our prayers are with you and I wish with all my heart the very best of blessings for you, for yours, for all of our troops. I pray that this will end soon. I am so sick of it.

I'm sorry. I know you don't need this. You live with it, and you and all of the troops are appreciated by so many. We love you and appreciate all you are giving up.

I paid half your Star off with $600.00. So just another $600.00 and you should be out of debt, I think. Your last 2 deposits have been around 866.00. Your Sunray State Bank loan comes out in an allotment.

How are Jose, Jamie, Brent, Barnes, and Koci? Please give them all my love.

The 2 letters I got from you the other day were a month old. I mailed Allie hers, and hopefully, you will get everyone's addresses that I sent you pretty soon. If you ever get the chance to drop Granny and Grandpa a letter, I know they'd be thrilled.

I love Tiffany. I can't wait for her to be here.

Please take care, son. I love you with all my heart.

Do you get to use the pillow any?

My love and prayers, always,
MOM

It's not really something of his. He never received it. But still, it's *ours*. Just like so many things are ours, now.

I add later, in my mind, a postscript. What I would write to him if I could. I miss you, Aaron, with all of me, all of the time. Every moment, I was, am, and will always remain so very proud of you, who you were, how you went down, what you stood for and those you fought for. For me. For us. For your Marines, your brothers. They awarded you the Silver Star, Aaron. They loved you too, and miss you. I guess I just never really believed that your time would come before my time. But son, you know, we are forever. By the grace of God I will join you some day. I'll meet the mystery of it all, too, and we will be together. How good it will be to see you again.

CHAPTER FIVE

THIS IS NOT A GAME

THE PHYSICAL AND EMOTIONAL TOLL OF WAR

Lieutenant Colonel Frank Correa, July 2003, on a medevac flight
of wounded troops. *Photo used by permission.*

The scene on the aircraft was hard to believe. We had row after row of litters stacked three- and sometimes four-high with patients. They seemed to go all the way to the back of the plane. The smell of unwashed bodies and infected wounds filled the air. Combat wounds are by nature dirty, and in spite of thorough cleaning, there are still a lot of infections. Some were amputees and missing parts of their bodies. One guy had stepped on a mine, lost part of his feet, and had small shrapnel wounds covering his face. Most of our patients had either gunshot or shrapnel wounds to the arms or legs. One of the most critical patients was a guy injured in a vehicle accident and had serious head wounds. Despite his swollen and discolored face, he was going to make it. He was lucky. We had another guy with a bad gunshot wound to the abdomen. His internal injuries were significant, and the best I could do was give him maximum doses of his pain meds to enable him to sleep as much as possible. Whenever he was awake I saw in his eyes the pain, fatigue, and fear he felt. I will never forget his expression, or him. Another guy needed pain pills and told me that the hospital had lost them along with all of his personal belongings. Ironically the thing he felt most upset about was their losing his pictures of him and his buddies in Iraq. I felt overwhelmed by the sheer number of patients we were treating, and I had been awake and on the go for the last twenty-four hours. Making critical decisions and keeping track of everyone when my mind and body screamed for sleep made the missions all the more difficult. But I knew I really had nothing to complain about because while our discomfort was temporary, many of the wounded faced a lifetime of hardships. For them, this trip was only the beginning.

> —Forty-four-year-old Lieutenant Colonel Frank Correa describing, based on notes from his April 2003 journals, his service as a medical crew director with the U.S. Air Force's 491st Expeditionary Aeromedical Evacuation Unit. During his five-month deployment, Correa and his crew cared for more than seven hundred troops injured in Iraq. After coming back to the States in August 2003, Correa returned to his job as a paramedic with the Los Angeles Fire Department.

WHAT'S GOING ON OVER HERE

E-mail

Sergeant Timothy J. Gaestel

Like most of the troops at the time, Sergeant Timothy James Gaestel was in high spirits. "Hey, dad this is your son," Gaestel began a hastily written e-mail home on September 21, 2003, while just south of Baghdad. "I finally get to write ya'll a letter. First off let me tell you we made it here safe and so far, but everything is going very good." The ground invasion of Iraq, only months before, was considered a military triumph, and the hostilities flaring up in scattered parts of the country since the fall of Baghdad seemed sporadic and containable. A twenty-two-year-old native of Austin, Texas, Gaestel had always wanted to be a soldier (both of his parents had served in the U.S. Army), and he was already on his second tour of duty—the first had been in Afghanistan—with the 1-319th Airborne Field Artillery Unit, 82nd Airborne. Despite the upbeat mood conveyed at the beginning of his message, however, Gaestel's e-mail was a stark reminder that the fighting in Iraq was far from over. "Now Dad, I know that you have already received a phone call that tells you I am okay," he continued, "but I want you to know exactly what happened [when our convoy was hit by a roadside bomb]. . . ."

We were heading south down highway eight and I was gunning for the 2nd truck. Byrd was driving and my chief was the passenger. We got off highway eight onto Ambush Alley the route we didn't take going up there. I was in the back of the truck with my 240B machine gun and the S-2 wanted to ride in the back of the truck with me since I was the only one back there. We were at the end of the convoy at this point so we were really hauling ass driving down the wrong side of the road and all that just so we could get to the front of the convoy. My buddy Eddie was a bad ass driver and keeps us for getting in wreck a few times. But still able to get the mission done. The X.O. truck was behind us and needed to get in front, not to mention the fact that I had his gatoraide I was supposed too through to him at the next time they passed us.

At that exact moment a loud and thunderous boom went off and pushed me all the way to the front of where my 240B was mounted. I knew something had just happened and when I turned around I could see to large smoke clouds on each side of the road. The first thing I had thought was I had just been hit in the back by and IED. It wasn't like I felt as if I was going to die, more like "man that really hurt." At that moment I reached around and felt my back and pulled my hand back and it was cover with blood, before that I honestly thought it had just hit my IBA. It turns out that it had hit my IBA and gone right through it.

I laid down on the back of the truck but this didn't seem like a good ideal and I didn't have my weapon and had to yell at the S-2 to give me my weapon, I didn't want an ambush to happen and for me not have my weapon. So I stood up on my knees and yelled again to him to man the 240B, he was scared but that's what happened when you don't ever get any kind of training and you sit in an office all day. This guy didn't react very well, when I showed him my back he started flipping out and yelling "oh, G you got him man, oh he's hit bad man." This is the last thing that you tell someone who has just been hit in the back and is bleeding. As you can imagine I was pretty pissed off at this point and I showed my anger toward the people in th town that we were driving through, I had my M-4 rifle at the ready and my trigger finger on the trigger and just waiting for someone to give me a reason to have me put it from safe to semi. I maintained my military bearing as well as one could in that situation. I sure wanted to shoot the bastard that had just set the IED off. The people in this town must have thought I was crazy because I was cursing and yelling and wanting someone to give me one reason why they shouldn't have me kill them. . . .

As we were making our way back to the FOB at that last street, I could no longer sit up straight and my back was killing me now. There was a Major who was our field surgeon waiting for me in the front of the gate to check me out. This guy didn't reassure me either. When I told him that I was okay he looked at me and said, "look son, you may have internal bleeding." Now I was scared. They rushed me to the Aide station, where I talked to some Sergeant Majors and the Col. and told them about the kites. In like 15 minutes, in my brown underwear, green socks up to my knees and a blanket, I was rushed out to the Landing Zone where a chopper took me to "cash 28" a hospital in down town Baghdad. The flight there was fast and I thought to myself, "how small our world was from being in an AC hospital from where I was living in a crappy army tent. The flight through Baghdad was amazing to you could see the whole city and all the building and stuff it was very strange. The helicopter piolet was a bad ass as well, he had to do a war time landing which is really fast and quick it was cool. Now Dad I hadn't seen a female in 21 days and so you could imagine I was excited when I looked down off the helicopter as we were coming in for a landing to see a very beautiful woman (it could be she is beautiful because I haven't seen a woman in awhile). Now when I landed a female, second Lt. took me into the ER room with no one else in the whole room except her and me. She came up to me and ripped off my blanket and grabbed my brown undies ripped those off to and gave me a capater. Now that was more painful than the IED and way not what I was thinking was going to happen when she grabbed my blanket off me. Then she gave me some morphine and I was good.

One thing that bothered me is the way they treated people, just because there always around stuff like that doesn't mean that they have to act like it's nothing to get hit in the back by a bomb. They did an x-ray of my back and found that I had two pieces of shrapnel in my back, I asked the doctor if I could keep the shrapnel and he said "yea sure, forever." They weren't going to be taking the shrapnel out. So yeah now your son is going to have two pieces of metal in his back for the rest of his life. I was cleaned up and taken to patient hold. A place that is something out of a movie. It was horrible to see all the soldiers with missing legs and arms and bandages everywhere. Shortly afterwards I was given some morphine and passed out. When I woke up Col. Smith CSM Burgos, LTC. Layton, CSM Howard and our Chaplin came in. The first thing LTC Layton said to me was "well me and the Sergeant Major were taking and you are the 1st person to receive the Purple Heart in the loyalty battalion since Grenada(1983). Its quite crazy the turn of events that have lead me here. A purple heart recipient, I guess all it means is that some guy got me before I could get him. We will joke about this all someday Dad. I told them I didn't want you all to find out about this because im not leaving Iraq and I dint want you to worry. I know your going too anyway but the reason I shared this story here was so you know what it's like to be here and that the people that im with all look after one another. I guess it's really crazy that I volunteered to stay even though I was hit in the back with shrapnel, and as soon as I can im going to return to my unit. I don't want mom to worry so don't read the detailed parts of this letter. I LOVE YALL and ill be home soon enough. Let everyone know what's going on over here, let them here it from a soldier. This is my First Letter Home.

LOVE ALWAYS
Your son
Spc. Timothy J. Gaestel

After recovering from his wounds, Gaestel remained in Iraq for seven more months before returning to the United States. In August 2005, after four years of military service, he was honorably discharged.

PROLIFERATION
Journal
Captain Robert Swope

U.S. Army Captain Robert Swope shipped off to the Middle East in the early spring of 2003 and served in Iraq for more than fourteen months, primarily with the 1st Armored Division's 2nd Brigade Combat Team. Swope was stationed mostly in Baghdad, and he and his unit were scheduled to return home in March 2004. But with more troops needed to combat the rising insurgency, their final homecoming was delayed for several more months. Swope kept a journal during his deployment, and in the fall of 2003 the twenty-five-year-old infantry officer began recording how dramatically Baghdad was changing. He was also concerned with what was turning out to be the most lethal new threat to U.S. forces.

October 15, 2003
I took my first trip through these streets in the middle of April when my platoon was tasked as a security escort to retrieve the wreckage of an Apache helicopter that had been downed earlier in the war and, I was told, later shot with one of our own Sidewinder missiles in an effort to prevent nearby Iraqi troops from acquiring the technology inside. Back then parts of the city still looked like an apocalyptic nightmare. Burned-out tanks, armored personnel carriers, overturned cars, and buses littered the streets. Rubble was everywhere.

Driving through these same streets today one sees a great deal of difference. Everywhere you look is a satellite dish, and Internet cafés have sprouted up across the city, both links to the outside world that were illegal under the previous regime. Outdoor restaurants and ice cream shops are crowded with business. It's a few hours before curfew starts, and the streets are still congested with vehicle traffic. Makeshift stands along the roads sell gasoline, cigarettes, sodas, and soap. The kids still chase you, except they picked up a little

English during the summer and can now say everything from "I love you" to "fuck you."

Perhaps the newest and most disturbing trend is the proliferation of improvised explosive devices. To date, more troops have been killed or wounded by IEDs or IED-initiated ambushes than any other cause. Unfortunately these devices are becoming increasingly sophisticated, with remote controlled detonators and elaborate concealment techniques, increasing the danger to both Coalition forces and the innocent Iraqis who happen to be nearby when one goes off, and who almost always bear the brunt of the damage.

November 8

Once a week on Saturday nights in the battalion theater, we have a professional development class or briefing for all the commissioned and noncommissioned officers in the battalion. Tonight's class is on the battalion's battle drill for what to do when encountering IEDs. The group discusses techniques that have been used to hide them as well as other issues relating to reacting to IEDs once they've been discovered, such as the ambushes that sometimes follow.

About five minutes into the discussion, a private comes into the theater and whispers to the sergeant major that the S3, the battalion's operations officer, is needed in the TOC. The S3 rushes out and then comes back to get the headquarters company commander who leaves with the scout platoon leader. The platoon leader comes back in with a disconcerted look on his face and vigorously motions for his platoon sergeant to get the hell up out of the meeting and leave with him.

The commander shakes his head when he's told what's happened and then quickly finishes his comments before releasing us. Stepping outside I hear that there has been an IED attack on one of the scout vehicles. A few minutes later I meet up with Joe, a friend of mine who is the battalion maintenance officer, and he tells me that two soldiers have been wounded, but that's all he knows. Joe and I head up to the roof of one of the buildings and hang out, drinking German near-beer and smoking Macanudo cigars in the moonlight. It starts to rain, one of the few downpours I've experienced in the desert, and the raindrops are cool on our skin but we don't leave. A little after midnight, we climb down the ladder, and ask the captain who gave the IED class if there is any more news on the scouts. He tells us the guys are okay.

November 9

I'm woken up early this morning by two fellow officers talking outside my room, discussing the death of one of the soldiers from the company I was in during the war, who died while manning a security position at the Baghdad airport last April. The weapons system of the Bradley Fighting Vehicle he was standing by accidentally discharged from an electrical surge, sending a 25 mm tungsten-tipped sabot round through his Kevlar helmet at point-blank range. It had been a sunny day at the airport and my gunner helped carry the stretcher. When he came back, his arms were covered in blood and he couldn't stop shaking. He put his hands to his head and then jerked back after he touched his face and realized his fingers were still wet. I helped him wash it off with a bar of soap from my toiletry kit, and poured water over him. I gave my extra uniform to one of the medics who attended the injured, and whose uniform had to be burned in a trash pit with all the other bandages and clothes. He spent the next day and a half being saluted as an officer. After the medevac helicopter left, I remember watching the dead soldier's squad leader walking back to his platoon area carrying his weapon cradled in both arms, a blank, uncomprehending and expressionless look on his face.

After hearing the other officers talk about the sabot incident, I realize that one of the scouts died overnight. My heart begins to sink into my stomach. Later that day on my way back from the base post office, I stop by the head-quarters building and inspect the Humvee hit by the IED. There are gashes in the steel of the vehicle and it's still wet from when some soldiers cleaned it up at 0200 in the morning. Because they didn't have a hose to spray down the vehicle with and flush the blood out, they ended up pouring five-gallon water jugs over the inside, soaking up the crimson liquid with strips of cloth torn from Army-issue brown T-shirts.

Next to the Humvee is a silver metal trash can with the smoldering re-mains of the rags and bloodied equipment that couldn't be cleaned, such as the dead soldier's boonie cap and his used compression bandages. A thin plume of white smoke rises up from it.

It turns out the soldier died before the medevac helicopter even landed to pick him up. A fragment from the bomb hit him in the back of the neck, sev-ering his spinal cord. I can't imagine how scared he must have been in those final moments as he saw his life slowly slipping away, bleeding to death and be-ginning to lose motor function. He was a private, twenty-two, and had only joined the unit about eight days earlier. It was his first mission out into the city.

TRY NOT TO WORRY ABOUT ME
E-mail
Captain Michael P. Sullivan

Along with the use of IEDs, American troops were confronted with another tactic that was less frequent but equally terrifying. "Now I don't want to scare you all, but I refuse to gloss this over, so let me tell you the story," twenty-six-year-old Captain Michael P. Sullivan began a December 12, 2003, e-mail to family members. Sullivan was stationed at FOB Champion in Ar Ramadi, Iraq, with the 313th Military Intelligence Battalion, 82nd Airborne Division. The day before Sullivan sent his e-mail, a car bomb detonated just outside the division's headquarters. "The damage was very extensive—it was a very large amount of explosives," Sullivan wrote. "The pick-up truck laden with aforementioned explosives was carrying three locals and one escort soldier. All of them in the vehicle were instantly vaporized by the explosion. The effects of the blast wounded 14 other US soldiers/contractors." Sullivan continued:

Frankly, I easily could have been killed or at least seriously injured—it really just came down to the timing. You see, whether it was targeted or not, it just so happens that the vehicle detonated right in front of our 313th MI living quarters—my house as it were. 20 feet away at the most. By a miracle of timing, I was not at that building at the time, but a lot of my subordinate soldiers were. I talk about timing, because we have a weight set just outside our living quarters which we utilize daily in the afternoons. We were planning on lifting yesterday at 1400. 30 minutes later, and I would have been standing outside that building, right in the blast. . . .

As it was, two of my soldiers were on the front porch at the time the vehicle drove by and detonated. They remembered how at the last second before the explosion, the escort soldier was frantically trying to escape the truck, but alas he was too late. Both soldiers on the porch were blown backwards through the front doors and into the building. Both suffered injuries, one fairly severe, but they survived. It took quite a while to mop up all the blood. The explosion of course blew all the doors and windows violently inward,

plastering everyone inside with a shit-storm of glass and debris. Again, miraculously, other than some hearing damage, everyone inside came out mostly
uninjured. It is incredible, because most that were inside have no idea how
the larger pieces of glass did not tear them apart. More of my Battalion colleagues were standing in front of the building next door—the concussion of
the explosion threw them 15 feet through the air, but they also came out
amazingly uninjured.

At the time of the explosion, I was working as usual in the Division Headquarters, which is about 100 meters away from where it detonated (still it was
damned close). Now remember, we hear loud explosions in the distance all
the time, day and night, so in the split second that it first detonated, my brain
registered that I was just hearing a mortar round or IED explode in the distance. In the next second, all the windows imploded, and the explosion was
louder than anything you can possibly imagine. The concussion was staggering. And understand, our wall was facing the explosion, and it was lined with
huge, tall windows. Everything went, and a maelstrom of debris, glass and
window frame came bursting into our workspace. Quite a few people were injured by the flying glass. My friend Matt was standing in the window at the
time and got blown about ten feet backwards. He luckily got away with just a
couple of scratches. Though some glass rained down on me, I was sitting in a
lucky spot and I somehow don't have a scratch on me. You have never seen
people move so fast in your life as they did when they were getting away from
those windows. At this point, it had become all very surreal. All I could think
to my self was: "Boy, that was close, what the hell just happened?" When we
looked back out the window, the horror really struck us in the 313th, as we
could tell the explosion originated from where our living quarters are located.

We grabbed our weapons and took off at a run for our house, still not quite
knowing what had happened. I knew that the explosion was way too large to
have been a mortar, but no one knew exactly what was going on. As we got
closer, you could see charred body parts scattered everywhere—although the
nucleus of carnage was at the building, some parts were thrown for hundreds
of feet, and may not have even been found yet. At one point, we ran right past
a head just lying there on the ground, looking up at us. There was an acrid
stench in the air from the expended munition—it is still in the air as we
speak. As we came up to the building, it was simply mass chaos, and the gawk-
ing onlookers were everywhere. Our injured were bleeding profusely, and the

other soldiers who were in the building were frantically performing first aid. The crater in front of the building was massive. Charred vehicle parts were scattered everywhere and will probably be found hundreds of feet away for days to come. Most of the portable toilets out front were blown apart—there was a person in one of them at the time of the explosion, but he was fortunately unhurt except for a ruptured eardrum. The Battalion Commander's vehicle, which was parked out front, was completely demolished. The remains of the escort soldier were strewn over the grill of the vehicle—we knew it was him, because along with his flesh, we found charred and bloody pieces of his uniform everywhere. Part of the debris hailstorm I mentioned earlier blowing through our building was also a spray of body parts . . . so at first, we just tried to go around and pick up the largest pieces and clear it out—a hand by the weights, part of a face by the back washing machines, intestines lying everywhere. Well, you get the idea. . . .

At some point yesterday, it really sank in for me just how lucky I was, just how lucky most of us were to have not been in a position to have been seriously injured. Timing was the only thing that saved us. That and a really strong building. . . . It was a lot to assimilate yesterday, and as I collapsed onto my bed last night, I shuddered at what could have been, what almost was, and I humbly said a small prayer of thanks for our being spared. I also said an agonized prayer for the family of our fallen comrade, who's Christmas will never be the same for the rest of their lives.

My close friend, CPT Mike Dean is the Company Commander of the soldier who was killed, and my deepest condolences go out to him today. We will have a memorial service for him tomorrow.

I won't go into the minutiae of how we are responding to this heinous attack, but know that the vigilance around here will be heightened in order to isolate this to a single incident. We will all hope this is the case, now and in the future.

Again, rest assured that I am perfectly alright, albeit a little shaken up— we all are. . . . Please let your minds be at ease and try not to worry about me. I am fine.

Please take care and try not to let this affect your holiday season. Everything will be okay—I will be in touch again soon.

All The Way
CPT Michael P. Sullivan

THE SMELL OF FRESH PAINT
E-mail
Sergeant Tina M. Beller

*In previous conflicts, U.S. troops rarely described the true brutality of war-
fare in their letters home. Strict censorship rules did not, for the most part,
allow it, but even during the fighting in Korea and Vietnam, when letters
were not screened by military censors, service members often withheld
graphic details. Now, however, in an age of twenty-four-hour cable media,
the Internet, embedded reporters, and satellite communications, Americans
on the home front are able to hear breaking news from a war zone almost
the moment it happens. Knowing this, troops are more likely to write home
with details—except for anything that might compromise operational security—about what really happened. On the morning of September 12, 2004
(Iraq time; it was September 11 back in the States), insurgents launched
mortars into the Green Zone, a highly protected area that housed the Iraqi
interim government, foreign embassies, and other administrative buildings.
Tina M. Beller, a twenty-nine-year-old sergeant in the U.S. Army Reserve
(350th Civil Affairs Command), was there when the predawn assault
began. Later in the day, Beller, who was two months shy of her eleven-
month deployment, e-mailed her parents in Pennsylvania to assure them
that she had not been injured.*

Dear Mom & Dad

I am sure by now you can read the news and watch the tube and know
that we were severely attacked with a barrage of rockets yesterday morning,
your night time. I guess we still have some diehard 9-11 fans here, those bastards.

At any rate, I am just writing to let you know that physically I remain un-
harmed. Emotionally and mentally, is a different story. I never would have
thought my day would have started out this way.

I was the first responder to a building within our compound that was hit
by a rocket. I was driving back into the compound around 0630 from my early
morning usual routine when the hair on my arms stood up. I suspected something was up, but couldn't identify since I had just arrived from the gym and

was too busy praying to Jesus that I hadn't been nailed by a rocket at the palace parking lot where I had been driving through just moments before.

I saw smoke in the distance and a man waiving his arms above him in the universal distress signal. I thought maybe something was on fire from an explosion. From inside the well-padded palace, I never thought any of the earlier impact rounds I heard were from down here where I lived. I thought it was just the palace being bombarded again. And for certain, I never thought we would have taken casualties. Iraqi workers—three.

The first Iraqi casualty I saw came briskly walking down the street toward me. He seemed very alarmed, sort of crazy. I could tell he was in shock. He reminded me of a Ping-Pong ball walking back and forth, talking, mumbling, although I had no idea who he was speaking to. His mandible was completely shattered inside the structure of his mouth. He made zero sense when he spoke. He just kept giving me sign language over his belly. I think he was trying to tell me someone was pregnant. Was that someone in the building? Wholly crap!

I was kind of worried. His head was abnormally larger than the rest of his slender body. The mixture of blood and spit that poured from his mouth looked really weird like a fountain, a bright red gurgling fountain. I later discovered he died as well . . . trauma to his head. Just even typing that . . . trauma to his head . . . I should have known he would pass. Yet I was so hopeful the all-mighty American Soldiers could save him.

His buddy, who sat cross-legged with his back to me in the now demolished living room was chanting and rocking. I couldn't figure out why he didn't hear me calling for him. I kept saying it to myself, and then I remember speaking out loud to myself as I scratched and pounded through the door that I couldn't budge all the way open, "Why isn't he listening to me, damn it? Why isn't he getting up?" The others say because the rocket blew his eardrum out and the poor guy couldn't hear me. The three of them were probably honoring their first call to prayer at that time when the rocket struck.

I still wonder to this moment, why in the hell didn't I just go in through the front window since it was all blown out, but they tell me not to second guess my actions or myself. Had I gone through the window, maybe then I would have seen the dead guy, the third casualty, camouflaged with soot and debris.

A Navy Seal, a medic, just happened to be walking by after his shift at the

Combat Support Hospital (CSH) ER. He took over for me obviously since he was far much more qualified than I. He really did all the work, not me. I just ran for help, got an ambulance and then at 0635 in the morning, I started screaming for help. "MEDIC, MEDIC. I NEED A MEDIC." In hindsight, I don't know why I was screaming medic when the Navy Seal had everything under control and was carrying a normal conversation with the two Iraqi wounded when the reinforcements arrived.

The weirdest thing of all was the absolute evil feeling that hit my body when I tried to bust through the door the first time, when I was alone with the casualties before the Navy Seal came. It actually stopped me in my tracks and I just paused. The Iraqi behind me kept nudging me in the doorway, but my legs were glued to the ground. A Vietnam veteran here with us explained to me last night what I felt was the presence of death. And my body didn't like it.

The general's driver showed up with a vehicle, and we put them in the Yukon and he made like a bandit for the CSH. I never did find out who came for the deceased. After somebody told me I was full of blood, I kind of thought I should go home and shower and get prepared for the next barrage of attacks. And without fail, they came too.

They hit while I was in the shower. I had been fine until this time not really reacting to what I had just seen and the little run I took to call for an ambulance. And that's when I went into shock myself or I did what they say is called coming down off the adrenaline high. It was all I could do to keep my little legs strong, but I finally just gave into the little trembles and just sat down in the shower and cried. A few moments before, I had realized that I had now washed my body two times and didn't know why the first time wasn't good enough. . . .

I made it back to my room after a long heaving cry and began to dress in my uniform. They found me in my room cleaning my weapon, yet I was shaking so bad I couldn't assemble my bolt and charging handle together correctly. I realized I needed to chill before I was going to defend us anywhere.

About four of us sat in our common room on the ground floor of our gigantic concrete house, which used to be inhabited by former presidential palace servants. Wearing our entire battle rattle, we just all looked at each other, like "wholly shit." There we sat, four women from the age of 24 to 40 something, from Staff Sgt. to 1st Sgt, gathered in the common room on the cold cement floor, both waiting and listening to explosions, radio traffic, and fifty cals (calibur) being shot off in the distance at one gate.

Since the attack, I have gone back once to see the area that was just barely lit by sunlight at dusk yesterday morning. Partial brain remains are still on the cement floor from the deceased, except now they are pinkish with cement gristle all folded into it and oven baked from the sun. Somebody tried to be discreet, but did a poor job in covering it up. The gate that was once there is all blown to hell. They have cheap yellow police tape around the place. Yeah, as if that's going to keep people out.

I found several pairs of men's sandals that were just blown about like they were nothing. And of course, pools of blood, some dark and brown, some still red and fresh, reminded me of the tragedy that occurred earlier that morning. I saw the pile of rocks that I tripped over in the morning dusk and chaos because I was trying to run and thought I was lighter than air, I guess. I saw the door that I couldn't bust through. I was glad to see somebody had. Upon later inspection of the attacked house, we found out the object behind the door was the remnants of the rocket. No wonder I couldn't get through. I saw all the cans of fresh paint that were stacked outside the building. The Koreans had hired these three Iraqi men to fix up the place for the Korean Embassy to move in. Guess the Koreans are going real estate shopping, huh?

But most of all, the veterans I spoke to last night told me I will probably smell paint sometime in the future, and it will remind me of this day, this horrible event. They also told me it wasn't my fault, and I couldn't have saved them since their injuries were far too great for my little hands. From what they had heard, I had done the right thing, the honorable thing. "Geez Beller, you didn't run back to your room and hide like a lot of them did," said one of our senior sergeants, a Vietnam veteran himself. "Just remember this, next time somebody comes up to you like they did today asking you about your story in disbelief, you look at them and ask them with a stone cold face, "Were you there? Then how would you really know what happened?"

I walked our compound in fear last night. I couldn't bear to think of walking by the place in the dark, even though it was the short way home. It was as though I were afraid some dark spookiness was going to jump out at me and steal my soul or something. The thought of the place so dark like it was in the morning resonates in my mind. And their horrified looks, their confused looks, the blood dripping on them, the sheer and utter pain mirrored on their faces, they all played like a silent movie in my mind all day yesterday, all night last night.

I slept like shit last night. I hope this isn't the beginning of what my Special Forces friend calls "the nightmares." Last night was the first time in my life I staunchly did not want to sleep alone. And that's a far cry for someone who is a both a restless sleeper and a sheet hog.

They told me not to write home about it. "We don't want it all over the internet." But even talking to all the right people isn't helping the heavy weight I am carrying on my tightened chest. And somehow, writing usually does. Even though I got my ass chewed and threatened with an Article 15 for not running all the way back to my quarters to get my gear BEFORE I went to the scene, "You could have been a combat liability to us, SGT, since you didn't have ANY of your gear with you," it really all doesn't matter in the big picture. Others here at my unit admitted the same things to me along the lines of, "Beller, we would have done the same thing you did, run to the emergency first—without a doubt." There's always a few ways of looking at things though, I guess. . . .

Keep well.

THE DAY OF THE DRAGON
Personal Narrative
Captain Robert A. Lindblom

Thirty-two-year-old U.S. Air Force Captain Robert A. Lindblom was deployed to Kandahar, Afghanistan, with the 41st Expeditionary Rescue Squadron from February through April 2003 to fly combat rescue missions and manage day-to-day flight activities. When tragedy struck his unit in March, Lindblom not only had to cope with the personal and operational ramifications of the sudden crisis, he had to help his fellow airmen find meaning in the sacrifices they and other U.S. forces were making in the region.

Staring straight ahead at the computer screen in front of me, I could not see the rest of the room with my peripheral vision, but I felt the eyes of everyone on me. The words hung in the air like a mirage. I knew what had been said, but my mind refused to accept it. The radio crackled again, repeating the same message.

"Roker, Roker, Komodo 11 is down!"

The transmission was meant for our command and control agency, nick-named Roker, but everyone monitoring the frequency would have perked up as I did when the call came through. The urgency in the voice answered everyone's unspoken question without actually saying the words: the crash was bad. It was no mere hard landing or rollover—someone was dead. As a flight commander back home, I had been responsible for training and equipping the preponderance of the forces we had in theater; four of the six crew members on board were my personal responsibility.

Komodo 11 and 13 were Air Force HH-60 helicopters assigned to Kandahar Air Base in Afghanistan. Their assigned task was to conduct combat search and rescue, or CSAR, missions—to recover the crews, of aircraft lost to enemy fire. This is the primary duty of these Pavehawk crews, and they're the best in the world. But U.S. military aircraft were rarely shot down in Afghanistan, and the HH-60s were frequently used for medevac missions to help individuals hurt either in ground combat or because of other, more mundane, reasons. Our primary responsibility still remained U.S. military forces, but it was not uncommon when things were quiet for our controlling agency, the Joint Search and Rescue Center, or JSRC, at Al Udeid Air Base in Qatar, to launch us to assist injured Afghan military and civilians. These missions were approved out of genuine humanitarian concern first and foremost, but they also had the side benefit of positively influencing the local populace. Nothing inhibits the spread of terrorism more completely than an act of kindness and goodwill, especially when it comes at great personal risk or expense.

On that particular day, we received word of two injured Afghan children. One had been burned severely and was in serious danger of losing an eye, and the other had significant head injuries after tumbling down a ravine. Although located in separate villages, they were close enough that we could recover both children and get them to competent medical care within hours, as compared to the days it may have taken for them to travel by land. The round trip was beyond even the Pavehawk's capacity on a single tank, however, and aerial refueling was required. That was the last normal report we received; Komodo 11 and 13 had commenced refueling operations with an HC-130 King aircraft. Now we learned the lead aircraft had somehow crashed in the course of that refueling. The details were still unclear.

All the men looked to me as I stood. As the unit operations officer, I ran the flying operations for the unit commander, Lieutenant Colonel Stein. More importantly, I was second in command behind him, and on that particular day I was in charge. Lieutenant Colonel Stein was flying on Komodo 11.

"Turn off all the computers and the morale phone," I directed out loud to no one in particular, but a few airmen quickly jumped to complete the task. To those remaining I said, "No one talks about this outside of the unit. No one contacts home. Understand?"

The JSRC finally responded to the initial call we had all heard. "Last calling Roker, say again."

With strained patience, a new voice I recognized as the aerial gunner on Komodo 13 came on the radio and tried for a third time. "Roker, this is Komodo 13. Komodo 11 has crashed. Repeat, Komodo 11 has crashed."

There was a moment of silence, then, "Roker copies."

That exquisite understatement belied the frenzy of activity I knew was stirring up on the other end of the radio call a thousand miles away. The team at the JSRC would quickly begin gathering as much information as they could and start coordinating recovery efforts for the six crew members they knew to be aboard. I was secretly relieved to have them in charge at this point.

Soon after Roker acknowledged the situation, the aircraft commander of Komodo 13, Lieutenant Spindler, came on the radio. "We've terminated refueling operations. We're landing to check for survivors." Roker acknowledged and requested exact coordinates of the crash. They were working to get overhead cover from some nearby fighters and a quick reaction force, or QRF, to secure the scene.

Komodo 13 was soon on the ground and silence reigned as he deplaned his pararescuemen, or PJs, to search the scene. I flexed my shoulders and unclenched my fists as I tried to reason with myself. Since they were refueling, they were most likely flying about 110 knots, or more than 120 miles per hour, when they impacted the ground. The odds of even one person surviving were not good, let alone all six of them.

Agonizing minutes ticked by without update until the PJs reported some bad news; they had found two bodies, both deceased. My heart sank with the announcement.

Komodo 13 suddenly recalled the PJs to the aircraft—there were a number of vehicles approaching the scene. My mouth went dry as I heard the radio crackle with Roker's response. "Intel confirms there are no friendlies in that area." Although that didn't necessarily mean the approaching trucks were hostile, it definitely increased the odds. When a warning burst from the gunner's GAU-2B mini-gun didn't serve to deter the approaching vehicles in the slightest, those odds were upped yet another notch.

In true cavalry fashion, a flight of Marine AV-8 Harriers arrived moments later. After taking a moment to positively identify our helo and the unknown vehicles, they began to make low passes over the scene to let the interlopers know there was significant firepower immediately available if they meant our helicopter or crew any harm. Ignoring this attempt at intimidation, the small group of vehicles continued to close the distance. The crew of Komodo 13 now identified two more sets of approaching lights. They were rapidly being surrounded.

The unknown persons had still not committed a hostile act, so the AV-8s could do nothing but look threatening. With odds continuing to mount against them, the crew of Komodo 13 wisely chose to crank their engines, board their PJs, and take off. They picked up to a hover with the nearest vehicle only five hundred meters away, climbing to a safe altitude just as the trucks arrived in their now-vacant landing zone.

Komodo 13 had to then fly in deteriorating weather over bad terrain in an effort to replenish, while airborne, their dwindling supply of fuel. When they finally succeeded in plugging with the HC-130, I breathed a sigh of relief. Their tanks had dropped to the point where they could no longer divert to any U.S. installation. Without gas they would have been forced to land on some mountaintop and we would have had yet another crew down in hostile territory. With full tanks, the aircraft commander elected to divert to Bagram, only thirty minutes away, instead of flying the ninety minutes required to make it back to Kandahar.

The AV-8s were also low on fuel by that point, but a flight of A-10 Warthogs had arrived to replace them. The A-10s made their own series of low passes, releasing flares each time they went by. Although harmless, that act was finally able to deter the curious locals; they soon returned to their vehicles and fled the same way they had arrived. Our equipment and our men, whether living or dead, were safe for the moment.

About that same time, the JSRC requested I meet them on the computer in our secure Internet chat room. They informed me the QRF had arrived on scene via CH-47 Chinooks.

There was a large debris field and it would take some time to search and secure it all. Aside from possible survivors, which were obviously our priority, there were weapons and classified information to be protected. The QRF spread out to begin this process, while we resigned ourselves to more waiting, and I kept a nervous eye on the television in the background. With all of the media focus on Iraq, Afghanistan was nothing more than a footnote on the news, but that might change with word of a fatal crash. With the sound turned low, I watched for any break in the stream of images from the larger war—a telltale map or photo of Afghanistan.

Within the next hour I received a phone call from Lieutenant Spindler, notifying me that they were down and safe. But he also told me that their aircraft had experienced power problems on the flight to Bagram and they were going to need our help coordinating approval to have Army mechanics work on the helicopter. I thanked him for the information and promised to work the issue. Before we hung up, he updated me on what they had seen at the crash site. Three bodies had actually been discovered, not just two as we had first thought, and I said a quick prayer for the remaining three airmen.

Soon afterward, the secure chat room flared with activity. Conflicting reports began to come in from the crash site via the JSRC. One minute they had found two survivors, the next they had found one more body and no survivors, after that there were indications they had two bodies and one survivor. Rescue operations work this way more often than not. In the desire to disseminate news as quickly as possible, sometimes the accounts become muddled and confused.

I tried to repress my sense of frustration as I was alternately heartened and discouraged with each passing report. Suddenly, someone shouted out, "There it is" and pointed to the television situated to my right, and we all watched as a banner scrolled across the bottom of the screen: "Air Force HH-60 Pavehawk helicopter crashes southwest of Kabul. Crew feared dead." I was furious; three of our people were dead, and possibly all six. How could they relegate their sacrifice to the same status as a record rainfall in Arizona or an overturned semi-truck in Virginia?

Shortly after the news broke on CNN, I received a request for a private chat from the JSRC—in this private cyber-room, others would not be privy to our discussion.

"Yes?" I posted.

"JSRC Deputy Director here," came the reply. "We're in direct contact with the QRF."

"Rgr," I typed, to show I understood.

"We have confirmation . . . six bodies recovered."

"Understand, no survivors?" I queried, just to be sure.

"Affirmative . . . all deceased."

Now it was official. Despite the meager hope I had attempted to hold on to, they were all gone, including Lieutenant Colonel Stein.

I stood stiffly. All eyes were on me—everyone knew there was news of some kind, although they could only guess at the details. "Gather everyone in the maintenance tent," I said. "Time for an update."

Standing before the small crowd of airmen just a few minutes later, I felt the burden of responsibility even more severely. No one spoke—the usual banter was replaced by an unnatural quiet and thoughtful, somber expressions. I silently cursed the moment I had accepted Lieutenant Colonel Stein's offer to act as his operations officer at Kandahar. I didn't have the depth of experience to handle these affairs, and I was certainly not the inspirational leader these men needed right now. I was afraid, terrified in fact, that I would make a mistake. Even worse, I worried that I would make no decision—falling victim to my own fear of error.

Finally, with a deep breath I began, "Komodo 13 has diverted to Bagram. They are down and safe, but their aircraft is hard-broke for power problems. They will have to remain at that location until we can figure out how to fix their helicopter and bring them safely back to Kandahar."

Nods of understanding greeted me as I braced for the next announcement.

"The QRF has completed their search of the crash site."

The group held their breath in unison.

"They have recovered all six bodies. There are no survivors."

Some bowed their heads. Others simply stared, lost in their own thoughts. One of the men began to cry silently.

I stood quiet for a moment, not out of any desire to allow them to absorb the news, but because I had no idea what to say next. I scanned the faces before me while I struggled to find the right words. As I searched their eyes, I realized that these men wanted to be led. In a flash I understood; my job was actually very simple—I had to act, to lead, that was all. I did not have to be perfect, I did not have to be right every time, but I had to lead. That is why the chain of command works the way it does—so men under pressure are relieved of the uncertainty that can otherwise cause paralysis in a unit.

Whether I wanted the responsibility or not was irrelevant; I had it now and it was my duty to pick up the mantle left by our commander and lead these men to the best of my ability. I realized as well that we needed something to strive for—a goal or a challenge. Without something to occupy our energy, the men would settle into a depressive funk.

"Sergeant Whitfield," I addressed the NCO in charge of maintenance. "What's the status of our third helo?" I knew as well as he did that our sole remaining aircraft was currently non-mission-capable. The engine gauges had proven unreliable, and the helicopter was unsafe to fly without them. But I wanted the announcement made to the group. He quickly confirmed the information for everybody.

"Gentlemen, we need to get that aircraft fixed. We still have a mission to do, and we cannot provide CSAR coverage with a broken aircraft. Can you fix it?"

"Yes sir," he replied with enthusiasm.

"If we can get that aircraft flyable, we can sit alert with one bird until Komodo 13 can get back home. We can fly with an Apache escort as our wingman if need be. How much time do you need?"

"Five or six hours, I think."

"Okay, let's get to it." The room was instantly energized.

I coordinated with the Army Apache unit colocated with us in Kandahar. Their commander assured me they were ready to support and would stand alert with us for as long as we wanted.

I worked with our maintenance officer to figure out how to get approval for Army mechanics to work on an Air Force helicopter. Master Sergeant Whitfield provided periodic updates on the status of our remaining helicopter. Progress was slower than expected, but he had every available man working on it. Arrangements were also made with our home unit concerning death notifications, and individuals were selected to pack the personal effects of the deceased to be shipped back home with the bodies and returned to the families.

We also began preparations for an all-post memorial that would take place two days later. In the interim, we felt it was necessary to organize a smaller, but no less important, ceremony as soon as possible, and we decided to postpone the standard flag raising in the morning and have it at noon. Instead of leaving the flag in its normal position, it would be raised once, then lowered to half-staff. Then I would read the names of our six comrades, followed by a moment of silence. The senior Air Force officer on base would say a few words, and we would close with a prayer.

Despite the shadow of tragedy still looming over us, the 0800 briefing the next morning was less somber, especially with the news that our lone helicopter was repaired and able to sit alert. There were also further discussions on plans to bring Komodo 13 to Kandahar. Not only did we need them desperately, the crew themselves wanted back in the saddle. But aside from the maintenance hurdle, there was also the problem of arranging the necessary escort. Having just lost one helicopter, the JSRC did not look favorably upon taking unnecessary risks with another.

After yet another round of debates with our controlling agency about the best way to return Komodo 13 to Kandahar, I sat down in frustration and rubbed my forehead. A young airman approached me with a small piece of yellow paper and handed it to me without comment. On it were the full names of all six crew members I had requested for the ceremony. As I studied the list before me, something inside snapped. Seeing the names of the deceased somehow made their deaths real for the first time. The oldest was forty-eight, and the youngest was twenty-one. Two of the crew members were engaged, one had gotten married only a few months before, three of them had children, one was a single parent, two were set to be promoted soon, one was ready to retire, and they were all my friends.

I knew them all—I knew them and I missed them terribly already. I could no longer hold back the weight of my own emotions. A childlike sob escaped first, and then the tears came, blurring the sheet of paper before me. I rushed out of the office with head bowed and crossed the short distance to our sleeping tent, grateful for the cool, dark, private sanctuary it afforded.

There I gave my emotions free rein—all the sorrow, frustration, and anger of the preceding twenty hours found an outlet for several minutes, until finally I regained some sense of composure. Although I began to feel back in control of myself, I made no effort to stop the deluge of tears until a knock on the door forced me back from the brink of my misery.

"Yes, come in," I said, wiping my eyes as best I could.

The door opened tentatively and there stood the airman who had handed me the piece of paper. "Uh, sir, they're getting ready for the ceremony."

"Okay, I'm coming," I replied.

The door closed as hesitantly as it had opened.

The short ceremony for the small contingent of Air Force troops at this Army base went essentially as planned. When I read the names aloud to the assembled crowd, I found myself unable to stem another flow of tears. This time, however, I wasn't alone—not a dry eye remained in the group before me. Other than our tiny unit, which comprised less than a quarter of those present, no one really knew the airmen who had been killed. Yet they shared in our loss, and they knew what it would feel like if it had been one of their own. There was a good amount of bonding and thoughtful reflection once the ceremony was concluded. I was surprised at how therapeutic the little display seemed to have been.

Soon after the memorial, I began to tire. I realized it had now been thirty-four hours since I had slept. Without the adrenaline rush of responsibility, my body had begun to shut down. I made arrangements with the NCO on duty to wake me if anything significant happened, then decided to try to get some rest. Lying in my bunk a short time later, I wondered if I could sleep with all that had happened. No sooner had that one thought passed my mind than I was unconscious. I slept for almost fourteen hours.

Two days later we still awaited the return of Komodo 13. The larger, all-base memorial ceremony, scheduled for that night, was the only major event that still remained. As the acting commander, I had a small speaking part in the ceremony, but otherwise bore little responsibility. The largest hangar on base was the selected location. It was still pockmarked with bullet holes and bomb-related damage from the early days of the war.

I was truly amazed, and touched, by the tremendous showing that night. In short order, it was standing room only and the ranks of mourners continued to swell. Even an entire battalion of Coalition soldiers stationed at Kandahar showed up dressed in their best uniforms. Although most of them would not even understand the words spoken, they wanted to show their support. Again, the powerful bond of fellow warriors struck me; they had not lost their own comrades, but they felt the loss nonetheless.

As the mournful wail of bagpipes began the ceremony, I felt another swelling of emotion. Determined not to lose my composure this time, I held my feelings in check through taps, a twenty-one-gun salute, a memorial slide show, the words of the chaplain, and my own speech. When it was finally over, I noticed a difference in our small unit. I caught small snippets of reminiscing as I mingled and even saw a laugh or smile now and then as stories were exchanged. We would never forget the sacrifice made by our departed comrades, but the closure provided by the ceremony signaled that it was okay to return to our mission and stay focused on why we were here.

The next day repairs began on our helicopter in Bagram. When the crew of Komodo 13 finally returned two days after that, it was a joyous reunion. The bonds of camaraderie had grown even stronger through the trauma we had faced together. Their return six full days after our first notification of the crash also marked the attainment of a priceless goal. After twelve hours for the crew to rest and recuperate, we were back on alert—full, 100 percent mission capable. The sense of pride was palpable. Other challenges still lay ahead, but the worst, we felt, was behind us.

In the weeks and months following the deployment, some questioned the loss of life on the night that Komodo 11 went down. Was there a reason for six U.S. airmen to die trying to rescue two Afghan children (who, we later learned, were successfully rescued by other American troops) from tiny villages that no one remembers? We grieved, and still mourn, their loss, but we refuse to accept that their deaths were for nothing. During the Kandahar memorial for the crew members of Komodo 11, I offered the following tribute to our fallen comrades, and I believe these words as strongly today as when I spoke them that night:

"The traditional image of a CSAR mission is flying into a hail of bullets to recover a young airman or soldier clinging to life after being wounded in direct combat with the enemy. Just because this was not that type of mission does not reduce in any way the importance of their sacrifice. The unfortunate reality of operations such as the one now performed by U.S. forces in Afghanistan is that we often do not see the results of our efforts. There is no way to ever know what tragedy we may have averted or catastrophes we may have prevented by our presence here. Every ally and friend we make now is one less enemy we have in the future. Although their mission did not succeed, perhaps the parents of those children will tell them someday of the brave men and woman who died attempting to save their lives. Perhaps that will be enough to convince one more person of the goodwill and intent of the United States of America. Perhaps that's one less enemy that will take up arms against us. That is why they flew their mission, and that is why they did not die in vain."

THIS IS NOT A GAME
Letter
Captain Ryan Kelly

While stationed in Kuwait and gearing up for combat, Company Commander and UH-60 Black Hawk helicopter pilot Captain Ryan Kelly and the members of his company in the 1-150th General Support Aviation Battalion 42nd Infantry Division (Mechanized), New Jersey Army National Guard, were eager to head into Iraq. (Kelly's letter voicing his frustration about the interminable waiting they had to endure in Kuwait appears on page 23.) Motivated by a desire "to give back to his country," Kelly joined the Army in 1992 at the age of twenty-two, and twelve years later he finally embarked on his first deployment to a war zone. On January 21, 2005, he sent the following letter to his mother from Camp Speicher, Iraq, expressing how the troops—and one soldier in particular—were reacting to actual combat.

Dear Ma,

They are called HERO missions. And they are the worst kind.

It's the body bag in the back that makes the flight hard. No jovial banter among the crew. No jokes of home. No wisecracks about the origin of the meat served at the chow hall, just the noise of the flight—the scream of the engines, the whir of the blades clawing at the air, the voice crackling over the radio and echo of your own thoughts about the boy in the bag in the back.

Yesterday I was in the TOC (tactical operations center)—it's where all the mission planning happens, briefings, maps on the wall, etc. Normally, after flying missions, pilots drift around the TOC with an air of satisfied indifference—similar to lions after devouring a zebra. I was talking with the operations officer, complaining that my pilots weren't flying enough, when a heavy-set, three pieces of cake after dinner man came in. Instead of the usual swagger, he was dazed. I asked him what was wrong. He told me he just finished flying one of the HERO missions. When we pick up friendly KIAs (killed in action), that is what we call it.

He told me he picked up a US kid killed in a car bomb. He tried to shrug it off as just another mission, but it was obviously bothering him. A few seconds later he left, but his look stayed with me.

Body bags must have been in the stars because later the Colonel announced that the heaters in the medevac helicopters were not working that well. In response, the medics, operating on a 'corn husk theory,' started zipping their live patients inside body bags to keep them warm during the flight. It can get very cold in the back of the Blackhawk because the wind seeps in through cracks in the window seals. However, the medics forgot to explain this to their patients who understandably freaked out. It's kind of funny, in a twisted sort of way. I guess being in a body bag is better than freezing on the way to the hospital. Why is death always so cold?

Things have hardened into routine here, like an old artery that's carried the same, tired blood along the same, tired path for years. Pump, return, pump, return, wake up, eat, work, sleep, wake up—back and forth, back and forth, BOOOM! Rocket attack. Pump, return, pump, return . . . We've worn a trail through the gravel with our boots plodding back and forth to the hangar.

If it weren't for the Army uniforms and the constant noise of helicopters taking off and landing, and the Russian 747-like jets screaming overhead every hour of the day, and the F-16s screeching around looking for something to kill, and the rockets exploding and the controlled blasts shaking the windows and the "thump, thump, thump" sound of the Apache gun ships shooting their 30mm guns in the middle of the night, and the heat and the cold, and the hero missions and the body bags and the stress, and the soldiers fraught with personal problems—child custody battles fought from 3000 miles away, surgeries on ovaries, hearts, breasts, brains, cancers, transplants, divorces, Dear John letters, births, deaths, miscarriages and miss-marriages— and the scorpions and the spiders who hide under the toilet seats, and the freakish bee-sized flies humming around like miniature blimps, and the worst: the constant pang of home, the longing for family, the knowledge that life is rolling past you like an unstoppable freight train, an inevitable force, reinforcing the desire for something familiar, the longing for something beautiful, for something safe, to be somewhere safe, with love and laughter and poetry and cold lemonade and clean sheets, if it weren't for all that Iraq would be just like home. Almost.

Last night, one of my soldiers showed up at the chow hall. I was surprised because he's been gone for a while. Two months ago he volunteered to be part of a security detail that escorts convoys to and from Kuwait and back again. The drive is a perilous 600-mile, one-way trip with roadside bombs, RPG attacks, ambushes and small arms fire.

The convoys are made up of security teams who speed down the highway in armored HMMVs, like cowboys herding columns of trucks stuffed with food, fans, etc. Foreigners—Japanese, Turks, you name it—drive the giant semis and risk capture and beheadings because the job pays big money. Some drivers earn $100,000 or more. Men like mine do it because they want to or because commanders like me order them to. My man earns about $40,000 a year.

The convoy escort mission passed to me like a foul smelling egg. The Army hatched the mission in an effort to spare more people the risk of convoying. The idea was to get a few permanent escort teams together instead of making whole units drive. It's a good idea, if you don't happen to be one of the poor suckers on one of the teams. Three men they wanted, three men. I was not happy. I was pissed off. Weren't we done with these awful convoys? I passed the news like a kidney stone to my first sergeant. We went through the horrible process of selection. Who would it be? Who could I afford to lose? Who was worth more to me alive? NO one should ever have to ask these questions. Fortunately, my men volunteered, sparing me the decision. I was—and am—so very proud of their bravery, mom. It nearly brought me to tears. After about two weeks, two of them returned unharmed and wide-eyed from the experience.

But not one man. He's still out there. The guys in the TOC tell me he'll be on a team for up to three months. That's a long time to let someone take shots at you. But it's war, and in comparison to what grandpa went through, a tame one. My man's missions are unpredictable. I never know if he's coming or going. He'll drift around the CP (command post) or the hangar for a week or so, turn a few wrenches on a helicopter and then suddenly I'll get a knock on my door at three o'clock in the morning. I'll open it and see him standing there donned in his body armor, helmet and rifle. He'll tell me he's leaving and my first sergeant and I will wish him good luck and God speed.

We'll all shake hands, I'll slap him on the back and he'll disappear. Then I won't see him for a few weeks. That's how it goes. That's our routine. Every time I send him off I feel like a father sending a kid off into the world, wondering when he'll be back again or if I'm going to write a death letter to his family.

For weeks I won't know if he's dead or alive, shot or blown up. All I will know is that he is somewhere between here, Kuwait, death and home. Then, as suddenly as he left, he'll reappear.

The last time he returned, he was flush with confidence and adrenaline. I caught him about three weeks ago regaling the guys about this latest trip; some Iraqi kids chucked a brick off an overpass and shattered a semi's windshield. The driver lost control and flipped the truck upside down. It crushed him to death. My man was unable to return fire because the kids melted into a crowd.

Despite the horror inflicted on someone else, the trip excited him. He announced that he liked driving on the convoys better than working in maintenance. He asked me if he could stay on the escort mission for the rest of our tour. I said, "hell, no," and that he could join the Goddamned infantry later, after we were safely back home. That exchange has become our second routine. He asks to go, I say, no. We both laugh and he leaves on another mission. He said he really likes it.

That was until last night.

I was eating dinner, like I usually do, when he appeared, interrupting me in the middle of a forkful of coleslaw. Something dark had happened. He was somber, deliberate and scared. Before I could say, "Welcome back," and "hell, no, you can't be an infantryman," he blurted out: "Sir, can I talk to you for a second?" When people say that to me there's a problem. Soldiers don't usually talk to me unless they are bitching or have something troubling them. God, mom, I've heard that phrase so many times.

He said he was driving back in a column of 12 armored gun trucks, secured by the fantasy that the enemy would never dare attack such a bristling display of American industrial might—replete with machine guns and automatic grenade launchers. He was thinking this when a huge roadside bomb exploded, engulfing a semi truck in flames, killing the driver and his passenger and spraying my man's HMMV with dirt.

The experience didn't rattle him. Worse, it changed him. He realized that this is not a game. He understands that there are people who are trying to kill him, and me, and anyone else unfortunate enough to stray down the wrong street. I think he wanted me to pull him off the mission and tell him he didn't have to go out on the road anymore.

But I didn't. He's become proficient, more of an expert on the tactics and tells of the enemy than anyone I could replace him with. So I made him stay. It's a cold decision, but the right one. Again, I felt like his father. "I think he's learning what this is all about," my sergeant said. Maybe we all are.

This morning I went to work and found a VFW magazine on the conference table. On the front cover was a picture of an injured 20-something solider, his face and forehead purpled with bruises, his lips swollen and cut, his left eye half-closed, his arm in a sling, fingernails black with dried blood, his thighs blotched with red abrasions and his leg wrapped in an ace bandage, amputated below the knee. He was sitting in a hospital bed with a half smile on this face. A blazing bold yellow headline scrawled across his chest read "wounded vets rebound." I opened the magazine and flipped to the story and saw a second picture of a wounded amputee. This one was of a young Navy guy lying in a hospital bed. His wife was sitting beside him. She was not smiling.

The caption under the picture read: "Navy Corpsman Joe Worley visits with his wife, Angel, while recovering at Walter Reed. A rocket-propelled grenade ripped off his left leg, but he said it was 'a fair trade for getting out of Iraq alive.' " The cut-line continued: "His sense of humor and positive outlook make him a favorite on the amputee ward."

Christ. What a terrible attempt at positive spin.

Tell everyone that I miss them. I think about them and you every day. I hope I'll be home soon. Peace is such a great and delicate thing.

Kelly returned to the United States in November 2005.

CLUSTERS

Poem

Captain Robert W. Schaefer

Just as troops find it cathartic to write letters and e-mails to friends and loved ones, many servicemen and women express their emotions through poetry. A formidable-looking Green Beret who has been deployed around the world, thirty-seven-year-old Captain Robert W. Schaefer jotted down the first draft of the following poem only days after the launch of Operation Iraqi Freedom (he would make only slight changes when he returned to the States). It relates to an incident that Schaefer observed firsthand.

Yellow
or were they
blue? White, red
ribbon everywhere—
Stay out.

But they were so small, plastic, barely three
inches across. They didn't look deadly. Two
soldiers wandered in curious. One
said: "I wonder what would happen if . . ."
          and gingerly tapped one
          with the toe of his boot

which then evaporated in a pink frothy cloud,
a bubble gum *pop*, then cotton candy chunks
arcing lazily through the air
landing with little wet thumps
muffled by the sand.

Then, he died—*just like that
just that quickly.*
One moment he was alive and curious
and the next, he was just a scattering.

But the second was still alive
And so, to help him, without thinking
          others ran into that minefield

pop
pop

We too now running, and I, fastest, first, frozen
by the sight of so much crimson-soaked clothing.
I didn't know where to start.

Covered with the blood of others,
later, I was
mistaken as a casualty myself.

But I would not let them take my uniform
they would still live as long as evidence
of them remained on my sleeves,
torn as they grasped for a few extra moments.

THE VIRTUAL SOLDIERS

Poem

Private First Class Allen J. Caruselle

"When we first got to Baghdad, the [Iraqi] men spread rumors that we had X-ray vision in our sunglasses and we would defile their women," U.S. Army Sergeant James A. Christenson wrote on April 5, 2004. "The kids would come up to us and ask to try on our glasses," Christenson continued,

all the while looking for secret buttons that would turn on the X-ray vision. They would walk around staring at each other with confused looks on their faces. My favorite one was the rumor about Marines being robots. They had no other explanation for the Marines being able to wear all of the hot and heavy clothes in this heat.

The comparison is an understandable one; decked out in full battle gear with audio/video communication systems, night vision goggles, laser scopes, and other high-tech equipment, American soldiers and Marines often appear, especially to the Iraqis or Afghans they encounter, like futuristic fighting machines. In the summer of 2003, while stationed in one of Saddam Hussein's former vacation palaces in Babylon, a twenty-one-year-old private first class named Allen J. Caruselle wrote the following poem reflecting on the degree to which technology had permeated and influenced military culture. Caruselle, a third-generation Marine and infantry rifleman in the 1st Battalion, 7th Marine Regiment, was on his first deployment to Iraq. He would be redeployed twice over the next two years. (The "digital camouflage" Caruselle mentions refers to the battle dress uniforms, or "cammies," most Marines now wear, which have a camouflage pattern that appears to be made up of digital pixels.)

We are the soldiers of the new millennium.
Our digital camouflage a testament to changing times,
Our ranks filled with the lost generation of video-pacified children,
Looking for the next great adventure.
We train on virtual simulators
To learn the proper methods of dealing with enemy tactics;
Civilians and children hiding machine guns behind teddy bears.
Disconnected from the battle zone by constant and clever training,
We are taught to live only in the between hours of liberty and leave,
Silicon knights out to save the world
From the newest threat of terror and disorder.
We step into the darkness.
Situation: Unclear;
Mission: Unknown.
This is the tenet by which we throw the dice,
And our very lives, into the raging storm.

ASHBAH, THE BAGHDAD ZOO, and THE HURT LOCKER

Poems

Sergeant Brian Turner

Inspired by both his father, an Army soldier during the Cold War, and his grandfather, a Marine who fought in almost every major campaign of the Pacific Theater during World War II, Brian Turner joined the military in 1998 and eventually became a sergeant in the U.S. Army with the 3rd Stryker Brigade, 2nd Infantry Division. Turner crossed the border into Iraq on December 3, 2003, and spent almost eleven months in Baghdad and Mosul. Nicknamed "the professor," Turner had earned a master's degree in poetry from the University of Oregon and composed numerous works during his deployment. (After the war, he returned to the States and became a teacher in California.) Turner kept the poems to himself, however, as he didn't want his men to think he was writing about "flowers and stuff." In fact, Turner's poems offer profound reflections on the haunting and nightmarish realities of warfare and the immense pain military operations can inflict on troops and civilians alike. "Ashbah," which is also the title of the first poem, is the transliteration of the Arabic word for "ghosts."

The ghosts of American soldiers
wander the streets of Balad by night,

unsure of their way home, exhausted,
the desert wind blowing trash
down the narrow alleys as a voice

sounds from the minaret, a soulful call
reminding them how alone they are,
how lost. And the Iraqi dead,
they watch in silence from the rooftops
as date palms line the shore in silhouette,

leaning toward Mecca when the dawn wind blows.

The following poem, "The Baghdad Zoo," is loosely based on stories that Turner heard concerning the damage and looting done to the city's main zoo during the March 2003 invasion of Iraq ("barchan dunes" are crescent-shaped sand dunes).

An Iraqi northern brown bear mauled a man
on a street corner, dragging him down an alley
as shocked onlookers cried for it to stop.

There were tanks rolling their heavy tracks
past the museum and up to the Ministry of Oil.
One gunner watched a lion chase down a horse.

Eaten down to their skeletons, the giraffes
looked prehistoric, unreal, their necks
too fragile, too graceful for the 21st Century.

Surreal. Dalmatian pelicans and marbled teals
flew over, frightened by the rotorwash
of Black Hawk helicopters touching down.

One baboon even escaped from the city limits.
It was found wandering in the desert, confused
by the wind and the sand of the barchan dunes.

The final poem is "The Hurt Locker."

Nothing but the hurt left here.
Nothing but bullets and pain
and the bled-out slumping
and all the *fucks* and *goddamns*
and *Jesus Christs* of the wounded.
Nothing left here but the hurt.
Believe it when you see it.
Believe it when a twelve-year-old
rolls a grenade into the room.
Or when a sniper punches a hole
deep into someone's head.
Believe it when four men
step from a taxicab in Mosul
to shower the street in brass
and fire. Open the hurt locker
and see what there is of knives
and teeth. Open the hurt locker and learn
how rough men come hunting for souls.

A CASE FOR BEING THERE
Personal Narrative
Major Paul D. Danielson, MD

*In May 2003, thirty-six-year-old Dr. Paul D. Danielson said goodbye to his
pregnant wife and eleven-month-old son in Massachusetts to deploy to Iraq
with the U.S. Army Reserve, Medical Corps, 912th Forward Surgical Team
(FST). Like many professionals who have to deal with intense stress and
suffering on a daily basis, Danielson and his unit used gallows humor as a
kind of emotional defense mechanism. But even though they were often*

cracking jokes in the heat (literally) of combat surgery, they were passion-
ately dedicated to providing the best care possible to critically injured troops
in and around Baghdad. Danielson wrote the following account about one
especially memorable patient months after returning home.

"Wakey, wakey, boyzzzz," Butter purred. "Someone mixed it up with hajji and we've got us some casualties comin' in." Butter was our overtattooed trauma nurse who earned his nickname on account of the gold second-lieutenant bars he wore. He was different. Most men who experience a midlife crisis quit a respectable job and go out and buy a Harley. Butter did it backwards. He woke up when he was forty and decided enough with the Jack Daniel's and motorcycle set. He figured he'd join the Army Reserve, and six months later he found himself in Mesopotamia.

The casualties turned out to be from an armored cavalry unit. These fellows always earned our respect. After dark they'd mount up and drive through the bad sections of town. They were trying to draw fire so that they could shoot back and put the hurt on the insurgents. Success with this tactic relies upon poor aim by the enemy and superior firepower by the Cav troopers. Unfortunately, during this particular mission an IED blew up one of their Humvees.

I batted my way out from under the mosquito netting and slipped on my flip-flops. I had stopped wearing my boots to trauma codes for two reasons. First, it got too difficult to wash the blood out of them. Second, it was too damn hot. Our two field operating tables were set up in a glorified closet in one part of the aid station. When you got an OR team in there and all the lights and equipment going, the temperature would be over 100 degrees Fahrenheit. Consequently, my uniform for patient care consisted of shorts, a T-shirt, and a sidearm. We'd add Kevlar and flak vests if the war came knocking a little too close. It went against all Army regulations. It was also against common sense as far as avoiding contact with bodily fluids. However, I viewed it as a calculated risk. Two of my cosurgeons were similarly clad, which did little to improve the reputation of the reservist medical corps in the eyes of the regular Army. Every time the sergeant major from the battalion walked through we had to have the defibrillator ready since he almost had an arrhythmia just looking at us.

The trio of yawning surgeons staggered down the hallway to the trauma bay. It was an open area in the front corner of the aid station with two litter stands in the center. The harsh fluorescent glow of two Bruce lamps strung from the ceiling illuminated the workspace.

While Butter's staff was spiking bags of IV fluid and opening up packs of dressings, the FST's first sergeant, Cueball, came in wearing his combat boots. We figured he slept in them; no one could lace up a set that fast. Cueball loved his docs and his enlisted, and all of us respected him. He was in his familiar role of playing bouncer in the trauma bay. He was giving the heave-ho to various wallflowers and rubberneckers who hoped to see some blood and guts. I never knew how all these trauma groupies got to the aid station so quickly. Of course, I'm being unfair in labeling them. They showed up to pitch in, and their assistance in moving patients, guarding EPWs, or just being "gofers" was indispensable.

The medical service corps lieutenant came over to meet us.

"Morning, El Tee." Warthog, my partner in general-surgery crime, grinned. "What are you doing up so early?"

"Sir?" the youngster replied, still no more certain on how to interpret us than the day we first met him in Kuwait. "I just came over from the TOC. I can report three or four definites coming, maybe more."

Warthog was about to ask him how many "definites" three or four actually meant, but decided it was too early to tease the young officer.

Our banter was interrupted as the walls rattled from the roar of a low-flying helicopter. There was a mass movement of people to the rear of the aid station.

I glanced over at Warthog, who looked positively meditative as we waited.

"The last moment of tranquillity, huh?" I observed.

His mind was on other thoughts. "I hope I covered up my pillow," he said, referring to the fine layer of silt that coated everything in the aid station after a helicopter landing.

Any sense of calm was gone a moment later as the first of the four-man litter teams burst through the door.

"I was worried he wouldn't make it to the CSH," the flight medic reported as he followed behind the second litter. "Two urgent surgicals. The first is an Iraqi interpreter with shrapnel all over. The second is a Cav officer with a near-amputation of his right upper extremity."

We followed the teams into the heart of the aid station, taking care not to slip on the blood trail. We exploded into the light and openness of the trauma bay, and then, just as a hush follows the roar of a wave crashing onto a beach, a soft hum filled the room to replace the clamor of our arrival.

I headed toward the second litter: white male, midthirties, eighty kilos, awake but looking "shocky." His uniform had already been cut away by the time I reached him. A new IV was being started and vital-sign monitors were being slapped onto his pale skin. My quick primary survey revealed that his right forearm was nearly amputated and his left foot had caught a sizable piece of shrapnel.

"We are going to take good care of you, Major," I said to the wounded officer. "But you're going to need an operation on your arm and foot."

"OK, sir," he said simply.

I was impressed by his calm. If my severed arm was hanging by a sinew, I would have been screaming my head off and crying like a baby. Not him. No tears in his eyes, and only a grunt here and there as we adjusted his tourniquet. He was 100 percent warrior.

Pooh, the orthopedic surgeon, appeared at the foot of the litter. As big as a bear and as gentle as the A. A. Milne character, he had left his lucrative sports-medicine private practice to come over to Iraq.

"He needs your magic, Pooh," I said.

"Nerves intact?"

He was already trying to decide whether to try to salvage the upper extremity or just amputate.

I frowned.

"We'll see." Pooh shrugged and shuffled off toward the OR to get ready.

Warthog and I turned away from our patients to confer in the narrow aisle between the litters.

"Mine's stable," he said. "But needs lots of debridement. He keeps asking about your guy."

It turned out that the Iraqi national was an interpreter. He had been studying to be a doctor until Saddam closed all the medical schools. When the U.S. Army arrived, the young man decided to put his English skills to work. On this particular evening, it was his knowledge of first aid in controlling hemorrhage that had kept the major alive long enough to reach us.

I walked a few steps down the corridor to the adjoining makeshift operating room. Looking in, I found the OR techs opening pans of instruments and the nurse anesthetists drawing up their induction medications.

"We're all ready for you," Mookie greeted.

"It's Pooh's show tonight," I replied.

I felt a bit disappointed. First, I was thinking about the major who was about to lose his arm. Second, I was depressed by the prospect of being idle. Pooh would be doing the amputation, and Warthog would be cleaning up the Iraqi interpreter's wounds. I could kill a little time doing some paperwork, coordinating the post-op evacuation of the casualties, and communicating with the CSH to give them a heads-up. After that, however, I would be back to thinking about home.

Half an hour later I was self-medicating my self-pity by eating an MRE. I had saved the peanut butter tube from one meal and the bag of shelled and salted peanuts from another. Now I could mix the two together, add them to the standard chow mein packet and season it with Tabasco. It gave the entree a little Thai flair. It was perfect comfort food at two in the morning.

Cueball came round the corner.

"You've got to have some," I offered, desperate to talk to anyone as a distraction.

"No thanks, sir," he grimaced. "But I was sent to find you. They want you to poke your head into the OR."

My mood immediately improved. I left the doctored MRE and thoughts of my family behind and headed to the OR.

Pooh looked up from the major's arm.

"His elbow is blown away," he said. "I think the only thing holding his forearm on is a bridge of skin and his median and ulnar nerves. I can't find his radial. And I think that this is his transected brachial artery."

I peered over at the sterile field. There was a huge gaping hole where the elbow joint should have been. The sharp, fractured ends of the bones of his arm and forearm protruded menacingly into the wound area. The stump of his brachial artery was in spasm. It stood up on end throbbing with each pulse.

It was a sticky situation. It is often possible to restore blood flow to an amputated limb. However, the efforts are useless unless the nerves will work. The nerves carry the messages to the muscles to make them move. They also carry sensory information back to the brain. There is little use in saving an extremity that won't work or that will constantly be getting injured without the owner's awareness. Moreover, the technology of prosthetic limbs had advanced so much that many patients have a better long-term outcome by having a mangled extremity amputated.

"Think we should try?" Pooh asked.

With two out of the three nerves identified and intact, I thought it was worth a shot. If it didn't work out, they could always just take the forearm off back at Landstuhl or Walter Reed.

"I'll scrub," I replied.

Once gowned and gloved, I started dissecting through the mess of damaged muscle and tendons to find the ends of the brachial artery. A portion of the vessel had been destroyed by the blast. In addition, the distal segment in the forearm had retracted several centimeters. It was apparent that the two ends would not reach one another. I needed a graft to bridge the gap.

Warthog showed up having finished with his patient.

"I could use your help. You want to get to work on this guy's groin?"

"I beg your pardon," he said indignantly. "He hasn't even bought me dinner yet. Let me also remind you that I wear Army green and not Navy white. I will not be a part of any of those 'don't ask, don't tell' activities no matter how . . ." His words trailed off as he went out for a quick scrub. A few minutes later, Warthog was flaying open the patient's thigh to harvest a piece of the saphenous vein. We would use it to replace the missing segment of artery. I continued to clean up the elbow area and tie off some bleeders.

The game was on and everything else was secondary. I became focused on the operation and lost touch with much of what was going on around me. I remember Cueball coming in asking for updates so that he could plan the timing of the medevac chopper. The anesthesia team asked about blood loss a few times.

I sewed in the bypass and removed the clamps. The patient's hand immediately pinked up, and the distal side of the wound started to ooze blood. I rested the pad of my gloved index finger on the shiny segment of vein and felt the thrill of blood coursing through the vessel. The graft was open. The repair was working. It was a moment to savor.

My silent celebration was interrupted by Mookie slapping, rather painfully, a loaded needle driver into my other hand. It was his not-so-subtle way of drawing me back to reality.

"Four-O nylon, sir," he announced, as he handed me the suture I would need for closing the skin.

"Screw you, Mookie," I shot back. "This is the closest thing I've had to sex in four months. Don't ruin the moment."

We finished quickly and dressed the wounds as Pooh put the final touches on the external fixation device. I then broke scrub as the recovery-room team came in to help package the patient for transport to the CSH.

I sat down on a medical chest in the corridor between the trauma bay and the operating room. After draining my CamelBak of tepid water, I leaned back against the wall and sighed. I am certain that I smelled to high heaven. I didn't notice, and it didn't really matter. By that point in the war everyone reeked.

Over the next few days we tried to figure out what happened to the major and his arm. Unfortunately, because casualties were evacuated out of the country so rapidly, the answer eluded us. In some ways, it was better not to know. Everyone was willing to assume that the arm was saved. Morale was so high that to consider the other possibility would have been too depressing, especially since that night was such a powerful justification for our being there.

Several months after getting home I was back at my civilian hospital sitting in my comfortable office when Pooh telephoned.

"Did you happen to see *Oprah* yesterday?" he asked.

"No, I missed it," I replied, worried that he had some psychological scars left over from the war that were driving him to watch daytime television. "Pooh, why in God's name were *you* watching *Oprah*?"

"No, no, I wasn't," he clarified. "But someone told me that she did a feature on some of the wounded U.S. soldiers being treated at BAMC in San Antonio. She interviewed a major who had had his arm saved. I pulled the transcript off the Internet, and I'll e-mail it to you. The name and dates seem to correspond. I think it's our guy, and it looks like his limb was salvaged!"

I swelled with professional pride that our operation had succeeded. However, it was what this officer said during the television interview that moved me. When I got home that night, I helped my wife put our two sons to bed before sharing the transcript with her. She sat down at the kitchen table to read. It was only a couple of pages of text, but in it the officer described lying on the battlefield after being wounded. He was staring up at the Iraqi nighttime sky bargaining with God for the chance to see his daughter again. Then, later in the transcript, the major went on to share his feelings of joy once he made it home safely and wrapped *both* of his arms around his family.

My wife looked up and dabbed her cheeks with the back of her hand. She had never complained to me about my mobilization although I knew how hard it had been on her. She had managed all the challenges: child care, work, pregnancy—you name it. She is a strong and optimistic individual, but even at that moment I knew she was dreading the day when I would be called for a second tour.

"You know," she said trying to smile. "I hated every minute of that deployment."

"I know," I said.

"But it was worth it, wasn't it?"

MEDEVAC MISSIONS

Journal

Captain Ed Hrivnak

After wounded troops are treated in a field hospital, those in need of additional care are flown out of Iraq or Afghanistan to a larger, more modern medical facility in another country (usually Germany or Spain). In many cases, they are patched up and returned to their units. But if their injuries are more serious, they are sent back to the United States for long-term assistance and rehabilitation. Thirty-four-year-old U.S. Air Force Captain Ed Hrivnak, assigned to the 491st Expeditionary Aeromedical Evacuation Squadron, Air Mobility Command, was a fireman living in Washington State with his wife, Jennifer (who is an Air Force Reserve flight nurse), before serving in Operation Iraqi Freedom. Hrivnak was a veteran of the Gulf War in 1991 and had assisted in peacekeeping missions that flew into Rwanda, Somalia, Bosnia, and other countries. But despite all that he had seen as a firefighter and during his previous military deployments, Hrivnak was still profoundly moved by the (mostly) young casualties he tended to day after day as part of a medevac crew. The following excerpts, which span from late March to mid-July 2003, are from Hrivnak's journal. (CCATT refers to the critical care air transport team, which treats patients with life-threatening conditions.)

First Mission

Our patient load is 11 − 7 + 2 and a duty passenger. That means eleven litter patients, seven walking wounded, and two attendants. Some can take care of themselves, some need lots of help. All have been waiting for us for a long time and need pain medicine and antibiotics. The patients include: gunshot wound (GSW) to the stomach, partial amputations from a land mine, open fractures secondary to GSW, head injury/struck by a tank, blast injuries, shrapnel injuries, and dislocations. The patients are mainly from the Marines and 101st Airborne (Screaming Eagles). Many were involved in ambushes.

One trooper confides in me that he witnessed some Iraqi children get run over by a convoy. He was in the convoy and they had strict orders not to stop. If a vehicle stops, it is isolated and an inviting target for a rocket-propelled grenade. He tells me that some women and children have been forced out onto the road to break up the convoys so that the Iraqi irregulars can get a clear shot. But the convoys do not stop. He tells me that dealing with that image is worse than the pain of his injury.

Back in Germany, the patients are off-loaded and we clean up our mess. Then a sergeant comes out and declares that we have to sign a paper stating we will not drink and drive in Germany. We look at him with anger. Our mission from start to finish was twenty-nine hours long. Most of us were up twelve hours prior to that, minus catnaps. Forty-one hours later and someone in peaceful Germany is worried we might drink and drive.

The field where we picked up the patients, we find out later, came under rocket attack six times after we left.

Another Mission "Down Range"
I've noticed that the most seriously injured are the youngest. The older, experienced soldiers do a better job of staying alive and avoiding the flying metal. One soldier I'm treating looks like a young boy. We talk for a bit as I assess him. I medicate him for his pain. It is the first of many infusions.

The morphine is not working, but it's the strongest stuff I've got. At some point during these adjustments I accidentally dislodge a Hemovac suction unit from one of his infected wounds. Foul-smelling, reddish-yellow fluid drains from the tube and drips off the litter. I start looking at his bandages to find the other end of the tubing. I open one bandage and find sand fleas where his toes use to be. I try my best to keep a straight face, but the sight nauseates me. Scott, one of my level-headed medics, finds the tubing and resets the suction, then cleans up the mess I made.

We finally get this soldier comfortable. Because we moved him so much,

I decide to reassess his extremities. I know there are parts of his leg and thigh missing from reading his medical record, but I can't tell from the thick bandages. The wounds were left open to allow them to drain. The dressings are wet and covered in a light layer of sand. I ask the soldier to wiggle the toes he has. On one side his toes move fine; on the other side there is no movement. What is left on that side is cold and hard to the touch. He looks at me and our eyes are locked. His eyes say, "Tell me I'm going to be okay. Tell me that I'm going to be fine, tell me I'm going to be whole again. . . ." These are some of the longest seconds of my life because I know he is counting on what I say to him.

I bend down below the litter to break eye contact. I act like I'm adjusting some of the medical equipment attached to him. My mind is racing. I have always been honest with my patients. Do I lie or tell him the truth? The seconds move so slowly as I fight my internal battle on what is right. I stand straight up and there are his eyes. I'm at the end of the litter and with the noise of the plane there is no way he could hear me speak. We are now communicating solely with our eyes and facial expressions. I'm sure less than two seconds passed before I gave him a big smile and a thumbs-up. Those two seconds felt like an hour. He broke into a big smile of relief and I felt broken for lying to him. He motioned to me and I walked to the head of the litter. I leaned in so he could yell into my ear over the jet noise. "Why do my feet feel so cold?" he asked. I yelled back, "There is a lot of swelling in your feet and the blood circulation is not so good because of the swelling. It is way too early in the game to tell how well you are going to heal. The swelling is going to affect your senses and ability to move." These were all true statements. I felt reassured with my answer. It is too early to say how this soldier will recover. But I still feel bad about lying.

Easter Day
Some come onto the plane with the thousand-yard stare. Some come on with eyes darting about assessing the new environment, maybe looking for an ambush or a booby trap. Some walk with a nervous jitter, some walk on like zombies. Some have eyes glazed over from a morphine-induced stupor. Once we are at cruising altitude, you can feel the tension drop within the aircraft.

I thought I was doing a decent job at nursing when my medical crew discovered a cure-all on our Easter Day mission. We had collected money at our staging base and bought frozen pizzas and cookie dough. Halfway through the flight we started cooking the pizzas. I walked from patient to patient and asked them if they would like a pizza. There were many looks of disbelief. These boys had seen nothing but MREs (field rations) for over three months. Then the smell of pizza started to drift from our aircraft ovens. (We have five small convection ovens on the plane.)

Our crew passed out the pizza to the faces of eager boys. They did not look like combat veterans anymore. Most of them had gleeful looks like young children at an Easter egg hunt. It was like we just gave them a little taste of home and America. They started to joke and laugh with each other. After the pizza we brought out the fresh-baked cookies (which takes a little skill in a pressurized cabin). The cookies were hot and dripping chocolate. I weaved between the seats and litter stanchions and let the boys grab the gooey cookies. You should have seen the looks on their faces. It was on this mission that I realized that there is more to treating the casualties of war than pushing drugs and dressing wounds.

A Mission to Baghdad

We were in Bravo alert and had been told that not much was going on. A crewmate and I were passing the time in our room watching BBC World News when a news flash came on describing multiple ambushes and fire-fights around Baghdad. Several hours later we were alerted for an urgent mission to that very place. We ended up loading thirty-eight patients, the majority of them combat injuries. The worst patient assigned to me was a Ranger who was nineteen years old, but looked to be about fifteen. He was on the litter prone, facing the two critical patients. His arms dangled over the side of the litter. As I walked by, his left arm reached up and grabbed my calf. He was loaded with morphine and difficult to understand. He was rambling, "Take care of my buddies. . . . TAKE CARE OF MY BUDDIES, don't worry about me and are they going to be okay? Are they going to live?" The critical patients he was facing were his friends. When we loaded the patients we had no time to take into consideration their relationships to one another. He was looking directly at his buddies while the CCATTs worked desperately to keep them alive.

As the flight continued, I got bits and pieces of what happened. Five Army Rangers were on patrol when a remote-control homemade bomb was deto-nated under them. Hidden Iraqi irregulars then sprayed the soldiers with small-arms fire. One Ranger died at the scene, and another died at the field hospital. We got the three survivors. My patient was the only one still conscious. Each time I walked by him, he reached up and grabbed my leg, always asking about his friends. I went over to the CCATT nurse, Brian, and asked him how they were doing. He told me, "I got one guy who is shot through the neck and is paralyzed. The other guy has multiple shrapnel wounds and a severe brain injury. These guys are messed up. I hope they killed the fuckers that did this."

Halfway home, I finally caught up on my other patients. I sat down to jot some notes on a patient's chart and fell asleep for a moment. Instantly I started dreaming and then woke up with a start. I had never felt so exhausted. I looked up to see the prone Ranger waving for help. He was in pain. I gave him a touch of morphine. As I leaned into him, he lamented about his friends again. I told him they were still alive. He then vomited on me. It was the perfect capper to an arduous flight. I have no memory of the patient off-loads—I was on autopilot at that point. We got into crew rest midday and I had disturbing dreams.

Faces of War

The Humvee is like the Pinto of the 1970s: it burns quickly when hit by a rocket. One GI told me he saw a Humvee burn down in less than three minutes. You can't get out of the vehicle fast enough when it is hit. I was transporting a medical officer who was stuck in such a situation. He was hauling medical supplies to Iraqi civilian hospitals when they were ambushed by an RPG. He was burned on most of his upper body and face. The tops of his ears were burned off. His arms and hands were covered in heavy bandages and ointment covered his red, peeling face. I sat and talked with him as we waited for an ambulance. This officer was prior enlisted, married, and has three children. He decided to become a medical officer to provide better for his family and to get out of the field. He told his family not to worry about him, because he would be serving in the rear with medical logistics. He would not be fighting on the front lines. (Where are the front lines in Iraq?)

He was not concerned about his burns, but he was worried about what his children were thinking. He said, "I talked to them on the phone yesterday. They didn't understand why I was burned. I promised them I was going to be okay—that I would be safe. The kids don't get it and I'm not sure how to explain it to them." I stared at his face and burns the whole time he was talking.

His face was an expressionless mask. I couldn't tell if he was tired like the rest of the patients or if the burns were causing his unvaried, mask-like appearance. The tone of his voice when speaking of his children was his only sign of emotion.

What does the future hold for these men who go home to their families mentally and physically different? And what of the critically injured who have a long future of VA hospitals followed by VA disability? How do they cope? How do they adjust? I feel obligated to stay out here and take care of the wounded. I want to do all I can to help them.

Battle Buddies

These Marines and soldiers are good at waiting. They see we are doing our best and rarely complain. One soldier, trying to be patient, went too long between morphine shots. He tried to gut it out. He did not want to slow the loading of the airplane. We loaded him on the bottom rack and he immediately grabbed onto the litter above him. I looked down at him and saw his knuckles turn white with a death grip on the litter crossbeam. Tears poured down his face but he did not make a sound. I grabbed the primary flight nurse and told him to give this kid some of the good stuff. The nurse said he would get the morphine when we were done loading the rest of the litter patients.

I can't blame this nurse. It was his first real casualty mission in the war. It is easy to lose sight of one patient and get caught up in what is going around you. I told the nurse to toss me a syringe of morphine and I would take care of him myself. When I returned to this GI, a battle buddy was holding his hand and talking softly to him. Their hands were locked like they were ready to arm-wrestle. I quickly pushed the morphine into his vein and apologized for letting his pain get to such a level. I felt like I had failed him. His buddy stayed with him, talking to him, consoling him, until the pain medicine took effect and the soldier's hand relaxed. These two were not in the same unit. They were not wounded in the same part of Iraq. They were brought together and bonded by their wounds. Their injuries made them part of a fraternity, a private brotherhood I felt privileged to witness.

ALARM RED

E-mail

Captain Lisa R. Blackman, Ph.D.

Even if troops emerge from a firefight or attack physically unscathed, the emotional damage can nevertheless be substantial. Watching buddies get killed or hideously maimed and realizing how close they might have come to dying as well, many servicemen and women are understandably traumatized by the experience. Dr. Lisa R. Blackman, a thirty-two-year-old U.S. Air Force captain from New England, worked as a clinical psychologist at the Al Udeid Air Base in Qatar, with the 379th Expeditionary Medical Group, 379th Air Expeditionary Wing, from September 2004 to February 2005. During her six-month deployment, Blackman regularly spoke with individuals who were suffering from the mental aftershocks of combat. Although she was limited in what she could reveal, occasionally she would offer her family and friends a glimpse of what the troops were going through in her (often short) e-mails home. "A quick word on guilt," Blackman wrote in a message dated October 11:

> No one ever feels like they are doing enough. If you are in a safe location, you feel guilty that your friends are getting shot at and you aren't. If you are getting shot at, you feel guilty if your buddy gets hit and you don't. If you get shot at but don't die, you feel guilty that you lived, and more guilty if you get to go home and your friends have to stay behind. I have not seen one person out here who didn't [check off] "increased guilt" on our intake form.

What most struck Blackman, however, was the extent to which the troops were unaware of their own psychological wounds. She wrote the following e-mail about these less visible injuries on October 29.

Lately I have had a string of combat trauma evaluations. Several have been Army troops passing through for R & R—they come here for a bit and then go back to Iraq or Afghanistan. As if this is a glamorous vacation site.

But, they are grateful to be someplace safe (and someplace with alcohol, which I will surely complain about at a later date). Anyway, each one presented with a different complaint. One guy wasn't sleeping, one gal was angry about "sexual harassment" in her unit, one gal was depressed, one guy just wanted to go home. Standard stuff.

I had no initial clue that the problems were combat related and no idea that I should be assessing for acute stress disorder or PTSD. None of these guys or gals said "I was in combat" or "I saw someone die." None connected these experiences to their symptoms. It was as if they didn't remember how hard and unusual it is to be at war. They're used to the danger. They've been out here too long. Why would a war mess with your mood, right?

Each evaluation started with the typical questions: "What brought you in today?" "When did the problem start?" "Have you ever experienced these symptoms before?" "How's your sleep?" etc. etc. etc. I kept asking questions and thinking that the symptoms did not add up. Something wasn't right. I wasn't getting the right reactions. Stories were incomplete. Affect was blunted. Level of distress did not match presenting complaint. Alarm red, people, alarm red.

At home I ask people if they have ever experienced or witnessed a traumatic event or abuse. But out here I ask, "Have you ever been in combat?" Apparently, this is a question with the power to unglue . . . because all four of these troops burst into tears at the mention of the word "combat."

And when I say burst, I mean splatter—tears running, snot flowing, and I literally had to mop my floor after one two-hour session. In other words, I mean sobbing for minutes on end, unable to speak, flat out grief by an otherwise healthy, strong, manly guy who watches football on the weekends and never puts the toilet seat down.

Each time I sit there with not a clue what to say . . . offering tissues . . . saying I'm sorry . . . trying to normalize . . . trying to say, "It was not your fault that so and so died" and "If you could have done differently, you would have" and "You had a right to be scared." And even worse, "You had to shoot back" and "Yes you killed someone, and you still deserve to go back to your family and live your life."

Next time you are hanging out with a friend, think about what you would do if he turned to you and said, "My boss made me kill someone, and I know I'm going to hell for it so why bother?" What would you say to "normalize" that?

I will probably never see these folks again. I have no idea if I have been helpful. Maybe I planted a seed of reprieve that will grow into self-forgiveness. Maybe I did absolutely nothing but sit here. Who knows?

I can't stop thinking about the fact that these folks have lost something that they will never get back—innocence (and a life free of guilt). My heart hurts for them.

Wish us well,
Lisa

TO THE FALLEN
E-mail
Sergeant John McCary

At some point during their deployment, many servicemen and women understandably become overwhelmed by the unrelenting strain of living in a combat zone. Twenty-seven-year-old U.S. Army Sergeant John McCary was serving in a human intelligence team attached to Task Force 1-34 Armor, 1st Infantry Division, in Al Anbar province in Iraq. In late January 2004, after a month of heavy casualties in his unit (several of whom were friends), McCary vented in an e-mail to his family back in North Carolina about the increasing ruthlessness of the insurgents and the random, horrific violence claiming the lives of his fellow soldiers. But despite his palpable sense of anger and frustration, McCary emphasized that he knew more than ever what he was fighting for amidst the chaos of war.

Dear all,

We are dying. Not in some philosophical, chronological, "the end comes for all of us sooner or later" sense. Just dying. Sure, it's an occupational hazard, and yeah, you can get killed walking down the street in Anytown, USA. But not like this. Not car bombs that leave craters in the road, not jeering crowds that celebrate your destruction. We thought we had turned the tide, turned the corner, beaten the defensive rush and were headed upfield, striding into the home stretch. But they are still here. They still strive for our demise. It's never been a fair fight, and we haven't always played nice.

But not like this. No one leaves the gate looking to kill, or looking to die. No one wakes up in the morning and says, "I sure hope blowing up a whole group of Iraqis goes well today." You may be worn out, hounded by hours on end of patrols, investigations, emergency responses, guard shifts, but you never wake up and think, today's the day we'll kill a whole bunch of 'em. There's no "kill 'em all let God sort 'em out." That's for suckers and cowards, people afraid to delve into the melee and fight it out, to sort it out like soldiers.

They've killed my friends. And not in some heroic fight to defend sovereign territory, not on some suicide mission to extract a prisoner or save a family in distress. Just standing out directing traffic. Just driving downtown to a meeting. Just going to work. All I can think is, "Those poor bastards. Those poor, poor bastards."

And the opposition, they've damned anyone with the gall to actually leave their homes in the morning, because they've killed their own, too. Indiscriminate is one word. "Callous" does not even suffice. What battle cry says "Damn the eight year old boy and his little sister if they're in the area! Damn them all!?" What do you say to your men after you've scraped up the scalps of an entire Iraqi family off the road, right next to the shattered bodies of your soldiers, held together only by their shoelaces, body armor or helmets? "We're fighting the good fight?" I don't think so. We're just fighting. And now we're dying.

It's nothing new, not really. I know what that look is now, the one on the faces of WWII soldiers coming back from a patrol, Vietnam vets standing at the Wall. But now it's us. You know the little blurb from Connie Chung that says "2 Coalition Soldiers were killed at a checkpoint today after a car bomb exploded while waiting in line?" And you think, "ah, just two. At least it wasn't like thirty. At least it wasn't in a movie theatre, or the town square."

Yeah . . . I changed my mind about that one. When you sit at the memorial service, gazing down at the display: a pair of laced tan combat boots, a hastily printed 8″ × 10″ photo, their service rifle, barrel down, their Kevlar helmet set on top of the buttstock, and you hear their friends say, "he talked about his son every night. He's two. He can hardly talk but his Dad just knew he would be a great linebacker." Or, "his wife is currently commanding a platoon elsewhere in Iraq. She will accompany the body home but has chosen to return to her own flock, to see them home safely though her husband will not join her. Our thoughts go out to their families." WHAT THOUGHTS?! What do you think? What good will you do knowing this? What help will you be, blubbering in the stands, snot drizzling from your nose, wishing you could have known beforehand, wishing you could have stopped it, pleading to God you could have taken their place, taken the suffering for them?

What do you say to the fathers of the men responsible, when you find them relaxing in their homes the next day, preparing for a meal? Should you simply strike them down for having birthed such an abomination? Or has the teeth-shattering punch in the face crunch of seeing a fallen comrade laid to rest sated your lust for blood and revenge?

Resolve, resolute, resolution, resoluteness. You feel . . . compelled, to respond. To what? On whom? Why? Will your children someday say, "I'm sure glad Dad died to make Iraq safer?" No. They died standing with their friends, doing their jobs, fulfilling some far-flung nearly non-existent notion called duty. They died because their friends could've died just as easily, and knowing that . . . they would never shirk their duties, never call in sick, never give in to fear, never let down. When you've held a conversation with a man, briefed him on his mission, his objective and reminded him of the potential consequences during the actioning of it, only to hear he never returned, and did not die gracefully, though blessedly quickly, prayerfully painlessly . . . you do not breathe the same ever after. Breath is sweet. Sleep is sweeter. Friends are priceless. And you cry. There's no point, no gain, no benefit but you are human and you must mourn. It is your nature.

It is also now undeniable, irrevocable, that you will see your mission through. You will strive every day, you will live, though you are not ever again sure why. Ideals . . . are so . . . far, far away from the burnt stink of charred metal. I, we, must see it through to the end. They have seen every instant, every mission, every chore, every day through, not to its end but to theirs. How can you ever deny, degrade, desecrate their sacrifice and loss with anything less than all you have? Their lives are lost, whether as a gift, laid down at the feet of their friends, or a pointless discard of precious life . . . I doubt I'll ever know.

I'm ok, Mom. I'm just a little . . . shaken, a little sad. I know this isn't any Divine mission. No God, Allah, Jesus, Buddha or other divinity ever decreed "Go get your body ripped to shreds, it's for the better." This is Man's doing. This is Man's War. And War it is. It is not fair, nor right, nor simple . . . nor is it over. I wish the presence of those responsible only to dissipate, to transform into average citizens, fathers, sons and brothers. I don't care about bloodlust, justice or revenge. But they . . . they . . . will not rest until our souls are wiped from this plane of existence, until we no longer exist in their world. Nothing less suffices. And so we will fight. I will not waiver, nor falter. Many of my fellows will cry for no mercy, no compassion. For those responsible, for those whose goal is destruction purely for effect, death only as a message, for whom killing is a means of communication, I cannot promise we, or I, will give pardon. With all, we will be harsh, and strict, but not unjust, not indiscriminate. And we will not give up. We cannot. Our lives are forever tied to those lost, and we cannot leave them now, as we might have were they still living.

We have . . . so little time . . . to mourn, so little time to sigh, to breathe, to laugh, to remember. To forget. Every day awaits us, impatient, impending. So now we rise, shunning tears, biting back trembling lips and stifling sobs of grief . . . and we walk, shoulder to shoulder . . . to the Call of Duty, in tribute to the Fallen.

—john

McCary himself survived his tour of duty and returned home in September 2004. He was honorably discharged from the Army in April 2005.

IN DUE TIME
E-mail
Captain Daniel Murray

Regardless of their patriotism or commitment to the cause, over time and with few exceptions, combatants in Iraq and Afghanistan begin to long for one thing above all: to return home to the United States. This expectation is the emotional ballast that helps them weather the hardships and dangers of war. And if this hope is suddenly dashed because of an unforeseen postponement, the blow to morale can be crushing. Twenty-seven-year-old U.S. Army Captain Daniel Murray deployed to Baghdad in February 2004 and served in what became known as the Multi-National Security Transition

*Command–Iraq. Murray worked closely with the new Iraqi Army and was
tasked with sustaining and controlling access to the Taji Military Training
Base, which had a five-mile perimeter and was a prime target for the insurgency. On August 1, 2004, Murray sent the following e-mail to his wife
when he learned that he would not make it back in time for them to celebrate their third anniversary together.*

Dear Sabina,

I am writing to tell you that I won't be home on the 15th, as I've been extended with a few other soldiers.

I spent the first 5 months here so busy I didn't even have time to use the
bathroom on numerous occasions. I heard my name today at least 100 times
before lunch. Everyone's problem was the most important. And after dinner,
ALWAYS, and after everyone else has gone home, was when the real emer-
gencies happened. Unannounced shipments of 100 or more vehicles were
not uncommon, nor were power outages for entire sections of the base. Iraqi
medics had to be escorted to their own hospitals with injured or sick patients. There was another riot at the dining facility, Central Issue Facility,
and fuel point. There were people freeloading on the base and consequently
had to be removed. These things have all happened, and they were all my
problems. The staff was 11 people on a good day. I had to hide like a fugitive
in order to get some of my work done. I gave way to not answering my door
when people knocked. When this failed and they started coming in, I placed
a sign on the door, forbidding entry. I then replaced this with a bar across the
door. My only solace became the hours between 0600 and 0730. If I was
lucky, no one would talk to me during that time. I kept telling myself that on
the 15th of August, I would be able to rest. The days where I was too tired to
think straight or sleep amplified my anticipation. I had a job to do and a mission to accomplish, and I did it gladly, knowing that it couldn't last forever.
Dreams of you and times past brought tears to my eyes as I reflected on my
inability to experience them firsthand at the time. The final day kept me
going.

Contingent upon my release was the thing I mistakenly placed my trust
in, that somebody was going to ensure that I could leave on the 15th.

But the above conditions pale in comparison, no, are happy compared to
the rest of this letter.

Fighting for my survival is exhilarating, but demands without mercy a strong personal fortitude. It doesn't stop simply because I am tired.

In the last 6 months, people have been trying to kill me, employing various methods. They've shot rockets at me. They've fired mortars at me, even while I talked to you on the phone. I now know what a bullet sounds like when it flies over my head; I know what it sounds like when it comes out of a gun when it is flying toward an enemy. I know how it feels to have to hide behind a pile of dirt while someone tries to shoot me, helpless to do anything about it, because if I did, I would put myself and my men at risk. Two times, I've cleaned up blast sites, where propane explosions have claimed the lives of 9 people and have destroyed an area of 16 feet around them. But that's only ground zero, as the entire facilities are now useless. The people who died did so quickly. I've identified their body parts, usually gobs of blood, tissue, and hair, up to 90 feet away. I've seen these people dragged out from under piles of debris. I've seen and stepped in pools of human blood, trying to help wherever I can. I've held an Iraqi survivor and my friend while he cried. I pulled a dead person killed by the blast and asphyxiated by deadly, burning chemicals out from under his personal debris pile. We put him in a bag first. I lifted the body into the bed of a pickup truck with people crowded around, making it difficult to maneuver around. I dropped it like I would a normal suitcase or other heavy object from habit, remembering that it was a body only too late. And the worst part is that it was the best I could manage.

I smelled it. Gas, metal, adrenaline, sweat, tears, torn building materials, fresh meat, unwashed blown-up body parts. I've seen hair and brains picked up onto a dustpan, scraped onto it with a stick and handed to me because no one knew what to do with it. I've had to think about securing the site later so thieves wouldn't come and steal the salvageable equipment and the dogs wouldn't eat any body parts we couldn't discover until the day time.

I've been on foot in the palm groves outside the base. I went to the bridge where 16 people have been gunned down over the last 3 months. One of them I knew well—we had worked together for 6 months—he died of a hole in his head. I had to be there for his workers when they were left without a leader. I had to provide for them at the same time hoping and praying they would make it back to work alive after their customary three days of mourning so they could continue payroll for the Iraqi Army.

And I did all of this because it was my duty.

I watched everyone but two other soldiers leave when they were scheduled to. I kept telling myself that I could see you in due time. I held onto this, not knowing how else to put one foot in front of the other. But someone has robbed me of this hope. Someone decided that I didn't warrant enough attention to be sent home to normal life with you. It was better for someone to be negligent, carelessly shirking the responsibility of making sure everyone else had replacements except me and a few of the soldiers.

The way it works, sweetie, is that I have to have someone to replace me before I leave. At headquarters, the person responsible for this puts together a list called a RFF, or Request for Forces. This document tells how many people we need and when we will need them. The person who submits it must do it three months ahead of time. Sadly, that person has not done that. That person is home now, with his family. I am still here. I wouldn't mind as much if I was still here because my job isn't finished and I had to complete it. I mind, however, because the fact remains that I am paying the bill for someone else's negligence. I, and more importantly, you and those I love and who didn't volunteer to join the Army, have been forced to bear bitter disappointment upon hearing news of my failed homecoming. The feeling of loss and permanence imbues my every thought. I try to shake it, but can't. I've learned that the only thing I can do to deal effectively with this is to withdraw from the world for a day, not being able to do anything else. Brooding seems the only comfort. And not caring about anything helps.

Sabina, I'm not sure when I'll be home. It could be anywhere from 30 to 90 more days over here. I'll let you know as soon as I find out.

I love you.

Dan

The extension, in fact, lasted just over three months; Murray did not return home to North Carolina until November 2004.

VETERANS

Personal Narrative

Second Lieutenant Brian Humphreys

A platoon commander with 2nd Battalion, 7th Marines, Second Lieutenant Brian Humphreys served in the vicinity of Hit, Iraq, for seven

*months, beginning in February 2004. After surviving his first ambush,
Humphreys described his visceral response to the incident once it was over
(the excerpt is from a longer narrative about his deployment, most of which
Humphreys wrote in the present tense):*

> *We have been under fire for nearly an hour and a half. We have fired
> over 2,500 rounds at enemy positions not more than fifty yards from
> our vehicles. None of my Marines has been hit. None of the vehicles
> has been hit. Not a broken windshield. Not a dent in an armored
> panel. Nothing. We have fought for our lives, and can scarcely believe
> it. Did that just happen? I think as we pull out of the traffic circle to
> the south, our weapons pointed in every direction, our pulses pound-
> ing. Another thought enters my mind before I have the chance to shut
> it out:* That was fucking awesome.

*Humphreys is hardly alone in writing about the initial thrill of being in
a war zone. As with previous American conflicts, troops on the front lines
frequently wrote in their journals and letters (and now e-mails) about the
almost intoxicating rush they experienced during their first days and weeks
in-country. And for many combatants, whether they fought in the Civil
War, World War II, Korea, Vietnam, Desert Storm, Afghanistan, or Iraq,
these feelings often changed over time. They would for Humphreys as well.*

B ANG, BANG, BANG. The sheet-metal door amplifies the sound of the
large fist striking it. Sergeant Graham is standing in the doorway, sil-
houetted by the white-hot afternoon sunlight.

"Sir, we have a unit in contact, two friendly KIA. The platoon is getting
ready downstairs."

"You've got to be shitting me" is my first response after being woken out
of a sound sleep. Death has visited us before, but it is not ubiquitous enough
to have lost its shock value. I throw my uniform and flak jacket on, grab my
rifle, and head down a flight of stairs. The platoon is already on the vehicles,
ready to roll with an ambulance.

"Interrogative, are you still in contact?" I ask by radio as my column of
Humvees speeds north.

"Negative," comes the reply. *That guy always has an impeccable bearing even in one word,* I think to myself while watching the sides of the road for wires and triggermen. He is the company executive officer. I am the boot lieutenant. The Marine Corps has yet to beat my slovenly tendencies out of me. Fate, cruel as it is, put us in the same company together.

The palm groves to our east that line the Euphrates River whip by. To the west of the asphalt ribbon are the scorched wadis used by insurgents to stage their attacks. Up ahead I see the telltale cluster of Humvees and Marines. I pull up to the first vehicle and find the patrol leader.

"Where do you want the ambulance?" I ask.

"Just have it pull up, we'll guide it in," he replies, as if we have arrived to help fix a flat tire. The ambulance in the middle of my six-vehicle column pulls forward, and I get out to find where the casualties are.

"What the hell is that?" I ask a Marine. Perhaps the explosion had some-how killed a farm animal of some sort who wandered out on the road. A sheep maybe? Or a cow. No, not big enough. Well, what is that and how did it hap-pen? The Marine gives his buddy's name and asks me to help find his head. *Fuck.*

We do not want the stray dogs that occupy Iraq with us to find our brothers. The corpsmen, with their blue latex gloves and body bags, scour the bushes for the last scraps of human tissue as waves of heat rise from the desert. The Associated Press dutifully reports that three Marines were killed in Al Anbar province in Iraq. Names have not been released by the Defense Department pending notification of next of kin. We will not read the two-sentence notice for several days. The Internet Room is always pad-locked while we wait for somebody to get a knock on the door half a world away.

At one point the casualties got so bad that it seemed the room was closed for a week at a time while notifications were made. Iraq is coming apart at the seams. Pictures of flag-draped coffins being unloaded from Air Force trans-ports surface on the back reaches of the Internet, as if they were a grainy celebrity sex video that decent people should avoid looking at. But I think otherwise. The images of flag-draped coffins show the end of war as we are meant to see it, and as we are meant to believe it. Uniforms, flags, patriotism, honor, sacrifice. In these images we are not street fighters struggling to sur-vive and kill in a distant gangland, but soldiers in the nation's service. They will help the families, I think. They will help us. In our own way, we too, need to believe.

Today, the Marines will have to wait to log on to their chat rooms, HotOrNot.com, MilitarySingles.com, and the online shopping sites. I myself have become something of a spendthrift in Iraq, ordering more books and CDs than I normally would. I have seen death enough times among people who had been indestructibly living only the day before. It is better to go ahead and buy the CD you have been meaning to get. There are reminders wherever you care to look. For instance, the pile of blood-soaked flak jackets sitting in the company's combat operations center, a low-tech jumble of maps and radios. The flak jackets' owners are either dead or in the hospital recovering from their wounds.

The executive officer reminds us that the flak jackets need to be sent back through the Marine Corps's supply chain as soon as possible. Somewhere, somebody will wash them and inspect them for damage, filling out all the necessary paperwork. It is the banality, even more than the carnage, that shocks. Our occupation grinds on. Others will assign meaning to our lives here, noble or otherwise. For us, though, there is a close meanness to the fight. There are no flags, no dress uniforms. We are fighting a rival gang for the same turf, while the neighborhood residents cower and wait to see whose side they should come out on.

Imperceptibly, we are coming to the end of our deployment. Time has stood still for months, with days and nights fusing together in the burning hot air of the desert. But now, our deployment is being measured in finite units of time. It takes getting used to.

Echo Company will remain in our forward operating base as a deterrent to the insurgents, but otherwise will have no dealings with the Iraqi people. Our only other mission is to keep our own supply lines open. One of the lieutenants jokes acidly that he knows a way to shorten our supply lines by fifteen thousand miles. Our forward operating base is still the target of the occasional mortar shell. Sometimes, if we are asleep, we do not even wake up, but death never quite leaves us, still creeping along the highways and wadis as we wear out the days.

Returning from a patrol with my platoon, I find a blue sedan riddled with bullet holes on the side of the highway. There are a few Iraqi soldiers standing around when we find it. We quickly learn the car belonged to Captain

Laithe, one of the senior men in the local police force. Connected, calculating, and English-speaking, he had collaborated with the Americans since the fall of Baghdad. I've wondered since I first met him why he cast his lot with us, what calculation he made, and whether we could even understand it—what mix of nobility and venality it contained. His future, however he imagined it, ended with the finality of death in a hail of bullets on the highway less than a mile from our forward operating base.

Not long before we leave, I am awakened out of a sound sleep again, this time at midnight. The company executive officer is at the door. We have another KIA. I feel the same shock I did the first time, only a certain numbness has developed, like a nerve deadened by repeated blows. Our turn had almost passed, and now this. I nod, and begin collecting my gear. One of my fellow platoon commanders is outside in the pitch black. It is the body of one of his Marines that we will go out in the dead of night to recover. I ask him if he is all right. I ask him if his Marines are all right. The worst thing, he says, is that by now they are used to it. It is better and worse at the same time. I realize that we have all come to accept the loss of familiar faces, to live with it, and cross the line of departure again the next morning. It is this acceptance, rather than the thud of hidden bombs, that has finally made us veterans, and will finish the words on the obscure page of history we occupy.

We head off in the pitch black, navigating the highway through the grainy green glow of our night vision goggles. We move north to a point just north of the place where we lost the two Marines in the bomb explosion months before. One of the Humvees in the patrol struck a land mine a short distance from the Iraqi National Guard post the Marines had been tasked with protecting.

The sun is rising above the river palm groves when the trucks arrive to remove the wrecked vehicle. The dead Marine's remains are loaded in another truck and driven north toward Al Asad Air Base. The remains will be laid in a flag-draped coffin and then secured in the cargo hold of a transport plane to be flown back to the United States. We, too, will soon go to Al Asad. We will then strap ourselves into the cargo hold of an identical plane to begin our own journey home. The scrawled memorials on barracks walls to fallen buddies will stay behind for the troops who replace us. They might read the awkwardly worded poems and epitaphs written in loving memory, and half-wonder who we were.

In the beginning of September 2004, Echo Company is finally packing up
to leave, and Humphreys concludes his journal with the following entry.

We are flying out of Iraq tonight, seven months after we arrived to crush the insurgency. We are leaving. The insurgents will remain behind without us. The contents of my pack and seabag are on the floor. To the left and right of me, fifty-five other Marines—privates, sergeants, and officers—have also dumped their worldly belongings onto painted squares for inspection by military police at Al Asad Air Base. Somehow, every transition in the Marine Corps involves dumping your trash on the deck. The first night of boot camp the drill instructors rooted through our measly belongings, the relics of the civilian world we were leaving behind. They used white latex gloves, as if they might catch something from the sticks of beef jerky and playing cards.

The military police just use black leather gloves. They do a perfunctory search for contraband, as defined by the 1st Marine Division on the "this-means-you" poster plastered to the wall. No lottery tickets or advertisements. No flags of foreign countries not manufactured for sale or distribution. No lizard hides. No sex toys. No rocks of any sort, no matter how sentimental. No shrapnel. No personal effects of enemy soldiers, to include body parts.

The drill instructors guarding the gates of the Corps were meant to keep us from bringing the civilian world into the war world. The military police are here to make sure we take nothing from the war world back, except ourselves. Many of the Marines are short-timers, with only a few months left in the Corps. They will return home and cross back over to the other side to continue their lives with friends who barely noticed they were gone.

For the rest of us, Iraq will be waiting for our return. We can leave, but the country and its war will remain. The war that began after the president's Mission Accomplished speech is too diffuse for us to make a noticeable mark on it. There is no end to where we are going. There is no Berlin, no Tokyo out there for us to push toward. We are simply part of a larger historical process that unfolds slowly and unpredictably, like rising smoke. How long the fire underneath us will smolder, or what the earth will look like when it has exhausted itself, is impossible to know for those of us who are in it.

The flight attendants on the chartered 747 parked at the edge of Kuwait

City International Airport greet us with hand clapping and squealed congratulations. I grunt some type of reply and make for a window seat. Back home, Sunday football kicks off with flags, uniforms, and exhortations to support our brave troops serving overseas, and to remember those who have made the Ultimate Sacrifice. I wonder numbly whether I am expected to bask in the adulation. I am weary. We fought. We survived, but some did not.

I do not need to be told to remember.

CHAPTER SIX

HOME

RETURNING TO THE UNITED STATES

Twenty-two-year-old U.S. Marine Corps Lance Corporal Robert E. Gordon III hugging his wife, Diana, after returning in February 2005 from his second six-month deployment to Iraq.

Photo by his mother, Christine N. Gordon; used by permission.

This week he's due home, this son of mine. I wonder: Is he nervous? Is he excited? This child who was so kind and sensitive, so caring of his mother. I can't even imagine what war has done to him. Is he expecting everything to be just the same as when he left? I remember some veterans saying they wanted everything to be exactly the same when they came home, and when it wasn't, it was a nasty shock. This week is full of questions, full of doubts, full of excitement. I walk around with a smile on my face. Despite my concerns, I get to see him, and hug him. To count his fingers and toes. To sit near, and just watch him sleep, and remember all the times I did the same thing when he was two, and ten, and fifteen. To pretend, just for a while, that he is not a grown-up soldier, in a war—that he is just my son, here, back in my home.

> —Becky Ward-Krizan, writing in April 2005 about the return of her son, twenty-five-year-old U.S. Army Reserve Specialist Richard Ward.

Just before getting on the plane that would take us stateside, a young airman said to us: "This flight is now an HR flight. HR means human remains. We have two deceased soldiers on this flight." I couldn't help but feel choked up by this news. We boarded the plane thirty minutes later, and then taxied out and did our usual combat takeoff, very fast, hard turns, and then leveled out far away from the airport. One soldier, a major, stood up and walked to the front cabin. He returned later with a crew chief. They stopped by the caskets and the major pointed to the bags in front of them. One piece of civilian luggage had rolled over and was pressed up against the corner of the casket. That bothered the major enough to do something about it. When the bags were cleared the major sat down again. He buried his face in his hands and wiped his eyes. I could see his chest rise and fall. He took one big sigh, rested his head and arms on his knees. I don't know if he knew the two soldiers going home. But in a way it didn't matter. I think we all knew them. We had just come from Iraq.

> —Twenty-five-year-old U.S. Army Sergeant James A. Christenson, writing about his flight home in May 2004 from the Middle East.

GOODBYE, AFGHANISTAN
Personal Narrative
Captain Cameron Sellers

Born in South Korea and adopted at a very young age by an American cou-
ple, Cameron Sellers was brought to the United States in 1970 and raised
in Arizona. Inspired by both a love for his new country and his adoptive fa-
ther's own military service, Sellers joined the Arizona National Guard im-
mediately after high school. (Tens of thousands of individuals serving in the
U.S. military are foreign born.) His first overseas tour of duty came in 2000,
when he was sent to Bosnia with a peacekeeping force. After the September
11 attacks, he was stationed at the U.S. Embassy in Kabul, Afghanistan, be-
ginning in the spring of 2002. During his four months in the Afghan capi-
tal, the thirty-three-year-old Army captain served in the Office of Military
Cooperation, which was tasked with rebuilding the Afghan National Army.
Sellers kept a journal that recorded everything from the more humorous mo-
ments — such as teaching armed Marines how to swing-dance — to a har-
rowing mortar attack on the embassy. In the final entry to his journal,
Sellers wrote about his seventeen-hour trip to the States, which proved to be
an unforgettable one.

The timing couldn't have been worse. Although my deployment was
over and I was cleared to leave, finding a ride home was proving difficult. Security had been amped up everywhere because the September 11 anniversary was approaching, and, only a few days before, a member of the
Taliban had pretended to be part of President Hamid Karzai's own security
team and tried to assassinate him. There was, however, one flight available —
a U.S. Air Force crew was taking the American ambassador to Afghanistan,
Robert Finn, and President Karzai to the States, where Karzai would address
the United Nations and then the U.S. Congress. After quickly calling some
contacts I knew at the embassy, I was — miraculously — placed on the flight
manifest.

On Sunday morning, September 8, Ambassador Finn and I were raced
through the city to an unidentified location on the presidential palace
grounds. The atmosphere was tense at the helicopter pickup site in light of

recent events, and when I saw President Karzai's palace guards in their dress uniform I wondered if there might be an assassin among them. An Apache attack helicopter appeared and began circling the palace as a Chinook landed to pick us up. Before I could even blink, the president's party, the ambassador, and I were whisked aboard the helicopters. Out of the corner of my eye I noticed a Navy SEAL I knew, and I was relieved because I had heard that he had been shot in the head during the assassination attempt against Karzai. First reports are often wrong, and it was great to see that he was alive and uninjured.

As Kabul was becoming a distant view, I realized that this was it. My adventure in Afghanistan was about to become a memory. From three thousand feet, the scars of war were hidden and Kabul looked like any southwestern adobe town. Looking out the window, I saw the dry Kabul riverbed snake through the middle of the city. I saw the old Ghazi stadium that was built to draw the Olympics, but was later used by the Taliban to execute prisoners.

The helicopters flew parallel to the Jalalabad Road and then turned north above the new Bagram road that the Soviets built in the 1980s as a secondary supply route from Bagram to Kabul. I was as familiar with that road as with the ones back home because I usually traveled it every week. I felt that I knew every pothole and bump. I remembered the illegal checkpoints where militias would shake down drivers for "tolls," the overcrowding of a refugee camp, and the kids running from their homes to wave to us as we drove by.

The Bagram road went through the Shamali plains. Someone had told me that the valley used to have hundreds of orchards and the plains were fertile for agriculture. And then the Russians cut the orchards down and scorched the agricultural fields to eliminate potential ambush sites. You could travel for miles and the only thing you would see were the dust clouds swirling. Once you trekked through the mountain pass from the Kabul plains to the Bagram Valley, the only signs of life were explosives specialists placing red-painted rocks around the land mines. Once in a blue moon, we would witness a camel caravan of Pashtun tribesmen traveling through the valley and wonder how they managed to navigate through the active minefields.

We touched down on the airstrip right next to the flight line. Once we landed, we immediately transferred to a C-17. While the layover at Bagram was pretty quick, I still had time to look out the window and reminisce about when I first arrived there, when it was just a lonely outpost. Soon after it became the main hub for the war on terror. Within minutes, we were at thirty-five thousand feet flying away from Afghanistan. As the plane leveled off, the U.S. Air Force showed President Karzai how we treat all foreign heads of state. For lunch we fed him a "Jimmy Dean," which consisted of a small can of ravioli, tuna fish, chips, and soda. While the food was lacking, the C-17 crew was hospitable, and they did the best they could under the circumstances to make our flight enjoyable.

The ambassador had told me that President Karzai was easy to work with, and he appreciated America's help for his people in rebuilding his country. While he was pro-American, he was not a patsy. A couple of friends of mine, who were in the initial meeting with President Karzai and the JTF (Joint Task Force) commander after a wedding party had been shot up by an AC-130 gunship in Tarin Kowt, told me that the president berated the JTF commander for not informing him of this mission as the previous commander had done. As quick as he was to chastise the JTF commander, he was just as quick to forgive and forget. The president told him that mistakes happen and "Let's move on."

Even though he is a Pashtun from the Kandahar area, I was told that he loved Masoud, the late Northern Alliance commander, and he wept when they visited his tomb in the Panjshir Valley. Watching him interact with people on the plane only confirmed what I had heard about Karzai. He had what we in the military call "command presence." He attracted the attention of those around him without making a scene; his very presence radiated a kind of quiet power, dignity, and strength. He transcended ethnic and regional politics, and people from all walks of life felt comfortable around him but were also respectful. I finally worked up the nerve to approach him myself, and he could not have been more gracious. In my later years, when my grandkids ask me what I said to the George Washington of Afghanistan, I will reply, "Hey, can I get a photo taken with you?" Oh well.

We flew to Rhein-Main, Germany, and transferred to Air Force Two for the flight to New York. Someone told me that President Bush had sent the plane for Karzai to use as a courtesy, and talk about first class! Wide aisles, plush seats, and tables. Everything had Air Force Two inscribed on it, and I was contemplating stealing some of it for keepsakes, but settled for just shooting some pictures. The only downside was the meal. It was chicken and rice. Hmmm, where had I had that dish before? Oh right, every day since the moment I had arrived in Afghanistan. The Navy SEALs just rolled their eyes when they found out what was for dinner.

Once we got to New York, the pilot flew past the New York skyline. What a fitting ending to a remarkable journey. The flyby of Manhattan put everything into perspective. I thought of the thousands of lives lost a year ago, and it was hard to fight back the tears. Once we landed, I stepped out on the staircase to breathe the air and to step on American soil. I could not believe my eyes.

In two days we would observe the first anniversary of September 11. I thought about everything I had seen and experienced in Afghanistan, and why I was there. As a reservist, I volunteered for this deployment when terrorists attacked my adopted country. A year ago, I wrote to my closest friends and relatives why I was volunteering for the war:

> By now you have heard that the Army has called me back to active duty. For me, duty, patriotism, and service started long before September 11. And my values started long before my parents instilled them in me when I was a little kid. It started fourteen years before I was born when 43,000 American servicemen were willing to die on a peninsula called Korea. For most of my life, I have been an average American who grew up with a pretty common life except for the first two years: I was born in Seoul, South Korea as an orphan. I was discovered in an alley and placed in an orphanage. A loving American family picked me to be part of their family when I was one year old, and they fought for me to come to the United States. Thus began the great life I've lived so far. But all of this would have never happened if the United States didn't come to the defense of South Korea in 1950. Every Korean of that generation knows their freedom was won by American blood. I, as a Korean immigrant, know I am indebted to those 43,000 Americans who didn't come home. I am indebted to their wives and kids for the scars they have endured because their husbands or fathers were no longer in their life. Our grandparents fought World War II so the Baby Boomers would never have to live through another Pearl Harbor. Now our generation will fight terrorism so that our kids will not have to live through another World Trade Center. I have all the confidence in our generation to rise to this occasion and exceed the expectation of our fathers and grandfathers. I have no doubts.

> Coming home, my feelings are as strong as they were one year ago.

SEA VOYAGE

E-mail

Captain Guy W. Ravey

While the majority of troops return to America on commercial and military aircraft, some—mostly Marines and sailors—make the long journey home by ship. Thirty-year-old U.S. Marine Corps Captain Guy W. Ravey, who had been flying combat missions in the Middle East, enjoyed the leisurely, seven-week voyage back to Hawaii on the USS Constellation. The time aboard ship gave him an opportunity to reflect not only on his own wartime experiences, but on those of other family members who had served in the military as well. While sailing through the jungle islands of Indonesia on his way home, Guy Ravey saw something that sparked a powerful emotional reaction, and on the evening of May 10, 2003, he sent the following e-mail from aboard ship to loved ones in the States.

Dear Family and Friends,

Tonight was special. Tonight we passed by the island of Halmahera. It is a seemingly insignificant blob of tropical land sitting right on the equator near New Guinea and the Philippines, but it holds a great deal of significance to the Ravey family. This is the island where First Lieutenant Will Ravey, US Army Air Corps, was shot down in August of 1944.

Grandpa Ken Ravey had mentioned the island to me a few times as I was growing up. He rarely, if ever, brought the subject of his brother up. Even as a child I could sense how raw and painful the memories of his loss still were to him. However, he would proudly and reverently tell me the stories of his big brother, and once or twice he mentioned how his brother had died in combat over an island I had difficulty finding in any atlas because it was so small.

I have hacked away at the subject of Great Uncle Will from time to time. I eventually did find Halmahera on an atlas and quickly determined there was probably very little chance I or anyone else I knew would ever go there. I found out through family ties that he had been a fighter pilot flying P-38 Lightnings with the 8th Fighter Group and had been on a mission escorting bombers attacking Japanese positions. The B-24 bombers were lumbering, slow giants that were easy prey for Japanese fighters unless the American escort fighters intervened. It was the P-38 pilots' job to pick fights and protect the bombers (B-24's had a crew of 10, P-38's had only one). The specifics of the story are probably known better by those closer to Will, but as far as I can gather, he jumped into a fight where he was desperately outnumbered and shot down a plane or two before he, himself, was shot down. Later it was discovered that he had survived the shoot down only to be captured and executed by the Japanese. His remains were recovered in the 1950's.

I learned from Grandpa that Will had been married and his wife was expecting a child when he died. That son has grown up and had his own children now (one son is my age). The Heises, though answering to a different name, are a dear part of our Ravey family.

The circumstances surrounding Will's death remain tragic. They are hauntingly similar to those concerning the death of my friend, Dan McCollum, last year in Pakistan. Dan was my roommate in flight school and one of my best friends in the Marines. His loss hurts me everyday that I live. In a bittersweet parallel to Will's story, Dan's wife, Jenn, was four months pregnant with their son when his KC-130 transport went down near Shamsi, Pakistan. Daniel Junior is a bubbly and happy infant who has his father's arctic-blue eyes and easy smile.

I went up on the signals bridge tonight and looked out at the dark silhouette of Halmahera on the horizon. I tried to imagine what it was like to be in this area fifty-nine years ago. The pilot in me wondered what the P-38 was like to fly, and how exciting it must have been to be where Will was and to do what he was doing. The combat I experienced was very different from his. He most likely endured malaria, unsanitary conditions, oppressive heat and humidity, and a determined, well-equipped enemy. Not to mention there was a war that endured four long years, not three short weeks. I felt a kinship, though, and not just because Will is my flesh and blood. Will was a fighter pilot, and he died doing what he loved.

I've often wondered how any person could sacrifice himself for others. I know it wouldn't be my first choice, but I think that the perspective I've gained over this deployment has given me a clearer picture of why it happens. I'm sure that it was not Will's intent to "die bravely while valiantly fending off hordes of enemy aircraft." That's the sort of stuff that gets written up in awards and history books to help assuage the loss his loved ones feel. What I think is closer to the truth, and much more difficult to comprehend, is that he didn't want to "foul up." We use a different "F-word" nowadays when we talk amongst ourselves in the ready room. It wasn't pain, torture, serious injury, nor even death that we feared most: it was failing. Failing to do our jobs. Failing to complete the mission. Failing to help our friends in the air or on the ground. Will dove into that formation of Zeros because it was his job. The fact that he died is tragic, but many bomber crews were probably saved that day because of what he did. The Ravey family endured a loss that day so that other families, families we will never know, could have their loved ones home to produce families of their own.

Dan's mission was to fly supplies and troops throughout Afghanistan and Pakistan during Operation ENDURING FREEDOM. He and his crew flew in perilous and demanding conditions not because they were trying to impress anyone, but because it was their job. The missions they flew helped feed, transport, and equip the forces responsible for crushing the Taliban and liberating Afghanistan. They died so that others could be free.

The weather at this latitude is hot and sticky, even at midnight, so I only stayed outside for a little while. I said a silent prayer for Will and for Dan, and then I went below. I felt strange. I'll tell you all this now and hope you understand: I felt happy. Being near Halmahera is the closest I've been to family in seven months. It felt warm and soothing. There are many more emotions I felt, and maybe someday I'll be able to express them better. Tonight, though, I am proud to have closed the loop within our family. I called Grandpa Ravey on the sailor phone aboard ship and spoke to him for four minutes: long enough to hear the lump in his throat when I told him where I was. I am proud to have been able to set eyes upon this place. In a way, I feel as though I'm bringing a part of Will's spirit home with me.

Love to all,
Guy

---

3 A.M. IN BANGOR, MAINE
Personal Narrative
Sergeant Michael A. Thomas

Beginning in February 2003, twenty-nine-year-old U.S. Army Sergeant Michael A. Thomas was stationed in Tallil with the 220th Military Police Company from the Colorado National Guard, which was attached to the

220th MP Brigade. Thomas had been raised in a family with strong roots in the military; his father had been a first sergeant in the Army, his uncle was one of the famed Tuskegee Airmen, and his stepmother was an Army recruiter. Thomas himself enlisted in the Army at the age of eighteen. As proud as he was to serve his country, by February 2004 (after having served a full year in Iraq), Thomas was more than ready to head back to the States and be reunited with his wife, Wendy. In the following account, Thomas relates how exasperating the journey was—and how meaningful, in the end, it turned out to be.

After months of extending our stay in Iraq, our unit was finally going home. The year had felt long enough. We had missed birthdays, births, anniversaries, Thanksgiving, and Christmas, and when the plane that was scheduled to take us back to the States was hit by a de-icing truck in Germany, we were left feeling as though we'd never return to our families.

We were ordered to deplane and had to wait for the next flight.

Sitting in the airport throughout the night, we called our families with the bad news. We waited for what seemed like an eternity before finally catching another plane.

Thirty-six hours after our scheduled arrival, we landed in Bangor, Maine. It was 3 a.m. We were tired, hungry, and as desperate as we were to get to Colorado, our excitement was tainted with bitterness. While we were originally told our National Guard deployment would be mere months, here we were—369 days later—frustrated and angry.

As I walked off the plane, I was taken aback; in the small, dimly lit airport, a group of elderly veterans were there waiting for us, lined up one by one to shake our hands. Some were standing, others were confined to wheelchairs, and all of them wore their uniform hats. Their now-feeble right hands stiffened in salutes, their left hands holding coffee, snacks, and cell phones for us.

As I made my way through the line, each man thanking me for my service, I choked back tears. Here we were, returning from one year in Iraq where we had portable DVD players, three square meals, and phones, being honored by men who had crawled through mud for years with little more than the occasional letter from home. A few of them appeared to be veterans of the war in Vietnam, and I couldn't help but think of how they were treated when they came back to the U.S., and yet here they were to support us.

These soldiers—many of whom who had lost limbs and comrades—shook our hands proudly, as if our service could somehow rival their own.

We later learned that this VFW group had waited for more than a day in the airport for our arrival.

When the time came to fly home to Colorado, we were asked by our commander if we would like to join the Veterans of Foreign Wars. Every hand in the unit went up eagerly—including my own.

Looking back on my year in Iraq, I can honestly say that my perception of the experience was changed; not so much by the soldiers with whom I served—though I consider them my saving grace—but by the soldiers who welcomed us home. For it is those men who reminded me what serving my country is truly about.

Thomas remains in the Colorado National Guard and was promoted to staff sergeant in August 2004. He is also now a proud member of his local VFW chapter.

THEODORE
Personal Narrative
Captain Montgomery Granger

As eager as returning servicemen and women are to see their friends and family members, reunions can be fraught with tension and anxiety. Jet-lagged troops are sometimes too exhausted to demonstrate the enthusiasm that their loved ones had been expecting. Couples who have argued via e-mail or over the phone during the deployment can be harboring hurt feelings that flare up once they're together. And military parents can find that their children are timid and even resentful when they first see their moms and dads. Troops who have left behind newborn infants are often especially concerned that their son or daughter won't remember them at all. Thirty-nine-year-old U.S. Army Captain Montgomery Granger, who was stationed in Cuba from January through June 2003, wrote the following account after saying goodbye to his wife and three young sons in New York, including one child who had been born only days before Granger departed.

The night before I deployed, I cuddled with Harrison and Benjamin and read them their favorite story (okay, my favorite story to read them): *Stop That Pickle!* It's a fun, silly book about a wayward pickle who faces certain . . . well, "consumption," but narrowly escapes due to his incompatibility with ice cream. I read it like a seasoned actor, and the boys chuckled and laughed along. At the end of each page there was a refrain that we'd all exclaim together: "Stop that pickle!"

Sandra came downstairs and saw us together. "Why don't you record that for the boys, honey?" she suggested.

I smiled and said, "Sure, that's a great idea. What do you say, boys?"

"Again!" Harrison said excitedly.

"Cool," said Benjamin.

"Great," I said. And we had a blast doing it once more—bigger, bolder, and better than before.

It got late, and I said good night to the big boys, and told them to be good to their mother and helpful with their new baby brother, Theodore. They promised they would. Kisses and hugs followed, and Sandra put them to bed. I went to peek on our newest boy and, quietly leaning against the door to his room, watched the rise and fall, rise and fall of his tiny chest as he slept.

"Yup," I thought, "he works. Our little miracle works."

Sandra came in and we hugged for a while, kissed gently, and then walked downstairs.

"I miss you already," she said.

"Me, too," I told her. "And the little fellas. I'm so scared Theodore won't know me when I get back, Sandra."

"He'll know you," she told me, with an intuitive wisdom that had me questioning my insecurity. But it bothered me, still.

"He won't know my smell," I said, "or my voice. I'll scare him when I get back, and he'll cry, and then I'll cry . . ." I was beginning to ramble.

"Don't worry," she said. "It'll be fine. I promise." There's one thing about my wife. She always keeps her promises. But this one was different.

I left my family forty-eight hours after Theodore was born. I wouldn't see him—or the rest of the family—again for six months. My second activation since September 11, 2001, would take me to the U.S. Naval Base at Guantanamo Bay, Cuba, or GiTMO, as we called it, as the field medical assistant for the Joint Detainee Operations Group (JDOG), to help run Camp X-Ray.

The toughest part about the mission was being away from home. But, thanks to modern technology, my family and I used e-mail, snail mail, and care packages to stay in touch.

For Father's Day, Sandra sent me a "talking" picture. It was a small, black plastic clamshell frame, with a picture of all three boys on one side and a speaker/microphone on the other. The older boys said together, and I could see them smiling and giggling as they recorded it, "HI, Daddy! We LOVE You! Happy FATHER'S Day!" I kept the frame open for a few more seconds, thinking that Sandra might have had something to say, and then I heard it: "Gggruuurgle, ggaaaaa, guh!" It was Theodore! These were the first sounds I had heard since listening to his soft, sweet whispering breath the night before I deployed.

The tour felt much longer than it was, but in late June, we finally returned stateside. All I could think of was how the boys would react, having not seen me for almost half a year. I wasn't too worried about Benjamin, who was six, but I was a bit concerned about Harrison, who was only three. Would he be mad? Would he recognize me? Would he even want to hug me?

As for Theodore, I really had no hope whatsoever. I felt sure he would cry if I tried to hold or nuzzle him. I had purposely left behind a shirt I had worn for several nights straight, which I asked my wife to wrap Theodore in each night so that he would remember my scent. Sandra told me that she had cleaned it after a few weeks. "It got bad," she said, after sensing my disappointment.

I had clung to that as my only hope, and now, in my dreaded vision, I saw myself home and Theodore wake up next to me, notice this completely unfamiliar monster, and then start one of those high-pitched baby screams that begins with a few moments of silence as he sucks more and more air into his tiny lungs before letting out a wail that would pierce my ears and heart.

Due to the uncertainty of my travel arrangements, my wife and the children weren't able to meet me when our unit arrived at the airport, so I hitched a ride with another soldier. Pulling up to our house, I saw trees adorned with yellow ribbons, and sidewalk chalk greetings in big bold letters: WELCOME HOME, DADDY. Next to that were smiling faces, an airplane, and a drawing of me in uniform.

But no one was there. I sat on the porch with my duffel bags and waited for my wife and children. Hours passed in my mind but only fifteen minutes had really gone by when I saw our minivan suddenly come into the driveway. I could see Sandra smiling broadly through the driver's side of the windshield. She was first out of the van—and first to get a welcome-home hug and kiss, squeezing me oh so tightly, and whispering in my ear, "I'm so glad you're home."

And then Benjamin jumped out, screeching, "Daddy, Daddy, Daddy!" I hugged him hard, and kissed his cheeks, and held his head against my belly.

Harrison stood in the doorway of the van, pouting. He looked at this strange man holding his brother and pretended to be angry. I knelt down to his eye level, smiling, and said, "Hi, Harrison. I missed you."

Harrison hesitated, and then I saw a twinkle in his eyes as he dove for me, crying. I held him a while, kissed his forehead, rubbed his back, and whispered to him, "It's okay, it's all okay. Daddy's home now." We broke our embrace, and I saw a crack of a smile form on his chubby little face. I started tickling his tummy and actually got a laugh out of him.

Then I saw baby Theodore, strapped in his car seat. He had rosy, fat, pink cheeks, a button nose, and blue eyes . . . looking at me. I stopped breathing for a moment.

I approached him cautiously, waiting for the crying, the tears, and the struggle to get away from this stranger. I carefully released the seat belt and moved slowly, as if I were about to pick up a rattlesnake. I was sure he would sense my nervousness and spring "the scream" on me.

I braced myself for the inevitable. He looked at me, blinked a few times, and then started twitching in the arms of this clumsy man who'd obviously forgotten how to lift him up like his mommy. He moved his lips and wiggled his body ever so slightly. But he wouldn't look away from my eyes. He seemed entranced, fascinated, almost as if he were in love.

I slowly took him from the car seat, and prayed my little prayer of forgiveness: "Oh, Lord, please help this little person forgive me my absence. And set me on the path of redemption and full fatherhood. . . ." Theodore gurgled, which made my heart jump, and I drew him closer.

I braved a kiss on his puffy cheek and then pressed his tiny body to my chest, with his head on my shoulder. I could swear I heard him sigh. He didn't cry. He didn't squirm. He just rested there, gently, as if it were the most normal thing in the world. As if, I realized with tears in my eyes, I had never gone away.

More than two years later, Granger would leave his family for a fourteen-month deployment to Iraq. After he returned in late November 2005, Granger added a brief epilogue to his account: "My final homecoming was wonderful, celebratory, and relieving. Theodore became attached to my hip, and was constantly giving me hugs during the first several weeks of my arrival. It was a dream come true for me. Who wouldn't love constant hugs from a three-year-old?"

WAITING FOR SHAWN

Personal Narrative

Paula M. Andersen

From the day her husband, twenty-five-year-old U.S. Army Specialist Shawn Andersen, was mobilized for duty in Iraq in April 2003, Paula Andersen pictured in her mind the precise moment he would be back in her arms. She envisioned herself at McCord Air Force Base in Washington with her young son, Andrew, and all the other families, each of them holding signs and flags and balloons as they waited with a growing sense of excitement and relief. Although Shawn was expected to serve in Iraq for a year with the 555th Combat Engineer Group (attached to the 4th Infantry Division), 14th Battalion, Alpha Company, Paula was elated to receive news in the middle of August 2003 that Shawn was returning from Iraq early. She would soon discover, however, that the homecoming she had so desperately yearned for would be nothing like the one that she had imagined.

On August 16, Alpha Company's Family Readiness Group (FRG) leader phoned me and said, "Paula, your husband is on his way home." My hands started trembling, and I asked her, "Are you sure? Are you sure?" Shawn was only about halfway through his deployment, but the FRG leader assured me that it was absolutely true, and that a few other soldiers from Alpha Company were all traveling home on the same commercial flight. The FRG leader said she would call back with more details when she had them.

I went to the store to buy Shawn his favorite foods and candies, as well as a sweatshirt and sweatpants, knowing he'd need to adjust to the colder weather in the Pacific Northwest. I also got him a bath sponge, figuring he probably couldn't wait to take a long hot shower.

On August 17, the FRG leader left a message telling me when the soldiers were due to arrive at SeaTac Airport in Seattle. The scheduled time was 12:15 a.m. that next morning. After calling her and confirming the flight information, I told our two-year-old son that his dad was on a big airplane flying home to see us. He replied, "Dada is coming home? Oh wow!"

Just before midnight, we walked into the airport with flowers, a disposable camera, and a small American flag. I noticed other soldiers in uniform and family members holding flowers, welcome home signs, and flags as well. One woman was holding a large sign that read WELCOME HOME 62ND MEDICAL. I knew that there would be other soldiers from other units on the plane; still at this point I did not recognize anyone around me.

About ten minutes later, I heard the crowd start screaming and clapping, and then I watched as wives and husbands ran to their spouses. I saw a lovely lady hug her husband for what seemed like five minutes and cry loudly. "I missed you," she said over and over. Soon, the line of passengers getting off the plane started to dwindle.

No one else was arriving. I began to feel embarrassed. An officer came up to me and asked me if my husband was a part of the 555th Combat Engineers. I said, "Yes." He told me that those soldiers had gone down to baggage claim where he said he thought many family and friends had also been waiting. I replied, "How could I have missed him?" By this time, my entire body was shaking. I don't remember what I was thinking except that Shawn had to be down there.

A soldier who had overheard me ask someone for Shawn Andersen, yelled out, "Hey Andersen, your wife is here."

"Oh, thank God," I thought. I didn't see him walking towards us at first, but finally he emerged through the crowd. And there he stood. He wore glasses, was quite tall, and had sandy brown hair, like my husband. But it wasn't Shawn.

"Oh my God, oh my God," I started saying aloud.

A short, dark-haired man, who had come to greet some of his fellow soldiers home, could tell I was distraught and asked me who I was looking for. I said, "Sergeant Shawn Andersen." (He had been promoted while he was in Iraq.)

He asked, "What company is your husband in, ma'am?"

"Alpha," I told him.

"This is Charlie Company." He then asked me, "Who contacted you about your husband being on the flight home?"

"The company's FRG leader," I replied.

He said, "Well, someone has made a very big mistake."

Shawn was not on the plane. He was not coming home. I turned and started walking very quickly to the escalators, running into a mother and her two small boys. I apologized and she let me past. "Oh God. Oh my God," I repeated to myself. I couldn't stop saying it. My arms were tired from holding Andrew and all of our things, and I just wanted to get to our car. I wanted to hide. I tossed the roses that we had for Shawn in a nearby garbage can. It took me what seemed like an eternity to pay for our parking ticket before walking to the car. Frustrated, confused, I couldn't find my cash, and then I couldn't find the ticket. I put Andrew in his car seat and called Shawn's parents to tell them what had happened. I talked with Shawn's father, who said, "Paula, you have got to calm down for Andrew's sake." That is when I realized what my son had been saying to me all along: "Mama, I'm scared. Mama, what's the matter?" I then knew I needed to keep my composure.

Over the next few days, I spent hours on the phone and even drove out to Fort Lewis to visit the 555th Combat Engineer Group's main administrative building to find out what had happened. No one had any answers. And then, on Thursday, August 22, I received a call from Shawn's father. The first thing he told me was, "Paula, Shawn is coming home." I was so confused. Obviously I had heard that before. "Now wait," he said. The tone of his voice indicated that something terrible had happened. "Shawn has been injured. All I know is that he has burns to his hands, legs, and face. He just called me from Kuwait." He didn't have any other information, and we didn't know how bad the injuries were. Later I heard from a notification officer who gave me a toll-free number I could call to get updates on where Shawn was being treated. After receiving initial care in Kuwait, he was transported to Germany.

On August 23, Andrew and I drove to Montana and stayed with my parents. I dialed another 1-800 number that the casualty office had given me, and this connected me to the hospital in Germany. A nurse called for Shawn, then handed the phone to him. Shawn's hands were wrapped, so it was hard for him to get a good grip, but at long last we were able to talk. Hearing his voice made my heart skip a beat, but he didn't sound the same. He was in deep pain. As hard as it was for him to talk, he wanted to make sure that we could see each other when they transferred him to the Brooke Army Medical

Center in San Antonio, Texas. "I'll be leaving in a couple days," Shawn said, his voice alternating between sounding normal one minute and distant and melancholic the next. I was now beginning to worry about his mental state.

After two days in Germany, Shawn was flown to the medical center in San Antonio, where he was quarantined for a few days before he was ready to receive regular visitors. On August 31, I flew to San Antonio, and when I arrived at the airport, I was met by the man who would be my liaison. He told me if I needed anything, he was the man to reach. I couldn't have asked for a more supportive person. After helping with my luggage and escorting me to the van, we were on our way to the hospital, where I would be seeing my husband for the first time in six months. "Are you ready?" he asked me.

My heart started beating so fast, and I choked out the word "Yes."

We took the elevator to the fourth floor where the Burn Unit was. He went to the nurses' station in the ward and told them that he was here bringing me to see Sergeant Shawn Andersen. He was first to walk into Shawn's room. I heard him say, "I have someone here to see you. . . ." Before I even stepped in the room, I started to cry. And there, in a hospital bed, lay the love of my life. He reached out to me, and his hands up to his elbows were wrapped. There were flash burns to his face and on his lips, and his hair was singed. I also couldn't help but notice how skinny he was. It looked like he had not eaten for months. I went to give him a light hug. I was afraid that if I hugged too hard I would hurt him in some way. Shawn cried. We said "hello" and "I love you" to each other.

The military liaison gave me his phone number and told Shawn to get well. He then left us alone to talk. Shawn kept repeating, "I'm so happy you're here with me." We talked for about an hour. He asked about Andrew and the flight. He told me about the wonderful nurse that he had and explained what the doctors had been telling him about his injuries. The main question was whether they would have to do skin-graft surgery on his hands. It was getting late, so I said that I would let him sleep, and I'd be back in the morning.

Every day we would talk on the phone with Andrew, who was staying with his grandparents, and he would say to Shawn, "Dada, you have boo-boos on your hands."

Shawn would say, "Yes I do."

Andrew would ask when he was coming home. Shawn would always tell him that Mama and Dada would be flying to Grandma and Grandpa's house soon and that he couldn't wait to see him.

In the days that followed, I would visit Shawn in the morning, leave for a little while so he could nap, go with him to physical therapy, and then walk laps with him around the ward. The nurses had insisted he get up and walk to keep his legs from getting stiff. We must have done a thousand laps, but it was my favorite time with him. We talked with each other, and we chatted with the nurses. It was an experience that I will never forget.

Shawn's primary nurse, Ms. Mary, showed me how to clean his burns and apply antibacterial cream to them. At first I had to turn my head away, and even after a few times I found it hard to look at his wounds. Sometimes Shawn's meds were already working and sometimes he didn't get them until later, so the scrubbings were very painful for him. He said, "Honey, you are going to have to look." He was right. I would need to be able to do this when he wasn't in the hospital.

Slowly he made progress, and he was becoming much happier. Day by day I felt I was getting my old Shawn back. After about two weeks in the hospital, Shawn was told he was well enough to leave (it turned out that surgery wasn't necessary), so he said his goodbyes to the nurses and we packed his things. As we walked down the hall, I could see into the rooms of other burn victims, many of whom were much worse off than Shawn. I couldn't imagine what their pain was like. I thought of the tiny burns I'd had from an iron or a hot pan, but to have that all over your body seemed unbearable.

Thanks to a kind lady who traded seats with me, I was able to sit next to Shawn during our flight to Great Falls, Montana. When we got off the plane, I walked slowly so that Shawn was ahead of me. I wanted Andrew to see him first. The nice lady on the plane walked alongside of me, and she was excited for Shawn herself. She knew that this father was going to be reunited with his little boy again.

The anticipation of seeing our son was agonizing for Shawn. He worried that when Andrew saw him, he might be scared to approach him. As soon as we turned the corner, I saw Andrew there with his WELCOME HOME DADA sign and I burst into tears. Shawn kneeled down toward Andrew, who rushed to him without hesitation. Shawn hugged him and then lifted him up, and the two of them had never looked happier. I gave Shawn's parents and sister a hug, and I watched as they all embraced him. I saw how thrilled they were that he was back and, although injured, at least still alive.

A month later we returned to Washington, and in November 2004 Shawn was awarded his Purple Heart. It wasn't until then that I found out that the five-ton truck he'd been traveling in near Tikrit had been lifted into the air when a roadside bomb exploded underneath it. Miraculously no one was killed, but everyone inside was badly wounded.

It took many months, but Shawn, except for some scarring, fully recuperated. He has stayed in the military, and he now works as a special agent in the Army's Criminal Investigation Division. At any time, he could be sent to Iraq again. If asked about going back to Iraq, Shawn will say, "If I have to go again, I have to go. It's my job." I couldn't bear to watch him leave a second time, especially for a war that I do not agree with. And I definitely couldn't handle waiting for him to return. One homecoming is enough.

A JOURNEY TAKEN WITH MY SON
E-mails
Myrna E. Bein

For every serviceman or woman killed in Iraq, it is estimated that seven times as many are wounded. Many of these troops—who return home paralyzed or with missing limbs, terrible burns, major head trauma, loss of vision, or other catastrophic injuries—face enormous physical and psychological hardships. They rely heavily on their families to help with their rehabilitation, and the process can be excruciating for their loved ones as well. At about 7:00 a.m. on the morning of May 2, 2004, Myrna Bein learned from her ex-husband that their twenty-six-year-old son, Charles, a U.S. Army infantryman, had barely survived an ambush in Iraq a few hours earlier. Charles had been riding in a five-truck convoy in Kirkuk when insurgents detonated a roadside bomb and then unleashed a barrage of gunfire on the American soldiers scrambling out of their crippled, flaming vehicles. One soldier was shot in the head, and ten others were injured. Metal fragments from the initial blast shredded the lower half of Charles's right leg, and he was ultimately flown to the Walter Reed Army Medical Center for long-term care. Charles's mother and his stepfather, Tom, visited him regularly in the hospital, and from the morning she heard the news about her son, Myrna Bein began e-mailing friends and family with updates on Charles's progress—as well as her own state of mind. (Bein also grew fond of another soldier, Specialist J.H., who had been with her son

when they were attacked.) The first time that Bein saw Charles was on Sun-
day, May 9, 2004—Mother's Day.

May 10

Yesterday afternoon I was finally able to see, touch, hug, kiss and comfort my
precious son. He arrived at Walter Reed Army Medical Center in Washington, D.C., on Saturday evening, May 8, at around 11 p.m. I got a call from the
Red Cross informing me he was there within thirty minutes of his arrival.
Charles called me around 6 a.m. on Sunday, May 9, to tell me he was scheduled for yet another surgical procedure that day and for Tom and I to delay
our initial visit until afternoon. . . .

When I first saw my son, I did not recognize him. His face was very thin
and drawn and he had about a week's growth of beard. There was a lot of pain
in his eyes. He grabbed my hand and would not let it go. . . . I'm a Registered
Nurse and I've seen a lot of people with amputations, so I know what to expect. But seeing my son's less than half a leg for the first time, wrapped up in
that big, bulky surgical bandage, was an experience of indescribable grief.
Seeing him maneuver so awkwardly in bed, and seeing the pain that he was
experiencing, just to do the simplest activity, was something I had tried to prepare myself for, but now I don't think I could have ever been prepared.

Once he was settled and medicated with morphine again, the pain began
to ease to what he described as a constant 4 out of 10. He never really complained about anything. He just gritted his teeth and did what he had to do.
"Mom, don't try to help me unless I ask you," he said, "I need to learn to manage everything for myself." His left leg is also very painful as he has numerous
smaller shrapnel wounds, which are sutured and the leg bandaged from toes
to hip. Charles said he's had many larger shrapnel pieces removed, but some
of the smaller pieces will just be left.

Charles held my hand and talked extensively to Tom and me. Much of
what he said, including thoughts and impressions, he did not want repeated
to anyone. He has begun to express that he would like to stay in the Army, if
possible, after he is fitted with his prosthesis and finishes his rehabilitation.
According to Charles, his orthopedic surgeons have told him they believe he
could do that, with a different MOS other than Infantry.

After several hours Charles asked to be taken to the Medical Intensive
Care Unit to try to see Spc. J.H. We called to the MICU and got permission
to bring Charles down. It took Charles approximately 30 minutes of pain and

maneuvering to get himself dressed in shorts and a T-shirt, put a sock and shoe on his left foot, and manage his transfer from his bed to his wheelchair. His determination and courage astound me. After another dose of morphine, Charles held onto his IV pole and pump in front of him, while Tom and I got his wheelchair down the hall, into the elevator, and down another set of hallways to the MICU.

I tried to prepare Charles, and myself, for what we could expect to find with Spc. J.H. Again, I've spent a lot of hours in ICU's in my time and seen a lot of heartbreaking situations, but nothing can compare to what I experienced yesterday. Spc. J.H. remains very ill and highly sedated. Charles asked me to get him as close to Spc. J.H.'s bed as possible where he was able to touch his hands, arms, and face. He talked to him for about thirty minutes. Charles was deeply affected by Spc. J.H.'s condition. Spc. J.H. and Charles were side by side when the IED exploded under their HMMWV. Listening to Charles speaking to Spc. J.H., I know that if he survives this, there will be a bond between Charles and him that will never be broken.

May 15

I thought I'd take the time to send another missive regarding Charles' condition. Unfortunately, he has had some very rough days since Friday. He went to surgery that day for what he thought would be his last procedure on his right leg, to create the best stump possible for his prosthesis. However, Charles has had an infection set in, caused by an organism common in soldiers returning with wounds from Iraq. The organism is *Acinetobacter baumannii*. It's a very nasty creature and resistant to almost all antibiotic therapy. The orthopedic surgery team working with Charles was only able to do part of the procedure they had planned, since the infection in the wound has caused too much inflammation in the soft tissues to proceed further at this point. The infection, coupled with the trauma of all the surgeries, is also causing Charles to feel very sick and to have very severe, unrelenting pain. . . .

I know Charles is having moments of despair and I can now, two weeks after the event, see the inevitable depression creeping in around his edges. The Walter Reed staff tell me that they've now seen enough amputees come through there from Afghanistan and Iraq to know that the depression, and its resolution, will generally follow a pattern. Apparently, Charles is on schedule. All of the wounded are followed by psychiatry and receive appropriate medication and counseling throughout the course of their care to deal with this life-changing event and the fear, anxiety, and grief that inevitably follow this type of injury. Thank God for that. I know the Army has learned a lot about taking care of the whole soldier since the days of Vietnam. Charles told me tonight, "I know this will get better." Tom and I are trying our best to support him through this horrible ordeal. Most of the time we feel pretty helpless, but we do what we can both in prayer and in practical matters to assist him where he needs it.

In spite of what I can see he's going through, I've never once heard Charles whine or complain. When the nurses and physicians ask, he rates the pain on a scale of 0–10, but he basically just grits his teeth and waits for it to eventually subside. He doses himself with morphine from his patient controlled IV pump and gets in his wheelchair and goes down to check on Spc. J.H. every day, because he's his buddy and they are in this together. He's pushing himself in physical therapy to do as much as he can, as soon as he can. My admiration for his courage and determination is so profound. . . .

There's great news about Spc. J.H. My husband, Tom, and I saw him on May 15, along with Charles. We rolled Charles and all his associated intravenous pumps and tubes downstairs to visit Spc. J.H. and his family. Spc. J.H.'s mother and brother were both with him. He had been transferred to an intermediate care unit, from the Medical Intensive Care Unit, and was being prepared for further transfer to a regular care unit as we were there. He was awake and for the first time he absolutely recognized Charles. As Charles rolled through the door of his room, you should have seen the look on Spc. J.H.'s face! He lit up like a Christmas tree. He was able to motion for Charles to come in. Spc. J.H. still cannot speak, but I believe that will come in a bit more time. The nurse in charge of the unit, a Major, said he was extremely encouraged by the progress that Spc. J.H. had made over the past 48 hours. Spc. J.H. nodded his head in response to questions, gave a thumbs-up sign, grasped Charles' hand very strongly and wouldn't let go, and made excellent eye contact. He was sitting up in a chair. He still has one nasogastric tube in place and many tubes for intravenous fluids, but when I touched him he did not feel as if he had a fever. He still has the evidence of many abrasions, etc. from the blast on his face and upper body. He was moving about in the chair to make himself more comfortable.

At times he would get a sort of panicked look in his eyes, which his brother attributed to "flashbacks." When that would happen, his brother and mother would speak very soothingly to him and he would return to normal. His brother said that Spc. J.H. has only just begun to realize that he is back in the U.S. and in a hospital. Charles emphasized to Spc. J.H. that they are both out of Iraq and "we made it." Charles updated Spc. J.H. on Spc. J.S. and Pfc. C.F. Charles also told Spc. J.H. that he had lived for a short time in Washington, D.C. and, "I know this town, man." I think that means he knows where the "chicks" are, but some things a mother is probably better off not inquiring about in too much detail ☺.

Last night, Charles wanted to try to go outside into the fresh air, so Tom and I got permission from his nurse to take him out onto the hospital grounds in his wheelchair. It was the first time since the incident that he's been outside of buildings, aircrafts, or vehicles. I thought it was very telling that Charles said that it felt "totally weird" to be outside without a weapon in his hand. He said he would have to get used to not feeling as if he had to be constantly alert to watching his back and the backs of others around him. He said he, too, is having flashbacks and that noises similar to the sound of the explosion are very upsetting. He knows all of this is a normal progression of his recovery from this event and injury. I think that talking about it is probably the best thing for him.

May 25 [to First Sergeant R.J., in Kirkuk, Iraq]
The expected depression and anxiety have now very obviously kicked in with Charles. His whole world has been totally turned inside out and he's having a lot of uncertainty about what he's going to be able to do in the Army, or out of the Army if he has to take a medical discharge. He fears that he is not far enough advanced in rank and that the Army doesn't have "enough invested in me yet" to really want to keep him. Charles has never been one to gravitate toward jobs that don't have a certain amount of adrenaline rush, so he fears the loss of his leg will very much limit him in doing what he would like to do in the Army. I've tried to remind him that he is an exceptionally intelligent young man and the Army must value that. I don't know if you may have any eventual influence over what happens with Charles' Army career, but if so, he could certainly use all the help he can get. I hope that once Charles actually gets up on a prosthesis and is walking again, he will have a brighter outlook. I also know that his depression is normal and a part of the process he has to work through to deal with this loss of his leg and change in his body image and lifestyle.

Donald Rumsfeld visited Charles a few days ago when he came to Walter Reed. Usually Charles opts out of the visits by the football players, Congressmen and Congresswomen, and others who pay frequent visits to Walter Reed. He has had limited energy and also has said he really doesn't care to be part of their "photo ops." However, he said that Rumsfeld came without press, just with his security personnel, and he did see him. He said his impression was that Rumsfeld was much older and smaller in physical stature than he had expected. He said that the visit to the injured troops at Walter Reed seemed to be a sort of "decompression" for Rumsfeld; a time without reporters, photographers, and probing, hostile questioning. It encourages me that Rumsfeld was taking the time to go and see for himself the ravages of this war. I know he must lose sleep at night over the cost of it. I hope he does anyway.

May 27 [to First Sergeant R.J., in Kirkuk, Iraq]

Dear 1st Sgt. J., I have wonderful news regarding Spc. J.H. I saw him last night, along with his mother and brother, when James and I visited Charles at Walter Reed. Spc. J.H. looked fabulous! He is talking up a storm now and appears totally normal, neurologically. Just before we saw Spc. J.H., the psychiatrist who's following both Charles and Spc. J.H. stopped by Charles' room to tell him that Spc. J.H. had begun speaking again that day. He thanked Charles for his support, regular visits, and continued communications with Spc. J.H. while he was so critically ill and coming out of his mental fog after the incident. . . .

Spc. J.H. continued to have a lot of questions and conversation with Charles regarding the specifics of the May 2 incident. Basically, Spc. J.H. remembers nothing except that he heard the explosion of the IED, and then found himself lying on top of Charles feeling pain in his abdominal area. Then he said he looked at his abdomen and saw "my guts hanging out." He could remember that he began firing his weapon. He has no memory of anything after that until he woke up at Walter Reed. He said he did realize that it was Charles coming to see him in the intensive care unit, even though he seemed only semi-responsive. . . . As far as I'm concerned, a true miracle has occurred with Spc. J.H. There have certainly been many, many people all over the world praying for his recovery. When I first saw him in the intensive care unit at Walter Reed, I had real doubt that he would survive; or, if he did survive, that he would ever be able to live a normal life. After seeing him last night, I now believe he will make a full recovery.

June 1

It's strange and ironic how my perceptions of what is "good" have changed since May 2. I don't have the awful feeling of personal dread watching the news on television or reading the newspaper now, because my son is not over there anymore in that hell hole. He's no longer trying to survive the politics or the fanaticism or the insanity that is Iraq and Afghanistan. Now, when I go to Walter Reed, I think how fortunate he is to have "only" lost his leg. As I've gone to visit him at Walter Reed, I've walked many times by the neurotrauma unit and said a prayer of thanks that he's not in there with a brain or spinal cord injury. Over the past three weeks on the orthopedic surgery ward, I've seen so many beautiful young men with such horribly mutilating injuries from this war: the Marine across the hall, with both arms gone up to his elbows plus a leg gone below the knee from a rocket propelled grenade; the young man in the patient computer room, typing out his E-mail with the one hand he has left. The almost ghostly apparition of a 20-something soldier I met on the sidewalk in front of the hospital one dusky evening, with a prosthesis on his left arm almost up to his shoulder, and his other arm absent at the same level, so affected me I had to stop and compose myself before I went in to Charles.

I'm not a sage, or a politician, or anyone with answers to all the hard questions. I'm just a mother. I know what I'm feeling down in my soul is what countless other mothers have felt over the centuries. I know the mothers in Iraq and Afghanistan feel the same thing. It's a timeless and universal grief. I see it in the eyes of the other women I meet at Walter Reed; that semi-shocked, "I'm trying to be brave and hold it all together" look. We recognize each other.

I know I'm going through a "normal" emotional process, but it feels pretty awful at times. It's not always like this; I know I'm tired and I had a bad night. I do feel God's love all around me, even in the midst of the suffering. I know that things will get better and that there will be blessings that spring from this experience for Charles, for me, and for others. There are already blessings and I am so thankful for each and every one of them. Most of all, I'm thankful to still have my son.

June 10

A sock did me in a few nights ago, a plain white sock. I'm doing so much better with the grief, but sometimes I just get blindsided again in a totally unex-

pected way. Some memory or sharp realization will prick at the places healing in my heart, and I feel the grief wash over me in a massive wave. Sometimes I almost feel I could double over with the pain of it. That's what
happened with the sock.

I had brought Charles' soiled clothes home from Walter Reed to wash.
Everything had gone through the wash and dry cycles and I had dumped the
freshly laundered clothes onto the bed to fold them. It was late and I was
quite weary, so I wanted to finish and get to bed to try for a better night's sleep
than I've been having lately. I found one sock . . . just one. I folded all the
rest of the clothes and still, just one sock. Without even thinking, I walked
back to the laundry room and searched the dryer for the mate. Nothing was
there. I looked between the washer and dryer and all around the floor, in case
I'd dropped the other sock somewhere during the loading and unloading
processes. Still, my tired and pre-occupied brain didn't get it. As I walked
back to the bedroom with the one sock in hand, it hit me like a punch to the
gut. There was no other sock. There was also no other foot, or lower leg, or
knee. I stood there in my bedroom and clutched that one clean sock to my
breast and an involuntary moan came from my throat; but it originated in my
heart.

I guess, as a nurse, I know too much. I know all the details of the physical
difficulties and long-term complications of life for an amputee that most others have no reason to comprehend. I know about the everyday activities of
daily living that the rest of us take for granted, and for which we never give a
moment's consideration, that Charles will now always have to struggle to accomplish. I do know he will eventually win the struggle; he is made of very
strong stuff. I'm in awe and so proud of his strength and determination. But
my "mother's heart" still feels very tender and sore. The wounds there are
fresh and bleed easily when disturbed. God's peace to you all. Myrna.

August 20

It's now been sixteen weeks since Charles was wounded in Iraq. Life goes on
and things settle down. Charles is very stable physically now. His right leg is
totally healed and the stump continues to atrophy and decrease in size. The
scars on both of his legs from the surgeries and the shrapnel remain red and
very noticeable, but are beginning to fade a bit. He has put on a bit more
weight and looks much healthier. Now he's in the midst of the long hard slog
of learning to live with the chronic remaining pain, adapting to a prosthetic

leg, and learning to achieve an active life again. On August 1st, he was in New York City with about twenty other soldiers from Walter Reed who were invited there by the Achilles Track Club to participate in a 5K race. Charles participated in the race on a hand cycle, as he's not yet able to attempt running. He finished the course and enjoyed the trip very much.

Charles' attitude remains generally very positive and he considers himself to be one of the "lucky ones." I know that's true as I travel back and forth to Walter Reed and see more and more wounded there. There are so many of them with terrible burns, often multiple amputations, deep and ragged scars, and mutilations. I still find myself especially shocked when I see the young female soldiers who are so severely wounded. This war has no front line and everywhere is a combat zone. There is no "safer place."

As more and more wounded come into Walter Reed, especially with so many traumatic amputations from improvised explosive devices and rocket-propelled grenades, the Prosthetics Department is fairly overwhelmed. The sheer number of amputees from all the explosive injuries, all needing artificial limbs made and adjusted frequently, means that there are long waits of days to weeks for Charles, back on his crutches and in his wheelchair when his "leg is in the shop." When this happens, his rehabilitation progress more or less comes to a standstill until his prosthesis is ready again and returned to him. I see his spirits sag when he is forced back into this mode and is unable to continue moving forward toward his goals.

At times I have to stop and compose myself before I go into Mologne House to meet Charles. Last week I had one of those times when I met a young father out with his two little sons. He had all of a leg missing and was pushing himself along in a wheelchair. His younger son, about three, was sitting on the young father's lap, while his brother, about five, skipped along beside the moving wheelchair. There are many other heart-rending sights and many shocking mutilations, but I will spare you the details. It's a humbling experience to move about the Walter Reed complex. The gritty determination of these wounded and the support they offer to each other puts a lot of the other details of daily life in clearer perspective. Regardless of your politics or how you may feel about this war, these wounded, and the dead, are an inescapable reality. I pray to God that we as a nation don't forget the sacrifices that are being made on our behalf. From now on, Veteran's Day will be a great deal more meaningful to me than just a day to take off from work and to fly the flag, if I remember.

I keep thinking a time will come when it doesn't hurt so much to watch Charles struggling to recover. Watching what is left of his right leg withering up and growing ever smaller is something I know is normal, but in my dreams at night I see him at about seventeen, running so smoothly and beautifully, and when I awake to reality I know how cruel this new "normal" is. Sometimes, still, when I see him I find my heart clutching and I have to take a deep breath and swallow hard to keep the tears at bay. My tears won't help him; hopefully my support and encouragement will.

God's peace to you all,
Myrna

In January 2005, a review board of Army physicians recommended that Charles be medically discharged because of his disability. Charles, however, successfully appealed the decision, and received a waiver so that he could stay in the Army. (He was promoted to sergeant in April 2006.) Knowing that he couldn't continue serving as an infantryman, he changed his specialty to military intelligence and was selected to begin studying to become an Arabic translator. His goal is to serve in a combat unit in Iraq, Afghanistan, or wherever else he is needed.

DEAR NEIL

Letters

Daniel Uhles

"You're back home this morning, sleeping in your own bed, and while that may not seem like much to some people, it is heaven on earth to me," Daniel Uhles wrote on May 11, 2004, to his twenty-four-year-old soldier son, Neil. While many parents have just one child in the armed forces to worry about, Daniel Uhles had two; Neil and his younger brother, Drew, had both joined the military when they turned eighteen. (Their older sister, Melissa, had served in the Gulf War and was later honorably discharged.) Neil enlisted in the Illinois Army National Guard, Drew joined the Marine

Corps, and in late 2003 through early 2004, both boys were in Iraq at the
same time. And, to the absolute joy of their parents, they were both stateside
by May 2004. Daniel Uhles continued his letter to Neil:

While I'll never be able to get into that psyche of yours, I know you've brought home some baggage you'll carry around for the rest of your life. You told us from the first days you were in Iraq, as did Drew, that the news accounts of the war were very inaccurate and that there was a more mellow side to those people. However, when you describe "incoming," it bothered us immensely, and I, for one, wondered why someone was trying to hurt such a nice person like our son. The only thing worse was multiplying that by two when Drew was there also.

You're down the hall sleeping. You're resting. We're resting. And now—finally—all seems right with the world for the Uhles family. When mornings and moments like these present themselves to me, I feel so guilty for having such a perfect family. Your brothers and sister and you were worth the wait for these moments. They're like rare diamonds to be enjoyed with a touch of misunderstanding. By way of defining that, I remember Jack Buck was asked in an interview what he would ask God when he got to see him. His answer, "God, why have you been so good to me?" The answer applies to me also.

You're down the hall in your own room. Mom's at work. Melissa, Sean, Heather, and Kelly are out there doing the same. And Drew is still holding vigil with his M-16, only for right now it's in the California desert. The cat's in my chair asleep, and I can hear the gurgling water in the fountain out front. A new day is dawning. My prayer is that never in your lifetime will you ever have to tell your children goodbye as they enter into that eternal nightmare we call war. Enjoy the solitude and beauty of the sun coming up, coffee perking, the sound of the wrens building their nest for the coming season, and above all, embrace those you love like there will be no tomorrow.

Neil, welcome home!

I love and salute you!!

Love,
Dad

Uhles's happiness, however, would be short-lived; in August 2004, Drew was redeployed to Iraq for his second tour of duty. On September 15, 2004, two uniformed Marines appeared at the Uhles home in Illinois and informed the family that earlier in the day, Lance Corporal Drew Michael Uhles had been killed in Al Anbar province by a rocket-propelled grenade. He was four days shy of his twenty-first birthday. Neil, who had fulfilled his commitment to the Guard, volunteered to go back to Iraq. Shocked by the decision, Daniel implored his son to reconsider.

November 3, 2004

Dear Neil,

I'm writing this letter knowing what I want to say but not knowing how to say it, so stick with me on this for awhile.

You already know that your mother and I really don't want you to volunteer for Iraq again, so that goes without saying, but our reasons for this are probably different than you can possibly realize, having been "over there" and not here in the good old US of A.

I'm sure you've jumped ahead and thought about what Christmas will be like without Drew, so try to imagine another one without BOTH of you here. Yes, I'm thinking of myself, but also I'm thinking of our family and extended family beyond our home, yard, village, and country. No one will think less of Neil Uhles if he says "No, I've done my share and now it's someone else's turn. My entire family has given enough." You're a hero, plain and simple!!

You've given a foreign country a jump start our country never had. You've given the Iraqi people a vision of working together to rid THEIR country of insurgents just as we did our country centuries ago in the United States. What more could they ask for than a year of a stranger's time to help them attain freedom?

Your feelings are not lost upon us, your mother and me, but please consider the consequences upon our older family members. I ask that you ease their burden in their last years here with us, and let them join Drew comfortably and free of everyday worry for you in your mission.

Lastly, I would ask you to take a deep breath, look at your ENTIRE life — past, present, and future — and say "Now I'm going to do something for myself! If it's school, so be it. If it's a career, so be it." I guess what I'm saying is, plan for YOUR future! "Will another year away be beneficial for what I want and not what someone else wants, or will it only help fill a void in a battalion's troop list?" My four years in the Air Force gave me the money I needed to go to school, plus it literally saved my life when the military found a tumor in my chest. But, your future is ready and waiting, and the "after-burners" are ready to kick in for a very intelligent twenty-five year old with an entire life ahead of him. (That's an Air Force term.) Will another year impede the take-off or put it on hold for yet another year? Don't be afraid of the future, and I certainly know you're not afraid of ANYTHING. All I'm asking is for you to take into consideration a multitude of other things and consider making a decision with the help of those who love you and of those you love the most.

Love,
Dad

Despite his dad's plea, Neil could not be persuaded and was unable to explain to his father why he felt so certain about the matter. Struggling to make sense of his son's reasons, Daniel asked his daughter, Melissa, and her reply was: "Dad, you just have to have been there to understand." In May of 2005, Neil embarked for Iraq and was stationed in Baghdad. He returned home in April 2006 and re-enrolled in college.

SHALLOW HANDS
Fiction
Corporal Michael Poggi

While some troops adjust relatively easily to postwar life and even express a desire to return to Iraq or Afghanistan, many struggle with everything from flashbacks, frequent nightmares, and aggressive behavior to substance abuse, persistent depression, and thoughts of suicide. A comprehensive 2006 study by the Army reported that one out of every three soldiers and Marines sought counseling for mental health problems within a month of coming home from Iraq (the percentage is not as high for veterans of the war in Afghanistan) and thousands indicated that they had contemplated killing themselves. Some veterans don't even realize that they are suffering from post-traumatic stress disorder (PTSD) until they have a total break-

down. Twenty-seven-year-old U.S. Marine Corporal Michael Poggi, a member of the elite 1st Reconnaissance Battalion, 1st Marine Division, fought in Iraq as part of a team of "ambush hunters" whose mission was to seek and destroy enemy forces lying in wait for U.S. convoys. When Poggi came back to the States in the summer of 2003, he saw many of his friends afflicted by PTSD, and he knew that he, too, was not unaffected by his months of intense combat. Poggi found it cathartic to write about the psychological repercussions of war, and a year after he returned home he wrote the following story, which is based on real events and characters but is not, he emphasizes, purely autobiographical.

I've been drinking steadily since coming back from the war. There's a caustic aftertaste in my mouth aggravating the queasiness in my stomach. Making my way through San Diego traffic to get to the airport, I know I shouldn't be driving like this. I park in the overnight lot and walk to the national terminal to catch a flight to Boston. This trip will be the first time I've been home in a long while.

I hate crowds, maybe because I am hung over, or maybe because they make me a critic of all humankind. I just can't help but think people are spoiled lambs walking around with their heads up their hinds, oblivious to the goings-on in the world. It makes me so damn sad. I look around the terminal and see people bitching and moaning about their flights. I don't know any Iraqi kids who complain about waiting for shit; they dream about not getting shot dead or killed by an explosion. Over there is some woman buying her kid a whole damn armful of candy while she holds her cup of Starbucks in the other hand. Some kid in Afghanistan just got his leg blown off by a land mine, but go ahead and pamper your ankle-biters with more shit they don't need! Half the world is starving! I watched people kill each other for dollar bills, why should you care? Fucking lamb.

I have been back from the war for a month. I spent most of it cruising around Southern California, harassing college girls with my tattoo stories and getting drunk. Thankfully I haven't woken up in a pool of urine lately. Nonetheless, I feel more alive than ever. Everything seems so different, so colorful. The sky is so vividly blue and white now, sunsets are beautifully orange, and the ocean a glimmering pool of I don't even know what. I don't ever recall noticing things this much. It's funny what being shot at does to a man. Yet, for some reason I can't stand to be in the presence of people anymore. Little inconveniences rub me raw, those polite phony smiles make me want to rip someone's face off when they say "excuse me" in that perky inaudible voice.

I eye everyone in the terminal as a potential threat, every nook and cranny an ambush. I want to stand in the center of the concourse and scream at the top of my lungs. So loud they burst, so loud all the cigarettes will purge themselves from my body. But I'm too damn tired to stand on a soapbox today; besides, it's a quiet anger, a pearled soreness beneath the breastbone that drives me insane, sore with every breath and with every swallow like the feeling of vomit in your throat. I don't know why I feel the way I do. It's not the booze. I know that for certain. It's something else, something that will have to wait until later. I hand over my ticket and board the plane. As I jostle into my seat, I quickly turn my head toward the window and try to think of other things.

Being there was pure, in the dust storms and blazing heat, the children looking up at you like you were God himself come to deliver them. Things were simple. The enemy is everywhere, hiding in every building, every palm grove, waiting to pounce on you when you let your guard down. The children, tugging at your leg, look up with desperate eyes. They will be slaughtered when they go home for collaborating with us. Still they hang on to the hope that for that brief moment we're there we will save them. Sometimes it is almost a nuisance when they'd crowd the vehicles and follow the patrols. I can't help but pity them; I'd give all I had to them if I could. Instead, it seems we're always leaving them when they need us most.

I landed at Logan International five hours later and took a cab to Bukowski's just off Boylston Avenue, by the Prudential Center. I love that place. No one knows it's there really, its windows naturally blend into the urban foliage, and you can watch the people wandering about on Boylston, oblivious to your observation. A great place for a thought or two, and getting drunk of course. I got smashed there that night. I was supposed to meet this girl I dated for drinks, but she never showed. I ended up calling my brother and my buddy Tim. We proceeded to get drunk. I kicked over a mailbox in front of a cop and began my "lamb" speech to everyone on the road. The cop just gave my brother the old "get him the fuck out of here" look. I nearly fought a few people on the way to the train station. I felt bad that my brother and Tim had to struggle with me to cooperate, but that passed quickly.

A few months before the war, I went to a palm reader. I don't know why, but I thought she might shed some light on things; curiosity I suppose. I don't remember how she looked, although I remember she wasn't some quack fat lady wearing purple. I do remember how she took my hand, how relaxing it felt when I gave it to her. Holding it gently, brushing the lines with the tips of her fingers, plying it ever so slowly, she told me things about my character I knew were true. Ever since, I look at my hands in a different light. I realize how soft and shallow the lines are, and how odd it is that someone you don't know could shake your hand and tell you when you're going to die, it was all so fascinating. Even if it was all bullshit.

They say the line running from your index finger that follows the fleshy tissue down around your thumb to the midpoint of your palm is the lifeline. It's supposed to tell you how long you'll live. I noticed mine stops halfway. I know a lot of guys in my unit with hands like rocks, deep crevices in them like they've been chapped or wind burnt for ages. It's supposed to be long. But mine isn't.

After days of drinking, I was strewn out on the floor of my brother's apartment in a bloody mess. When I finally came to in the morning, I felt like killing myself. Not because I was depressed, or regretful, but because I was hallucinating and delirious. I thought I was going crazy. Spiraling down into the void, I stumbled around the apartment, completely disoriented and confused, slamming down water and vitamins, hoping that the delirium would pass, and it did not. I started to scream, first in my head, where the battle was, then out loud. So loud my brother came running down from his bedroom to see what was going on. I can only imagine what he was thinking when he saw me balled up in the corner, quivering and weeping assurances to myself.

It took me two days to get over the breakdown. I just walked around in a trance and sat watching television on the couch. My brother came home from work one afternoon and put an end to it. He sat next to me and told me that our dad had called and wanted to see me. He wanted me to go as soon as possible. I had been waiting for this to happen. I was ashamed to look and feel this way in front of my father.

He had always been proud of my service. He served with the Army in Vietnam, and he's seen his share. He was of the old school that seems withering today, one that preaches conservative compassion mixed with blue-collar sense of duty. He taught me about nature, from back when I was a little boy in the car seat pointing at the hawks circling the highways, to the days as a teen when we took long walks in the woods and talked philosophy. The musty pic-

tures of a bearded adventurer line a desk stacked with nature guides and animal skulls, a living tribute to the man. I would spend lots of time at his desk as
a kid, picking up and staring at the skulls, reading the guides, and playing with
the samurai swords he'd bought so many years ago in Southeast Asia.

Now I was supposed to put myself before his expecting eyes and hide the
shame and booze. It was almost too much to bear as I stood on his porch and
rang the bell after minutes of hesitation. He opened the door, hugged me in
a powerful embrace, and then led me in.

The living room was as I'd remembered it, but the fireplace mantel had
been transformed into a shrine to me, and I winced. We moved to the kitchen
and sat down for coffee. He could barely contain his excitement, but I could
see his intuition told him something was wrong.

"You look good, Tommy," he said, grabbing my shoulder. I thanked him
and sipped my coffee, but I knew he was lying. I looked like shit and felt like
the sewer.

"So you've been back for a few days I hear. Staying with your brother . . .
How's your head?" he asked with a smirk.

"It's doing fine now, Pop," I replied quietly.

"Good, just go easy, Tom, you know you get out of hand with that stuff."

"I know, Pop. I know," I said. *He had no idea.*

"So did you . . . you know."

"Kill anyone?" I answered.

He nodded.

"Yes," I said blankly. Truthfully, it hadn't bothered me that I had killed
someone, or more than one for that matter. It was us or them and the fact that
it was them means I am here drinking coffee with my dad and not buried in
the sand thousands of miles from here and that's that.

"You did the right thing, boy." He sighed. "If you ever want to talk about
it, I know where you are coming from. I had to do the same in my day."

"Thanks," I said. The room went quiet, and I could hear someone raking
leaves two houses down. It made me smile for a moment. I always liked this
time of year. The smells and sounds seemed more alive in autumn, even as
the leaves were dying; another paradox to ponder.

We talked about the family for a long while, and then I looked at my
watch.

"It's getting late, Dad, I think I better get going," I said, standing up. "I'll
be back tomorrow."

Dad grabbed me on both shoulders and forced me to look him in the eye. I noticed the calloused old hands; I noticed the grooves in them as they reached for me, deep and wise . . . unlike mine.

"Not everyone is going to understand what you've done, Tommy. It's your job to be patient. You've got to understand that most people in this country have never left it. They never will. But you, you have seen what's out there. It's up to you to make them understand. So take it easy with the booze. Relax and clear your head out." He patted me on the shoulder as I stepped out. I waved goodbye and started the two-mile walk to my brother's apartment in the moonless cool night.

Most of the trees were bare now, and I couldn't avoid the childlike draw of kicking through the coating of dry leaves on the streets as I walked down the neighborhood's narrow roads, my hands shoved deep in my pockets. I traced the shallow lifeline of my right palm over and over again with my fingers, and I couldn't shake off the thought of mortality that it caused. I remember the palm reader told me to "live every day to its fullest" and to "enjoy every moment"—the kind of shit you tell to someone with terminal cancer. I couldn't help thinking that I wasn't meant to live for long, and my life was a void of nothing, except the anger and frustration of not knowing what I was doing with it. I felt contempt for everyone around me, and I knew it; I carried it like a loaded pistol just aching to pull the trigger.

I began drinking heavily again. I tried to escape. I spent a night in jail. How it happened I couldn't recall in truth. All I know is what patchwork memories I can muster through the inebriated haze and what they tell me about when I did pull that trigger. I guess I had taken too many shots too fast and assaulted the barroom in a tirade. My friends had called the police. Can't blame them, but I'll never go back to that shit hole again.

My brother bailed me out to take me to the hospital, then left since he had to get to work early. The doctor in the emergency room looked at my hand, then back up at me with a disappointed look. "It's definitely broken, my friend. There appear to be several hairline fractures spiderwebbing off of the major point of impact. Luckily there are only minor contusions on the outer edges and on your palm when you obviously braced a fall." He sighed and injected more Novocain into my wrist as he swabbed the cuts with Betadine solution. I tried to look away, but out of some grisly curiosity I watched as he cleaned the wounds, cutting and peeling the skin back. I wanted to see what had become of the hand that told so much. It wasn't telling shit now. It was wrapped up and numb.

I stumbled out of the emergency room at four a.m. and hailed a cab, my hand in a splint, arm in a sling. Fuck if I'd go back to my brother's place. He'd been pretty cool with everything, I owed him that, but he didn't need my baggage. I checked my wallet to make sure I had enough funds, and told the cabbie to take me to the Adams Inn in Quincy. It's an old motel down by the Neponset. I could get a room facing the river and watch the muddy water and highway traffic.

I went back to my brother's apartment later that day, after some sleep and some Percocets. I grabbed all my bags and penned a note telling him where to reach me. I found a message from my dad. He wanted to see me today. I tossed it in the trash on the way out the door. There was no way I could see him like this. There was no way I could face anybody like this.

I did end up in a room overlooking the river. I set up my laptop on a nightstand, and with my good hand began typing furiously. I imagined my hand blown off in the war. The thought made me laugh out loud at the irony. I hadn't been wounded in combat, yet here I was at home, hand split open and broken.

Everything I typed was angry. I thought that after I had the opportunity to vent a little, it would end—it would stop—but it did not. It kept going; from the lambs in the airport and their spoiled children to my mom's death, to my brothers' success and my failure, to my credit card bills and my high car insurance. Everything was fucked up. I wrote page after page and stopped only when I had to urinate or refill my whiskey-coke. On the way back from the bathroom, I paused to read the last page of what I'd written:

Fuck it. Fuck it all. Fuck the lady bitching at the line in the DMV . . . a few hours out of your life isn't going to kill you. Fuck my ex-girlfriend and all her boring ass phone calls about her brother and friends and backaches and fucking cramps. Fuck that wannabe businessman yacking on his cell phone like he is somebody. It's all just so amazing to me. All of them, heads stuck so far up their asses they can't see daylight. I hate them for their ignorance; their bliss . . . yet I am amazed that in our country, we can have a war with a thousand casualties, and nobody hardly notices. I FUCKING NOTICE. I notice the kid in the wheelchair rolling through the mall with his Dad proudly pushing and his Mom tearing up. I notice the guy with the fake leg at the bar who I used to serve with and buy his beers and recall old times. I notice the ones without the scars and prostheses, the ones with the eyes that stab right into you, the eyes that see through you. I notice because I have them too . . . and every time I notice one of them, I notice ten mindless ignorant people; people who talk about birthday parties and dry cleaning, and meetings at work. People who go home to sit down for dinner and ask their kids how school was, and never once consider that their kid could be in Iraq in a year and that chair would be empty forever. You can't talk to them about the horror of a dead child's lifeless mutilated body staring back at you from the void, knowing you took part in that end, or laugh at the humor and terror in your weapon jamming in a firefight where every crack and pop of the incoming rounds has you shaking and ducking for cover. You know they don't even know what you really do in the military in the first place, so when you talk about the chow and the bullets and the asshole Gunny, they just look at you and nod. So you just sit there and smile politely, thank them for their homecoming, and try to get out of there as soon as you can, before the bitterness and anger seep through. I'm bitter at their weakness and their ingratitude. I'm bitter at their fucking lives and their petty complications. I'm bitter I couldn't be ignorant as well. FUCK IT ALL.

It was amazing how it flowed from my fingertips, and into this. Though "this" wasn't anything. I knew I'd delete it tomorrow when I woke up, but I was shocked at how true it was to me. I turned to the bureau mirror and stared into the face of the man looking back at me. I saw an animal—a predator no doubt—but I saw a pathetic excuse for a man first.

I looked at the bottle of whiskey I'd emptied while I typed, and in a moment of clarity, realized—I am an alcoholic. The thought bothered me more than anything I could have ever imagined. A wound a thousand times deeper and more painful than any shrapnel or bullet graze, it was a wound to the heart. I started to weep apologetically to my reflection, seeking some response but getting none. The people we killed, the shit that went down. It all rushed back to me in a moment. I questioned some of the kills. I thought of the civilians caught in the crossfire. I wept more. I looked down to my iodine-stained wrappings, I envisioned the lifeline's shallow groove tainted brown, and I wondered again why it was so weak. Maybe the palm reader was right to say I should live life to its fullest. I won't live long this way at all.

Poggi is still in the Marine Corps and was promoted to sergeant in January 2004.

DOVER

Personal Narrative

Colonel Marc M. Sager

Home to the active-duty 436th Airlift Wing and the reserve 512th Airlift Wing, Dover Air Force Base in central Delaware is the largest and busiest military cargo port in the United States. Dover's C-5 Galaxy aircraft, which are almost as long as a football field and weigh up to a million pounds, provide one quarter of the nation's entire strategic airlift capability. But Dover AFB is unique not only for its aircraft, but for what happens on the base itself in times of war and other national crises: U.S. servicemen and women killed in Iraq and Afghanistan are brought to Dover's Charles C. Carson Center, the largest mortuary in the U.S. military, to be identified and prepared for burial. The Center, named after one of its former directors, operates seven days a week and can handle up to eighty-five bodies a day. While stationed at Bolling AFB in Washington, D.C., Marc M. Sager, a fifty-three-year-old colonel in the U.S. Air Force's medical service corps, had an opportunity to visit the Center in the spring of 2004. Despite all that Sager had seen during his almost twenty-two years in the military as a medical administrator, he was still overwhelmed by the experience. Immediately after leaving Dover, Sager began writing the following account.

To say a mortuary is beautiful sounds odd, but the Charles C. Carson Center truly is. Once inside the main doors you are immediately struck by the large curving wall in front of you with several engraved panels of names and dates chronicling many of our nation's most memorable and tragic events—Beirut, Space Shuttle *Challenger*, Desert Storm, Somalia, USS *Cole*, Pentagon September 11, 2001, and so on. There is a vaulted, translucent ceiling above that lets in the sunlight and illuminates a large, bubbling fountain underneath.

We were met by the mortuary director, Karen Giles, and Lieutenant Colonel Susan Hanshaw from the Armed Forces Institute of Pathology. It was immediately apparent how proud they were of the new facility, but even more so, in being part of this necessary, but by no means glamorous, aspect of service to our country. Every time they referred to a deceased soldier, sailor, airman, or Marine it was always "the fallen hero." At first this seemed like one of the politically sanitized phrases that many of us have used in various settings over the years, but as the visit continued, it became clear to me that this was the phrase everyone used, and that it was also the most appropriate.

The mortuary is located on the flight line so aircraft can pull up directly to the receiving area. Once the transfer cases, which contain the fallen heroes, are off-loaded, they are taken into an explosive ordnance disposal room that has walls about ten inches thick. The transport case cover is taken off and the remains checked for any loose ordnance that might have been missed overseas. The remains are then run though an X-ray machine that looks like the ones at airports to inspect checked baggage. The value of this screening became clear. Just the week before a live grenade was found in the body armor on the remains of one of the soldiers.

Once the remains have been determined to be safe, they are taken to the fingerprint area, where we met two FBI personnel from Quantico, Virginia, who rotate every six days to work at the mortuary. The day before remains arrive at Dover, the names and other information are provided. The agents then pull fingerprint files from an FBI computer in Martinsburg, West Virginia, which contains all active-duty military and literally millions of other sets. From fingerprints the remains are taken to dental. Here again, all of our dental records are on file and can be used as a match. Everything is state-of-the-art. The radiology techs, who do the full-body X-rays, told me that the new system was eight to ten times faster than the old film method, and images can now be captured on a CD-ROM. When we were finished in radiology, it marked the end of the "easy" part of the tour, as no remains were being processed while we were there. That was not the case as I looked across the hall into the autopsy room, our next stop.

A full autopsy is performed on all the fallen heroes. No longer can we simply provide families with the statement "Killed in Action." Families want to know exactly what happened to their loved ones, so for medical and legal reasons a full autopsy is performed. Again, as an MSC, I wasn't sure how well I would handle this, but knowing what these brave men had sacrificed, my concerns seemed pretty trivial. There were two autopsies being conducted when we arrived. The medical teams performing them were very professional and careful how they handled the remains. The room itself had ten bays, a high ceiling with bright lighting, and lots of air circulation. When we exited this room we entered the embalming area that is a mirror of the autopsy room. Here two of the staff were preparing the remains of another fallen hero. It sounds odd to say, but I could see the pride these professionals took in their work. Everything that can be done to make the remains look "normal" is done. From here the remains go to "cosmetology," where expert makeup personnel restore the faces to look as natural as possible.

It was comforting to see Critical Incident Stress Management team members at the mortuary. These CISM teams are there to support mortuary team members at the point of stress. Even the most seasoned staff members have moments when the blunt trauma of war is overwhelming, and there is a constant need for a calming, healing presence for the caretakers.

Our fallen heroes are now ready to be put back in uniform. Since almost all the deaths are combat related, no one arrives with their dress uniform. Here another group of dedicated experts goes to work. Service records are used to verify rank, branch of service, and medals. There is a complete "military clothing store" at this location. Shirts, socks, underwear, pants, blouses are all available from every branch of the service, in any size you can imagine, and they also have every ribbon from every service. Unit patches and pins are also on hand. The staff can make the ribbon rack and name tags right there in less than a day. When we walked through, eight fallen heroes from the Army, Navy, and Marines had just finished being put back in uniform.

On separate racks are the personal items that each of these fallen heroes was carrying at the time of death. To me, this was the most poignant aspect of the visit: pictures, money, keys, watches still on Baghdad time, AT&T calling cards, driver's licenses, and military photo-ID cards—they all brought home how young and vibrant these individuals were and, most of all, that they were real people, not statistics. The staff explained that the personal items accompany the remains.

We had noticed in the clothing area a trash can filled with Marine dress-uniform coats. We later met the master gunnery sergeant responsible for ensuring each fallen Marine's uniform is properly prepared. He had inspected the coats, he felt the workmanship was not up to par, and he was not going to allow his comrades to be sent home in anything less than perfection. Every extra step to honor these fallen heroes is accomplished; every oak-leaf cluster, star, and device is polished before being put on the ribbon. Every belt buckle and badge gets a luster to it. Uniforms are altered and pressed to fit as perfectly as possible.

Once the remains are dressed, they are moved to the final preparation area and placed in caskets. There are even coffins that contain no metal for Jewish personnel or anyone else who wants a wooden coffin. There were cremation urns available too, if that is the family's desire. No detail is overlooked. That day there were seven caskets waiting for escorts to take them home. They would be gone by the next evening.

As we came back up front, Ms. Giles took the time to explain how important some of the other people in the process were, such as the folks who arrange for airline tickets for the escorts and handle the arrangements for the caskets. Over and over we heard, "We are a zero-defects operation. We can't let anything go wrong because the families of these fallen heroes are waiting."

It was a day of many emotions. Most people will never get a chance to see what we saw, and probably would not want to. I'm glad I did. I realized once more that casualty numbers are the sanitized, amorphous representation of what I had just seen. Each number was in fact an individual person—someone's spouse, parent, sibling, sweetheart, or friend—who had joined the military to serve his or her country and paid the ultimate price. I especially thought of the parents of these fallen heroes. The remains I viewed that day were kids as young as my two sons, both in their twenties, and I kept thinking of their mothers and fathers waiting for these bodies of their children, their babies, to come home.

Every person I met at the mortuary exuded pride in what they did and their role in ensuring the families got back their loved one in the best manner possible; appropriate and in keeping with the sacrifice they performed for this country. It is obviously a highly stressful working environment, but the core mortuary staff, along with the temporary duty personnel and those from other agencies, are focused on their duty.

They have to be—there were eight more fallen heroes arriving the next day.

TAKING CHANCE
Personal Narrative
Lieutenant Colonel Michael R. Strobl

After they are brought to Dover Air Force Base, all fallen soldiers, Marines, airmen, and sailors are escorted home to their families and loved ones by a uniformed member of the U.S. armed forces. In mid-April 2004, thirty-eight-year-old U.S. Marine Lieutenant Colonel Michael R. Strobl, a manpower analyst assigned to the Combat Development Command in Quantico, Virginia, accompanied the body of a young Marine killed in Iraq to his final resting place in Wyoming. Strobl wrote the following description of his journey to Wyoming in a small, spiral notebook on his way back to Virginia.

Chance Phelps was wearing his Saint Christopher medal when he was killed on Good Friday. Eight days later, I handed the medallion to his mother. I didn't know Chance before he died. Today, I miss him.

Over a year ago, I volunteered to escort the remains of Marines killed in Iraq should the need arise. Thankfully, I hadn't been called on to be an escort since Operation Iraqi Freedom began. The first few weeks of April, however, had been tough ones for the Marines. On the Monday after Easter I was reviewing Department of Defense press releases when I saw that a Private First Class Chance Phelps was killed in action outside of Baghdad. The press release listed his hometown as Clifton, Colorado—which is near where I'm from. I notified our battalion adjutant and told him that, should the duty to escort PFC Phelps fall to our battalion, I would take him.

I didn't hear back the rest of Monday and all day Tuesday until 1800. The battalion duty NCO called my cell phone and said I needed to be ready to leave for Dover Air Force Base at 1900 in order to escort the remains of PFC Phelps. I called the major who had the task of informing Phelps's parents of his death. The major said that the funeral was going to be in Dubois, Wyoming. (It turned out that PFC Phelps only lived near my hometown during his senior year of high school.) I had never been to Wyoming and had never heard of Dubois.

With two other escorts from Quantico, I got to Dover AFB at 2330 on Tuesday night. First thing on Wednesday we reported to the mortuary at the base. In the escort lounge there were about half a dozen Army soldiers and about an equal number of Marines waiting to meet up with "their" remains for departure. PFC Phelps was not ready, however, and I was told to come back on Thursday. Now at Dover with nothing to do and a solemn mission ahead, I began to get depressed.

I didn't know anything about Chance Phelps; not even what he looked like. I wondered about his family and what it would be like to meet them. I did push-ups in my room until I couldn't do any more. On Thursday morning I reported back to the mortuary. This time there was a new group of Army escorts and a couple of the Marines who had been there Wednesday. There was also an Air Force captain there to escort his brother home to San Diego.

We received a brief covering our duties and the proper handling of the remains, and we were shown pictures of the shipping container and told that each one contained, in addition to the casket, a flag. I was given an extra flag since PFC Phelps's parents were divorced.

It turned out that I was the last escort to leave on Thursday. This meant that I repeatedly got to participate in the small ceremonies that mark all departures from the Dover AFB mortuary.

Most of the remains are taken from Dover AFB by hearse to the airport in Philadelphia for air transport to their final destination. When the remains of a service member are loaded onto a hearse and ready to leave the Dover mortuary, there is an announcement made over the building's intercom system. With the announcement, all service members working at the mortuary, regardless of branch, stop work and form up along the driveway to render a slow ceremonial salute as the hearse departs. On this day, there were also some civilian workers doing construction on the mortuary grounds. As each hearse passed, they would stop working and place their hard hats over their hearts. This was my first sign that my mission with PFC Phelps was larger than the Marine Corps and that his family and friends were not grieving alone.

Eventually I was the last escort remaining in the lounge. The master gunnery sergeant in charge of the Marine liaison there came to see me. He had a pouch with Chance Phelps's personal effects. He removed each item: a large watch, a wooden cross with a lanyard, two loose dog tags, two dog tags on a chain, and the Saint Christopher medal, which was on a silver chain. Although we had been briefed that we might be carrying some personal effects of the deceased, I was taken aback. Holding his personal effects, I was starting to get to know Chance Phelps.

Finally we were ready. I grabbed my bags and went outside. I was somewhat startled when I saw the shipping container, loaded three quarters of the way into the back of a black Chevy Suburban that had been modified to carry such cargo. This was the first time I saw my "cargo," and I was surprised at how large the shipping container was. The master gunnery sergeant and I verified that the name on the container was Phelps's, and then they pushed him the rest of the way in and we left. Now it was PFC Chance Phelps's turn to receive the military—and construction workers'—honors. He was finally moving towards home.

As I chatted with the driver on the hour-long trip to Philadelphia, it became clear that he considered it an honor to contribute to getting Chance home. He offered his sympathy to the family. I was glad finally to be moving, yet I was apprehensive about what things would be like at the airport. I didn't want this container to be treated like ordinary cargo, but I knew that the simple logistics of moving around something this large would be difficult.

When we got to the Northwest Airlines cargo terminal at the Philadelphia airport, the cargo handler and hearse driver pulled the shipping container onto a loading bay while I stood to the side and executed a slow salute. Once Chance was safely in the cargo area, and I was satisfied that he would be treated with due care and respect, the hearse driver drove me over to the passenger terminal and dropped me off.

As I walked up to the ticketing counter in my uniform, a Northwest employee started to ask me if I knew how to use the automated boarding-pass dispenser. Before she could finish, another ticketing agent interrupted her. He told me to go straight to the counter, then explained to the woman that I was a military escort. She seemed embarrassed. The woman behind the counter already had tears in her eyes as I was pulling out my government travel voucher. She struggled to find words but managed to express her sympathy for the family and thanked me for my service. She upgraded my ticket to first class.

After clearing security, I was met by another Northwest Airlines employee at the gate. She told me a representative from cargo would be arriving to take me down to the tarmac to observe the movement and loading of PFC Phelps. I hadn't really told any of them what my mission was but they all knew. When the man from the cargo crew met me, he, too, struggled for words. On the tarmac, he told me stories of his childhood as a military brat and repeatedly said that he was sorry for my loss. Even here in Philadelphia, far away from Chance's hometown, people were mourning with his family.

On the tarmac, the cargo crew was silent except for when they gave occasional instructions to each other. I stood to the side and saluted as the conveyor moved Chance to the aircraft. I was relieved when he was finally settled into place. The rest of the bags were loaded and I watched them shut the cargo-bay door before heading back up to board the aircraft. One of the pilots had taken my carry-on bag himself and had it stored next to the cockpit door so he could watch it while I was on the tarmac. As I boarded the plane, I could tell immediately that the flight attendants had already been informed of my mission. They seemed a little choked up as they led me to my seat.

About forty-five minutes into our flight, I still hadn't spoken to anyone except to tell the first-class flight attendant that I would prefer water. I was surprised when the flight attendant from the back of the plane suddenly appeared and leaned down to grab my hands. She said, "I want you to have this," as she pushed a small gold crucifix, with a relief of Jesus, into my hand. It was her lapel pin and it looked somewhat worn. I suspected it had been hers for quite some time. That was the only thing she said to me the entire flight.

When we landed in Minneapolis, I was the first one off the plane. The pilot himself escorted me straight down the side stairs of the exit tunnel to the tarmac. The cargo crew there already knew what was on this plane. They were unloading some of the luggage when an Army sergeant, a fellow escort who had left Dover earlier that day, appeared next to me. His "cargo" was going to be loaded onto my plane for its continuing leg. We stood side by side in the dark and executed a slow salute as Chance was removed from the plane. I then waited with the soldier and we saluted together as his fallen comrade was loaded onto the plane.

My trip with Chance was going to be somewhat unusual in that I had an overnight stopover. We had a late start out of Dover and there was just too much traveling ahead of us to continue on that day. (We still had a flight from Minneapolis to Billings, Montana, then a five-hour drive to the funeral home. That was to be followed by a ninety-minute drive to Chance's hometown.)

I was concerned about leaving him overnight in the Minneapolis cargo area. My ten-minute ride from the tarmac to the cargo holding area eased my apprehension; just as in Philadelphia, the cargo guys in Minneapolis were extremely respectful and seemed honored to do their part. While talking with them, I learned that the cargo supervisor for Northwest Airlines at the airport is a lieutenant colonel in the Marine Corps Reserve. They called him for me and let me talk to him.

Once I was satisfied that all would be okay for the night, I asked one of the cargo crew if he would take me back to the terminal so that I could catch my hotel's shuttle. Instead, he drove me straight to the hotel himself. At the hotel, the lieutenant colonel called me and said he would personally pick me up in the morning and bring me back to the cargo area. Before leaving the airport, I had told the cargo crew that I wanted to come back to the cargo area in the morning rather than go straight to the passenger terminal. I felt bad for leaving Chance and wanted to see the shipping container where I had left it for the night.

The next morning, the lieutenant colonel drove me to the airport, and I was met again by a man from the cargo crew and escorted down to the tarmac. The pilot of the plane joined me as I waited for them to bring Chance from the cargo area. The pilot and I talked about his service in the Air Force and how he missed it.

I saluted as Chance was moved up the conveyor and onto the plane. It would be a while before the luggage was loaded, so the pilot took me up to board the plane where I could watch the tarmac from a window. With no other passengers yet on board, I talked with the flight attendants and one of the cargo guys. He had been in the Navy and one of the attendants had been in the Air Force. Everywhere I went, people were telling me about their relationship to the military. After all the baggage was aboard, I went back down to the tarmac, inspected the cargo bay, and watched them secure the door.

When we arrived at Billings, I was again the first off the plane. The funeral director had driven five hours up from Riverton, Wyoming, to meet us. He shook my hand as if I had personally lost a brother.

We moved Chance to a secluded cargo area, and it was now time for me to remove the shipping container and drape the flag over the casket. I had predicted that this would choke me up, but I found I was more concerned with proper flag etiquette than the solemnity of the moment. Once the flag was in place, I stood by and saluted as Chance was loaded onto the van from the funeral home. I picked up my rental car and followed Chance for five hours until we reached Riverton. During the long trip I imagined how my meeting with Chance's parents would go. I was very nervous about that.

When we finally arrived at the funeral home, I had my first face-to-face meeting with the casualty assistance call officer (CACO). It had been his duty to inform the family of Chance's death, and I knew he had been through a difficult week.

Inside I gave the funeral director some of the paperwork from Dover and discussed the plan for the next day. The service was to be at 1400 in the high school gymnasium up in Dubois, population about nine hundred, some ninety miles away. Eventually, we had covered everything. The CACO had some items that the family wanted inserted into the casket, and I felt I needed to inspect Chance's uniform to ensure everything was proper. Although it was going to be a closed-casket funeral, I still wanted to make certain his uniform was squared away.

Earlier in the day I wasn't sure how I'd handle this moment. Suddenly, the casket was open and I got my first look at Chance Phelps. His uniform was immaculate—a tribute to the professionalism of the Marines at Dover. I noticed that he wore six ribbons over his marksmanship badge; the senior one was his Purple Heart. I had been in the Corps for more than seventeen years, including a combat tour, and was wearing eight ribbons. This private first class, with less than a year in the Corps, had already earned six.

The next morning, I wore my dress blues and followed the hearse for the trip up to Dubois. This was the most difficult leg of our trip for me. I was bracing for the moment when I would meet his parents and hoping I would find the right words as I presented them with Chance's personal effects. We got to the high school gym about four hours before the service was to begin. The gym floor was covered with folding chairs neatly lined in rows.

There were a few townspeople making final preparations when I stood next to the hearse and saluted as Chance was moved out of the hearse and into the gym. A Marine sergeant, the command representative from Chance's battalion, met me inside. His eyes were watery as he relieved me of watching Chance so that I could go eat lunch and find my hotel.

At the restaurant, the table had a flyer announcing Chance's service. Dubois High School gym, two o'clock. It also said that the family would be accepting donations so that they could buy flak vests to send to troops in Iraq.

I drove back to the gym at a quarter after one. I could have walked; you could walk to just about anywhere in Dubois in ten minutes. I wanted to find a quiet room where I could take Chance's things out of their pouch and untangle the chain of the Saint Christopher medal from the dog-tag chains and arrange everything before his parents came in. I had twice before removed the items from the pouch to ensure they were all there—even though there was no possibility anything could have fallen out. Each time, the two chains had been quite intertwined. I didn't want to be fumbling around trying to separate them in front of his parents. Our meeting, however, didn't go as expected.

I practically bumped into Chance's stepmom accidentally and our introductions began in the noisy hallway outside the gym. In short order I met Chance's stepmom and father, followed by his stepdad and, at last, his mom. I didn't know how to express to these people my sympathy for their loss and my gratitude for their sacrifice. Now, however, they were repeatedly thanking me for bringing their son home and for my service. I was humbled beyond words.

I told them that I had some of Chance's things and asked if we could try to find a quiet place. The five of us ended up in what appeared to be a computer lab—not what I had envisioned for this occasion. After we had arranged five chairs around a small table, I told them about our trip. I told them how, at every step, Chance was treated with respect, dignity, and honor. I told them about the staff at Dover and all the folks at Northwest Airlines. I tried to convey how the entire nation, from Dover to Philadelphia, to Minneapolis, to Billings and Riverton expressed grief and sympathy over their loss.

Finally, it was time to open the pouch. The first item I happened to pull out was Chance's large watch. It was still set to Baghdad time. Next were the lanyard and the wooden cross. Then the dog tags and the Saint Christopher medal. This time the chains were not tangled. Once all of his items were laid out on the table, I told his mom that I had one other item to give them. I retrieved the flight attendant's crucifix from my pocket and told its story. I set that on the table and excused myself. When I next saw Chance's mom, she was wearing the crucifix on her lapel.

By 1400 most of the seats on the gym floor were filled and people were finding seats in the fixed bleachers high above the gym floor. There were a surprising number of people in military uniform. Many Marines had come up from Salt Lake City. Men from various VFW posts and the Marine Corps League occupied multiple rows of folding chairs. It turned out that Chance's sister, a petty officer in the Navy, worked for a rear admiral—the chief of naval intelligence—at the Pentagon. The admiral had brought many of the sailors on his staff with him to Dubois to pay respects to Chance and to support his sister. After a few songs and some words from a Navy chaplain, the admiral took the microphone and told us how Chance had died.

Chance was an artillery cannoneer and his unit was acting as provisional military police outside of Baghdad. Chance had volunteered to man a .50-caliber machine gun in the turret of the leading vehicle in a convoy. The convoy came under intense fire but Chance stayed true to his post and returned fire with the big gun, covering the rest of the convoy, until he was fatally wounded.

After the admiral spoke, the commander of the local VFW post read some of the letters Chance had written home. In letters to his mom, he talked of the mosquitoes and the heat. In letters to his stepfather, he told of the dangers of convoy operations and of receiving fire.

The service was a fitting tribute to this hero. When it was over, we stood as the casket was wheeled out with the family following. The casket was placed onto a horse-drawn carriage for the mile-long trip from the gym, down the main street, then up the steep hill to the cemetery. I stood alone and saluted as the carriage departed the high school. I found my car and joined Chance's convoy.

All along the route, people had lined the street and were waving small American flags. The flags that were otherwise posted were all at half-staff. For the last quarter mile up the hill, local boy scouts, spaced about twenty feet apart, all in uniform, held large flags. At the foot of the hill, I could look up and back and see how enormous the procession was. I wondered how many people would be at this funeral if it were in, say, Detroit or Los Angeles — probably not as many as were here in little Dubois, Wyoming.

The carriage stopped about fifteen yards from the grave, and the military pallbearers and the family waited until the men of the VFW and Marine Corps league were formed up and the school buses had arrived, carrying many of the people from the procession route. Once the entire crowd was in place, the pallbearers came to attention and began to remove the casket from the caisson. As I had done all week, I came to attention and executed a slow ceremonial salute as Chance was being transferred from one mode of transport to another.

From Dover to Philadelphia, Philadelphia to Minneapolis, Minneapolis to Billings, Billings to Riverton, and Riverton to Dubois, we had been together. Now, as I watched them carry him the final fifteen yards, I was choking up. I felt that, as long as he was still moving, he was somehow still alive. Then they placed him at his grave. He had stopped moving.

Although my mission had been officially complete once I turned him over to the funeral director at the Billings airport, it was his placement at his grave that really concluded the mission in my mind. Now, he was home to stay and I suddenly felt at once sad, relieved, and useless.

The chaplain said some words that I couldn't hear and two Marines removed the flag from the casket and slowly folded it for presentation to his mother. When the ceremony was over, Chance's father placed a ribbon from his service in Vietnam on Chance's casket. His mother removed something from her blouse and put it on the casket. I later saw that it was the flight attendant's crucifix. Eventually friends of Chance's moved closer to the grave. A young man put a can of Copenhagen on the casket and many others left flowers.

Finally, we all went back to the gym for a reception. There was enough food to feed the entire population for a few days. In one corner of the gym there was a table set up with lots of pictures of Chance and some of his sports awards. People were continually approaching me and the other Marines to thank us for our service. Almost all of them had some story to tell about their connection to the military. About an hour into the reception, I had the impression that every man in Wyoming had, at one time or another, been in the service.

It seemed like every time I saw Chance's mom, she was hugging a different well-wisher. After a few hours at the gym, I went back to the hotel to change out of my dress blues. The local VFW post had invited everyone over to "celebrate Chance's life." The post was on the other end of town from my hotel and the drive took less than two minutes. The crowd was somewhat smaller than earlier at the gym but the place was packed.

The largest room in the post was a banquet/dining/dancing area and it was now being renamed "The Chance Phelps Room." Above the entry were two items: a large portrait of Chance in his dress blues and a wooden carving of the Eagle, Globe, and Anchor, the Marine Corps emblem. In one corner of the room there was another memorial to Chance. There were candles burning around another picture of him in his blues. On the table surrounding his photo were his Purple Heart citation and his Purple Heart medal. Above it all was a television that was playing a photomontage of Chance's life from small boy to proud Marine.

As had been happening all day, indeed all week, people were thanking me for bringing Chance home. I talked with the men who had handled the horses and horse-drawn carriage and learned that they had worked through the night to groom and prepare the horses for Chance's last ride. They were all very grateful that they were able to contribute.

After a while we all gathered in the Chance Phelps Room for the formal dedication. The post commander told us of how Chance had been so looking forward to becoming a life member of the VFW. Now, in the Chance Phelps Room of the Dubois, Wyoming, post, he would be an eternal member. We all raised our beers and the room was christened.

Later, a staff sergeant from the reserve unit in Salt Lake grabbed me and said, "Sir, you gotta hear this." There were two other Marines with him and he told the younger one, a lance corporal, to tell me his story. The staff sergeant said the lance corporal was normally too shy to tell it, but now he'd had enough beer to overcome his usual modesty. As the lance corporal started to talk, an older man joined our circle. He wore a baseball cap that indicated that he had been with the 1st Marine Division in Korea. Earlier in the evening, he had told me about one of his former commanding officers, a Colonel Puller.

So, there I was, standing in a circle with three Marines recently returned from fighting with the 1st Marine Division in Iraq and one not-so-recently returned from fighting with the 1st Marine Division in Korea. I, who had fought with the 1st Marine Division in Kuwait, was about to gain a new insight into our Corps. At that moment, in this circle of current and former Marines, the differences in our ages and ranks dissipated—we were all simply Marines. The young lance corporal began to tell us his story.

His squad had been on a patrol through a city street. They had taken small-arms fire and had literally dodged a rocket-propelled grenade that sailed between two Marines. At one point they received fire from behind a wall and had neutralized the sniper with a SMAW (shoulder-launched multipurpose assault weapon) round. The back blast of the SMAW, however, kicked up a substantial rock that hammered the lance corporal in the thigh, missing his groin only because he had reflexively turned his body sideways at the shot.

Their squad had suffered some wounded and was receiving more sniper fire when suddenly he was hit in the head by an AK-47 round. I was stunned as he told us how he felt like a baseball bat had been slammed into his head.

He had spun around and fallen unconscious. When he came to, he had a severe scalp wound but his Kevlar helmet had saved his life. He continued with his unit for a few days before realizing he was suffering the effects of a severe concussion.

The staff sergeant finished the story. He told how this lance corporal had begged and pleaded with the battalion surgeon to let him stay with his unit. In the end, the doctor said there was just no way; he had suffered a severe and traumatic head wound and would have to be medevac'd.

The Marine Corps is a special fraternity. There are moments when we are reminded of this. Interestingly, those moments don't always happen at awards ceremonies or in dress blues at Birthday Balls. I have found, rather, that they occur at unexpected times and places — next to a loaded moving van at Camp Lejeune's base housing, in a dirty tent in northern Saudi Arabia, and in a smoky VFW post in western Wyoming.

After the story was done, the lance corporal stepped over to the old man, put his arm over the man's shoulder, and told him that he, the Korean War vet, was his hero. The two of them stood there with their arms over each other's shoulders, and we were all silent for a moment. When they let go, I told the lance corporal that there were recruits down on the yellow footprints tonight who would soon be learning his story.

I was finished drinking beer and telling stories. I found Chance's father and shook his hand one more time. Chance's mom had already left, and I deeply regretted not being able to tell her goodbye.

I left Dubois in the morning before sunrise for my long drive back to Billings. It had been my honor to take Chance Phelps to his final post. Now he is on the high ground overlooking his town.

I miss him.

MEMORIAL DAY
Letters
DeEtte and Rex Wood

Late in the evening on November 1, 2004, U.S. Marine Lance Corporal Nathan Wood e-mailed his family from Iraq to let them know that he was about to participate in a massive operation. "Hey guys whats up," he began, im doing good dont worry so much the big hit hasnt gone on yet but very very soon within the next week or so. I cant tell you the exact date over the internet but its coming soon. Technically i cant even tell you the city but you already know wich one im talking about. It is going to be very interesting to see how this turns out because im not even sure anymore, but dont worry. . . . if you hear on the news about 3/1 Lima company thats me and my guys so keep an eye out. . . . Also listen for stuff about a train station. . . . If i dont get to talk to you all for awhile i love you and ill try to write or call when i get a chance.

The city was the insurgent stronghold of Fallujah, and the train station was going to be transformed into a forward base by the Marines. Eight days had passed since Nathan's last message, and there was still no word from him. On November 9, his mother, DeEtte, sent him the following e-mail with the subject heading "Are you still alive":

It is 11:30 am Tuesday the 9th. I watched the news till 1:00 last night and there was nothing new. I woke up at 5:00 and still nothing new. At 10:00 I watched a news conference and heard that there were quite a few casualties. I searched the internet and could not find anything specific. I did find that there were 3 marines and 6 soldiers killed. One soldier interviewed said there were a lot of troops injured. I hope you are ok. All I can do is watch and hope no one knocks on our door. According to the news conference they say you are ahead of schedule. That gives me hope that the heavy fighting will be over soon but I know you will still not be safe till you come home. I'll keep praying. . . .

The knock that DeEtte feared more than anything in the world came almost twelve hours later; a few minutes after 11:00 p.m. on November 9, 2004, three casualty notification officers arrived at the Kirkland, Washington, home of DeEtte and Rex Wood and informed them that their nineteen-year-old son had been killed in Fallujah. Nathan had been shot while conducting a door-to-door sweep through an apartment complex the morning (Iraq time) of the ninth, and he died instantly. For parents, like the Woods, confronted with the trauma of losing a child, the grief can seem endless and all-consuming. Some try to cope with the pain by writing a letter to *the deceased, expressing how much he (or she) is still—and always will be—loved and missed. On the first Memorial Day after Nathan's death, both of his parents wrote letters to their son after visiting the Garden of Remembrance in Seattle. His mother's letter follows.*

Dear Nathan,

Today is May 30, 2005, Memorial Day. You have been gone for almost 7 months. Sometimes I still don't believe it. I never really understood what Memorial Day was about until this weekend. I was browsing through the mall and felt so angry that the stores were taking advantage of this holiday to push their sales. I wish I was still naive and could celebrate as though it were a "holiday weekend." I will never look at this weekend the same. Today I share in the grief that many other families have known since losing someone they love fighting for their country. Your name has been added to the Garden of Remembrance in Seattle. There are more than 8,000 names listed on this wall since WWII. I am very proud to see your name among so many other American Hero's. I want you to know that seeing your name in stone will never replace the real memories I have of you. I will always miss your crooked smile, your red cheeks and freckles, your smell and most of all I will miss never being able to hug you again.

Since you have been gone I have been in contact with some of your fellow marines. Your friend Derrick has adopted your father and I to be grandparents of his wonderful boys. Derrick and his wife had a baby boy on February 16, 2005. They thought so much of you that they now have a Nathan of their own. We will enjoy watching Nathan and his big brother Trent grow up. Jacob and his wife Priscilla will soon be having a child of their own. Garret too is doing well. His parents call us often to see how we are doing.

Anne Larson, Nick's mother and I email often. She too is taking the loss of her son just as hard. We do take some comfort knowing that you and Nick died together. I have recently been in contact with Michael's mother, Karen. I am hoping that some day we can all get together to share memories of our brave son's.

Not a day goes by that I don't think of you. I never knew that love could hurt so much. There are so many things that spark a memory of you—a song, a boy in a baseball cap and baggy pants, a skateboarder. I wish I could spend another summer at the cabin with you. I know that when you were there you were in heaven. When I think of you now I know that you are on the lake fishing with your friends and I know that someday I can join you. Until then little man I love you and I hold you close to my heart.

Love,
Mom

Nathan's father wrote the following:

To my son, my hero Nathan R. Wood

With memories of a little boy who brought me such happiness playing in the yard with his dog, playing catch in the back yard and trying his best to help his father in anyway he could.

To the little boy who wore my shoes and gloves that were five times the size of his own hands and feet trying to be like me. One who would ride with me in the mountains of Montana on my motorcycle and spend all day with me just being happy to be in those mountains and to do a little fishing and talking.

As you got older into your teens I lost you because I couldn't seem to remember what it was like to be a teenager and we grew apart. You became your own man and became a Marine. On that day of graduation at MCRD I felt so proud of you, you had made it and you knew you would, you were a true Marine.

As I told you on the phone while you were in Iraq, it is strange how the farther away you are the closer that we seem to be getting. I longed for the day that you would come back home so that we could start again and be close once again but that day will never come.

Today as we stand in front of this memorial wall with your name etched into it, I feel a great emptiness inside knowing that I will never get to tell you I love you and to thank you for all that you have done. You have given the greatest sacrifice for your family and your country. You have given more in your short life then I will ever be able to give in my entire lifetime and that son is why you are my hero.

When I see the pain and loss in your mother since your passing I would gladly change places with you so that she could hug you and smile once more. I will never forget you and I hope that you are in a better place. I miss you.

Dad

THE HARDEST LETTER TO WRITE

Journal

Staff Sergeant Parker Gyokeres

Members of Staff Sergeant Parker Gyokeres's family have served in every major American conflict since, in his words, "the defense of Jamestown in 1609." Gyokeres himself was deployed to Iraq to provide "force protection" for the air base in Tallil from November 2003 through March 2004 with the U.S. Air Force's 332nd Fighter Wing. His younger brother, Zachary, also a staff sergeant in the Air Force, was assigned as a flight engineer on a combat rescue helicopter in Afghanistan shortly before Parker left for Iraq. During his five months in Tallil, Parker Gyokeres wrote hundreds of pages of journals, all of which he e-mailed to his wife, relatives, and other loved ones back home. (He has another excerpt featured on pages 134–39.) Gyokeres downplayed the risks he faced, and the majority of his journals detailed the more offbeat and humorous incidents that helped him endure the monotony of life on an air base in the middle of the desert. But there are also moments in his journals when the true nature of war reveals itself in all its cruelty. Perhaps the most serious of his entries is the final one, which, even after he e-mailed it to friends and family months after returning home, he continued to edit. Gyokeres was no longer writing for them. He was writing for himself.

Hello all,

This has been, by far, the hardest letter to write. I returned home to the dichotomy of being universally welcomed with open, respectful, grateful arms—by a country that is increasingly against why I was ever in Iraq. I performed my mission well and have great pride in my actions, and those of my peers, but I can also understand why people are questioning if there is any long-term hope for Iraq and its people. The reason we were sent there in the first place will require a lot more study, but that's another book for another person.

The main issue for me has been adjusting to a life without the dear friends I served with and whom I grew to love—and, without whom, I felt lost, alone, and unable to relate to others. I am told this is normal. That did not, however, make it easier. And I know I'm doing better than many for whom I care deeply. They hide it well, but they are struggling.

The world I returned to was disorienting, confusing, and frustrating to me. The racket and clutter of daily life gave me a tremendous headache. I now know why some people choose to simply unplug and move into the woods. Obviously we heard our share of noise in Iraq, some of it sudden and terrifying, but overall it wasn't so incessant. Wherever I walk today I feel like I'm surrounded by a barrage of electronic trash—music blasting everywhere, cell phones ringing, people chatting away and having the most inane conversations, and all of it louder than when I left for Iraq. Over there, we had the comforting simplicity of a routine. There was a purity to our lives. There were life-and-death implications to our actions, but all we had to worry about was our friends and ourselves. I'm not saying that either we or our jobs are any better or worse than anyone else's back here, but just different. I'm slowly acclimating to a civilian world and the speed of modern life, but it has not always been pleasant.

For a while I truly wished I was still in Iraq. As much as I looked forward to leaving, when I got back to the U.S. a part of me wanted to return immediately. My wife was upset to hear me say that, for a while, I preferred a war zone to a home life. Again, I am not alone. Some of my friends and other returning veterans I know have talked about this as well. Departing Tallil was like leaving a family. We also left behind memories, some of them beautiful and some horrific, that left a deep impression on us.

Traumatic, life-changing, or profoundly spiritual events can bond people together in ways that are hard to explain. My friends and I shared all three. I do not want to overstate my own situation or suggest I was in grave danger. I was not. But there are experiences I had and things I saw that were extremely disturbing. The worst, by far, came only two days after we arrived at Tallil, when I had my first opportunity to work in our visitor control center at the base. I had been on duty for only a few hours when a call came over the radio that there was a local ambulance en route to pick up an Iraqi bombing casualty. Moments later an Army Humvee arrived carrying two soldiers who identified themselves as the ones tasked to meet the ambulance. They explained to me that they were there to transfer to the Iraqis a body—the body of an eight-week-old infant killed by a bomb set off by insurgents.

I will never forget the sight of those soldiers reaching into a grossly oversized body bag, folded into quarters, and then removing a package no bigger than a travel pillow. It was anointed in oils and wrapped in ceremonial muslin dressings for a religious burial. Instantly a hush fell over the small group as the child was gently carried from the back of that beaten-down, ugly Humvee and solemnly placed on a nest of blankets inside the Iraqi ambulance. Both vehicles then slowly pulled away, leaving a semicircle of terribly scarred people in its wake. I felt like somebody had punched me hard in the stomach.

You do not forget moments like these.

Just over a week later, a critically wounded man arrived at the base in a gutted Iraqi ambulance with four other men. One of his companions, whom we were told was his brother, whispered into his ear, and held the man's head and smoothed his matted hair, while he rocked back and forth, clearly in great emotional distress. The man's injuries were sickening. His hands were stumps, and all his wounds were terribly infected. His breathing was very slow, incredibly labored, and punctuated with large, gasping heaves. There were black flies everywhere, and he looked sallow, sunken, and transparent, a husk of a man covered in fresh scabs and badly drawn tattoos. I recognized some of the tattoos as those of the infamous Fedayeen, the brutal terror thugs of Saddam's regime. If there was ever a "Bad" guy I would encounter in my life, those tattoos told me all I needed to know. Here was a man who looked fifty but was probably only thirty, and would never see thirty-one. He had lived a hard life and would meet a hard death, and I stood and watched, without remorse.

One of my fellow force protection escorts (who is a medic at Wilford Hall, the AF's largest hospital) did an appraisal. While snapping off her gloves, she said, "This man is going to die whether he's given treatment or not, and there isn't a single thing any hospital can do about it. It's too late." It was a brutal statement, totally lacking in compassion, but it was an honest and logical one that we all at the time readily accepted. There was one among us, however, who felt that even if the man was going to die, he wasn't beyond mercy. As the first medic climbed out of the ambulance, the second one quietly placed gloves on her hands and with grim determination climbed *into* that reeking, fly-infested, and urine-soaked ambulance, alone. She looked at us with cold flint in her eyes, as if *daring* us to do something different, and began waving a small piece of cardboard over the dying man's face to keep the flies away. As we stood there stunned by her compassion, she began to do the unthinkable, as a small, lone female in a vehicle full of hostile, frustrated Muslim men. She began to pray for him.

As I realized what she was up to, I became concerned for her safety—a little at first, and then more so as each second passed. She was female, and if

these men became offended it would be very hard to get her out of that ambulance uninjured. As I moved closer to the door of the ambulance to reach
in and snatch her out if things went south, I discreetly slid my weapon sling
into my hands, behind my back. The men asked our interpreter what she was
doing. He said, "Praying." Immediately, they all laughed out loud at her for
being so foolish. Our interpreter shot back at them, "No, no, don't laugh,
she's doing this because she believes only God can help him. She's trying to
help your brother. Where is your faith?"

At that, the men instantly fell silent and looked chastened. The man's
brother shakily took off his shoes and knelt inside the tiny ambulance with his
forehead against the filthy floor and began to pray for his dying brother. The
other three took off their shoes where they stood, amongst at least fifteen
armed escorts, medics, and translators, and knelt on the ground in the direction of Mecca and began to pray to Allah. The fearless faith of one person
changed the hearts of four angry men with a single silent prayer. Those men
were humbled and suddenly very different as they prayed fervently to Allah.

Later, when I asked her how she could do what she did, all alone and
oblivious to her safety, she said to me in a strong voice, "I *wasn't alone* in that
ambulance."

It took a week of wearing a mask of brittle bravado for me to finally begin
talking with my friends about what I had seen. I had been furious with God
for allowing so much pain into our world, for allowing people to act like soul-
less animals and kill infants, for allowing all of this to happen in the first
place, and I felt physically sick having witnessed what evils man is capable of.
The courage of this extraordinary woman gave me something to cling to.

These are the people I left behind.

Many of us also came to admire and even love some of the Iraqis we met.
Yes, there were troops who grew to distrust and hate them, especially as tensions escalated and it was harder to tell the good guys from the bad guys. But
a lot of us had very positive experiences with the locals. They genuinely
wanted us to remember them as happy, intelligent, fun-loving people and,
most importantly, as friends. I have heard many times, "You need to come
back years from now and visit us with your family." To be torn from a place
that has become so much a part of your own life and where so many intense
memories are rooted is much harder than people might imagine.

As difficult as things were when I got home, sitting here now I fully realize how blessed I am—and was over there. Our base in Tallil was relatively

safe, far from constant mortar attacks, car bombs, and truly wicked people try-
ing to do desperate, vicious things to us. Others had it much, much worse.
They are the true heroes of this war. And they are the ones I think of most as
I write this.

One friend of mine at Tallil, who was very full of life and sang in the little
church choir we had organized, was temporarily transferred to a base closer
to Baghdad and in a considerably more dangerous area. When I saw her
again, it was as if only her ghost had returned. She never came back to the
church—or to us. She pretty much kept to herself, and it was painful to watch
this once gregarious woman become so distant and reserved. Others reached
out to her, but to no avail.

I saw her in passing one day, and I finally asked her how she was doing. I
was genuinely interested to hear the truth, her truth; for it was obvious that
there was a real event, or perhaps many, that had caused her to withdraw. She
suddenly grew dark, and a cold expression, like the sudden remembrance of
a lost loved one, came across her face. Instantly I knew I had screwed up and
had carelessly trampled on an unseen line. I wanted to take it back, but it was
too late. The awkward silence was broken by her curt reply, which, in so
many words, was not only her answer to the question but an indication that
the conversation was over entirely: "I don't want to talk about it." She then
turned and walked away.

We never spoke again.

In hindsight, and knowing the subject might still be raw, I should have
waited before asking—or given her time to approach me or someone else.
Until I came home and watched as other friends wrestled with their emotions,
it was the first time I had seen how debilitating weeks of trauma and stress can
be. It was a sobering realization, and I wondered how many others like her
have we created in these last few years? How many others live with the shocking and barbaric images of war that are seared into one's memory forever? I
pray that they will find someone they can confide in and unload this burden
so that the pain they carry with them is lessened over time. My writing gave
me an outlet while I was over there, and it continues to help me now.

I was fortunate not only because I had it easy compared to so many other
troops, but because my wife supported me during my angry, confused, and
sleepless times. I cannot thank her enough for this, and she has always been
there for me and never stopped loving me. This is all that matters, and I do
not want to leave her again or make her go through all the anxieties and wor-

ries that she silently endured as well. My wife could not understand how I could become so close to people I had served with for such a relatively short period, and she was upset about my apparent inability to leave it all behind. But it was for my own well-being that she was concerned, and not out of jealousy. Most importantly, she knew when to listen and when to let me work through my emotions.

This is perhaps the most important thing any loved one or friend can do. Those of us coming back from Iraq or Afghanistan are not looking for sympathy. We might be reluctant at first to talk about what we've been through, good or bad, and some troops might never be able to open up, which is certainly their right. There are also things about war that people will never comprehend unless they have experienced them firsthand. But I hope that those who need to will reach out, and it's helpful knowing that there are people who care about us and are at least making an effort to understand.

Your support has made this journey an incredible one for me, and I couldn't have gone through it alone. Thanks for joining me—and thanks, above all, for listening.

Parker

ACKNOWLEDGMENTS

The morning after National Endowment for the Arts Chairman Dana Gioia launched Operation Homecoming, our agency received a heartfelt thank-you letter from former NEA literature fellow Richard Currey. Having served as a medic in Vietnam, Currey knew well the benefit of unburdening oneself through story about the trauma of war. His letter was soon followed by more from World War II, Korean War, and Vietnam War veterans. They commended the NEA for creating a program that they wished had been available following their combat years.

Currey soon joined our team of thirty-four distinguished writers who taught workshops, recorded war literature, penned essays for our website, and evaluated the writing submitted to the program.

While it is hard to reduce fifty workshops to a few examples, we recall in particular Mark Bowden's brilliant explication of Orwell's "A Hanging" and how he had constructed *Black Hawk Down*; Victor Davis Hanson taking a room of Marines, soon to deploy to Iraq, back in time to how the Greek hoplites fought in phalanxes; on the USS *Carl Vinson* in the Persian Gulf, Jeff Shaara's passionate discussions of historical fiction and his re-creation of the boyhood moment with his father at Gettysburg when *Killer Angels* was born; Marilyn Nelson, with her quiet, calming voice of peace, talking about the kinship of poetry and meditation, and the responsibility to oneself and one's community to be a chronicler; Bobbie Ann Mason's reflections at Camp Lejeune on the Vietnam Veterans Memorial and the stories beneath the carved names, including those of the families left behind; at Fort Bragg, Stephen Lang's evocative reading of a workshop poem about a fallen soldier's empty boots, written by a Special Forces troop too overcome by tears to recite it himself. For such exchanges, we are deeply grateful to every writer who participated.

But the greatest thanks goes to the men and women in uniform, and their families, who welcomed Operation Homecoming into their lives. They readily accepted instruction about the craft of writing as well as critiques of their own efforts. Though it was often heartbreaking to read the ten thousand pages produced, the most difficult task for our editorial panel was evaluating the submissions with the knowledge that only 5 percent could be included in the anthology.

After an intensive reading of the panel's recommended pieces, Andrew Carroll conceived of the anthology as an epic narrative, ordered the entries accordingly, edited them for length with the approval of the submitters, and wrote insightful headnotes to establish historical context—all this and more, without compensation. A true man of letters, Carroll exhibits in his writing a scholar's intellect and a war correspondent's immediacy.

Following a competitive process skillfully managed by literary agent Miriam Altshuler, Random House was chosen as our publisher and—to our good fortune—Nancy Miller as our editor. Senior vice president and executive editor at Random House, Nancy has an exceptional ability to discern where a narrative is waning. And to anyone who says editors don't know how to line edit anymore, we offer Nancy as clear proof that Maxwell Perkins has his inheritors. We also appreciate the support of Gina Centrello, president and publisher of Random House; Tom Perry, associate publisher; Sally Marvin, director of publicity; Jynne Martin, assistant director of publicity; and Sanyu Dillon, director of marketing.

Without the financial support of The Boeing Company, Operation Homecoming would have been a modest program that reached a handful of bases rather than an international program of lasting importance. In particular, we would like to thank Jim Albaugh, president and CEO of Boeing Integrated Defense Systems; Mary Foerster, vice president of communications; and Pat Riddle, director of advertising and branding, for their unfailing support. Their commitment to enhancing the lives of our nation's service members is readily apparent.

At the Southern Arts Federation, Executive Director Gerri Combs has embraced our program and its mission; Betsy Baker played a key role in selecting the publisher; and David Dombrosky worked seamlessly with us on base logistics.

Of course, this program would not have been possible without the cooperation of the Department of Defense. The DOD allowed the NEA to solicit writing directly from the troops but had no role in selecting submissions for this anthology. Without the efforts of more than one hundred DOD and civilian base employees, this program would not have succeeded.

The National Council on the Arts, the NEA's advisory board, has been an unwavering supporter of Operation Homecoming. NEA Senior Deputy Chairman Eileen Mason and Government Affairs Director Ann Guthrie Hingston provided valuable guidance in executing the program. Communications Director Felicia Knight and her staff attracted unprecedented national media attention to the project. Thanks also to NEA staff Claudia Nadig, Hope O'Keeffe, Dan Stone, and especially Rebecca Turner Gonzales and Monica Glockner.

Most important, the success of Operation Homecoming is the direct result of the vision and commitment of NEA Chairman Dana Gioia. In a small federal agency of 150 employees, he created an artistic program for military communities during a time of war. There was no road map for how to do such a thing successfully; he found a way nevertheless. Refusing to allow this program to be politicized, Gioia stressed from the first day that our responsibilities were to the troops and their families—and to the freedom of artistic expression.

—Jon Parrish Peede
Director, Operation Homecoming

GLOSSARY

A-10	(Thunderbolt Warthog) Ground support aircraft
ANA	Afghan National Army
Apache	(AH-64) attack helicopter
ASOC	Air support operations center
BIAP	Baghdad International Airport
Black Hawk	(UH-60) combat helicopter
C-130	Military transport aircraft
CENTCOM	U.S. Central Command
Chinook	(CH-47) tandem rotor helicopter
CJTF	Combined Joint Task Force
CPA	Coalition Provisional Authority
CSH	Combat support hospital
DOA	Dead on arrival
EPW	Enemy prisoner of war
FOB	Forward operating base
HEI/HE	High-explosive incendiary rounds
Hero mission	Recovery of deceased troops
HH-60	Special operations helicopter
HUMINT	Human intelligence collector (interrogator)
Humvee	(HMMWV) High-mobility multipurpose wheeled vehicle
IBA	Individual body armor
IED	Improvised explosive device
JAG	Judge advocate general

KIA	Killed in action
LZ	Landing zone
MCRD	Marine Corps recruit depot
Medevac	Medical evacuation
M-4	Military assault rifle
M-16	Military assault rifle
MI	Military intelligence
MOS	Military occupational specialty
MRE	Meals ready to eat (field rations)
NVG	Night vision goggles
OEF	Operation Enduring Freedom (the War in Afghanistan)
OIF	Operation Iraqi Freedom
PTSD	Post-traumatic stress disorder
PUC	Person under control (prisoner)
RPG	Rocket-propelled grenade
S2	Battalion or brigade intelligence staff officer
SAF	Small-arms fire
Stryker	Infantry carrier vehicle
TOC	Tactical operations center
WIA	Wounded in action
Zulu	Greenwich mean time

Military Ranks

A list of common abbreviations in text, in alphabetical—not rank—order.

CO	Commanding officer
COL	Colonel
CPL	Corporal
CPT	Captain
1LT	First lieutenant
LTC	Lieutenant colonel
NCO	Noncommissioned officer
PFC	Private first class
PVT	Private
1SG	First sergeant
SPC	Specialist
SSG	Staff sergeant
XO	Executive officer

CREDITS AND PERMISSIONS

INDEX OF CONTRIBUTORS

INDEX OF TITLES

ANDREW CARROLL is the editor of several critically acclaimed and nationally bestselling books, including *Letters of a Nation, Behind the Lines,* and *War Letters,* which was also made into a PBS documentary. Carroll is the founder of the Legacy Project (www.warletters.com), a national, all-volunteer effort that honors veterans and active-duty troops by seeking out and preserving their letters and e-mails for posterity. He edited *Operation Homecoming* entirely on a pro bono basis.

ABOUT THE TYPE

This book was set in Electra, a typeface designed for Linotype by
W. A. Dwiggins, the renowned type designer (1880–1956). Electra
is a fluid typeface, avoiding the contrasts of thick and thin strokes
that are prevalent in most modern typefaces.